The author, Michael McClintock, spent several years on this investigation. He has a growing reputation as an expert in the field of US foreign policy.

The American Connection

Michael McClintock

A Companion Volume on El Salvador
Michael McClintock has written a companion volume to this
book called *The American Connection, Vol. I: State Terror
and Popular Resistance in El Salvador* (Zed Books, 1985)

The American Connection

Volume II:

State Terror and Popular Resistance in Guatemala

Michael McClintock

Zed Books Ltd.

*The American Connection, Volume Two: State Terror and
Popular Resistance in Guatemala* was first published by
Zed Books Ltd., 57 Caledonian Road, London N1 9BU, UK,
and 171 First Avenue, Atlantic Highlands, New Jersey 07716,
USA, in 1985.

Cover designed by Andrew Corbett.
Printed in the United Kingdom at The Bath Press, Avon.

First reprint, 1987.

British Library Cataloguing in Publication Data

McClintock, Michael
  The American Connection.
  Vol. I. State terror and popular resistance
  in Guatemala
  1. Central America—Politics and government
  2. United States—Politics and government 1945-
  3. United States—Foreign relations—Central
  America
  I. Title
  972.8′052   F1436

  ISBN 0-86232-258-8
  ISBN 0-86232-259-6 Pbk

Contents

Tables

Part 1: The Unchanging Pattern: Repression, Resistance and Revolt

1. From Spanish Conquest to Secret Police

Repression, resistance and revolt have been the experience of the Guatemalan people since the Spanish Conquistador Pedro de Alvarado began his mission of conquest in 1524. Once the territory was occupied, the conquest attained, the population depleted by disease and the sword, a structure of government, to establish and defend a new social order, was built on the ruins. The Captaincy General, or Kingdom, of Guatemala extended through what are now the five states of Central America and the Mexican state of Chiapas. It remained under Spanish rule for nearly 300 years.

The colonial government served as the arbiter in dividing the spoils of the conquest, the land and the labour of the disinherited Indians, and would endeavour to create institutions to fix the conquered in a position of perpetual servitude. Colonial law and administration served above all to ensure that the Indian population provided unending and limitless labour to the new overlords, and to counter Indian resistance by force of arms. To the Indian peasantry, by far the majority of the population even today, independence, in 1821, brought little change. The social order remained largely as before, and the instruments of government through which the Indian was obliged to labour without cease, remained much the same. The subjugation of the Indian peasantry to the descendants of the conquistadors, to later waves of European immigrants, and to the mixed-race, Spanish and Indian, *ladinos* would remain at the core of Guatemalan social structure.

The characteristic systems of forced labour were the *encomienda*, which reduced entire communities to serfdom at the disposal of members of the new landed elite, and later, the *repartimiento*.[1] The latter was a system of centrally administered labour levies based on a requirement for every Indian adult male (16 to 60) to perform an annual quota of labour. Available labourers were distributed in groups to work on the large estates, in the mines, on the roads, or at the service of religious orders. The *repartimiento* was a reform of the *encomienda* system in that it formally required some remuneration for Indian labourers. Both were systems whereby the state guaranteed the availability of Indian labour.

Just as land grants were distributed to the participants in the conquest, and to the European immigrants who followed, the state granted the services of Indian labourers to the non-Indians who required them. Reflections of colonial systems of forced labour persisted after independence and on into the 20th Century, from the vagrancy laws of the late 19th and early 20th Centuries, to systems of press-gang recruitment, forced labour, and debt servitude in the Guatemalan plantation agriculture of the 1980s.

The means to uphold the new order brought by the conquest, and ensure the submission of the Indian population to demands for their lands and labour evolved from reliance on small contingents of Spanish troops, to the development of city-based militias, raised largely from the *criollo* population (the offspring of Spanish parents) and the new *ladino* population. These militias were developed as the principal enforcement arm of colonial government, their pre-eminent purpose, to pre-empt, or put down, Indian revolt and, ideally, to reduce the Indian population to total subservience.

The colonial militias, direct ancestors of the national armies which developed after independence, proved ineffective in pre-empting revolt or guaranteeing the permanent submission of the Indian population. They did, however, serve to successfully put down the scores of revolts that erupted under Spanish rule, revolts which, while usually localized and small in scale, continued on a sporadic but persistent basis, even after independence and into the 20th Century. Only after Spain's disastrous showing in North America in the Seven Years' War, and ensuing vigorous steps by the Spanish crown to improve its colonies' means to defend themselves against rival European powers, did the militias of Guatemala acquire a military function beyond that of keeping down the Indians.[2] Notwithstanding their occasional commendable performance against English forces, notably at Roatan Island in 1782, or successful engagements with pirates (also generally English) Guatemala's militias, which by law excluded Indian membership, remained primarily oriented to defend the social order against Indian revolt.

Although the militias, and subsequently the national armies of the region, were the ultimate guarantors of the social order, containment and control of the Indian population was equally facilitated by mid-16th Century innovations in the structure of government itself, a part of the 1542 reform package known as the "New Laws". Their most striking effect was to restore some measure of control over local affairs to the Indian towns previously subjected to the absolute domination of the *encomenderos*. Implementation of the measures was the task of Guatemala's second governor, Alonso López Cerrato (1548–54):

> Power over community matters had been taken from the indios cabezas [the Indian leaders] and given to the encomendero. Cerrato...established

a formal governmental structure for Indian towns patterned after the Spanish *cabildo* [town council].[3]

The principal members of each Indian community were themselves to choose members of local government for fixed terms of office: four town council members, a clerk, and two mayors (*alcaldes*). The new system allowed for semi-autonomy in local government and provided a basis for Indian communities to establish (or maintain) a corporate identity. At the same time, the new system institutionalized means whereby each Indian community could be dealt with as a collective unit, and induced to comply with its obligations to the state through threat of sanctions against the community as a whole.

Colonial government delegated to the Indian community's own authorities personal responsibility for the community's fulfilment of its duty to provide labourers to local estate-owners; for guaranteeing the collection of tribute; and for seeing that what we would now call a civil police function was carried out. At that time the function of *policia* included enforcement of public health and safety standards, moral behaviour, and maintaining the streets and buildings in good repair — and appearance. Policing was carried out by members of the Indian communities themselves. Service in local government was in accordance with a concept of mandatory social service; those elected were obliged to serve. Policing was administered by local councils through a system of mandatory, fixed-term service as constables by the young men of each community on a rota basis; a system still in force in some parts of Guatemala. The power of the central government was reserved for those occasions when local government failed to ensure the community's collective compliance with its obligation to provide tribute, tax, and labour levies. Communities' non-compliance with the dictates of central government could be met with punitive action, carried out by armed men on horseback sent out from the cities. Community leaders were carried off to imprisonment, goods were confiscated, or houses burned. More serious punishments were meted out after open resistance or revolt.

The essentially democratic, close-knit nature of the Indian communities influenced both the way their members could be coerced, and the pattern in which resistance and revolt regularly flared. Revolt was frequently sparked by the arrest of community leaders, or by increases in the quotas demanded for tax, tribute or labour. Generally strictly localized, the Indian revolts usually had limited objectives. In 1679, for instance, the Indians of Totonicapán determined to send a delegation to the capital to complain that labour demands were impossible to fulfil.[4] Provided with raw cotton, the community had been ordered to produce an impossible quota of spun thread. Even before the delegation left their village the community's leaders were clapped in jail. It was this that transformed discontent into direct action: as the prisoners were being

5

taken to Huehuetenango the community rose en masse, rescued their leaders and gave their captors severe beatings. A few days later the community was punished by a squad of militia-men from the capital.

The Totonicapán case illustrates a perennial form of collective resistance short of open revolt, still occurring in Guatemala in the 1970s (before the present open civil war) when communities frequently rose up and surrounded police posts in order to free a jailed leader. More widespread and serious revolts, sometimes taking the form of a caste war, can be illustrated by a rebellion that broke out in 1803 in Cobán, in what is now Alta Verapaz, once again in the 1980s a centre of Indian rebellion. Tribute, a form of annual head tax, was demanded on the basis of a quota assigned collectively to each community: while nominally based on the number of adult males between 18 and 50 years of age, account was not always taken of the actual population, and disregarded the deaths of former tribute-payers. In Cobán the quota had not been adjusted to take into account the death of 180 tribute-payers in a 1799 epidemic. The surviving adults were obliged to raise an amount equal to three times the normal levy. A petition requesting an adjustment, dealt with only in December 1802, was rejected. Three months later the 14 Indian communities surrounding the *criollo/ladino* town of Cobán rose up, captured the town, burned much of it, and broke open the prison, freeing their imprisoned leaders. Authorities and townspeople took refuge in a fortified convent until the militia arrived from the capital. When the revolt collapsed reprisals were taken against participant communities: villages were burned, some leaders were executed, others were taken into captivity.

The pattern of localized revolt, followed by repression and reprisal, a short sharp shock of exemplary violence, after which the punitive force would withdraw to the cities, persisted up to the middle of the 20th Century. News of the overthrow of Guatemalan *caudillo*, President Jorge Ubico, in 1944, and of the creation of a "revolutionary" government, prompted the Indians of Patzicia, Chimaltenango, to rise against their local overlords. In their enthusiasm, and thinking they would be supported by the new regime, they murdered 14 *ladinos* — singled out both because of their race and their particular role in oppression under the Ubico government. Ironically, the first major public order crisis of the new revolutionary government was the Patzicia rising. In a manner not noticeably different from that of the colonial and 19th Century periods, a contingent of troops was sent out from the capital and reprisals claimed the lives of 47 Patzicia Indians.[5]

Patzicia notwithstanding, the Creole and *ladino* elites of the 20th Century had considerably more sophisticated means for dealing with a rebellious Indian peasantry than did their colonial ancestors. This more elaborate legal and military apparatus was integral to the introduction of new forms of commercial agriculture, and the drastic transformation of the economy in the late 19th Century.

Change came slowly after Guatemalan independence from Spain in 1821, with many colonial administrators remaining in place and the leading figures of the erstwhile kingdom anxious to avoid disruption of public order or the status quo. Elite factions eventually coalesced — as throughout much of Spanish America — into Conservative and Liberal parties, and open conflict between them soon followed. Conservatives came to stand for keeping things as they were; preserving the institutions of the colonial period, the prerogatives of the Church, and the traditional economy. The Liberal ideal was to foster Guatemala's entry into the international community, the aggressive promotion of commercial agriculture for export, and the creation of a secular state in which the Catholic Church would be stripped of its legal privileges and economic power. In Central America, Liberals also stood for the concept of the federation of the former provinces of the Captaincy General of Guatemala in a single state.

A series of Liberal warlords dominated Central America, from the creation of the United Provinces of Central America in 1823 — after the collapse of Mexican imperial ambitions — until the federation's dissolution in 1838. The defeat of the Honduran Liberal General Francisco Morazán that year by the forces of Guatemalan Conservative General Rafael Carrera spelt the definitive breakup of the formerly united provinces into independent states, and ushered in a period of over 30 years of Conservative rule in the new state of Guatemala.

Rafael Carrera, of Indian descent and an illiterate, rose to power on the wings of an Indian rebellion sparked by the 1837 cholera epidemic; after the Church and the Conservative elites fomented rumours that the anti-clerical Liberals then in power had poisoned the wells and propagated the plague. The Indian rebellion ultimately became a Conservative rising against the Liberals.[6]

Until Carrera's death (peacefully, in bed) in 1865 and the victory in 1871 of the Liberals (led by Miguel García Granados and Justo Rufino Barrios) there was little change in Guatemala's economic order. Rafael Carrera, a classic "man on horseback", ruled by force of arms and personality, backed by the great landowners, the Church, and the wealthy merchants, and in their behalf. There was no great expansion or transformation of agriculture or industry; the traditional elites retained their privileges and the mass of the population remained on the margin of society, called upon only for their labour and to fill levies for Carrera's rag-tag army. The Indian communities remained much as they were in the latter days of Spanish rule; they continued to provide labour, but colonial laws which protected their communal lands remained largely intact, even if sometimes honoured in the breach.

Economic Reforms and a New Security System

Drastic changes in the Indian communities' relation to the land, and to the landed elites, only came about when the Liberals took power after 1871. As in El Salvador (and elsewhere in Latin America) Liberal rule spelled major changes in patterns of land tenure and usage, as the Liberals used all the powers of the state to promote commercial export agriculture. Expropriation and redistribution of the Indians' communal lands, and of the vast agricultural holdings of the Catholic Church, provided the wherewithal for agrarian transformation. The corporate or communal handholdings, deemed by Liberal ideology to be an obstacle to development and progress, were, after expropriation, redistributed to private agricultural entrepreneurs, including immigrants drawn by offers of cheap land or outright grants, largely conditional on a commitment to turn the land to coffee production. As the coffee estates grew the Indian communities were progressively disinherited.

Between 1870 and 1920, aspiring planters are estimated to have taken possession of over one million hectares of land (1 hectare = 2.47 acres) previously classified as state, church, or Indian communal lands.[7] Coffee exports nearly tripled, from 113,000 *quintals* (about 100 pounds) in 1870 to 290,000 in 1880, rising to 543,223 in 1890 and 846,679 in 1915.[8] By 1913 the Liberal governments' favouring of immigrants had resulted in German nationals owning 170 farms and producing 358,000 of the total 525,000 *quintals* of coffee exported that year. With their own river route to the coast, planters of the German enclave centred on Cobán in the north-eastern highlands of Alta Verapaz, were virtually independent from the rest of the country. In El Salvador, 1870s legislation breaking up and dispersing the communal lands was fully implemented; by the turn of the century most traditional peasant communities there had lost their lands to private estates; many communities had disappeared, their population dispersed as labourers. In Guatemala the process was more gradual, and the absorption of Indian lands less complete. In many areas communities retained *de facto* use of a portion of their traditional lands, although often without formal title, right up to the 1944–54 "revolutionary" period.[9] But in Guatemala — as in El Salvador — the growth of the coffee estates required the state's intervention to ensure the supply of labour to the new entrepreneurs.

A major political repercussion of Liberal economic reforms was the development of police and military institutions to enforce compliance with new laws regimenting the rural labour force, and to maintain order when resistance flared as traditional ways of life were disrupted by the exigencies of commercial export agriculture. The new labour requirements were in part guaranteed through the institution of debt bondage, a pre-existing system newly regulated by the Liberal government of Justino Rufino Barrios (1873–85). The 1877 *Reglamento de Jornaleros* (Regulations for Farm Workers) established categories of rural labourers and a legal basis whereby farm workers would be obliged to pay off all outstanding debts — to the estate owner's satisfaction — before they could leave employment there.[10] The 1877 law also provided for its own implementation by prescribing that every farm labourer must carry a pass-book recording his debts, and ordering the arrest of those who failed to do so; departure from employment required a clear pass-book. An 1878 decree signed by President Barrios tightened the grip of commercial agriculture on the Indian peasantry by providing for imprisonment as vagrants of those peasants who could not prove they were wage labourers on private estates.[12] Under an 1894 decree, peasants who ran away or failed to perform satisfactorily would be arrested by local authorities and, at the discretion of the estate owner, required to return to work, or remanded to the custody of the army to carry out forced labour on the roads.[13]

Enforcement of new legislation obliging the Indian peasantry to work on the expanding private farms devolved largely on local authorities, but was also a primary responsibility of each provincial governor (*Jefe Politico*). Both the Liberal philosophy, tinged as it was with Positivism, and the practical necessities of the coffee economy are expressed in an executive order of 3 November 1876,[14] issued to governors by President Barrios, stressing the importance of increased production to the nation, and insisting that, on request, estate owners must be provided levies of labourers as required from "the towns of Indians of your jurisdiction". The progress of the nation is said to suffer from the lack of labourers, resulting in "the loss or paralyzation of capital". The fault is found to lie with the Indians; putting them to work on the estates is described as necessary both for the advancement of the nation, and of the Indians:

> The President understands that should the commercial farmers be left to their own devices, without counting on the efficient cooperation of the agents of Government, their efforts to build enterprises will always fail, given the shiftlessness of the Indian classes, which are, moreover, so prone to deceit. . .

The remedy is to place the Indians in "continuous contact with the white classes" so they learn to work, and become "useful and productive for agriculture. . ."

As agricultural entrepreneurs gobbled up Indian communal lands, security systems of increased sophistication were required to enforce legislation introduced to regiment the rural labour force and guard against the danger of agrarian revolt. In El Salvador, expropriation of Indian lands was both more rapid and more comprehensive, tensions were acute, and Indian resistance prolonged; steps were taken after 1870 to both strengthen the army and organize a national police force to maintain law and order in the coffee-growing areas. In Guatemala, measures to increase the state's control in rural areas concentrated on building a national army. The creation of a permanent police force in the capital of Guatemala in the 1870s was less a response to any serious threat to public order than a modern civic amenity, like the new naptha gas street lighting inaugurated in the same period; there would be no institution comparable to the Salvadorean National Guard, the paramilitary police force created in 1912 explicitly to keep order in the countryside.

Before 1871 Guatemala could not truly be said even to have a national army, a deficiency keenly felt by Liberal presidents seeking to maintain order and boost production, and ideologically committed to reunifying Central America (under Guatemalan leadership) either through diplomacy or by military domination.[15] Before the 1870s Guatemala's army — or armies — were largely ad hoc affairs, evolved in part from the Spanish colonial militia system but considerably less structured, and departing from the colonial pattern of excluding Indian troops.[16] Post-independence Guatemalan armies incorporated *criollo* and *ladino* personnel of the traditional city-based militias; these led the dragooned Indian conscripts who provided the bulk of the forces. Most of the 19th Century armies were city-based, and in no sense national: they were still effectively local militias, or ill-armed mobs. As late as 1840 the militias of the cities of the western Guatemalan highlands, backing secession of their "Republic of the Highlands", fought an army raised by President Rafael Carrera (and lost).[17] The army commanded by Carrera during the next 25 years of his government shrank and swelled at short notice in response to the caudillo's immediate requirements (including foreign expeditions, such as the invasion of Nicaragua in 1857 to assist in the defeat of American filibuster William Walker, and war with El Salvador in 1863).

The creation of a true national army was a priority for both the governments of Miguel García Granados (1871–73) and Justo Rufino Barrios (1873–85); few advances to that end had been made in the first 50 years of independence. The law laid down to govern the organization and discipline of the colonial militias by the Spanish crown under Carlos III was still in force, unmodified, in 1871 as the basic law of the army.[18] García Granados modified these 18th Century Ordinances to bring them partially into line with the requirements for a national army modelled on modern European military establishments.[19] Despite the Monroe Doctrine the principal model was Spain. In 1873 Justo Rufino Barrios took a first step towards the establishment of a professional army; he contracted a Spanish military mission to set up and staff a military academy for training professional military officers.[20] A Military Code to replace earlier legislation was decreed in 1878 [21] and a law detailing army organization followed in 1892.[22] Like the Liberal Constitution of 1879 these codes and ordinances remained in force until 1945; they provided the legal framework for the army's development and operation, including provision for compulsory military service and conscription.

The creation of a national army was just one of the modernizing achievements of the late 19th Century. In his 12-year rule, Justo Rufino Barrios also presided over the transformation of the agricultural economy and the creation of much of the infrastructure considered necessary to a modern state. A railway had been built linking Guatemala City to the Pacific port of San José; telephone and telegraph services were operating in the capital, the latter linked to the world by undersea cable; and Guatemala City was given a police force.[23]

Haste to regularize the military establishment was matched by the enthusiasm to create more modern police institutions. Before 1871 the basis for implementation of the police function was the system of local government itself: colonial and early post-independence laws delegated the "policing" of towns and communities to the people themselves, as a civic duty to be performed and organized locally, not a function of central government. Created by decree in 1872 Guatemala City's new police force — called for a time the Civil Guard (*Guardia Civil*) — was ostensibly modelled on the Spanish Civil Guard, although in practice it appears to have borne little resemblance to its model.[24] Problems with the Civil Guard led President Barrios in 1881 to create a new "Model Police" for the capital, with a new body of regulations to govern their conduct. If only the police had been able to read the new regulations some good might have come out of the "Model Police". Patrolmen were obliged to tell their name and number, respectfully, to any person requesting them; to assist ladies "of whatever social class or condition"; to deny animals (and "burdened men") the use of the sidewalks; to ensure ox-carts were not driven but led, and that animals were not mistreated. Lost children and animals were to be taken home.[25] The force was to number 150 patrolmen and about 50 officers. Officers were subject to military discipline, and the Director responsible to the Minister of War.

It was in setting up the "Model Police" in 1881 that Guatemala first received United States security assistance, although the circumstances under which the New York City police force released Sergeant Joseph H. Pratt for his mission remain obscure. Sergeant Pratt began service in Guatemala City on 2 October 1881, and set about organizing the 150-man force along the lines of New York City's finest. With its officers kitted out in frock coats and men admonished to use club or revolver only in circumstances of "absolute necessity", the force so impressed President Barrios that he created a special tax to finance its operation.[26] Although officers were described as "well-uniformed, well-groomed, and each . . . provided with a manual of instructions"[27] Sergeant Pratt's protégés did not retain their high reputation very much longer than the ill-fated Civil Guard.

In the final analysis the new police institutions appear to have progressed little under either Justino Rufino Barrios or his successor, José Reina Barrios (1892–98). And under the long rule of Manuel Estrada Cabrera, from 1898, when he replaced the assassinated President Reina, to 1920, when he himself was overthrown, the civil police concept introduced by Sergeant Pratt appears to have disintegrated altogether. Some civil police organization endured in the capital, but the police forces of the previous decades were apparently subordinated to a vast and shadowy secret police apparatus at the service of Estrada Cabrera alone — a theme of Nobel Prize winner Miguel Angel Asturias' great novel, *El Señor Presidente*.

Best known for his omnipresent secret police, Estrada Cabrera did little to sustain his predecessors' efforts to develop a modern army. In 1919 Military Intelligence (G-2) reports filed by the US Military Attaché assigned to Central America (then based in Tegucigalpa, later in San José) described an army of about 6,000 men, noting that with the exception of a crack 500-man Presidential Guard [28] "most [of] these men, who are Indians, are badly fed and equipped and are very poor shots, with very little training, and no system of sanitation".[29]

Under Estrada Cabrera even the officer corps was demoralized, and subject to persecution by the President's *Policía Secreta*. The story-line of Asturias' *El Señor Presidente* centres on the President's use of the secret police to keep rising army officers under surveillance and purge them if they offered a threat to his absolute power. When, in 1908, a bomb failed to assassinate Estrada Cabrera, and the attempt was blamed on the cadets of the *Escuela Politécnica*, the academy was shut down for four years; all the cadets were jailed or exiled, many tortured, and some cadets and officers were killed. For a time, this episode halted the Guatemalan army's advance towards professionalism. Whether or not the cadets — or progressive junior officers — were involved in the assassination attempt, the affair fuelled Estrada Cabrera's suspicion of the modernizing officer corps, and may have been a factor in his subsequent, sometimes ludicrous, restrictions on the training permitted Guatemalan officers. In 1919, for instance, a French Military Mission arrived in Guatemala, invited by the Guatemalan envoy in Paris who, unfortunately, had not previously received the final approval from Estrada Cabrera. The US Military Attaché described the scene:

> [The President] received the Mission (three Captains and an Artillery Major) very cooly and has practically ignored them ever since their arrival. They are not allowed to carry out the project work, and are compelled to remain idle about the barracks, not even having been permitted to unpack the machine guns which they brought with them for purposes of instruction.[30]

According to US military intelligence, the social standing of the Guatemalan soldier, and even of the officers, in 1919 approached zero.

> ... there has been little ambition on the part of the youth of the Republic to adopt the career of arms. The ranks are composed usually of barefooted, ignorant, untrained Indians and halfbreeds who come from the lowest social stratum. Many of the officers are of the same social standing. As a result of this condition, the spirit of the people towards the army may

be described as one of no enthusiasm whatsoever. The soldiery is not accepted in social circles except for a few educated higher officers.[31]

Despite its failings, the army under Estrada Cabrera provided a relatively efficient mechanism for internal control of the Republic, with detachments based throughout the rural areas and in principal towns and cities. Military commands (*Comandancias de Armas*) were established in each of the 23 provinces, with 215 local command posts around the country, and 88 garrisons in the larger towns, at the ports and on the frontiers.[32] Although the Presidential Guard was armed with modern Mausers and a battery of Hotchkiss mountain guns, other troops were reportedly armed with an odd assortment of antique weapons (although US military intelligence reported that the President had 30,000 Mausers still packed in their original crates as a "reserve" armoury).[33]

After Estrada Cabrera's overthrow in 1920 measures to modernize the army were rapidly introduced. The *Escuela Politécnica* was again given the resources, and the prestige, required to train a professional officer corps, while the rural network of army commands was reinforced, extending the degree to which the central government and the army could monitor and control local affairs even in remote areas. By 1922 US military intelligence estimated that garrisons were manned by "from 10 to 20 men in even the smallest towns throughout the Republic" — an apparatus much like that developed in neighbouring El Salvador the decade before through the creation of the National Guard.[34]

The fall of Estrada Cabrera was also followed by the reorganization of the existing police apparatus, and the burning of police files and records.[35] Only in 1925 was a wholly new structure established, building on the capital city police force to establish a National Police. The 1925 police ordinances declared the police to be a civil, not a military institution, responsible for maintaining public order, protecting persons and property, and co-operating with the courts in the prevention and investigation of crime. The 1925 legislation made the first provision both for a National Police force under central government control, and for a special subdivision, the judicial police (*agentes de justicia*), a corps of detectives which would perform the political police function well into the 1980s.

The institutional basis for a functioning civil police organization was in place in Guatemala after 1925, but the army remained the principal instrument through which government exercised its coercive power within the country. Although the police would be further developed into efficient auxiliaries to the military in the subsequent decade, it was the expansion of the military role in domestic affairs that most characterized the regime of the next great *caudillo*, General Jorge Ubico.

Jorge Ubico: Order and Progress

General Jorge Ubico, President of Guatemala from 1931 to 1944, in 14 years of virtually unchallenged personal power, was responsible for major changes in most aspects of government, particularly in those related to internal security and the security system; changes in some cases paralleled by those of his contemporaries, Somoza and Martínez. Ubico took radical measures to extend central government control throughout the country on a variety of levels; some of these changes have had a persistent influence on later developments in the security system.

The Municipal Law (*Ley Municipal*) was rewritten in 1935 in order to abolish what had been the cornerstone of local government in colonial and 19th Century Central America: the autonomy of the *municipio*, or township, whereby municipal government was at least nominally an expression of local consensus. The elective post of mayor (*alcalde*) was eliminated, and municipal *intendentes*, which would take over its functions, were appointed directly from the capital.[36] These *intendentes*, responsible to the central government, directed all aspects of municipal administration, including the police function. Ubico's Departmental Law (*Ley de Departamentos*), which covered the powers and duties of the *Jefes Políticos* (Political Chiefs), the appointed governors of the departments, drew largely from the previous statute of 1879. The Political Chiefs remained central government's strong arm, with a new element being added: their supervision and direction of municipal government through the *intendente* system. Municipal *intendentes* were required to submit monthly reports to the Political Chiefs, who were also given responsibility for carrying out Ubico's plans for improving public health and sanitation, promoting export agriculture, and, above all, improving communications. In this last area the new law placed special emphasis on the imperative of making the roads safe, with Political Chiefs being empowered to try and sentence within 24 hours any captured "road agent".

Ubico would apply his new system for control of local government to the enforcement of new measures regulating the lives of the Indian peasantry. A long-standing tax called the *vialidad*, requiring two weeks labour on the roads — or payment in lieu thereof, beyond the means of the peasantry — was efficiently put to use, with Indian labour gangs conscripted to build and maintain Guatemala's slowly growing road network.[37] A police measure introduced, and enforced, by Ubico which more directly benefited the private estate owners — the 1934 vagrancy law — required peasants who owned less than ten *cuerdas* of land (about one acre) to provide, on pain of arrest, proof that they had worked for wages at least 100 days each year, the days worked being registered in a booklet to be filled in by farm owners or administrators. In the absence of such proof, dependent on the land-owners' good will, the peasant-labourer could remain tied to an estate quite as effectively as under previous debt bondage systems (formally abolished by Ubicio).[38]

The changes in administrative law regulating local government and Indian labour were accompanied by the building of a network of local army command posts throughout the country which gave the army at least a scattered presence even in remote areas, most of them linked by telegraph to the capital. Ubico also militarized the national road-building department, the telegraph system, and even the sanitation workers, making existing staff members of the army and placing them under military discipline.[39] The same measures were taken at about the same time in El Salvador and Nicaragua.

Deployment of the army in local command posts and Ubico's vigorous measures to use the army to enforce law and order were major features of the security system at that time. As with other Ubico initiatives, turning the army to police functions was established by law. A 1935 code of army regulations for times of peace declared that all towns "whose importance so requires it" should have a local army commander through whom the army is "to lend assistance to the civil authorities". Their duties are "the conservation of order in all towns, ranches and villages" and the pursuit of "criminals and deserters".[40]

As an arm of the central government against highwaymen and "bandits" the military security network appears to have been exceedingly efficient; a quote from a United States military intelligence report on the theme is representative of other contemporary observations:

> Banditry has never existed in Guatemala to any great extent. The traditional military control of all sections of the country has served as a most effective check... Since General Ubico took office the death penalty has been enforced against highway robbers. It has had a most salutary effect upon the lawlessly inclined element.[41]

Observers of Guatemala's army had had their eye on Ubico for some time before he reached the heights of power. He had seen active service in the 1906 border war with El Salvador, which gave him an important military credential; served as *Jefe Politico* and *Comandante de Armas* of Alta Verapaz department from 1907 to 1909, and then of the department of Retalhuleu from 1911 to 1919; and as head of the National Sanitary Commission during an army campaign to eradicate yellow fever, a successful campaign, modelled on US army programmes in the Panama Canal Zone, for which Ubico was highly praised.[42] By 1919 Ubico had a reputation as a "modernizing", professional officer, and the Estrada Cabrera regime (1898–1920) was beginning to totter. US military intelligence reported the cracks in the regime, adding that Estada Cabrera "is making preparations to meet any emergency, and is reorganizing the army in a very quiet but none the less significant manner".[43] This involved the appointment of a commission of senior army officers, including Colonel Jorge Ubico, described in the report as "unscrupulous but efficient" and "of presidential timber".

Dating from his yellow fever campaign, the then Colonel Ubico was well known to the United States military establishment in Central America. He was one of the first of Guatemala's rising officers to benefit from US training, and, after 1920, was instrumental in shifting Guatemalan military training and organization from Spanish and French military models to the United States'. Kenneth Grieb writes that toward the end of the Estrada Cabrera regime Ubico "spent several months on a training assignment with the United States Army" and returned to Guatemala in 1920 "in time to participate in the coup that installed General José M. Orellana in the Presidency".[44] As Orellana's Minister of War (1921–23) Ubico was responsible for replacing French Army instructors at the *Escuela Politécnica* with US army "advisers" (in 1931, as President, Ubico appointed US army Major John Considine, then serving as an instructor, Director of the *Escuela Politécnica*).

Whether or not influenced by Ubico's affinity with the US army, steps taken by the end of his first year as War Minister (1921) to modernize and revitalize the Guatemalan army were lauded in US military intelligence reports:

> From the entirely useless force I saw here in June, the army has been developed in a few weeks into a really good military machine. . . The old pompous colonels have disappeared and have been replaced by comparatively young men, well trained in the Polytechnic School, and having none of the arrogance and conceit of the old time leaders.[45]

Ironically, by the end of the Ubico regime in 1944, US intelligence was reporting the state of the army in terms remarkably similar to those applied to Estrada Cabrera's forces, calling it an army of ancient, useless officers and hopeless inefficiency. In the 1920s, however, Ubico was seen as the model soldier, the only doubts expressed being about his reputation for cruelty:

> 43 years old, of unmixed Spanish descent [Ubico] has the reputation of being extremely vindictive and cruel, so much so that this is practically a tradition about him. Very pro-American and a very able military commander.[46]

When Ubico reached the Presidency in 1931 many — not least the army's officer corps — saw his avowed dedication to economic development and public order as holding great promise. One of the most effusive testimonials in this regard was made by a future President of Guatemala, then Colonel Miguel Ydígoras Fuentes:

> All the inhabitants of the country with very rare exceptions hope that

General Ubico will be a kind of Messiah... What is certain is that he will hang everybody who steals anything from the nation, for he is a bitter enemy of that kind of thing. As for myself, I am very well satisfied, for now the greatest ambition of my life will become a reality, that is the Army of Guatemala will become a real army and not a mob, badly dressed, badly clothed, badly organized and badly... everything. It was General Ubico who, when he was Chief of Staff and I his aide, initiated the reorganization of the army...[47]

While Ubico's initial measures tended to place the army in an unprecedented situation of privilege, rationalization of the army's internal security function was matched by the creation of a sophisticated political police system and the reorganization of the uniformed National Police, a body created in 1922.

In 1932 the National Police had 800 personnel in the capital, including 60 detectives, then termed *Policía de Seguridad*, or security police. Another 600 were distributed among the 23 departments, largely restricted to the departmental capitals and under the direct command of the *Jefes Políticos*. Ubico also placed under National Police administration the *Resguardo de Hacienda* (Treasury Guard), renamed *Policía de Hacienda*, a force of some 400 men charged with halting clandestine liquor distillation, and the only civil police force that operated in the rural areas. US military intelligence commented on the former Treasury Guard's reputation for brutality since its creation in the 1920s, and the potential for Ubico to transform it into a disciplined force:[48]

We find government officers, clothed with wide powers of search and seizure, traveling armed about the country and frequently committing serious abuses. General Ubico in placing this organization under police discipline and training is taking another step in the right direction.

Force levels of the National Police, and the Treasury Police, did not change dramatically from their 1932 levels during Ubico's regime, and, indeed, would not change significantly until the 1960s.

By 1933 the police were already being described as highly efficient in both conventional law enforcement and as a political police. Ubico's Director of Police until 1937, General Roderico Anzueto, is known principally as the architect of Ubico's greatly feared secret police network, and remembered as a man

with a reputation for brutality, ruthlessness, capriciousness, and cunning who was considered responsible for much of the torture and the excesses that characterized the police and the prisons.[49]

Ubico kept a tight rein even on Anzueto, to the extent of reviewing with him lists of ongoing investigations and of prisoners, reportedly in daily meetings.[50]

The results were much admired by US intelligence, which in early 1933 described the police as an excellent force "highly trained and commanded by army officers", adding that its director, General Anzueto, "has an excellent secret service and little goes on within the country that is not immediately learned by both Anzueto, and his superior President Ubico".[51] The US intelligence reports remark on the futility of the effort of exiles living in Costa Rica to send in anti-Ubico handbills by mail, an objective "which will hardly be achieved in Guatemala, when it is realized that ALL mail is read in Guatemala, before being delivered. . ."[52] The effectiveness of such a police system in crushing Communism in the country was also noted by US intelligence:

> Since, early in 1932, the attempted communist outbreak was nipped in the bud, and the ringleaders tried and shot, there has been a complete absence of communist activity in Guatemala.
>
> The Government realizes that the country, with its 85% illiteracy, would provide a most fertile field for communist endeavor. Therefore, it may safely be asserted that as long as the present Government remains in power — with its well organized spy and police service — Guatemala will be scrupulously avoided by communist agitators. Without outside inspiration and guidance communism cannot exist in guatemala.[53]

Although none of the US intelligence reports attempt to estimate the numbers involved in secret police work, a 1935 report grasps at one indication of the scope of "secret" operations: its budget. The G-2 report of 22 July 1935 encloses a copy of a decree of 10 June 1935 that orders the Treasury to disburse $6,000:

> in favour of the National Police Headquarters to cover the cost of secret expenditures of the said organization during the months of March and April of the current year, at the rate of Q. [Quetzal] 3,000 monthly, to be charged to item No. 8810 of the current budget (signed by Ubico, 30 April 1935).[54]

Military Attaché Colonel N. W. Campanole comments that "for a small country like Guatemala, the expenditure of $36,000 per annum for this purpose is quite large." It is likely, furthermore, that other funds were available where required.

Ubico's ever keener interest in police organization, both political and conventional, was paralleled by his progressive neglect of the conventional military; the pattern was much the same in El Salvador under General Martínez during the same period. By 1941, US intelligence reported the state of the army as appalling, presenting it as in a state of decrepitude if possible worse than that reached in the last years of Estrada Cabrera, another past master of secret police organization: "With an octogenarian, illiterate Secretary of War and a preponderance of hopeless incompetents on its active list of 67 general officers."[55]

In assessing the relative weight of the civil and military components of the security system, the most important factor, however, is not the preponderance of ageing relics in military command structures, but the superior resources, training and prestige accorded Ubico's National Police and to army officers whose careers had meshed with police development. The National Police tended to recruit from among army veterans and to retain personnel more effectively than the largely conscript regular army, with its rapid turnover. The police, in addition, received supplementary military training, including the use of both pistol and rifle. By the early 1940s it was reported to be of considerably higher quality, as a body of fighting men, than units of the standing army, particularly the police units based in Guatemala City, some 50% of the entire force.[56]

Guatemala's October Revolution: A Decade of Reform

In May 1944, in neighbouring El Salvador, young officers, university students and middle-class protesters overthrew the Martínez regime after weeks of street demonstrations in demand of reform. In June 1944, Guatemalan political exiles gathered in El Salvador, and university students inside Guatemala went into the streets demanding similar changes. The street demonstrations culminated in a general strike on 24 June, declared by the students but backed by much of the urban middle class. Ubico responded by declaring martial law and demonstrators were shot dead in front of the National Palace. On the following day the general strike escalated, gaining support from virtually all the businessmen in the city, who closed their shops in support, and its object quite patently veered from demanding reforms to ousting Ubico from power. On 30 June Ubico reported his intention to resign, but appointed a hand-picked military junta to serve in his place. General Federico Ponce Vaídes rose to the occasion and was duly elected President by Ubico's hand-picked legislative assembly. After 108 days he was tumbled in what is known as the "20 October Revolution", in which disgruntled junior officers joined the middle classes to bring in an entirely new regime. A second military triumvirate then took provisional power until a new Constitution could be drafted and civilian Juan José Arévalo, elected President in December 1944, took office. Approved on 13 March 1945, this new Constitution ushered in a period unique in Guatemalan history, during which two democratically elected presidents would serve in succession and major changes would be made in Guatemalan society.

19

The elected governments of Presidents Juan José Arévalo, a civilian, (1945–50) and Colonel Jacobo Arbenz (1950–54) were memorable for the restoration of democratic procedures for the election of local and national government, and for their practical encouragement and support for the political organization, and participation in the democratic process, of population sectors hitherto excluded from either formal or informal political participation. These measures, for the first time, gave democracy some concrete meaning for the Indian peasantry, although they were not uniformly successful.

Inseparable from these political reforms were social and economic measures designed to irrevocably — if gradually — ameliorate the economic oppression of the peasants and the urban labouring classes. Legislation was introduced to open the way for both rural and urban labour organization, to establish new conditions for labourers, and, finally, to alter the pattern of land ownership itself by means of an agrarian reform. The revolutionary period also saw some changes in the Guatemalan security system, both police and military, changes most immediately apparent in the immediate aftermath of Ubico's (and Ponce Vaídes') overthrow.

Throughout the Ubico period, annual reports prepared by the Ministry of the Interior began invariably with the phrase: "In the course of the year, public order remained inalterable throughout the nation." The report issued to cover 1944, written by the new "revolutionary" government, appropriately began: "In the course of the year, public order was altered throughout the nation."[57] The security system itself was profoundly — though not permanently — changed as a consequence.

The elements of Ubico's contribution to the Guatemalan security system can be considered broadly as: the introduction of rigid central control of community policing; the extension of the military internal security infrastructure into the hinterland; and weaving a web of secret police agents within an integrated national police organization. In the ensuing period of democratic rule, which lasted ten years, secret police largely disappeared to be replaced by a new, relatively respectable security apparatus. The National Police were purged and renamed but remained much the same. The army itself largely turned away from its recent rural police function and developed characteristics more appropriate to a modern military institution.[58]

The changing role of the army after October 1944 was reflected in formal demands by the young officers who participated in ousting Ponce Vaídes. Decree No. 17 of the short-lived triumvirate, issued in November 1944, declared the precepts of the new army, which were later to be restated in the new Constitution of 1945:

> Within the new organization . . . there will be an effective guarantee for the members [of the armed forces] to the effect that their profession remains

organized on solid bases that cannot be destroyed by the caprice of the President, who will not concern himself with the technical or professional organization of the military, the responsibility for which will be delegated to the *Consejo Superior del Ejercito*, in order to ensure the social and professional position the Army deserves.[59]

This, if nothing else, indicates that the desperate measures of the young officers of 1944 involved institutional military interests, and either a defence of classic military values or aspiration to those values. The Constitution subsequently provided for the army's *Consejo Superior* (Supreme Council) to be elected by the army's officers and chiefs (*jefes*), and for the Congress to appoint the Chief of the Armed Forces from a slate of three officers chosen by the Army Council. In a sense, then, the first democratically elected civilian regimes of 20th Century Guatemala were bound to live with an unprecedented delegation of power to the institutional military. Civilian President Juan José Arévalo, moreover, appointed army officers to serve as Ministers of Defense, Communications, and the Interior (or Government), as well as to serve as departmental governors and, for the first time, as diplomats.[60]

By the completion of Juan José Arévalo's first year in the Presidency, professionalization of the army had been promoted by the expansion of the *Escuela Politécnica*; the creation of a school founded for young people seeking entrance to the academy (*Escuela de Aspirantes*); and the founding of a non-commissioned officers school, (*Escuela de Aplicación de Armas y Servicios*). Foreign training was encouraged, perhaps to Arévalo's later regret, and 78 officers sent on scholarships to study in the United States and the Panama Canal Zone. Arévalo in his speech to Congress on progress achieved in 1946 had warm words for US military assistance:

> The activities of the North American Military Mission are worthy of praise and the collaboration they have lent to the development of the reorganization of the Army very valuable. Its members have worked with zeal and enthusiasm on the commissions to which they were assigned.[61]

As the army distanced itself from the police function, professionalization in the police proper advanced. After the fall of Ubico and Ponce — in part because it had so firmly supported both — the National Police had disintegrated. Reorganized as the Civil Guard under the Arévalo administration, in 1945 a school was founded for aspiring members, with facilities for 100 students to be provided with a grant of 15 quetzals (about $15) a month for living expenses; a radio station, the *Voz de la Guardia Civil* (Voice of the Civil Guard) was created and an educational centre built for the National Guard which included a theatre, radio studio and a cinema.[62] A Civil Guard magazine editorial described the break-up of the previous police system, the public indignation against former police officers, and their temporary replacement by volunteers from among university students and middle-class supporters. The picture given is strongly reminiscent of the first days of the new regime in Nicaragua after Somoza was overthrown, though without the attendant grievous consequences of Nicaragua's bloody and bitter civil war. The volunteer youngsters are even called "*muchachos*" (the boys), as in Nicaragua:

> A police institution was rapidly created to take over from the brave . . . *muchachos*, most of them university students and Boy Scouts, who [initially] directed traffic and kept order during the day and made dangerous rounds in the treacherous darkness of those tempestuous nights. The members of the old police were pointed out as the principal enemy of the revolutionary triumph. The bulk of them were found in their headquarters. The rest had dispersed; each one . . . was sought with fury by the people, who remembered the abuses committed by the overthrown government. The secret police who had . . . defended the private interests of the tyrant fled for the borders. Since the Revolution no more has been heard of these agents . . . [What the people demand is] a new guard, a model guard, an efficient respectful and energetic guard that would respect the rights of the people and control the outbreaks of reactionary counter-revolutionaries.[63]

Avévalo turned to the United States for help in building the new police corps, which obliged by sending an instructor from the Federal Bureau of Investigation, at United States' expense. Although the Civil Guard's own publication and Arévalo's speeches give an unrealistically exalted idea of the new Guard, there was in fact a clean sweep of the old police system, with few former National Police personnel permitted to join the Civil Guard, and a determined effort to end the more appalling abuses of the Ubico period. Reform was encouraged by a persistent campaign of denunciations of torture and killing of prisoners committed by Ubico's regime, previously hushed by the victims' fear of retaliation. By 1945 the Civil Guard numbered 1,496 with more than half of them based in the capital. The reorganized Treasury Guard remained a force of about 500 men.[64]

Sociological studies of Guatemalan communities tend to confirm that there was a general change in the tenor of police action during the "revolutionary" period, particularly as it related to local government. According to one scholar's monograph on San Luis Jilotepeque:

> Police interference withs the citizenry was cut down. For example, in a fairly dramatic episode in 1948 the mayor arrested and incarcerated a lieutenant of the Guardia Civil who had entered and searched a private house in violation of Article 37 of the Constitution of 1945.[65]

While the abolition of Ubico's all-powerful secret police, the restructuring of the National Police and a revision of the role of the military were major developments between 1944 and 1954, reaction to Ubico's alterations of local government also led to significant structural changes during the same period and later. The most fundamental change wrought by Ubico at local level was the *intendente* system. Ideally, this system might have served as a means whereby government could take local power from the local economic elites' control and successfully implement national reform programmes. Ubico, however, does not seem to have made use of the replacement of the previously elected mayor by centrally appointed *intendentes* to that end, but only as a means to reinforce the traditional economic structure and prevent disruption of the social fabric. One of Ubico's most long-lasting public order measures, for example, was to grant, in 1936, "All proprietors of rural estates (*fincas*), their administrators or legal representatives, the status of agents of the government", empowered to bear arms and make arrests. The farms covered by the decree were specifically defined as those producing cash crops, and not the peasant farmers' subsistence plots.[66] This law effectively granted police powers to Guatemalans who owned large rural properties, a situation that continued during the Arévalo administration and was modified only under the Arbenz regime. Similar provisions were reinstituted in the late 1960s in the context of the rural counter-insurgency offensive.[67]

The 1944 revolution abolished Ubico's *intendente* system, reverting to the earlier system of autonomous municipal government by means of the *Ley Municipal* of 1946. Revulsion against the abuses of Ubico's centralist political regime ensured that local autonomy would be a fundamental part of the new order, with only passive control of the purse strings remaining available to the central government as a means to enforce the implementation of its policies. In practice the restoration of local autonomy as a measure against abuse may have backfired. When the "revolutionary" central government sought to bring about important changes in the country's social and economic structure it found itself hamstrung in many rural areas where the local elites retained their old influence. In the optimistic, effervescent political milieu of the Arévalo and Arbenz period the impetus of central government policy — backed by a solid sector of the armed forces, vigorous new political parties, labour organizations, and the new government agencies charged with implementing the agrarian and other reforms — sufficed to some extent to push these through. The new political context also favoured the entry of non-elite sectors, including the peasantry, into participatory politics at the local level. Yet even in the most active period of the Arbenz government, some rural areas remained virtually unaffected and effectively closed to the central government's social programmes. In these regions, local government remained firmly under the control of the traditional elites; outside political organizations, labour federations and central government alike were shut out. In the northern department of Alta Verapaz, for instance, an area of largely German colonization which, in the early 1950s, had Guatemala's highest percentage of Indian population (93.4%) and illiteracy (92.5%) even nominal representatives of the "revolutionary" political parties strongly opposed bringing the Indians into local political life, to the extent of systematically opposing literacy programmes:

> Many informants expressed themselves as opposed to [literacy] training for Indians, lest the latter develop political and social ambitions . . . ostensibly pro-government officials of Cobán spoke of the Indian with disdain (and treated him in the same way).[68]

Ubico's *intendente* system had, furthermore, brought about the disappearance of all posts traditionally held by the Indian communities' council of elders, or *principales*, and the destruction of these communities' traditional forms of self-government. Henceforth Indians served, if at all, in relatively menial municipal posts. In many areas the 1944 "revolution" changed none of this:

> After 1945 the office of intendent was abolished, and the government of San Antonio (Sacatepéquez) was restored to its former position of local autonomy. There was no return, however, to the pre-1943 system, and the Indian continued to be excluded from any position of political power.[69]

In certain areas, then, the situation of the peasantry under Arévalo and Arbenz remained much the same as before. Local autonomy there meant only that in their efforts to keep things as they were, agrarian elites were unhampered by the interference of local representatives of central government. But this resistance to change was not the norm, and enclaves such as the coffee lands of Alta Verapaz, among the most resistant to reform, were the exception and not the rule.

The social and economic reforms pursued by the Arévalo and Arbenz governments were, in fact, significant. Their achievements, and failures, have been amply documented. Here, there is need only to note the points in which the reforms of the "revolutionary" period clashed most significantly with the interests of the United States, and, in particular, with those of the United Fruit Company.

The US United Fruit Company's Empire

Coffee became the mainstay of the Guatemalan economy by the 1870s, and would remain so. Bananas came late as a plantation export crop, and even by the 1940s represented only about one-third of the export income provided by coffee,[70] yet they were the nation's second export. Banana production was promoted by the introduction of a tax exemption for their export in 1901, and in 1906 the US-owned United Fruit Company (UFCo) signed its first banana purchase and sales agreements. The Company subsequently received a government grant of 170,000 acres of land around the town of Bananera, in Izabal department, near the Atlantic Coast.[71] United Fruit's banana empire in Guatemala had its beginnings in railway building. Late 19th Century Liberal governments had raised funds to bring in foreign contractors to build railroads from Guatemala City to the Pacific Coast ports of San José and Champerico, and had begun a line from the Atlantic port at Puerto Barrios. The contract for the last 60 miles to the capital went to Costa Rican based railwayman and banana grower Minor Keith, who, in partnership with two US entrepreneurs, had founded UFCo in 1899, incorporating it in New Jersey.[72] Land grants, exclusive rights to operate the railway, and virtual ownership of Puerto Barrios were the concessions granted by the Guatemalan government in exchange for completing the railway. In 1912, United Fruit's railway subsidiary, under the name International Railways of Central America, was granted control over the other railway lines in the country.

Under a 1930 agreement the Ubico government made further extensive land grants to UFCo on the Pacific Coast, in exchange for the construction of a Pacific Coast port. The port was never built,[73] but the plantation based at Tiquisate would expand to cover much of the southern half of the department of Escuintla. UFCo had, by that time, long monopolized commercial banana growing in Guatemala and was the nation's largest landowner, with some 555,000 acres — much of it dedicated to livestock — of which 85% was described as an uncultivated reserve against banana disease.[74]

By the 1950s, although coffee remained the principal export crop, UFCo dominated a broad sector of the Guatemalan economy. Its domination of the transport and communications infrastructure earned it the nickname of "*El Pulpo*" ("The Octopus"), both for its stranglehold on the economy and the many tentacles of its involvement.[75] The Company controlled the nation's sole Atlantic port and its railway system, enjoying preferential rates and scheduling for shipping its own products. In the absence of a highway to the Atlantic (completed only in the mid-1950s) it controlled all shipping to that coast. United Fruit also owned the Tropical Radio and Telegraph Company, which virtually monopolized telegraph and radio communications, and a great many other enterprises.

The first clashes between the US/UFCo and the Guatemalan reformist governments of 1944–54, followed the promulgation of the 1947 Labour Code, and subsequent strike action against United Fruit and its subsidiary companies. The new labour code legalized the organization of farm workers into unions, for the first time in Guatemala, although initially limiting these rights to workers employed on large farms.[76]

Opposition to the new labour code was led by the United States government, which protested against the regulations permitting the creation of agricultural workers' unions, and strike action, on farms employing 500 or more, or commercial enterprises employing over 1,000 agricultural and other workers. This issue illustrated the level of US domination over the Guatemalan economy by the 1940s. The Department of State protested, in May 1947, on the grounds that the law discriminated against US enterprises, since:

> the only concerns [in Guatemala] with more than 1,000 employees are the United Fruit Company, the Compañía Agrícola de Guatemala, and International Railways of Central America, all American enterprises. With one possible exception, the only employers of more than 500 agricultural laborers are the American owned Compañía Agrícola de Guatemala and United Fruit Company.[77]

The Arévalo government denied discrimination, pointing out two nationally owned farms and seven privately owned farms with more than 500 workers.[78]

Conflict escalated inevitably as a consequence of the 1952 agrarian reform law and expropriations that began in 1953. The first redistribution of land affected state owned farms — a heritage of the confiscation of the estates of German nationals during World War II — granting titles to peasant co-operatives organized among farm labourers. Expropriation of private lands followed, with compensation paid in bonds and based on the value previously declared by the owners for tax purposes (many owners, including United Fruit, had under-declared their plantations' value). The agrarian reform law provided for the expropriation of idle or under-exploited land; such as the vast tracts held as "reserves" by United Fruit, much of them prime agricultural land turned over to cattle ranching or just left fallow. By June 1954 expropriation orders had been issued affecting 1,002 plantations, totalling 2.7 million acres. About half of the land was actually handed over to peasant co-operatives and small-holders, with the estimates of the numbers of beneficiaries ranging up to 100,000 peasant families.[79] Decrees were issued to expropriate 387,000 acres from UFCo holdings on the two coasts, and offered compensation based on the company's own tax declarations of the value of the land: $1.18 million. The United Fruit and the US government denounced the offer, and demanded $16 million in compensation.[80]

It remains for historians to wrangle over which was the main factor that precipitated the United States overthrow of Arbenz' government with the bombing raids and mercenary invasion of June 1954. The *economic* threat to US interests posed by Arbenz' agrarian reform was, of course, apparent to all. The refusal, even by the more moderate Arévalo government to crush left-wing influence on labour organizations, and control strike action on the plantations (and UFCo's railway company) had already been the object of sizzling cables from the State Department to Guatemala City since 1949.[81] The expressly *political* threat perceived by the US was gauged both by Guatemala's new economic policies and domestic committment to broad political pluralism, and its international shift towards non-alignment, just at the time when the US was demanding the total exclusion of left-wing philosophies or political ideologies, and their adherents, from the political life of the Americas.[82] Identification by the US of individual members of government and leaders of labour organizations as "known leftists", the legal registration of left-wing political parties, allowing them to participate in electoral politics, and Guatemala's deviation from the blind support offered by other American states for US anti-Communist initiatives in international fora, were all signals registered by John Foster Dulles' State Department that, with or without UFCo's tribulations, might well have prompted intervention.

2. Castillo Armas; the CIA and Resurrection of the Secret Police

Overthrow of Arbenz: US Involvement

The overthrow of the democratic government of Colonel Jacobo Arbenz in June 1954 has been described in numerous contrasting accounts by participants, apologists, and critics. It is no longer possible to challenge attribution of the major role to armed forces of the United States — directed by the Central Intelligence Agency (CIA) — since Dwight D. Eisenhower's proud boasts, in his 1963 memoirs, of having ordered the successful operation contradicted earlier, pious denials by US officials. In a speech to the American Booksellers Association, Eisenhower even explained his decision to authorize the CIA to supplement its B-26 bombers and P-47 fighters (which began bombing and strafing Guatemala City on 18 June) with US Air Force planes flying out of Nicaragua, until Arbenz resigned on 27 June.[83] All recent accounts are in agreement that it was the army's refusal to defend the Arbenz government — and its withdrawal to barracks — and United States air power that forced Arbenz to resign, and not the contingent led by Colonel Castillo Armas. On 18 June 1954, Castillo Armas did cross the border from Honduras with his rag-tag force of several hundred mercenaries and personal followers, but remained some six miles from the Honduran border (in the town of Esquipulas) until it was clear that the army would offer no resistance, and that the regular air sorties over the capital had worn down Arbenz' will to resist. He finally reached the capital *not* at the head of the "Liberation Army" but in Ambassador John Peurifoy's Embassy plane. The operation's success in winning the army's sullen acquiescence has been discussed largely in terms of its growing disenchantment with the isolation imposed on Guatemala by the US embargo on military equipment (which, after 1948, blocked arms sales from the US and its allies) and fear that Arbenz would agree to arm the peasant unions to defend the regime as a militia independent of the army (the institutional interests of the military were seen to be in jeopardy in other areas, too). The United States' official motive for intervention — that Arbenz was a Communist — appears to have had little credence within the army itself, and Arbenz' social reform programme was not a major factor in its position. A perhaps underestimated factor was the respect much of the officer corps held for Colonel Castillo Armas, a man with ferocious ideological views, which on at least one occasion led to his imprisonment by the Arbenz government (and "escape", clearly with inside help); a view borne out after the capitulation of Arbenz and the eventual showdown between the army and the "Liberation" forces.[84]

When Arbenz resigned he handed control of the government to a military junta headed by a close supporter, Colonel Carlos Enrique Díaz. Díaz was forced out two days later, on 29 June 1954, reportedly on the direct demand of US Ambassador Peurifoy, pressure meanwhile being exerted by continual bombing of the capital. Díaz was replaced by Colonel Elfego Monzón, who immediately flew to a meeting with Castillo Armas in San Salvador presided over by Ambassador Peurifoy. On 3 July Castillo Armas flew in triumph to Guatemala City, attended a party with the five junta members at the US Embassy on 4 July, and on 8 July was elected President of the Republic — by the five junta members: all in all a busy week in Guatemalan history.

The Castillo Armas government's achievements were primarily negative; existing political parties and labour unions were dissolved, and much of the social and economic legislation of the previous ten years annulled:

> Executive orders repealed the Law of Forced Rental and the 1952 Agrarian Reform Law. 99.6% of all land expropriated under the law was returned to its former owners, including UFCo [United Fruit Company]. Virtually all beneficiaries of the agrarian reform were dispossessed, and all cooperatives dissolved. Literacy programs, branded tools of Communist Indoctrination, were suspended, and hundreds of rural teachers fired. The government ordered the burning and proscription of 'subversive' books such as the novels of Guatemalan [Nobel prize winner] Miguel Angel Asturias. . .[85]

Up to 9,000 Guatemalans were detained by the new regime, many of them tortured and held without trial for several years; 8-10,000 fled into exile.[86]

What is perhaps most striking in the pattern of repression in the months after the "Liberation" is the *traditional* form it took: in the main, short-term political imprisonment or exile. By 1960s standards there was surprisingly little bloodshed, and no persistent pattern of political killings by the government, despite its hyperactive anti-Communism and the total lack of protection or redress from its arbitrary security measures. Killings did occur, mostly of peasants known for their leadership of agrarian unions; the murderers were primarily local

Castillo Armas' followers in areas affected by agrarian reform and peasant direct action.

Some of the killings were clearly motivated by revenge and took particularly savage forms in a foretaste of the institutionalized terror of the 1960s. In the first days of July 1954, for example, local landowners in the Bananera area grabbed leaders of the local peasant union, murdering at least five of them; one source reported that trade unionist Alaric Bennet was publicly mutilated and killed in Bananera and his severed head mounted on a post in the town square.[87] In his study of San Luis Jilotepeque, social scientist John Gillin gives a less dramatic account, saying of the "few literate and 'enlightened' young Indian men" who had become leaders in the peasant unions: "All of these leaders have been removed from the scene as a result of the Liberation, several in hasty executions carried out in Chiquimula."[88] Once Castillo Armas was firmly installed, however, the killings appear to have ground to a halt. While in the immediate aftermath of the takeover the "Liberation" government clearly sanctioned summary executions on a limited scale, there are no convincing reports that large-scale killings continued thereafter. A reasonable estimate, on the basis of conversations with some former members of the Arbenz government, would place the toll of peasant and labour leaders and political activists killed in the immediate aftermath of the invasion at about 300. Most victims of the Castillo Armas regime suffered torture, imprisonment and exile, but not summary execution or "disappearance"; a relative "softness" that might seem inexplicable to Guatemalan army officers accustomed to the post-1960s standards of repression. In 1954 there was neither an apparatus, nor a counter-insurgency orientation encouraging wholesale murder along modern lines. Certainly at that time the army would have had no part in it.

The army, in fact, moved in August 1954 to pull the teeth of the scruffy band of mercenaries and self-declared patriots of Castillo Armas' "Liberation Army", both to stop the disorder created by their vigilante-style operations, and to put an end once and for all to the boasts of its leaders that it would become a permanent civilian militia. The Guatemalan army in 1954 was not prepared to tolerate any kind of permanent armed civilian force, particularly when the expectation that Arbenz would create and arm such a force had been a major factor in the army's complacency as the Arbenz government crumbled and Castillo Armas flew in to take power.

On 4 August 1954, the officers of the army general staff met the Director of the Military Academy to plan an operation intended to teach the "*Liberacionistas*" who was boss. The same day the Director led a cadet force to disarm the main force of the "Liberation Army", then barracked in the Hospital Roosevelt in Guatemala City. After a pitched battle, in which some 50 "*Liberacionistas*" were killed, the rest were disarmed and marched through the city with their hands on their heads.[89] Castillo Armas survived this trial of strength, but by 1956 the paramilitary groups backing him were almost entirely dissolved, and military disquiet at the existence of rival armed forces assuaged. Castillo Armas managed to save face when the army agreed to the expulsion and exile of the cadets involved in the humiliation of his paramilitary forces, but the army won the final round when the 1956 Constitution pointedly prohibited the existence of civilian militias outside the control of the armed forces.[90] Exiled cadet leaders were permitted to return to the army after the assassination of Castillo Armas in July 1957; some of them subsequently participated in the young officers' revolt of November 1960 which provided the nucleus of Guatemala's future guerrilla movement.[91]

The destruction of progressive political parties and labour unions, and the rolling back of reforms appeared complete by 1955. There was no turning back the clock in regard to the people's consciousness of what they had lost.

> In 1955 there were no political parties and no political arguments. Everyone was for the incumbent president, Castillo Armas, and against the Communists. But 10 years of political activity have opened people's eyes and minds. They are aware of social and economic issues even though they may not want, for the moment, to discuss them in political terms.[92]

Castillo Armas and successive governments offered no substitutes for the institutions smashed upon "liberation", nor any satisfaction to the aspirations raised under the previous regime. Until 1963, the main concern of the post-invasion government was seemingly to throw up successive obstacles to the insurgent explosion thought to be just around the corner; from laws against Communism to measures banning former President Arévalo from stepping on Guatemalan soil. The administrative vacuum created by the destruction of Guatemala's democratic government was progressively filled by the army, culminating in its outright takeover of all areas of government in 1963, and ensuing rule by a self-proclaimed government of the armed forces. From that moment the ruling Movement of National Liberation party's (MLN) stop-gap measures to guard against creeping revolution were replaced by a systematic regearing of the security system to meet such a threat by plain force. The security system built in the 1960s progressively dominated all aspects of political life.

Richard Bissell, one of the top CIA officials responsible for implementing Jacobo Arbenz' overthrow in 1954, was later, as CIA Director of Plans (Operations), responsible for the Bay of Pigs invasion of Cuba. Quoted by several sources in the 1960s, after his resignation in the wake of the Bay of Pigs fiasco, Bissell described the overthrow of Arbenz as "an unqualified success".[93] Some ten years later, in a conversation quoted by Leonard Mosley, in his study of the Dulles family, he qualified this assessment:

> Guatemala was a complete success in the sense that the tactical object was achieved. . . It was done more or less on time and on budget. . . Whether having placed a friendly political leader in power and having got rid of Communist influences, you can then turn the situation around in the country is open to question. We got Arbenz out. We substituted Armas. But I think most people would argue that from the day he was installed nobody has been able to make much of a success of Guatemala.[94]

From Secret Police to Counter-Insurgency: 1954-63

Castillo Armas presided over a police system almost entirely oriented toward countering subversion, at its core an intelligence system set up by the United States. A 1956 classified survey of the security system produced by the US International Cooperation Administratio (ICA) — AID's predecessor — described the single-minded political orientation of all sectors of the police system:

> the ever present driving thought is the 'alert' to communist activity and attack . . . the preparedness and functional operations are more and more directed toward . . . near obsessive-compulsive acts closely bordering on the neurotic.[95]

Within hours of Castillo Armas' triumphal appearance in Guatemala City a "Committee Against Communism" (*Comité Contra el Comunismo*) appeared on the scene and immediately took charge of the records of the departing government. In the course of those first few days this "Committee" also acquired extensive records of the political parties and labour organizations active during the previous ten years and considered by the new regime, and more decisively, by the United States, to have been tainted with "Communism". The 1956 ICA report said blandly that the *Comité* was "apparently extremely effective in intelligence operations" and had dealt with the records of "thousands" of Communist Party members and pro-Arbenz labour and political organizations. The reported efficiency of the "Committee Against Communism" was astonishing: "Having processed some 600,000 documents without a loss, this unit's records and records control are most excellent."[96]

This was in dramatic contrast to the same survey's assessment of the Record Bureau of the National Police in 1956, regarded as a shambles of disorganization with "piles of documents, files, etc. dumped on the floor".[97]

The mysterious identity of the members of the "Committee Against

Communism" was revealed when, years later, the CIA operatives involved in tumbling Arbenz got around to writing their memoirs. CIA official David Phillips, in *The Night Watch*, revealed that actually it was him and CIA counter-intelligence officers who sorted the records and determined how they could be put to use:

> I returned to Guatemala for a one-month temporary duty assignment . . . as part of a team [to] assist the new government in sifting and evaluating the documents left behind when Arbenz and his friends abruptly went into the foreign embassies. The papers we found were an intelligence gold mine, filled with nuggets of information. . . The CI-nicks — counter-intelligence officers — who worked with me were ecstatic. These were pearls which could be fondled for years.[98]

The "Black List"

The names of suspected Communists compiled by the "Committee's" personnel from the previous government's records, and political parties and labour organizations served as the basis both for immediate and for long-term action, and were incorporated into a legally established "register" of "all those persons that in any form have participated in communist activities". The register, set up under the provisions of the 24 August 1954 "Law Against Communism",[99] was immediately known as the "Black List" and informed sources estimated that by November 1954 it included names and information on 70,000 suspects.[100] Names from the membership lists of the pro-Arbenz political parties, teachers' associations, peasant unions, and, of course, the small Communist Party (*Partido Guatemalteco del Trabajo*, PGT) went directly into the "Black List". The "Law Against Communism" declared that mere inclusion of a person's name in this register constituted a "grave presumption of dangerousness" and besides banning them from public office or employment, authorized the culprit's indefinite imprisonment without charge or trial.[101]

The "Black List" was unusual in that it was acknowledged to exist, and gave keepers of the list enormous powers to indelibly mark Guatemalans as suspect in accord with the flimsiest criteria. The relative sophistication of its data base and the records control system set up by the United States in 1954 may have dazzled the Guatemalans into thinking they were fully informed on all possible subversives in the country. The list certainly appears to have persisted as an index of potential subversives through the 1960s, 1970s and into the 1980s. Individuals marked as "dangerous" over 20 years ago have seemingly remained on the books of the intelligence agencies as permanent security threats, even when they have withdrawn from political or union activities entirely or lived in exile for decades. The steady trickle of elderly exiles who are detained and murdered shortly after returning to Guatemala to attend the funeral of a relative, or to settle urgent business matters, (and often arrested at the airport on arrival) implies that the "Black List" compiled in 1954 by the "Committee Against Communism" continued to be operational under the post-1960s security terms whereby to be suspect is to be dead.

In 1954, intelligence and political police operations were controlled first by the "Committee Against Communism" and then by a "National Security Council" which absorbed the "Committee" as a permanent agency under the name of "Department of Defense Against Communism". The intense preoccupation with internal security under Castillo Armas is illustrated by the practice of holding "Presidential Intelligence Conferences" at 9 am every day at the Casa Presidencial at which Castillo Armas could consult with heads of the new Security Council, Army Intelligence, and of the conventional police forces. As a 1956 report notes, intelligence was assessed, policies determined, and operations co-ordinated at these 9 am meetings.[102]

In 1956, the head of the Defense Against Communism department was a 28 year old civilian who had formerly worked with the "Committee Against Communism" and was also assistant director of the National Security Council — in effect the real head of the Security Council, since the nominal head was a civilian attorney appointed by the President but not operationally involved in security work. The department had a staff of around 30 and a mandate covering all aspects of intelligence work.[103]

A second component of the Security Council was a Department of Security supposedly modelled on the US Secret Service. Its 36 staff members acted as a security escort for the President as well as carrying out intelligence work concerning threats against him. The third component was, in essence, a resurrection of Jorge Ubico's *judiciales*, the Judicial Police traditionally serving as Guatemala's secret police. As the 1956 ICA report noted, Ubico had removed the "organic investigative unit" from the conventional law enforcement apparatus to create "an autonomous agency called the Policia Judicial, which exists today as a key intelligence unit..."[104] In 1956 the Judicial Police force level was 184, and it was considered the main source of manpower for the footwork of intelligence and the detention of "political criminals".[105]

The "conventional" law enforcement agencies were dominated by the National Police, a renamed, reorganized version of the Civil Guard, with about 2,000 men, over half of them based in the capital city area. As with the forthrightly political police, the National Police was also "acutely geared to security against subversive activity and communist attack, with the primary police function taking a secondary role".[106] The degree of disorganization and sheer sloppiness predominating in the conventional law enforcement sectors of the National Police is illustrated in the ICA report, which describes a visit to one department in police headquarters where the eight personnel were all "reading comic books, newspapers, or with head on table 'resting' ".[107]

The three top-ranking officers of the police were described as having "one driving thought", "the maintaining of a constant alertness to communist attack and subversive activity", and as relatively efficient in ensuring that even at the lowest levels, traditional police roles were skewed to the regime's political priorities. The Civil Guard had formerly fielded groups of Mobile Guards in rural areas, primarily to deal with such problems as cattle rustling; in 1956 the 14 groups of Mobile Police were described as dedicated primarily to checking on local people suspect as "possible communist agents".[108] The 663 men of the Treasury Guard (*Guardia de Hacienda*, translated as "Border Patrol" in the ICA report) patrolled borders and ports of entry, to combat the smuggling of contraband, but also had a new role as an intelligence source: "It also carefully checks suspicious persons as possible subversive agents and gathers security type information."[109]

The 1956 ICA report concludes that conventional law enforcement is almost an incidental concern of the revamped Guatemalan law-enforcement agencies, but that the priority should indeed be stabilization of the political situation, with civil law enforcement to come later:

> It may be assumed . . . that the primary police function of protecting life and property, and preserving the peace, is in reality a secondary function of the police administration and executive management. Operations top level planning, intelligence gathering activities are singularly directed toward alertness and preparedness against 'the threat of the communists', instead of being directed against the army of criminals.
>
> In spite of the lack of professional policemanship . . . the National Police force is performing a good job in maintaining a high degree of preparedness against subversive activity and attack. Its fulfillment of its police function is at best to be rated as fair.
>
> If a stability in the country's security against subversives is attained, then it may well be a two to a four year period before the desired level of law enforcement is achieved.[110]

Recommendations for assistance to the Guatemalan police services in 1956 centred primarily on the need to polish their performance in the political police area, in "special investigation work", "to be utilized for the identification of unlawful organized underground activities". Assignment to Guatemala was urged of an:

> Investigative Specialist qualified to advise and assist in training and organizing 'civil police' personnel in special investigation work including methods of investigation, following up undeveloped leads, training in physical and technical surveillance, utilization of scientific aids and techniques in special investigations, developing and preserving physical evidence, [and]. . . To teach detailed techniques in interrogations, interviews. . . .[111]

The Investigations Advisor was also to become operationally involved in "special investigations" work, "supervising and directing the most complicated, involved types of investigation".[112] In late 1956 a police advisory programme began, headed by David L. Laughlin and an Investigations Advisor named Popa; the relation of Public Safety investigations advisers to US intelligence agencies is discussed in Volume I.[113]

After 1958, the Guatemalan government passed under the Presidency of General Miguel Ydígoras Fuentes (a former Ubico minister) until his overthrow in March 1963. The security system changed little either in numbers or in quality during this period. In July 1962 the US government instructed its embassies in seven countries, including Guatemala, to draft local "internal defense plans", within which they were to "briefly summarize the military, police, intelligence, and psychological aspects of internal defense", point out particular "vulnerabilities" to subversion in their countries, and propose actions "to reduce susceptibility of subversive insurgency".[114] The Internal Defense Plan for Guatemala described civil police forces in 1962 as ill-organized and ill-equipped to deal with guerrilla activity or any large scale public disorder, and remarkably, considering the CIA's efforts in 1954, with "no intelligence system worthy of the name". The National Police, with some 3,000 men, remained the major civil agency, and was considered corrupt and inefficient, little changed since police assistance began in 1956.[115]

The quality of the political police, too, apparently had hardly improved, gaining little from its technical head start in the heady days of US support for Guatemalan anti-Communism under Castillo Armas, and suggesting that no structural reforms were made then that in any way differentiated the secret police from Guatemala's traditional secret police. Indeed, the assessment of the various secret police branches in the 1962 survey suggests they were as unsavoury as any of their predecessors. A Department of Special Investigations (DIE) replaced and worked closely with the Judicial Police, still the major secret police body — although newly divided into supposedly separate "common crime" and "political crime" sections. The estimated 150 officers and men of the Judicial Police were said to be primarily "employed by the President and other high officials in the investigation and harassment of political opponents and in the carrying out of this or that unsavoury assignment". They were described as "feared and despised by virtually everyone in Guatemala except those whom they serve", and by their equally despicable counterparts in the DIE. The DIE agents, "like those of the Judicial Police, are considered little better than hoodlums".[116]

One pre-1963 development that merits mention was the emergence, as an active part of the internal security apparatus, of the army's Military Police, from its original internal role (protecting military installations, enforcement of military regulations and discipline) to a paramilitary force increasingly called upon to "supplement and in some cases supplant the civilian police".[117]

> In times of emergency, particularly when the 'law of public order' invests the Minister of Defense with primary responsibility for the establishment and maintenance of public tranquility, the military forces in general, and the Military Police in particular, are called on. . . The Military Police, which is the military body first used in situations calling for military intervention, are relatively well trained and paid and their discipline is good. Members of this body are carefully selected for this duty from among new Army recruits on the basis of physical condition and background. . .

Despite the utility of the force, the report added that the Military Police are in general "feared by the people, for they will not hesitate to employ firearms if provoked", and cited a recent example in which Military Police guarding the Congress were heckled by students from the law school across the street who had "congregated illegally": "in short order, three students were sprawled dead on the sidewalk."[118] After 1963 the Military Police expanded enormously and were fully integrated into the regular forces of the internal security system.

All in all, 1962 policy papers assessing Guatemalan security concluded that training and assistance to civil police forces should be continued, particularly in riot control and counter-guerrilla operations, but that the emphasis of security assistance should be on military co-ordination of security operations, with the September 1962 Internal Defense Plan recommending increased "in-country advisory assistance in the field of security and intelligence" and "counter-guerrilla training within all echelons of the armed forces". Assistance was proposed to "establish effective professional intelligence channels within the military forces" and to "establish operational plans for the joint operations of all law enforcement agencies and military units." Having dealt with civilians in the years since 1954, security assistance would increasingly rely on buttressing the army's own apparatus and its takeover of the civil law enforcement system.[119] As the army itself regeared under the government of the armed forces that overthrew Ydígoras Fuentes in March 1963, more scope for radical revision of the other sectors of the security section could be undertaken as adjuncts to the army itself, with massive increases in United States assistance flowing to both sectors.

Notes to Part 1

Chapter 1

1. For a useful summary see Ralph Lee Woodward, Jr., *Central America: A Nation Divided* (New York: Oxford University Press, 1976), pp. 42–5. The *encomienda* was officially replaced by the *repartimiento* system under the "New Laws" of 1542; in practice the *repartimiento* system came into effect gradually, but remained law in Guatemala into the 18th Century (although abolished in other parts of the Spanish colonies a century before). After independence it was replaced by new legal forms of forced labour, as discussed further below.

2. The Bourbon Reforms under Carlos III (1759–88) included a programme for vigorous expansion of the Spanish American militias, with new ordinances providing for more efficient, professional forces. See Lyle McAlister, *The "Fuero Militar" in New Spain* (Gainesville, Florida: University of Florida Press, 1957).

3. Rolando H. Ebel, "Political Modernization in Three Guatemalan Communities", in Richard Adams, (ed) *Political Changes in Guatemalan Indian Communities* (Middle America Research Institute, Publication No. 21, New Orleans, 1957), p. 144.

4. Severo Peláez Martín, "Los Motines de Indios en el Período Colonial Guatemalteco", in *Estudios Sociales Centroamericanos*, March-August, 1973, p. 208. The Totonicapán incident, the 1803 Cobán rebellion and many others are described in this study.

5. The figures of 14 *ladinos* and 47 Indians killed were given in the annual report (*Memoria*) of the Ministry of Government for 1944.

6. For a wonderfully eclectic collection of contemporary documents on Carrera see the voluminous, never completed *Diccionario Histórico-Enciclopédico de El Salvador*, by Miguel Angel García (San Salvador, 1938, the volumes appeared at varying dates).

7. Roger Plant, *After the Earthquake*, (Latin America Bureau, London, 1977), p. 68. Coffee exports in the 1850s averaged just 95 quintales per year.

8. Ibid.

9. As in El Salvador, legislation attacking Indian communal lands came in several stages. 1882 legislation required communities to register and pay rent on their traditional lands (most did not); more disastrous was the 1887 legislation requiring all land to be registered as under private ownership.

10. See Plant, op. cit., pp. 69–70 for a summary of the provisions. Debts were also inherited. See also Richard Adams, *Crucifixion by Power*, (University of Texas Press, Austin and London, 1970), p. 177.

12. Richard Adams, *Crucifixion by Power*, p. 177. This was Decree 222 of 14 September 1878.

13. Ibid., p. 176. This was Decree 243 of 1894.

14. *Circular*, dated 3 November 1876, from President Justo Rufino Barrios to the *Jefes Políticos*. Unless otherwise noted, all decrees, edicts and executive orders are taken from the government record, *La Gaceta*. Adams, (*Crucifixion by Power*) op. cit., p. 177, cites a similar circular from 1894 expressing the President's concern that *mandamientos de mozos* (groups of peasants forcibly recruited to work on the farms) "should be equally distributed among the various farm-owners of the department."

15. Justo Rufino Barrios' military adventures included war with El Salvador in 1875, which hoisted Liberal Rafael Zaldívar into the Presidency there, and, again, in 1885, when Barrios was himself killed in the first battle. His successor (and nephew), President José Reina Barrios (1892–98) continued the trend, invading El Salvador in 1893. President Manuel Estrada Cabrera, who as Minister of Government succeeded Reina Barrios after his assassination in 1898 (and remained in power until he was deposed in 1920) conducted a brief war with El Salvador in 1906.

16. Lyle M. MacAlister, op. cit.
17. The short-lived "*República de los Altos*" incorporated Quezaltenango, Sololá, Huehuetenango and San Marcos.
18. Noted in the comments of the Commission that prepared the new code to President Barrios on completion of their task; reproduced in the 1951 edition of the Code. See *Codigo de Justicia Militar de la Republica de Guatemala*, (Editorial del Ejercito, Guatemala, 1951).
19. These included decrees defining precisely who should be considered to enjoy the privileges of the jurisdiction of military law and military courts (the *fuero militar*).
20. The *Escuela Politécnica* was founded in implementation of Decree 86, 1873. See also Richard Adams, op. cit. p. 239, for an account of the García Granados and Rufino Barrios governments' efforts to create a national army.
21. This was a decree of 1 August 1878; see *Codigo de Justicia Militar de la República de Guatemala*, (Editorial del Ejército, Guatemala, 1951) for Decree of 1 August 1878 and reforms through 1950.
22. *Reglamento del Ejercito*, (Guatemala, 1892).
23. See, for example, Ralph Lee Woodward, op. cit., pp. 151–72.
24. The Guard was established by decree of 7 December 1872, its regulations were dated 7 April 1877. See Adalberto Pereira Echeverría, *La Policía*, thesis, Universidad Autónoma de San Carlos, Guatemala, 1951. See also International Cooperation Administration, *Report on the National Police of Guatemala*, (Washington, D.C., 1956), which notes that the creation of the new police system was followed by "some 12 years wherein the police took or were granted strong measures to control emergencies, becoming increasingly abusive with the public."
25. Pereira, op. cit. The regulations — extensively quoted by Pereira — were dated 12 September 1881. See also Police Lt. Col. Oscar González Díaz, "Development and Present Activities of the Police of Guatemala", in the *International Police Academy Review*, November 1970 (Washington D.C.) for a historical outline of the police, and reference to the failure of the Civil Guard experiment. The 1872 regulations issued by the Rufino Barrios government for the Civil Guard, also described by Pereira (op. cit.) are similar in spirit to those for the "Model Police", but perhaps even more unrealistic. The Guard's principal obligation was "the conservation of public order"; a wide range of tasks to this end are outlined. Article 22, section 7, for example, requires the police "To lend immediate assistance to any resident between 8 in the evening and 6 in the morning... to call a doctor, a priest, a scribe or other person needed by a sick person or similar circumstances, or to purchase an article from a pharmacy..."
26. Oscar González Díaz, op. cit., and International Cooperation Administration, *Report on the National Police of Guatemala*, op. cit.
27. International Cooperation Administration, *Report ...*, op. cit.
28. G-2 Report, 20 March 1919. National Archive, Washington, D.C., Record Group 165. All G-2 Reports cited were consulted at the National Archive, and are located in Record Group 165.
29. G-2 Report, 17 July 1919.
30. Ibid., 20 March 1919.
31. Ibid., 20 March 1919.
32. Ibid., 20 March 1919 and 17 July 1919. G-2 pointed out that 2,000 of the army's approximately 6,000 men were based in Guatemala City, and that 111 of the local command posts were manned by a lone commander without a garrison. The army's force level was broken down into 4,935 soldiers, 649 officers, and 358 *musicians*(!!).
33. G-2 Report, 20 March 1919 and 17 July 1919.
34. Ibid., 26 October 1922. Estrada Cabrera's fury after the assassination plot was such that he had the old *Escuela Politéchnica* torn down. It was reopened in June 1912 under the name *Academia Militar* in a new building designed as a *Cuartel de*

Artilleria (Artillery Barracks) within which it remained (interrupted by earthquake damage from 1917 to 1920) until the 1970s. After Estrada's overthrow it was again named *Escuela Politécnica*. By 1920 the Academy is officially reported to have trained 1,686 cadets and, from 1920 to 1965, 2,139 are reported as having been enrolled. For a potted history see "Apuntes Históricos de la Escuela Politécnica", in *Revista Militar de Guatemala*, July-December 1965, pp. 39–40.

35. International Cooperation Administration, *Report...* op. cit., reports the burning of the files; see Pereira, op. cit., for a detailed discussion of subsequent police reorganization.

36. See *Ley Municipal de 1935*. The municipal council (*Junta Municipal*), consisting of *sindicos* and *regidores*, continued to be elective, but even these elections were subject to the approval of the *intendente*, often an outsider and a *ladino* (non-Indian) even in largely Indian communities. *Intendentes* were appointed by the President on the recommendation of the *Jefe Politico* of the department. The *intendente* system was perhaps not all bad, since in some areas local community affairs were previously wholly dominated by the local economic elites. According to Richard Adams (op. cit. p. 176): "Ubico appointed intendentes... The intendentes did not occupy a post indefinitely; Ubico did not want them to become too involved in the welfare of the local upper class." This may understate the degree of self-government under the traditional system (at least in the wholly Indian communities) and overstate the *intendentes'* role in *countering* local elites' control over local affairs. Since a main Ubico economic objective was to develop commercial export agriculture, the traditional agricultural elites' privileges were in fact reinforced in many ways.

37. Kenneth Grieb, *Guatemalan Caudillo: The Regime of Jorge Ubico, Guatemala 1931–1944*, (Athens, Ohio: Ohio University Press 1979).

38. Adams, op. cit., p. 178.

39. US military intelligence reported in 1932 that the Guatemalan army's strength (active service) was 6,783 men, not including the "active reserve" with "114 Telegraph and Telephone officers (coopted)". (G-2 Report, "The Military Establishment: Strength of the Army and Police" (as of July 1932), dated 8 September 1932.) A later report (3 January 1936) commented on all highway workers and sanitation workers being placed under military discipline, and on the army's active involvement in road-building for military purposes: "Graduates of the Polytechnic School are ... building roads in the vicinity of the Mexican and Salvadorean borders with a view of their serving active defensive positions now being mapped." ("Militarization of Public Works Sector", No. 62, 3 January 1936). This is an early instance of what came to be termed military "Civic Action".

40. "*Reglamento para el servicio del ejército en tiempo de paz*", 1935: as in the revised civil administrative system, local commanders were required to make regular reports to departmental commanders. Article 332 of the regulations determines that "All Departmental commanders will daily report by telegraph to the President and Minister of War" summing up any unusual events in the past 24 hours as reported by local commanders.

41. G-2 Report, 24 January 1933. In his mammoth study of Ubico, Kenneth Grieb observes that during his period as Jefe Político and Comandante de Armas of Retalhuleu from 1911 to 1919 Ubico carried out a "revitalization and reorganization of the security forces in the state". That, and his "orders to execute all suspected bandits", pacified the region, but earned him "a reputation for efficiency and cruelty" (Grieb, op. cit., p. 6).

42. Grieb, op. cit., pp. 6–7.

43. G-2 Report, 20 March 1919. This conjunction of adjectives — unscrupulous, efficient and presidential — in a military "who's who" report is startlingly similar to a report on Anastasio Somoza shortly after his appointment in 1933 to head the National Guard of Nicaragua: "He is energetic and clever, but none too honest, and should, provided his political inclinations do not interfere with his duties as commander of the guard, make an excellent officer in charge of that organization"

(G-2 Report, 18 November 1933).

44. Grieb, op. cit., p. 6. See also pp. 74–5 for Grieb's account of Ubico's role (as Minister of War) in introducing US army staff; and pp. 45–6, citing Major Considine's report of 2 May 1931 to the US Secretary of War citing Ubico's directive requesting him to "make the Escuela Politécnica as near like West Point as was possible under conditions here".

45. G-2 Report No. 199, 24 December 1921.

46. Ibid., No. 24, 8 August 1922.

47. Ibid., No. 391, enclosing a copy of a personal letter from Col. Ydígoras Fuentes to the former Military Attaché in Guatemala, dated 1 January 1931 and marked "for publication if desired".

48. G-2 Report, 4 November 1932. Almost ten years later another G-2 Report described the *Policia de Hacienda* 462 men as "a tough lot of men, inured to service in the field". For details of National Police force levels and deployment in 1932 see G-2 Report, 8 September 1932, citing a report by National Police headquarters to the Minister of Government and Justice. In the same report, however, Military Attaché A.R. Harris notes the continuing major role of the army in the rural police function ("In practically all of the small towns and villages in the Departments police duty is performed by the local garrisons".)

49. Grieb, op. cit., p. 28.

50. Ibid.

51. G-2 Report, 24 January 1933. According to the same report: "The Police Force, both of Guatemala City and the larger towns, is excellently, although somewhat over-organized, is highly trained and commanded by army officers. It serves as an effective check against disregard of the rights of citizens. The Present Chief of Police, General Anzueto, is a close friend of General Ubico."

52. G-2 Report, 5 July 1935.

53. Ibid., 25 January 1933. The extent to which a "Communist Plot" had existed in Ubico's Guatemala in 1932 is questionable. Ubico moved against labour organizers and political activists as an apparently direct response to the January 1932 uprisings and ensuing massacre in El Salvador, arresting 76 Guatemalans and Salvadoreans, and executing ten. See Adams, op. cit., p. 467, which describes those arrested and/or executed as "'radical' . . . organizers whom he accused of being Communists".

54. G-2 Report, 22 July 1935.

55. Ibid., 24 June 1941, by Lt. Col. J. H. March; the report was made in the context of Ubico's deal for secret compensation for the use of Guatemalan airspace by the allies during World War II.

56. "This part of the force especially is of a much higher type than the army", reported military intelligence on 18 November 1940.

57. *Memoria del Ministerio de Gobernación*, 1944, (Guatemala, 1944).

58. The changing role of the army after 1944 is summed up in an excellent study by José Luis Cruz Salazar, *El Ejército como una Fuerza Política*, produced in mimeographed form by the Guatemalan Universidad Autónoma de San Carlos' Institute of Political Science in 1971.

59. Ibid.

60. Ibid.

61. Arévalo also thanked the US army for grants of 9,000 beds and mattresses and large quantities of uniforms. (See Arévalo's *Informe* (report to Congress) on the achievements of fiscal year 1946.)

62. Juan José Arévalo, *Informe*, 1946.

63. *Revista de la Guardia Civil*, 2 July 1948, "La Institución Policiaca Revolucionaria, una Guardia del Pueblo". The *Guardia* were, in fact, a bulwark against counter-revolutionaries; in what was surely its finest hour, on 18 and 19 July 1949 the Guardia held out against a 12-hour assault by the rebellious Presidential Guard until loyal army units joined them in defending Arévalo and crushed the rebellion.

64. *Memoria del Ministerio de Gobernacion*, 1945.
65. John Gillin, "San Luis Jilotepeque", in Richard Adams, (ed), *Political Changes....*, p. 25.
66. *Código Penal*, Artículo 154, Decreto No. 2164, 29 April 1936.
67. Decree No. 386, 19 May 1947, under Arévalo, exempts public officials, including mayors, municipal councillors and "diverse guards" from licencing requirements for bearing of arms, and reaffirms the definition of the Ubico Penal Code categorizing private landowners as "agents of authority" authorized to use firearms: "The administrators and owners of rural farms and their legal representatives can use within said farms, in their capacity as Agents of authority, their firearms, but only in those cases prescribed in Article 154 of the Penal Code."
68. Kalman Silvert, *Guatemala: A Study in Government* (Middle American Research Institute, Publication 21, New Orleans, 1954) p. 71. See also Arden R. King, "Cobán: 1944–1953", in Richard Adams, (ed), *Political Changes...* op. cit.
69. Robert Ewald, "San Antonio Sacatepéquez, 1932–1953" in Adams, *Political Changes...* op. cit., pp. 16–19.
70. Grieb, op. cit., p. 183.
71. North American Congress on Latin America (NACLA), *Guatemala*, NACLA, New York, 1974, p. 19.
72. Ibid., p. 124.
73. Grieb, op. cit., p. 185. The agreement was to build a port with wharf facilities for two ships, and a rail spur linking up with the rail network within five years. UFCo reneged on the prior agreement, shipping its produce overland on its subsidiary railway to Puerto Barrios. In 1936 Ubico agreed to drop the demand for compliance with the agreement on the grounds that an outbreak of banana disease (*sigatoka*) on the Atlantic Coast in 1935 had severely strained the company's resources. This notwithstanding, United Fruit's failure to fulfil its obligations was a grievance that would fester throughout the revolutionary decade of 1944–54, and provide added impetus to moves to expropriate United Fruit's lands in the agrarian reform.
74. NACLA, op. cit., p. 20.
75. Grieb, op. cit., p. 181.
76. See further below, chapter on popular organization for a summary of peasant organization after 1944.
77. *Foreign Affairs of the United States, 1947*, Vol. VIII, p. 705, Department of State to the Guatemalan Embassy, 28 May 1947.
78. Ibid., p. 706, Secretary of State to the Embassy in Guatemala, 24 July 1947.
79. NACLA, op. cit., p. 20. Adams *Crucifixion by Power*. pp. 396–400, cites agrarian reform records indicating the *expropriation* of 600,000 hectares between January 1953, when it began, and June 1954, when it ended (in all, about 1,482,000 acres), with beneficiaries of land grants ranging from 54,000 to 100,000.
80. NACLA, op. cit., p. 20.
81. For a summary of US grievances as of mid-1949 see *Foreign Relations of the United States, 1949*, Vol. II, pp. 650–3, which reprints a cable from the Acting Secretary of State to the Ambassador in Guatemala, dated 14 June 1949. It includes the text of a Memorandum enumerating Guatemalan government actions in previous months which "reflected a lack of concern for traditional good relations between Guatemala and the United States". The Ambassador was instructed to express US concern to Arévalo at the Guatemalan government's "rendering of cooperation and assistance to pro-Communist elements in Guatemalan national life [and] disregard of the rights of legitimate American interests established in the country..."
82. Ibid. The June 1949 Memorandum suggests a certain hysteria was already building up in the State Department over the Arévalo government's ideological/political composition, in full knowledge of its potential international repercussions — Guatemala was the first in Latin America to break ranks in the anti-Communist line-up of the post-war years — and that in the long run this was more significant than moves against US economic enterprises in Guatemala. Conversely, it was

precisely those economic moves, first to challenge through organized labour, and then to expropriate the property of American enterprises, that were seen as the proof of the ideological pudding, and that Guatemala was, indeed, falling to the Communists.

Chapter 2

83. The 1954 operation is summed up concisely and with a fresh and objective perspective in Thomas Powers *The Man who Kept Secrets: Richard Helms and the CIA,* (Pocket Books, New York, (1979)), pp. 107–10. Powers describes the raids after 18 June as "militarily insignificant while contributing to widespread fear of all-out raids" (p. 109). On 22 June CIA director Alan Dulles requested further aircraft of Eisenhower after two of Castillo Armas' P-47's went out of commission: "With the President's okay Richard Bissell then negotiated the 'sale' of US Air Force planes to the Nicaraguan Air Force, the CIA pilots flew additional sorties, and on June 27 Arbenz resigned." (p. 109). A more detailed account is in NACLA, *Guatemala,* (New York, 1974).

84. Col. Carlos Castillo Armas had been trained at the US Army Command and Staff School at Fort Leavenworth, Kansas, and had worked with the CIA out of Nicaragua and later Honduras in propaganda against the Arbenz government and in preparation of a paramilitary "invasion" force. CIA official E. Howard Hunt wrote in his memoirs that Castillo Armas was chosen by the CIA to head the "Liberation" because other prospective candidates had been ruled out, and "our (US) paramilitary people . . . were impressed with Castillo's qualities as a military leader." (Cited in NACLA, *Guatamala,* p. 68.

85. NACLA, *Guatemala,* op. cit., p. 72. The Law of Forced Rental (*Ley de Arrendamiento Forzoso*) of December 1949, although little implemented, had provided a mechanism whereby landless or nearly landless peasants could petition for the right to rent at a rent limited by law, land from neighbouring private estates.

86. Ibid., p. 75.

87. Comité Guatemalteco de Defensa de los Derechos Humanos, *La Violencia en Guatemala* (Mexico: Fondo de Cultura Popular, 1969) p. 18. Killings were reported in those areas where land reform and peasant direct action — primarily in the form of land takeovers and occupation — had most threatened large private landowners. Actions by peasant organizations to forcibly take over private farms were reported most frequently in 1953 and early 1954, and were a major factor in unifying the non-Indian landowners against both Indian and peasant organizations, and the government which ostensibly tolerated their actions. John Gillin writes that *Union Campesina* peasant leaders were blamed for several violent attempts to take over private lands and even for murder, but adds that most of the reports of alleged depredations by the peasants and their organizations were made considerably after Castillo Armas' coup in 1954, and therefore suspect. (See John Gillin, "San Luis Jilotepeque. . ." p. 26, in Richard Adams, *Political Changes. . .,* op cit.)

88. John Gillin, op. cit.

89. This affair has gone largely unmentioned in more or less "official" histories of Guatemala, perhaps as best forgotten; it is referred to in several studies on Guatemala, but details of the attack and the "hands on their heads" description were given to the author by a witness now in exile.

90. A 1956 US government survey said: "After the Armas regime came into power, there were numerous persons and organisations which were extra-legal and acted in a quasi-police manner, informing and making arrests. With the adoption (March 1, 1956) of the new constitution of Guatemala, these units and persons 'officially' came to an end. Even though there appeared to have been a tacit but reluctant approval of these activities, a high Guatemalan official expressed his (sincere) pleasure at the termination of such." (In ICA, *Report on the National Police of Guatemala,* 9 April 1956, op. cit.) p. 50. Other, more critical, studies also report that the independent armed groups of June-July 1954 rapidly withdrew. The "*Liberacionistas*" subsequently formed the political party *Movimiento de Liberaciónal,*

Nacional (MLN, Movement of National Liberation). Their teeth pulled by the army in 1954, in the 1960s they provided manpower for the army's own irregular auxiliary forces. The 1956 constitution's limits on armed civilian groups would, notwithstanding, be reiterated in the 1965 constitution, which in Article 215 stated that "The organizing or functioning of militias other than the army of Guatemala is punishable."

91.   For reference to the role of the previously exiled cadets in the 1960 revolt, see Luigi Einaudi, Brian Jenkins and Cesar Sereseres "US Military Aid and Guatemalan Politics". (Manuscript paper for the California Arms Control and Foreign Policy Seminar, March 1974), pp. 22–3.

92.   John Gillin, op. cit., p. 26.

93.   Richard Bissell in "The Science of Spying", NBC television programme, 4 May 1965, transcript in NACLA, *Guatemala*, p. 73.

94.   Leonard Mosely, *Dulles: a Biography of Eleanor, Alan and John Foster Dulles and their Family Network* (Dial Press, New York, 1978) p. 459.

95.   ICA, *Report on the National Police. . .*, op cit., p. 55. Elsewhere the survey refers to an "almost neurotic hypersensitiveness to communist activity" (p. 48).

96.   Ibid.

97.   Ibid.

98.   David Atlee Phillips, *The Night Watch* (Robert Hale, London, 1978), p. 52. See also Thomas Powers, op. cit., p. 418. Phillips' speciality in the 1950s was propaganda, although he subsequently rose to prominence as CIA station chief in the Dominican Republic in 1965, head of the Chile Task Force against Allende in 1970, and, eventually, head of the CIA's Western Hemisphere division. The CIA team both processed documents and devised a permanent record system; Phillips notes that one of the files opened was on 25 year old Che Guevara, who had sought asylum in the Mexican Embassy. Phillips describes his major task in Guatemala as collecting information tending to justify Washington's claim that Arbenz was a "Soviet Puppet", or, at least, pro-Communist. According to Powers, Phillips played a key part in compiling documentation presented to congressional committees compiling and "selectively editing" documents to be presented to congressional committees in justification of earlier charges against the Arbenz government and of his overthrow, as well as in the preparation of virulently anti-Communist books and pamphlets published under Castillo Armas' auspices in Guatemala.

99.   *Ley Preventiva Penal Contra el Comunismo*, 24 August 1954. The introduction to the law establishes its purpose as "extirpating Communism"; to "repress the Red conspiracy, its activities and plans, and to fight and pursue it to its final redoubt."

100. The figure of 70,000 is provided in Norman La Charite, "Political Violence in Guatemala, 1963–1967: its social, economic, political and historical origins and its patterns and sequences" (American University, PhD dissertation) p. 80. Much of the documentation gathered by CIA counter-intelligence officers, including the membership records of pro-Arbenz labour and political organizations, can be consulted on microfilm at the US Library of Congress manuscripts division. In Guatemala these lists of members of perfectly legitimate trade unions, peasant leagues and political parties were not examined for the purposes of scholarship, but provided the principal data base for the "register" of suspect persons. The lists would be used as proof of "Communist" guilt for decades, and, once the "death squad" counter-terror policies of the 1960s were introduced, used as a guide to selective murder. By that time the lists compiled by people like David Atlee Phillips and his counter-intelligence team had been vastly expanded and up-dated.

101. Banning members of certain suspect organizations from public employment was, of course, then in force in the US itself, and it remains in force elsewhere, for example, in the Federal Republic of Germany by means of the *Berufsverbot* law.

102. ICA, *Report. . .* op. cit., p. 4.

103. Ibid., p. 30. The various secret police agencies' budget was not published; although

the National Police requested a "Confidential Fund" of $30,000 for fiscal year 1956–57. The Department for the Defense Against Communism received direct funding from the Presidency, not accounted for in the general budget.

104.   Ibid., p. 3; the Judicial Police were "Largely concerned with intelligence and arrests of subversives. It will also, at will, take over investigative jurisdiction of some crimes."

105.   One criticism of the security system in the ICA 1956 report was that the Judicial Police, as the only detective force in the system, was virtually uninvolved in conventional law enforcement. The vacuum required either the creation of a separate detective corps in the National Police, making the Judicial Police responsible for intelligence (secret police) work alone, or that it specialize strictly in criminal investigations, leaving political matters to other agencies. ICA *Report...* op. cit., pp. 53 and 66.

106.   Ibid., p. 1; "In spite of the lack of professional policemanship ... the National Police force is performing a good job in maintaining a high degree of preparedness against subversive activity and attack. Its fulfillment of its police function is at best to be rated as fair." (p. 2).

107.   Ibid., p. 5.

108.   Ibid., p. 7.

109.   Ibid., p. 4.

110.   Ibid., p. 2.

111.   Ibid., p. 3.

112.   Ibid.

113.   Public Safety Program, *Phase Out Report*, 1974, Appendix "Public Safety Advisors Roster".

114.   Freedom of Information Request 1979: US Department of State Cable, 6 July 1962, for information to all diplomatic posts. "Subject: Special Group for Counter-insurgency"; the message announces the creation of a "Special Group-Counterinsurgency" to co-ordinate programmes of counter-insurgency for "friendly countries", and gives the terms of reference for the "internal defense plans". Planning for counter-insurgency was to have two components, but security assistance was an immediate priority: "Development of measures designed to eliminate causes of discontent or to immunize the population from appeals to conspiracy and violence" are "largely long term in character", as they might involve "correction of basic social, political and economic injustices". Actions for immediate results, however, "in a country confronted with an internal security threat" are "shorter-range actions [which] may reduce both the effectiveness of insurgent and subversive operations and communist appeals to the population for the instigation or support of violence" through the "development of effective police and/or military capabilities to maintain internal security".

115.   Freedom of Information Request, 1979: US Embassy Cable, Guatemala to Department of State, 29 May 1962, assessing local police forces, No. A-125, "Secret". The Embassy's assessment of progress in Guatemala contrasted remarkably with those made within the Public Safety Program itself. A comment by his superior on the "End of Tour Report" of David L. Laughlin, Chief Public Safety Advisor in Guatemala from December 1956 to April 1960, concluded that "as a result of the US program of assistance to the internal security forces of Guatemala since late 1956, these forces have been able to make advances in their administration, organization and operations which might have otherwise taken from twenty to thirty years to accomplish". (See ICA, "Completion of Tour Report" by David L. Laughlin, 27 April 1960; including comment by Herbert O. Hardin, Chief of Latin America Branch, Public Safety Division, ICA/W.) Freedom of Information Request, 1979, US Embassy Cable, Guatemala to Department of State, 29 May 1962; the cable added that "The recent chiefs of the Judicial Police, Ranulfo González Ovalle (assassinated on January 24, 1962) and Jorge Córdova Molina ... have been men of limited intelligence and ruthless and often unwise in action."

Part 2: Counter-Insurgency Emerges

3. The Bay of Pigs and After

In 1960 a considerable sector of the Guatemalan army was antagonized by an arrangement between President Ydígoras Fuentes and the United States for a paramilitary force to train in Guatemala for the Bay of Pigs invasion of Cuba. Many officers were particularly galled as Ydígoras had not even consulted the high command before unmarked United States aircraft began coming and going between the Panama Canal Zone and the south coast invasion headquarters at a farm in Helvetia, Retalhuleu. As one authority writes, the military were concerned not only on nationalist grounds, but because "whatever payoff was to be had was clearly received solely by Ydígoras and the owner of the farm, (Roberto) Alejos".[1] This discontent, combined with unhappiness over the galloping corruption of Ydígoras' regime — what many saw as his incompetence to govern — and finally and decisively, his introduction of divisive favouritism into the ranks of the military itself through inequitable promotion practices, and offering political spoils to his personal supporters in the officer corps.[2]

A combination of these and other factors spurred a revolt on 13 November 1960 by more than 120 young officers and an estimated 3,000 soldiers. The rebellious officers took control of the military base at Zacapa and most of the eastern military zone and demanded Ydígoras' resignation.[3] True to the traditional style of their revolt, a military coup in defence of institutional military interests, the officers refused to bring civilian supporters into the fray, and according to one account turned away a group of 800 peasants who appeared at the gates of the Zacapa base requesting arms to support the revolt.[4]

At the time, the participants apparently saw their action in entirely non-ideological terms. Many of the leaders were graduates of US counter-insurgency courses, including the two who became most famous, Lieutenants Luis Turcios Lima and Marco Antonio Yon Sosa, who subsequently became the driving force in Guatemala's later guerrilla movement. The 1960 revolt, however, was neither left nor right, but guided by nationalist, military criteria. Lieutenant Yon Sosa, who had been trained at Fort Gulick in the Canal Zone, said later that "At the time [they] had no distinct ideology. That is why we talked with people on the right and left — anyone who was in agreement with toppling the Ydígoras government."⁵ Lieutenant Luis Turcios had spent six months in the elite US Army Ranger School at Fort Benning, Georgia, in late 1959 and early 1960. He described the instruction received as very good "from the military point of view", but explained that he also enjoyed "the officers' club, 15-ounce Texas steaks, good clothes, the best equipment. Plenty of money too. What worries did I have!"⁶

A major factor behind the coup attempt appears to have been the military's concern that the US presence in Retalhuleu with their secret training camp and air strip represented a loss of sovereignty for Guatemala, and a threat to the military. If, indeed, this threat precipitated the coup, its crushing certainly bore out the young officers' fears that the Guatemalan army had increasingly come to enjoy its prerogatives on the sufferance of the United States.

Since the revolt threatened the Cuban invasion plans, the US had a particular motive for helping out Ydígoras, and United States B-26 bombers flew from the Retalhuleu base and up from the Canal Zone to bomb army installations held by the rebel officers in Zacapa, further inflaming the army's nationalist sentiments, but quelling the revolt within four days.⁷ As one study puts it, "The CIA had between eight and sixteen B-26 bombers in Guatemala which were painted with the markings of the Guatemalan Air Force", all involved in smashing the coup.⁸ The young officers who fled into exile across the border to Honduras after the aborted coup subsequently formed the nucleus of a guerrilla group they called the Revolutionary Movement of 13th November, MR 13. They returned to Izabal and Zacapa departments in the north-east in the early months of 1962. Guerrilla warfare in Guatemala began on 6 February 1962 with attacks on the offices of the United Fruit Company in Bananera.⁹

As a military offensive, MR 13's operations in February 1962 were a failure, but, the political repercussions were immense, triggering massive support in Guatemala City expressed through strikes and demonstrations, particularly by the university students. The killing of at least 20 protesting students in the second week of March, with several hundred wounded, spurred demands for Ydígoras' resignation both from the right and the left. A joint manifesto issued by the three main political parties — the National Liberation Movement, the Christian Democratic Party and the Revolutionary Party — called for the formation of a civil-military junta to replace Ydígoras and restore order.¹⁰

So began Ydígoras' downfall. On 16 March he ordered the army out to patrol the streets of Guatemala City and, with the sole exception of the foreign minister, replaced his entire Cabinet with army officers. On 30 March 1963, one year later, Ydígoras was deposed by the army, headed by the Minister of Defence, Colonel Enrique Peralta Azurdia.

The coup occurred without bloodshed; Ydígoras virtually fell under his own weight, helped on by the aura of corruption and incompetence surrounding his administration. Besides, both the Guatemalan army and the United States were eager to see him go, and recently declassified material has suggested the US had a considerable role in persuading the army the time was ripe.[11] The Ministry of Government's annual report on political developments (1963-64) declared that intervention had been necessary to save democracy from the "misgovernment" of Ydígoras, and from "the frank danger of being devoured by the forces of international communism".

The army's senior officers issued a manifesto on 31 March, justifying the coup as a response to Ydígoras' incompetence in confronting the "permanent subversion of pro-communist sectors" and "communist infiltration". The latter was apparently a reference to the return of former President Juan José Arévalo to Guatemala a few days before the coup, and fears that Ydígoras would allow him to run as a candidate in the up-coming Presidential elections. According to the manifesto, by abusing the liberties of the Constitution, the "Communists" threatened to infiltrate the government and political parties, and this would have the "logical result" of their taking over the Government "within apparent legality, only to later install a communist regime".[12] The threat of Arévalo sweeping the field in the elections scheduled for October 1963 did, indeed, worry the army, and seems to have been an important consideration. A later CIA report summing up political developments in 1963 tends to confirm this:

> A military regime headed by Col. Enrique Peralta came to power in March 1963 following the ouster of President Miguel Ydígoras. The coup, provoked by the entry into Guatemala of ex-President Arévalo, who is anathema to the military, received wide popular approval or acceptance. Subsequently the government has prohibited political activity, instituted stringent antisubversive measures, dissolved the congress and maintained the state of siege.[13]

The military declared in its manifesto that the powers of government were to be assumed by the army as a whole, and that its hierarchical chief, Minister of Defence Colonel Enrique Peralta Azurdia, would serve as Chief of State — not "President" — and would exercise executive and legislative powers on behalf of the armed forces.[14] The constitution was declared in suspension (and, therefore, civil rights as well) although the courts would still apply ordinary legislation. A "Provisional Charter of Government" (*Carta Provisional de Gobierno*) would serve in lieu of the Constitution and establish the ground rules of the armed forces' government. Finally, the military suspended all political parties, and called upon "all Guatemalans" to join in building democracy and the "eradication of Communism from Guatemala".

A New Head of State

Colonel Peralta, a 55 year old infantry officer, and graduate of the Chilean War College, had worked closely with the US military mission during World War II when he served as deputy director of the *Escuela Politécnica* with Lieutenant-Colonel Glass of the US army as Director. As had military intelligence reports many years before on Jorge Ubico and Miguel Ydígoras Fuentes, a 1940 resume by Lieutenant-Colonel Glass filed with military intelligence correctly marked then Lieutenant-Colonel Enrique Peralta Azurdia for greater things:

> In my opinion [he] is capable of being the outstanding officer of the Guatemalan army, if given the chance. He is studious, tactful, loyal, a hard worker, admires the United States and its institutions. I would especially desire to have him in any command of mine in peace or war.[15]

Peralta Azurdia's service record after the war also gave him considerable experience outside Guatemala, with service as military attaché in Chile, Costa Rica, Panama, El Salvador, Guatemala and Washington, D.C., as Ambassador to El Salvador, Costa Rica and Cuba, and as Chief of Delegation at the Interamerican Defense Board at Fort McNair, Washington, D.C.

Although he was clearly close to the United States, and his *coup d'etat* found favour in Washington, Peralta was too nationalistic and too intelligent to repeat the mistake of Ydígoras Fuentes by over-enthusiastically, or clumsily, ceding Guatemalan prerogatives to the United States.[16] Peralta Azurdia drew very systematically upon US assistance to restructure Guatemala's security system, without a radical expansion of the advisory personnel, material, or dollars already flowing in through the various security assistance programmes.[17]

Peralta's early speeches as Chief of State set the tone of the new orientation to internal security. Unlike Ydígoras Fuentes' shrill denunciations of Cubans in the woodwork, and expectation that whatever happened the US would bail him out, Peralta determined to use United States support not in embarrassing "fire-brigade" actions like the US bombing runs of November 1960, but to develop a reorganized security system sufficient in itself to permanently crush the small guerrilla movements. Peralta was also perhaps the first professional and nationalist military leader who saw the Guatemalan army's role in ideological terms. He believed in the Cold War and the rhetoric of anti-Communism, and rated the threat of Communist infiltration or indoctrination of the people as the greatest and most immediate threat facing the country and the army. The threat was from both within and without the country, and the army was its sole hope of resistance.[18] As Peralta put it in a 1963 speech:

We must be united as never before, as solid as granite, to attack the communist movement, because these people are devious and only the Army that has better organization than they have can oppose their ambitions to power. We have the elements of force necessary to smash any outbreak of subversion arising out of communism, directed by international agents.[19]

Peralta's first major speech to the nation expressed the major priority of his administration, quite unambiguously, as the crushing of the opposition groups that had harassed the Ydígoras government. These were: the guerrilla groups formed by the junior officers of the 13 November 1960 revolt, threatening the unity of the army itself, and, other opposition groups that intended "to bring communism to Guatemala":

Security and order are indispensable prerequisites for the realization of the values of economic and social evolution. Whosoever disturbs the public order will be rigorously repressed. Those who intend to bring communism to Guatemala will be destroyed without pity.[20]

Among Peralta's first actions was the restoration of basic anti-Communist measures that had lapsed or been derogated since Castillo Armas' assassination, chief among them Decree Law No. 9, the Law for the Defense of Democratic Institutions (*Ley de Defensa de las Instituciones Democráticas*), which was to revive Castillo Armas' "Black List" by creating a "National Security Archive" of political suspects. Known as the "Black Book" (*Libro Negro*), it drew upon the data base of the earlier "register" and included:

... the names of union organizers, members of revolutionary parties, anti-government activists as well as officers and leaders of cooperatives, agrarian reform committees, unions and parties from the 1944-54 period. Denunciation of a peasant or labourer as "communist" by a *comisionado militar*, local notable or any government supporter was sufficient cause for entry in the Book.[21]

As under Castillo Armas, suspicion was sufficient cause for arbitrary arrest or exile. As before, the Judicial Police were the major political police body, and "infiltrated and spied upon middle and lower sector political parties, unions and associations, and kept a particularly close surveillance over student organizations and activities."[22] For a brief period after the end of the Peralta regime, the abuses of the *judiciales* were much remarked upon in the press. President Julio César Méndez Montenegro, in an interview immediately after his inauguration in July 1966, discussed torture by the Judicial Police and promised the press that it would be "radically and definitively eradicated" (it wasn't), and referred to secret, Judicial Police cells, one of which was known as the "Tiger Cage" (*La Tigrera*), saying their use would be discontinued (it wasn't).[23]

While the techniques of repression applied by Peralta's government were almost entirely traditional in nature — political imprisonment, torture, and exile — major structural changes in the security system were implemented during his three years in power. Under Peralta manpower available to the army for counter-insurgency operations (including irregular army auxiliaries) more than doubled; special counter-insurgency units were created in the conventional armed forces; a mobile military police force was organized for rural areas; police and military forces were integrated under a single military command structure; a sophisticated communications network was set up, consisting of networks within each security service feeding into a single, co-ordinating nexus in the National Palace; the Guatemalan security horizon was extended to include all the Central American isthmus, through the creation of the Central American Defense Board, based in Guatemala. Finally, a presidential security agency was established to run the centre for inter-agency and international communications, and to combine and co-ordinate the resources of the police and the military intelligence apparatus.

In Pursuit of Counter-Terror

United States counter-insurgency doctrine encouraged the Guatemalan military to adopt both new organizational forms and new techniques in order to root out insurgency more effectively. New techniques would revolve around a central precept of the new counter-insurgency: that counter-insurgent war must be waged free of restriction by laws, by the rules of war, or moral considerations: guerrilla "terror" could be defeated only by the untrammelled use of "counter-terror", the terrorism of the state. The acceptance of both innovations for Guatemala's security system was the first long step of Colonel Enrique Peralta Azurdia's military government. The preparation of the organizational basis, both conventional and irregular, for launching unlimited "counter-terror" dominated the security system throughout his three years of government. The US security assistance programme's introduction of sophisticated wherewithal for sowing the "counter-terror", such as computers, submachine-guns, or helicopters, was, in its influence on events, secondary to the Guatemalan military's wholehearted adoption of the US doctrine that it is correct and necessary for governments to resort to terrorism in the pursuit of certain ends.

United States military assistance to Guatemala after 1963 served mainly to strengthen core units of the conventional military forces and create regular army units specialized in counter-insurgency as preconditions to developing a vast force of irregular army auxiliaries. There was also an effort by the US military to build regional organizations of Latin American armies under its leadership and promote such bodies as the Inter-American Defense Board as a regional forum through which US allies would ratify US defence policies for the region as their own.

From the first months of his government, Peralta actively championed co-ordinated regional efforts to promote counter-insurgency doctrine and vigorously promoted both the Inter-American Defense Board (IDB) (where he had been Guatemala's chief of delegation) and the gestation of the Central American Defense Board, CONDECA (*Consejo de Defensa Centroamericana*). Peralta saw CONDECA as a potential means of putting IDB recommendations into action, as he noted in a speech soon after the 1963 coup:

> . . . A plan for the Defense of the Continent has been drawn up by the Inter-American Defense Board, presenting as the single and exclusive enemy Russia. The Central American Isthmus, in this Plan for the Defense of the Continent, is considered as a unit, not as five or six separate units. As a consequence, we have always had in mind the idea that what is required is a military organ formed of representatives of all the Armies of the Isthmus, to put into practice the recommendations formulated by the Inter-American Defense Board.[24]

The creation of CONDECA, by a treaty signed in Guatemala City on 14 December 1963, followed a series of preparatory meetings, beginning in 1961, between Defense Ministers and Chiefs of Staff of the region. Peralta himself gave particular importance to the second meeting of regional Defense Ministers, in Managua, Nicaragua, in 1963, when army representatives had agreed to co-ordinate military and police operations against Communism and to "a complementary provision referring to the interchange of information and a unified intelligence service in all of Central America as a contribution to the fight against Communism."[25] CONDECA's statute, as subsequently agreed by member states, made it a body of the Organization of American State's regional body, ODECA (*Organización de Estados Centroamericanos*), its stated purpose "the coordinated use of the Armed Forces or Security Forces" of the region "for the maintenance of peace and of collective security".[26] In his inaugural speech at the first meeting of CONDECA, in Guatemala City in 1964, Peralta lauded its potential for "immediate action" against subversion, and as "a rampart for the protection of the democratic system".[27]

The purpose of the US Military Assistance Program (MAP) in Guatemala during the Peralta administration (in the words of a 1966 US government report on "Internal Security Programs") was "to assist Guatemala to establish and maintain armed forces capable of maintaining its internal security against internal violence and incursions inspired and supported by Castro-Communist elements . . .".[28] Assistance was "aimed at the improvement of the organization, intelligence training, transportation and communications, (and) the replacement of obsolete weapons . . ." and had been dramatically increased after the 13 November 1960 young officers' revolt:

> . . . the proposed FY 1962 MAP as submitted to Congress in January 1961 showed a total program of $787,000 . . . However, before the FY 62 MAP was implemented there were increases (on 2 January 1962) made in training and material which more than tripled the original FY Program.[29]

The revised budget included new provisions for training and material intended to reorganize and equip a large portion of the Guatemalan military for a new counter-insurgency role; MAP was

> to include support for 3 additional Infantry Battallions, 4 T-33's, 2 C-47's (both aircraft particularly suited to counterinsurgency operations), trucks, arms, ammunition and radios plus training for a total of $2,666,000.[30]

Ydígoras Fuentes' Cabinet shuffle after the March 1962 disturbances placed the army in firm control of most of the government defence funds and the new American largesse, with Peralta, as Minister of Defense, in charge of it all.

The FY 1963 MAP budget approved in January 1963 at $1,667,000 was in turn revised upward on 19 March, two weeks before Colonel Peralta's coup, to a total of $2,524,000. Assistance to the Guatemalan military was further boosted in 1963 by "windfall" funds provided under an AID "Civic Action" budget, boosting the total dollar value of assistance by $325,000 to the unprecedented figure of $2,849,000. 1963 was the first year AID funds went to the army,[31] and almost matched the $382,000 provided for its Public Safety operation in Guatemala that year. Total funding for assistance to the Guatemalan armed forces dropped after 1964, but a US government assessment of the Military Assistance Program reported in 1966 that four elite infantry battalions designated "MAP units" had reached "full strength" under the Peralta administration.[32] Each battalion had been provided with weaponry including "pistols, .30 and .50 caliber machine guns, 60 and 81 mm mortars, and recoilless rifles" and been trained in "counter-guerrilla operations, small unit tactics, and riot-control . . .". Training was provided in four ways, "by MILGROUP advisors, by Mobile Training Teams from CINCSOUTH, at schools in Panama, and at schools in the United States", with an average of $636,000 disbursed each year under Peralta for training programmes.[33] This did not include Mobile Training Teams (MTTs) flying in from Panama which were apparently not funded from the Guatemala MAP budget. There are no declassified reports on the number of MTTs working in Guatemala, the personnel allotted each MTT, the time they spent in Guatemala, or the overall cost of that area of the assistance programme.

The four army battalions reorganized and equipped by the MAP between 1963 and 1966 were the two principal infantry battalions based in Guatemala City: *Brigada Mariscal Zavala* and *Brigada Guardia de Honor*; the *Brigada General Manuel Lisandro Barrillos* in Quetzaltenango, and the *Brigada Capitán General Rafael Carrera* at Zacapa, in the north-eastern military zone where the guerrillas were based.

By the time Peralta Azurdia left office the *Brigada Mariscal Zavala* was reported at "97% of planned capability", and the *Brigada Guardia de Honor* at "98%". The 1966 progress report said the key battalion for taking counter-insurgency into the mountains of Izabal and Zacapa in the north-east, the *Brigada Capitán General Rafael Carrera* "will be at 100% of planned capability with FY 1966 deliveries"[34] just in time for the October 1966 counter-guerrilla offensive.

Smaller units more especially created for counter-insurgency warfare, and ready for action by early 1966 included the 1st Airborne Infantry Company, consisting of elite paratroops modelled on US Army "Rangers", "approximately 98% equipped"; the 1st Special Forces Company, called the "Kaibiles", modelled on US Army "Green Berets"; a counter-insurgency force described enigmatically as "a CT Detachment" — "CT" teams in Vietnam at that time were "Counter-terror" teams — and a "Counter-Intelligence Detachment" which "attained 100% capability with the arrival of FY 1965 material".[35] One source reports a total force, by about 1966, of over 700 "airborne and airmobile troops" in the Special Forces and "Airborne Infantry" units, the elite of Guatemala's counter-insurgency forces:

> These units are considered, along with the two city brigades, to represent the best trained and undoubtedly the most mobile — principally because air force C-47's and helicopters are at their disposal for tactical operations throught Guatemala.[36]

A further major contribution of the MAP in preparing the armed forces for counter-insurgency was to provide aircraft and training for Guatemala's Air Force. MAP built up an air transport squadron and two "Special Air Warfare" squadrons between 1963 and 1966 with provision of T33 trainers and B26 bombers for "ground support", C47's as troop transports, and multipurpose helicopters. Ironically, helicopters initially provided under the "Civic Action" budget, with the aim of forming a "Civic Action Squadron", were reallocated, before they even got off the ground, and became a "Special Air Warfare/Reconnaissance Squadron":

> Due to the increase in internal security operations, it has now been

designated an independent Special Air Warfare unit with the composite missions of coastal patrol, target location, psychological operations, medical aid, evacuation and trooplift. The two H19s funded in FY 64 and delivered in FY 1965 have materially increased the ability of this unit to perform its tasks. Delivery of the H19 funded in FY66 will bring this squadron to 100% of force objective equipment. Remaining MAP assistance will be chiefly pilot/mechanic training for H19 crews and the replacement of attrition loss.[37]

A final addition to the army's counter-insurgency capabilities under Peralta, and the focus of initial moves against the guerrillas, was an army command centre at the Zacapa military base charged with integrating police and military security forces into a joint counter-insurgency apparatus, and co-ordinating forays into guerrilla redoubts in the Sierra de Minas. Contrary to public declarations by members of the US military mission that Peralta had "held back" in hitting out at the guerrillas, the 1966 classified report suggested that his methodical approach had been rather effective:

> ... in the latter part of 1965, the Army established a joint command in the northeast area of the country to deal with the first serious wave of guerrilla raids. While the Army was unable to eliminate the guerrillas, by December of 1965, they had been so badly harrassed that the threat to the area was very much reduced.[38]

A secret CIA report from about the same period gave a similar positive assessment of Peralta's efforts to take the army into the rural areas, but warned that "The qualified success of the military in the rural areas is not matched by security force capabilities within the city."[39]

Total funds allocated to the Public Safety, (*civil* police assistance) programme jumped dramatically after the Peralta coup, along with the MAP funds, but police assistance remained very much the junior partner in the overall security assistance programme. Over two-thirds of the funds provided under the Peralta administration went to pay for the presence of Public Safety Advisors, and the overseas training of Guatemalan police officers.[40] By 1966, however, police personnel had not expanded significantly, neither had its quality noticeably improved. A 1966 US government report concluded that "the conditions and capabilities of the police are only moderately improved over what they were in 1957 when the Public Safety Program began."[41] The same report noted that although police assistance had been provided throughout the period "police reforms were not achieved, and ... the police were not becoming the 'first line of defense' ..."[42]

While the main forces of the conventional law enforcement system remained virtually unaffected by the Public Safety Program, the expansion of the contingent of Public Safety Advisors based in Guatemala had a major impact on two specialized areas within the security system linking the civil and military communications and intelligence networks, as discussed in Volume I. The complement of two advisers in 1962 was raised to four in 1964, including training, communications and investigations advisers. Both communications and investigations advisers worked directly with the civil and military intelligence apparatus.[43]

Military domination of security assistance (apart from the intelligence and communications areas) was partly because the Guatemalan army desired to maintain its own position unchallenged, without any possibility of an elite police corps emerging as its competitor. As one US report put it in the early days of the Public Safety Program, "It may be well to keep in mind that a 3,000 man police force with good communications and ready mobility will constitute a formidable force that is almost half the size of the country's armed forces . . ."[44] Police assistance planning in the 1960s took into account the Guatemalan military's reluctance to support a too efficient *civilian* police. A 1966 report notes that "the Guatemalan military in Zacapa [the major guerrilla problem area at the time] strongly opposes counterinsurgency operations by the police"; consequently the report urges consideration of:

> how US police assistance might be provided most acceptably, including the possibility that assistance through MAP for creating a police capability under the aegis of the Army might be the way to proceed in Zacapa and elsewhere.[45]

This is precisely what was done, in addition to militarizing the police command structure and some of its conventional forces.

While material assistance to the conventional forces of the Guatemalan army and the civilian police forces during the Peralta administration should not be underrated, the major change in the security system in this period concerned not arms, equipment or technical expertise, but organization, adding to the army's regular force of some 8,000 troops a body of more than 1,000 elite "Military Police" and an over 9,000 strong force of irregular army auxiliaries (the *Comisionados Militares*). Both the new Mobile Military Police and the irregular Military Commissioners became key factors in counter-insurgency action in the countryside.

The Paramilitary and Counter-Guerrilla Terror

The organization and deployment of irregular paramilitary forces and the use of terror tactics to crush both violent and non-violent opposition were the hallmarks of counter-insurgency operations in the 1960s. A contributor to RAND Corporation studies on Guatemala in the early 1970s attributed the "success" of counter-insurgency operations in the 1960s in large part to "the utilization of paramilitary civilian groups" and "the psychological impact of terror tactics". The author maintained that probably "the most decisive factor in the [guerrillas'] defeat" was the successful effort "to organize and mobilize local civilians in support of regular military operations".[46]

Counter-insurgency specialist David D. Burke made a similar assessment during United States congressional hearings in 1968. The army's irregular forces were described as "a potent force, though one which has not worried about the niceties of who is or who is not a communist", adding that "the army asserts it exercizes control over this force of irregular troops." Burke, an academic, shared the general view of the period that the "niceties" need not be observed in counter-insurgency as long as operations were effective; "Although the methods of the rightists raise grave issues, still, in combination with effective military action, they have reduced insurgency to a very low level indeed."[47]

A 1980 study of Guatemalan counter-insurgency, produced within the US military establishment, arrived at similar conclusions on the efficacy of paramilitary irregulars and terrorism in counter-insurgency.[48] The study was apparently concluded in the late 1970s, as one of its basic tenets: "it appears that the Guatemalan government has succeeded in putting down the insurgency within its country", would have seemed unrealistic by 1980.

United States Air Force Major Vicente Collazo-Dávila outlines the major innovations in the historical development of the counter-insurgency apparatus in Guatemala as involving the special training of regular army units, the development of an irregular civilian militia to assist the army, and the pursuit of a civic action programme. The "militia forces" were devised to "provide local security and attempt to destroy the guerrilla infrastructure" and worked closely with regular units "on both military operations and in the acquisition of intelligence". These irregular forces "were armed and supplied by the government, and were mainly composed of small landowners." They were "indiscriminate" in carrying out "counter-terror" operations: ". . . it has been reported that thousands of peasants died or were tortured . . . Many of the individuals, if not most, who were killed or tortured by the irregulars were innocent peasants . . ." Major Collazo-Dávila also describes special assassination squads in the countryside and the cities,[49] "set up (or at least supported)" by the army in the mid-1960s, including the famous White Hand (*Mano Blanca*), NOA (*Nueva Organización Anticomunista*) and CADEG (*Consejo Anti-Comunista de Guatemala*) which we shall hear of later.

Major Collazo-Dávila writes that Guatemalan counter-insurgency programmes were effectively adapted from "current counterinsurgency doctrine". The contribution of US aid to the counter-insurgent effort was considered to have been "decisive" because the Guatemalan government had been wholly co-operative, and "totally dedicated to the task at hand". The resonse to the threat of insurgency was summarized as follows:

> The government . . . replied with various countermeasures based on a coordinated political, administrative, military, police and intelligence effort. The organizational and propaganda threat was countered by civic action, right-wing counterterror, a low-level police effort, and a concerted intelligence effort.[50]

Similar frank acknowledgements of the nature of the counter-insurgency offensive and the US's decisive role in its direction came from within the military assistance establishment inside Guatemala in the 1960s. When the chief of the US Military Mission in Guatemala, Colonel John Webber, was assassinated in January 1968 *Time* magazine stressed the intimate involvement of the United States military assistance programme in the army's organization of ". . . armed local bands of 'civilian collaborators' licensed to kill peasants whom they considered guerrillas or 'potential guerrillas' ".[51] *Time* criticized the nature of the counter-insurgency operations, and particularly the use of "counter-terror", a technique which it attributed both to the military advisory programme and to Colonel Webber. According to *Time* Webber himself claimed to have introduced the concept of paramilitary terror to Guatemala:

> . . . it was his idea and at his instigation that the technique of counter-terror had been implemented by the Guatemalan Army . . . There were those who doubted the wisdom of encouraging such measures in violence prone Guatemala, but Webber was not among them. 'That's the way the country is', he said. 'The Communists are using everything they have, including terror. And it must be met.'[52]

Colonel Webber did not, of course, devise the doctrine of counter-insurgency, but he was responsible, as head of the US Military Assistance Program in Guatemala, for promoting the doctrine giving practical guidance in counter-insurgency to his counterparts there. In the course of their overseas and in-country training Colonel Peralta Azurdia and thousands of other Latin American army officers had studied the US army's counter-insurgency doctrine from the time it took shape at the beginning of the 1960s. Evidence suggests that well before the coup in March 1963 Peralta and the army general staff had decided that the army's priority would be to regear the security system along the lines recommended by the US advisory programmes.

The documentary record of the decisive influence of United States counter-insurgency doctrine in Guatemala after 1963 ranges from general articles on "counter-terror" and the organization of irregular "counter-guerrilla forces" reprinted by the Guatemalan army in its own military review, to mimeographed documents outlining the application of the doctrine in Guatemala's peculiar political milieu. Representative of the general promotion of "counter-terror" and paramilitary organization within the army was an article, reprinted from the US army's *Military Review*, in the *Revista Militar de Guatemala* in October 1966 reviewing guerrilla and counter-guerrilla tactics, and outlining the advantages of forming "guerrilla-type" irregulars and "combatting guerrilla terrorism with counter-terrorism". "Counter-guerrilla" forces are to be formed from local people with some special motivation to fight, thus enjoying the same tactical advantages of the guerrillas, but "better trained and equipped so that it has even more mobility, commitment and idealism than the guerrilla itself".[53]

A confidential US Army document, giving specific instructions on structuring a security system for counter-insurgency, (precisely matching the development of such a system in Guatemala) surfaced inside that country at the end of the Peralta administration and a photocopy of the original mimeographed paper has survived. Widely circulated within the army under Peralta the undated document is a rather poor Spanish translation of a US Army "Guide for Counterinsurgency Planning" and attributed to the US Army School of Special Warfare at Fort Bragg.[54] Much of the text matches documents cited in Part 1, Volume I on the basic "gospel" of counter-insurgency, and closely parallels the steps taken in Guatemala to prepare and launch counter-insurgency after 1963.

Counter-insurgency is to proceed through a sequence of preparatory, clearing and holding phases. The preparatory phase is clearly reflected in developments between 1963 and 1966: in theory this phase was to include enactment of emergency legislation, registration of the civil population with military authorities and an identity card system devised; special training for counter-insurgent operations for police and conventional military units; new "semi-military" or "paramilitary" forces to be created, organized and trained by the army and, wherever possible, "composed of former military and police personnel". This "armed militia" is to serve the army as guides, maintain vigilance, and in other ways support the counter-insurgency operations in the community, "including limited offensive actions". All local paramilitary forces' operations are to be co-ordinated through the army command structure, with all local intelligence data channelled systematically to the "national agencies of intelligence/security".

In phase two, offensive actions are to be launched to clear the insurgents from the specific area. Conventional forces, in collaboration with the local "armed militias", are to "dislodge or eliminate" insurgent forces. The primary task of the local irregulars being the identification and destruction of guerrilla political and administrative structures.

In the "holding" phase, armed local irregulars are to be institutionalized, with communication links directly to central authorities. They are to assist the regular army in continual counter-guerrilla offensives, and in the investigation of the local population, in order "to determine who are the insurgent elements and locate the local leaders". Civilian irregulars are to continue to assist in systematic information gathering; to participate in propaganda campaigns and demonstrations in support of the authorities; and to assist in "population control" measures. These latter are to include monitoring movements through the area, and controlling the entry of medicines, foodstuffs and other goods into the region, that might be passed on to insurgents by sympathizers.

Another document variously attributed to the military assistance programme or the CIA, outlines a virtually identical procedure for implementing counter-insurgency doctrine in the special context of Guatemala.[55] This paper, pointedly anonymous, was widely circulated both within the Guatemalan army and the *Movimiento de Liberación Nacional* (MLN), the right-wing political party which provided most of the recruits for the army's new irregular forces. This document stresses the indispensability of foreign security assistance for successful counter-insurgency in Guatemala, and even comments that accepting such aid is no infringement on Guatemalan sovereignty.

> This training can be requested from government to government or through the intermediary of the corresponding international organization (Organization of American States, Interamerican Defense Board, Central American Defense Board), without it in any way placing in question the sovereignty of our country (Guatemala) . . . military assistance . . . is indispensable to achieve effective results . . . The government of the Republic through the Minister of National Defense can request the most modern equipment, the war material most appropriate for waging a war of this nature, as well as training of civil and military personnel in foreign schools . . .

Lip-service was also given to "civic action" and economic development as facets of counter-insurgency: "The government should develop a program of economic and social development of such magnitude as to be capable of healing the wounds of the past, [in] the zones affected by fratricidal fighting, tending to raise the standard of living of the inhabitants."

More relevant to the development of the counter-insurgency apparatus in Guatemala, is reference to the creation of irregular forces to fight the guerrillas, and their central control by the army (as we have seen, independent civilian militias were a traditional sore spot with the army):

> A paramilitary organization should be created, charged with combatting

the guerrillas with their own systems, their own tactics, and on their own ground . . . [these forces] should function as a paramilitary organization and never as a militia apart from the armed forces. Their members should be men of the political ideology contrary to that held by the guerrillas; it being required not only that they claim to hold such views but that they prove it.

Finally, the role of special army command centres in counter-insurgency operations was emphasized, perhaps to reassure the army that they would retain complete control of these "counter-guerrillas":

All of the operations of the antiguerrilla struggle — propaganda, violent action, intelligence — should be coordinated by a Counterguerrilla Operations Centre, in charge of the execution of plans . . .

Mobile Military Police: Functions

To develop the extensive paramilitary forces prescribed by counter-insurgency doctrine, the existing security system required some adjustment. The greatest changes would have to be in the rural areas, where the bulk of the paramilitary forces were to operate. To risk creating such a force, the army first needed to ensure that its conventional apparatus in the rural areas would suffice to co-ordinate and control all future counter-insurgency activity. So, just as the military under Peralta Azurdia improved and expanded its conventional forces, it also took methodical steps to develop its own police-type capabilities in the countryside.

One of these was to militarize the "Mobile National Police", a small rural police force attached to the National Police. The Military Police's entry into the civilian police area was formalized by Decree Law 332 of 2 June 1965, dissolving the Mobile National Police and creating in their place the *Policia Militar Ambulante* (PMA) or Mobile Military Police, "to lend police service in the rural areas of the Republic".

The duties of the new Mobile Military Police (PMA) were to include not only general police functions ("preventing crime, the persecution and capture of criminals and repression of offenses in the towns and rural circuits"), but also to provide their services to "owners and administrators" of private estates, and keep a sharp eye on the peasants. In fact, Articles 5 and 6 of the Decree are couched in terms almost identical to late 19th Century police legislation in which the rural police role is clearly stated as the defence of commercial agriculture and the containment of the peasantry:

[The PMA shall] lend assistance, in cases of emergency, to the owners or administrators of estates, haciendas, agricultural lands, forests and all rural properties . . . [and] Observe all activity that tends to inflame passions among the peasant masses or in the rural communities and, when necessary, repress through licit means any disorder that should occur.

PMA regulations also provided for the contracting of PMA personnel as guards, initially for service on large private farms, but later for industrial establishments too, and as bodyguards to business and political figures. A virtually unlimited number of army reservists could be called upon in this way without affecting the normal PMA force level or budget. Salaries of additional PMA personnel thus contracted as guards were paid via the Defense Ministry, but loyalty to their private employer could be guaranteed by additional payments.

Although the number of such additional PMA personnel is unknown, by 1966 normal PMA forces were well over 1,000 and constituted, to all intents and purposes, an elite counter-insurgency corps within the army, their police duties and specialized training placing them in closer contact with the rural population than any regular units of the armed forces. The central base of the PMA was established in the southern city of Escuintla, and was reported to control a highly mobile force of 800 men for "rapid deployment" as a rural anti-guerrilla strike force.[56]

But the creation of the PMA was only a secondary feature of the army's expansion of its role in directly policing internal security. A far more significant force was built out of the military commissioner system, organized in 1938 as a means to enforce military conscription. This system eventually provided the administrative framework within which the army's irregular auxiliaries were integrated. The Presidential Decree of 9 July 1938 had created unpaid part-time posts whereby military commissioners were to serve as "agents of military authority" with a primary duty of filling quotas for military recruitment in rural areas. Every *municipio* had a military commissioner who could appoint assistant commissioners (*comisionados auxiliares*) as required. Military commissioners did not bear arms, had to be residents of the jurisdiction within which they worked, were generally army veterans, and often were both recommended for appointment, and employed, by local land-owning elites (their official duties were quite limited). The network of commissioners was under the command of the head of the Military Reserve Department (*Servicio de Reservas Militares*).[57]

The potential for military commissioners to serve as the long arm of the army at the local level was recognized even in the 1940s and 1950s, but apart from serving as the instruments of forcible conscription (grabbing able-bodied Indians for service in the army) their role was traditionally the largely passive one of reporting major local problems to their military superiors. Abuses attributed to the military commissioners before 1963 were generally not linked to security work *per se*, but to their use of the threat of violence or conscription at the behest of local landowners and other notables, a logical development since they were often their employees and served as farm administrators or labour contractors in addition to their part-time, unpaid service as commissioners. This link with the local elites continued after 1963. As one authority on the subject writes:

> While the comisionados were formally responsible to departmental reserve commanders and the military hierarchy, in reality local notables... controlled the selection and deployment of comisionados. This informal arrangement made the local commissioner a truly powerful individual: he wielded public authority as well as influence derived from his close association with the local elite structure.[58]

After the March 1963 coup the military commissioners' role changed radically, first in the areas most threatened by guerrilla insurgency, and eventually throughout the country. Within three years the post changed from a largely symbolic representation of the army, to an active instrument of the army in counter-insurgency. First came the rapid expansion of the ranks of military commissioners and their auxiliaries. Under the Ydígoras Fuentes' regime, most of Guatemala's 300 odd *municipios* had at least one military commissioner, concerned almost exclusively with conscription; under Peralta Azurdia they grew to over 9,000, were armed, and performed a multiplicity of tasks.[59]

Reliable statistics on local level military commissioner strength in the 1960s are available only for the Department of Jutiapa. By 1965 there was a total of 971 commissioners in Jutiapa alone (not an especially guerrilla-prone area) with "approximately one for every 50 adult men".[60] In contrast, in 1974, the National Police contingent for the entire Department of Jutiapa totalled 60.[61] After 1963 military commissioners and their assistants were to be found "in every population centre: towns, villages, hamlets and even among the scattered settlements of plantation workers", and the full extent of the commissioner system was described as "a closely guarded secret".[62]

The official standing of the commissioners also changed in 1965 with a new army law placing them on an active status equivalent to that of the standing army, allowing for payment as a normal condition of service (the 1960 army law had defined the commissioners as part of the army's *reserve* force).[63]

The change in the commissioners' role after 1963 was as dramatic as the network's sudden growth. Under Peralta Azurdia's government, and the army's administration, they were expected to become an active part of the counter-insurgency apparatus, "observing, and reporting the presence of insurgents, political organizers and strangers; accompanying military patrols to seek out insurgents; (and) questioning, detaining and ordering the arrest of suspects".[64] Traditional political privilege enjoyed by the commissioners was supplemented by real coercive powers to accompany the new responsibilities. Identification cards issued to commissioners gave the holder virtually unlimited power "to interrogate and hold suspects, as well as to carry a weapon".[65]

The adaptation of the commissioner system to an active security function was most pronounced and immediate in the south coast and the eastern areas, particularly in the north-east where guerrilla activity was concentrated. There a commissioner came to be what Richard Adams described as a virtual "one man army, who moved from one settlement to another, on the lookout for guerrillero activity."[66]

In the north-east the commissioner network was co-ordinated from a regional command centre at the Zacapa military base and a force of some 2,000 commissioners and assistant commissioners was raised to work with the regular army. These were the forces described at the time as secret "civilian" vigilante death squads; legally, the *comisionados militares* and their deputies were part of the army's active duty forces, and answerable to regular army superiors (and the military court system) for their actions. Furthermore, they were closely supervised by the regular army and generally went into action side by side with the regular army or PMA forces. Their "civilian" status, however, was widely reported. One 1974 study by RAND Corporation specialists on the military in Latin America described the role of the *comisionados* in Zacapa:[67]

> . . . the Zacapa military zone headquarters provided comisionados militares, private citizens deputized by the army, with weapons and credentials for them to operate. The comisionados, in turn, organized and armed a civilian irregular force that numbered some 2 000 men. Who were these vigilante "soldiers"? Some of them can be described simply as gunmen whose political preferences, if they existed at all, are unclear and probably were secondary to their desire to shoot . . .

While this account suggests that the civilian irregular force raised by the commissioners in Zacapa (as elsewhere throughout the country) was in some way an "independent" force for which the army was not accountable, the truth is, that members of these irregular forces raised by the *comisionados militares* were duly deputized by the army as assistant commissioners, with the same credentials described above and the same extraordinary police powers, and that the army controlled and co-ordinated their counter-insurgency activities.

Just as the Mobile Military Police worked closely with the rural elites, the commissioner system built upon the local rural power structure and protected the interests, lives and property of the local elites. In the more than 4,000 settlements located entirely within the boundaries of large private agricultural estates, for instance, military commissioners and PMA contract guards alike were likely to be employees of the farmowner, since, vis-a-vis counter-insurgency, the interests of the army and the large landowners were considered identical. As one US government source put it, these "organized farms" are a form of company town that can "develop sizeable security units of their own ..." Central government involvement in local security is thus "largely unnecessary from the viewpoint of the farm owner".[68]

As military commissioners and their assistants were given a free reign at the local level, the posts became particularly attractive to the lesser landholders and small town militants of the extreme right-wing political parties. Under the revised military commissioner system, the special ideological affinity between the military government and the rural elites permitted a decentralization of the security system within a framework established and co-ordinated by the regular army. A head of military commissioners in a township, in co-ordination with the local command post or garrison of the regular army, could depute as assistant commissioners an unlimited number of local residents, from the local plantation owner, to hired bodyguards and gunment traditionally employed by large landowners.[69]

The special relationship, already mentioned, between the army and the right-wing political party, National Liberation Movement, (MLN) was welded by the MLN's provision of recruits to the army's new paramilitary formations. The army, in turn, gave local MLN leaders recruited as military commissioners considerable discretionary powers within their counter-insurgency duties, and several sources have remarked that the distribution of Civic Action resources was palpably distorted to the benefit of MLN militants, as a form of patronage for their services in the security network.[70] One must not, however, disregard many MLN supporters' very real ideological motivation to join in the counter-insurgency programmes' anti-Communist "crusade" and, of course, simultaneously to be in a position to protect their control of the economic wealth of the area in question. The large and medium landowners comprising the bulk of MLN membership were vulnerable to guerrilla action and, indeed, had the most to lose. They neatly filled the role counter-insurgency doctrine allotted to a highly motivated minority group that could be organized as army auxiliaries.

Naturally, the MLN used its collaboration with the army to further its own political ends, and there is no evidence that the army high command disapproved of this. The army appears to have been a full party to the appointment of MLN militants as military commissioners and their consequent role as arbiters of ideological purity in the countryside, in charge of culling "guerrillas" and "guerrilla supporters" from the population. One source remarks that, within the new security system, the army and the military commissioners would target for assassination "peasants (who) refused to work against the guerrillas" and that support of the MLN was one criterion by which peasant sympathies were assessed: "The only sure way not to be accused of being a guerrilla was to join the MLN . . ."[71] In the north-east the MLN was integrated into the security system to the extent that:

> A civilian irregular operating in the northeast could be a member of the MLN, a military commissioner licensed by the army, or a member of La Mano (a death squad), any two or possibly all three.[72]

The MLN's role should not, however, be overestimated. Its main contribution was its provision of manpower to the army, and it should not be forgotten that commissioners who were also party members were responsible first to the army, and the army had the coercive (and legal) power to enforce its discipline throughout the network. As it turned out, there was little conflict between the party and the army until the 1970s.

The Army's Role Transformed

The Peralta government was above all a watershed in the relation of the military to society in Guatemala, and marked the emergence of the army as a coherent political institution capable of dominating the country's political life. This involved the transformation of the army from simple gendarme and power-broker — the traditional arbiter of politics and stepping-stone enabling individual strong men like Ubico to attain personal power — to the permanent, institutional wielder of the powers of the state. By its overwhelming concern with the threat of insurgency, and mild commitment to extend the scope of central government intervention to promote "development", between 1963 and 1966, the Peralta government placed the Guatemalan army in much the same position as the Salvadorean army had reached in 1932, and power and privilege unlimited lay before it.

The new powers of the military in the spheres of economic management and public administration, as well as many of Peralta's policies in this area, clashed with the time-honoured views of the traditional landed elite and the MLN: that the role of government was best limited to "punishment and protection"[73] (not taxation and regulation). These differences between some sectors of the civilian elites and the military were, however, largely buried under a common perception of the single burning issue facing Guatemala — the threat of subversion and insurgency — and the common conviction that Peralta Azurdia had the right approach to the problem: "Those who intend to bring Communism to Guatemala will be destroyed without pity", as he put it in his first speech to the nation as head of state. Expressed less dramatically, the convergence of the civilian elites and the military after Peralta came to power was based on "a thorough shared commitment to maintaining the existing mass/elite boundaries".[74] Differences between

69

the various elite sectors of Guatemala over shades of ideology or economic policy were and are secondary issues, easily submerged in the broad consensus over how best to organize counter-insurgency and permanently eliminate future threats to privilege.

It should be noted that while the MLN's co-operation was useful to the army, and the army's counter-insurgency plans convenient for the MLN, the Peralta government was not especially close to the MLN in its policies. Several excellent studies of the three year government have pointed out the military's affinity under Peralta to policies of direct intervention in economic affairs, including tariff controls, increased taxation and other measures which were anathema to the MLN's membership among the landholding elite.[75] Such policies were of advantage to a more "modern" elite sector whose wealth was of more recent origin, based on the development of a light manufacturing industry relying on import substitution, new agro-industrial enterprises in frontier areas (made possible by army-backed land grabs), and the exploitation of newly accessible mineral resources. At the same time, the military began to claim a larger piece of the economic pie, through social welfare benefits accruing to the military institution as a whole; the placement of military personnel within all sectors of the government bureaucracy; and through a relatively new pattern of private partnership by senior officers in business ventures. By the 1970s these senior officers had capitalized on the military's new position as a springboard by which they themselves joined the ranks of the most wealthy sectors of the population, a goal no longer limited to the rare, individualistic officer who fought his way into the Presidency, but one which could normally be expected to crown a successful military career.

Communications and Intelligence: Role of the US

The vastly expanded military and paramilitary network built under Peralta tied into a final structural innovation in the security system: a central communications and intelligence nexus for co-ordination and control of all facets of the security system. It was in the development of this part of the security system that United States military assistance meshed most closely with the work of US advisers attached to the (civilian) Public Safety Program.

Already in late 1962 a mobile army training team had organized and outfitted a special "Counter-intelligence Detachment" for the Army General Staff; according to a November 1966 inter-agency report:

> The unit attained 100% capability with the arrival of FY [Financial Year] 1965 material. The detachment is designed to provide the Guatemalan Armed Forces with a capability in counter-espionage, counter-subversion, counter-sabotage and personnel security.[76]

The establishment of a central intelligence agency and command centre drawing on both military and civil intelligence resources was, however, mainly the responsibility of civilian advisers, and, indeed, was the most significant assistance provided by personnel of the Public Safety Program. The development of communications networks within the security forces was a major part of Public Safety's official brief and by the end of the Peralta administration resulted in nationwide networks within the National Police, the Detective Corps, and the Treasury Police. Public Safety also reported in a classified paper that communications assistance had gone to smaller police agencies and to irregular forces: "Limited advisory guidance was occasionally rendered to small agencies such as Immigration, Customs and Para-Military Units."[77]

Public Safety Communications Adviser Alfred W. Naurocki wrote in his 13 October 1966 "End of Tour Report" that his activities had involved improving the communications capabilities of "the police and security organizations", including creating a system for "inter-agency telecommunications coordination" linking police bodies, local army commands, and the Presidential Staff at the National Palace.[78]

In May 1964 an agreement, signed by the United States and Guatemala, provided for security assistance within the US Public Safety Program for the development of a communications centre at the highest level of government to link Guatemala with other Central American states and the United States facilities in the Canal Zone. The agreement also covered assistance in organizing a presidential intelligence agency to operate the inter-regional station, and the completion of communications links tying it to all areas of the civil and military security apparatus. The agreement specified that the project would be completed on 30 June 1966, Peralta's last day in office.[79]

Within months of Naurocki's arrival in Guatemala, in August 1964, Peralta created a "Presidential Intelligence Agency" based in the *Casa Presidencial* and combining civil and military intelligence resources. By October 1964 the new agency was already operating and making Guatemala's own contribution to a "Central Security Telecommunications Network" that was described in a Public Safety report ten years later:

> Radio-teletype network initiated in October 1964 for the exchange of criminal and security information among the Central American and Panamanian Republics. Each of these countries owns, operates and maintains its respective station equipment under the control of the major security group in that country. In Guatemala the "*Centro Regional de Telecomunicaciones*" (Regional Telecommunications Centre) under the Casa Presidencial controls and operates the station.[80]

By spring 1966, Naurocki's communications work had placed the "Regional Telecommunications Centre" in command of a fully operational system linking civil and military security forces within the country, and quite correctly described as a "High-Level Security/ Administrative Network". Established for "both administrative and general emergency situations" it was a VHF-FM intra-city network controlled directly by the "Regional Center":

> The network interconnects on a private frequency the principal officials of the National Police, Treasury Police, Detective Corps, Ministry of Government, the Presidential House, and Guatemalan Military Communications Centre.[81]

Naurocki collaborated closely with the Military Assistance Program on the integration of the police and military components of the communications system. A November 1966 inter-agency report praised "the cooperative relationship existing between the USMILGRP and Public Safety Communications Advisors who are consulting on police and military communications plans . . ."[82]

When Colonel Peralta stepped down on the inauguration of a civilian President on 1 July 1966, both the international and national components of the communications assistance programme agreed upon in 1964 were complete. One major change remained to be made: the Presidential Intelligence Agency which had controlled the "Regional Telecommunications Centre" was moved out of the *Casa Presidencial* and changed its name — a move apparently designed to assist the military to evade any effort the new President might make to place it at his own service. Under the direction of the Minister of Defense during the civilian government which lasted from 1966 to 1970 the "Presidential Intelligence Agency" became the "Guatemalan National Security Service" (*Servicio de Seguridad Nacional de Guatemala*). To outsiders it was still the "Regional Telecommunications Centre" but its offices were now based next door to the *Casa Presidencial*, in the Presidential Guard annex within the National Palace complex. Known popularly as "*La Regional*" the agency co-ordinated military and civil security services and placed them at the disposal of the Defense Minister and the Army General Staff. Its dominant role is graphically illustrated in one 1974 Public Safety Program document that slipped through the declassification process, an organization chart entitled "Organization of Security Forces". Answerable after 1970 only to the Guatemalan head of state, the "Regional Telecommunications Center" appears in a box at the head of all other military and civil elements of the security system.[83] This is the agency which has consistently and conclusively been denounced as the nerve centre of the security system and of its extra-legal activities. Officially termed "Presidential Intelligence Agency", "Presidential Security Service" (under General Laugerud's Presidency) or "Special Communications Services of the Presidency", there is overwhelming evidence that it runs the Guatemalan government's counter-terror assassination programme. It also retains its original regional communications function, keeping the Guatemalan military in daily contact with the United States army's Southern Command in the Canal Zone, and with their military counterparts in Honduras and El Salvador.

Whether the Regional Telecommunications Centre was designed from the start for internal communications, intelligence and co-ordination of military operations cannot be known in the absence of a further round of declassified documents. The circumstantial evidence afforded by the sequence of events would imply that it was, since its creation coincided with the creation of the presidential intelligence agency located in the same offices, and it has been popularly associated with government assassination squads since at least 1966.[84]

A further bit of circumstantial evidence may be found in the career of the Public Safety Program's Communications Adviser responsible for setting up the Regional Centre as a domestic and international security nexus: Alfred W. Naurocki. From 27 June 1964 to 13 October 1967, Naurocki served as *regional* communications adviser for Public Safety for all of Central America and part of the Caribbean, although he was based in Guatemala City. "Extensive travel to (Central American) countries was required and completed" writes Naurocki in his "End of Tour Report"; in the course of his tour of duty Naurocki was sent to the Dominican Republic after the US intervention there in 1965 and, subsequently to Jamaica for a short stay, in both cases "to assist the police and security agencies in fulfilling their telecommunications needs". Although Naurocki left Guatemala and the region in 1967, he returned as Communications Advisor in 1970, shortly after Colonel Carlos Arana Osorio assumed the Presidency, and remained there until mid-1973, shortly before the end of the Arana administration.[85]

Public Safety Program assistance with the Guatemalan Regional Telecommunications Centre and the explicitly intelligence oriented agencies of the army (Section G-2, military intelligence) and the police (the *Policia Judicial*) was administered both by the programme's communications adviser, and "investigations" advisers. The secret report by retired US Ambassador C. Allan Stewart, already cited, observed that during his visit in 1967, "investigations" advisers for Public Safety in Central America worked out of the "CAS" offices — "CAS" standing for CIA in the 1960s[86] — and only nominally for the Public Safety Program.[87] In Guatemala, Investigations Adviser Dave Wright was said to work exclusively on "efforts to improve GOG [Government of Guatemala] intelligence capability". While Public Safety reports credit the Communications Adviser with, from 1964 to 1967, having established the Regional Telecommunications Centre (National Security Service) Ambassador Stewart indicates this was also a major area of concern for the Investigations Advisers to the extent that he:

... works with the intelligence unit of the National Police but spends the majority of his time with the Security Service which coordinates intelligence activities of the National Police and Army.

After Naurocki's return to Guatemala in January 1970 the number of Public Safety advisers increased to its maximum strength of seven, which was maintained until the end of 1972. Naurocki, as well as two advisers who arrived after Arana's inauguration, Jack Forcey (in Guatemala from July 1970-October 1972) and Gerald D. Brown (from August 1971-October 1972), respectively "Administration" and "Rural", reportedly served in similar capacities in the "Civil Operations and Rural Development Support", CORDS, programme in Vietnam, according to a 1974 NACLA study of Guatemala, citing US Government *Biographic Register* and *Foreign Service Lists* (which identified 25 US Foreign Service and AID officials stationed in Guatemala between 1964 and 1974 who had also served in Vietnam).[89]

Although the Vietnam link has generally been pointed out in studies that have sought to show that counter-insurgency technology was developed in the "laboratory" of Vietnam and re-exported around the world, the shuffling of Public Safety technology and personnel between Guatemala and Vietnam also appears to have moved in the opposite direction. There is no doubt that Public Safety advisers were key in setting up the clandestine operations centre at the Guatemalan National Palace (the Regional Telecommunications Centre) and assisted the security services extensively during the 1966-67 state of siege, when "counter-terror" assassinations first mushroomed in Guatemala. And some advisers from that period appear to have subsequently turned up in Vietnam's CORDS between 1967 and 1970.

The identification of security assistance personnel cross-over between Guatemala and Vietnam is indicative primarily of the standardized nature of counter-insurgency doctrine and its implementation in trouble-spots around the world. More striking evidence that a single counter-insurgency doctrine was being implemented in both countries is to be found merely by examining the parallel organizational and tactical innovations applied in the two countries, making the apparent interchangeability of assistance personnel seem almost incidental. As has been pointed out before, security innovations were not a matter of personal inspiration, but the implementation of institutionalized doctrine imparted by one great power to the security forces of its allies.

Similarly, speculation as to precisely which US agencies claimed the primary allegiance of advisers may serve only a secondary and prurient interest. Even if US advisers to Guatemala's security system had always and only been career police administrators, their assistance in developing Guatemalan security communications system and organizing centralized intelligence and command centres could be expected to have been consistent with contemporary counter-insurgency doctrine. This would have been written into their brief. The implementation of this doctrine in the 1960s required the development of conventional and irregular security forces knit tightly into an integrated command structure — an impossibility without sophisticated communications systems. Centralization, under military control, of intelligence collection, analysis, and communications was similarly prescribed and equally indispensable.

It is unnecessary to belabour the Vietnam experience and the Vietnamese connection to conclude that counter-insurgency doctrine, as imparted by the United States civil and military assistance agencies, had a tremendous influence on Guatemala's security system and a devastating impact on Guatemala's people. It is beyond dispute that US security assistance between 1963 and 1966 was directly responsible for creating the Regional Telecommunications Center; that US Investigations Advisers were assigned to the National Security Service operating from the Regional Telecommunications Center; and that, since 1966, this communications/intelligence agency has continuously been the centre of command directing covert state terrorism.

4. Launching Counter-Terror

Although less active in the rural areas by 1965, at the beginning of that year the guerrilla movement carried out a series of spectacular assaults in the capital city itself, and for the first time directed its action at the US security assistance programme's installations and personnel. In June 1965 the CIA advised Presidential National Security Adviser McGeorge Bundy that special measures were being taken in the light of "communist intentions to take direct action against US Personnel and installations". Security was "increased sharply", and the Marine Corps complement in the Embassy "has been more than doubled and emergency radio and telephone facilities have been installed... "[90] The same memorandum informed Mr Bundy that the creation of a special group within the police force to deal with counter-insurgency had been recommended in order to provide the capital with a rapid reaction force to deal with growing urban terrorism. By October 1965 the National Police had deployed the new force, described as a counter-guerrilla unit of 31 members for rapid deployment to deal with "emergencies" in Guatemala City; its special training provided by the Public Safety Program.[91] That a serious problem existed in the capital — particularly for the US security advisers —is illustrated by a CIA chronology of guerrilla activities in the first half of 1965:

> In January (1965) there was an attempted assassination of the Chief of the US Army Mission and the USAID motor pool in Guatemala City was burned to the ground. In February a terrorist in Guatemala City, who had intended to assassinate Peralta, threw a grenade at a crowd of people and into a Guatemalan army truck causing several casualties... Terrorists on March 20 assassinated a police officer who had a reputation as a terrorist, on March 25 threw a grenade at an Army truck which bounced off in the street and killed a girl, and on March 31 machinegunned a Guatemalan army building and planted bombs around the city causing several casualties. On May 2 the consulate was sprayed with machinegun fire and bombs were thrown elsewhere in the city. At noon, May 21 the Vice Minister of Defense was assassinated near his home ...[92]

Peralta's final adjustments of the security apparatus took place after the 15 September 1965 promulgation of a new Constitution (which again proscribed Communism) and the announcement that presidential elections would take place the following March.[93] In December 1965 Public Safety received a special request from Peralta for previously unprogrammed police advisory assistance; the United States responded immediately with the "detailing to Guatemala for temporary duty of an expert in anti-terrorist techniques . . ."[94] In March 1966, the Peralta government requested and received considerably more emergency assistance in the military sphere:

> In response to a request from the Minister of Defense on March 1, 1966 for a special team to provide advice and training in riot control, and in counter-guerrilla and anti-terrorism techniques, an eleven-man MTT [Mobile Training Team] was dispatched by SOUTHCOM and between March 12 and April 12 gave instruction and training to over three thousand armed forces personnel. The special training was desired by the Government of Guatemala because it anticipated that violence might be intensified as the day of the Presidential election approached.[95]

A further area of preparation for a change of government was the army's escalation of propaganda activities to communicate to the public its unflinching dedication to smash subversion, and warn that those not with the army would be considered against it. The army itself was fed continual pep talks, as, for example, the following editorial from the army's magazine, *Ejército* (October 1965):

> As our Armies in acts of patriotic faith build schools, give bread to children, medicine to the sick . . . the communists agitate, steal, kidnap, rape, burn, and destroy . . . Our people are then before two roads: either with their Armies in the labour and struggle to confront Communism, or with the standard bearers of the anti-nation, whether through their actions or their collaborationist indifference . . .

Colonel Miguel Angel Ponciano, former Chief of Staff under Peralta, who resigned his post in order to run for the Presidency, went a step further in a December 1965 interview when he spoke not only of cooperation with the army in general, but through armed army support groups; "the definitive liquidation" of the rebels, said the Colonel, should involve all citizens, "with no less than the formation of voluntary civilian militias".[96] In his January 1966 Aviation Day speech Air Force chief Colonel Manuel Octavio Zea Carrascosa expressed similar sentiments, warning that to win the "harsh and definitive battle (between) liberty and slavery, free determination or subjugation by the transpersonalist state", the Army must count on "the valiant and dedicated collaboration of all those true Guatemalans who have their hearts in the right place". The Cold War boils down to "a fight to survive in a world within which in a short time there will be no room for both ideologies" (*Ejército*, January 1966).

Considerably before the March elections and, in effect, as their precondition, the army required all candidates' agreement to a nine point "pact". In return the army would guarantee "the exchange of power and the tenure of the new government during the period 1966-1970 as long as the conditions of the pact are fulfilled." As an agreement that substantially eroded the prerogatives of whosoever became president, it was in the interest of the army, and the civilian politicians, that it remain a deep, dark secret. To the dismay both of the army high command and the newly elected President, Julio César Méndez Montenegro, the new Vice-President Clemente Marroquin Rojas (eccentric editor of the newspaper *La Hora*) published the text.[97]

The agreement covered three basic themes: 1) the internal affairs of the military were not to be meddled with; 2) the government could govern, but could not alter certain laws or diverge from certain anti-Communist policies, and 3) the war against subversion was to remain under strictly military control.

Leaving its own internal affairs to the army involved a commitment that the Minister of Defense was to be recommended by the army general staff for appointment by the President and that the "constitutional government . . . will prevent all political interference with the army." The army was to "exercise full autonomy in its integration, organization and administration" and this was specified in some detail: for example, no retired army personnel could be returned to active duty without the Minister of Defense's consent.

The government was required to protect the property and persons of the civil and military functionaries of the Peralta regime, and guarantee their immunity from "repressive action of any kind, be it administrative, judicial or otherwise". And, under the watchful eye of the military:

> Those elected will comply with the Constitution of 1965 and the laws that proscribe communist activities, either individual or collective, as well as those activities that tend to foment this ideology in the nation; these laws may not be derogated.

The government was, furthermore, to be one of "national unity", permitting the participation of all capable individuals, "with the absolute exception of communist elements, those with communist sympathies or those with proclivities toward this ideology".

Finally:

> The fight against subversive groups and factions will continue. In no case and under no pretext will the new government enter into any understandings or pacts with such groups, and it will give the army all of the collaboration necessary to eliminate them.

Counter-Terror Takes Off

Almost immediately after Julio César Méndez Montenegro's inauguration as the new civilian President on 1 July 1966, the army requested a vast expansion of US security assistance through both Military Assistance and Public Safety Programs, and launched an intensive campaign of "counter-terror" against "communist elements, those with communist sympathies, and those with proclivities toward this ideology." According to a US government report,[98] on 30 July 1966 Colonel Arriaga Bosque, Méndez Montenegro's new Minister of Defense (chosen for him by Peralta and the army high command) requested "urgent special assistance . . . in the form of equipment and MTT's in preparation for a campaign against the guerrillas"; this assistance was immediately provided. The equipment included arms and ammunition, plus M-1 carbine cartridge magazines and grenades, C-rations, and the loan of four helicopters. The US also provided the Guatemalan army with personnel to fly and maintain the helicopters: "The problem of insufficient pilots and maintenance crews was solved by sending a helicopter MTT to Guatemala from SOUTHCOM (the Southern Command based in the Canal Zone)". The same report notes the special effort of US SOUTHCOM to comply promptly with requests — "we have expedited delivery of MAP [Military Assistance Program] equipment and furnished counter-insurgency MTT's" — and that the commodities and helicopter crews requested on 30 July had arrived in Guatemala within two weeks.

Documentation on how many army MTTs were present in Guatemala in the first months of the new government has not yet been declassified; news reports of the period, however, have claimed that relatively large numbers of US Army Special Forces personnel (grouped in MTT units of from 12 to 36 men) were in Guatemala City and in the north-eastern departments of Izabal and Zacapa, the areas which were to be the focus of the first major counter-insurgency offensive.

Working closely with US advisers was the newly appointed commander of the Zacapa-Izabal military zone, Colonel Carlos Arana Osorio, charged with preparing forces for counter-insurgency (and "counter-terror") in the area. Colonel Arana was close to Defense Minister Colonel Arriaga Bosque (both were 1939 graduates of the Guatemalan military academy) and for two years prior to his appointment in Zacapa had been Guatemala's military attaché in Washington, D.C.[99]

Funding for the MAP rose from its programmed 1966 budget of $994,000 to nearly double at $1,745,000; IMET funding rose from $270,000 to $320,000. Further extensive grants and credits for commodities were provided under the Foreign Military Sales (FMS) and Excess Defense Articles (EDA) programmes (see Table 7.1).[100] Figures released for the costs of the overt aspects of the assistance provided , however, may not have indicated the full cost of the MTTs rushed to Guatemala in late 1966, or of all commodities provided in this period. The 1966 funding level for the Public Safety Program was nearly tripled for fiscal year 1967, rising to $644,000, and showed a marked change from assistance patterns in previous years.[101] $438,000 of the budget went toward commodities grants which for the first time included firearms and ammunition (1,300 carbines and 1,250 .38 revolvers and 510,000 rounds of ammunition), and portable radio equipment (89 sets) described in a Public Safety report as "equipment of the Vietnam Village Hamlet type".[102]

The installation of a tractable, powerless civilian government benefited the army since it served to shield it from public responsibility (or accountability) for the excesses of the coming counter-insurgency campaign. Counter-terror, in its new aspect of massive secret detention and murder of political prisoners, was launched a few days before the Presidential elections. On 3 and 5 March 1966, in which became known as the case of "the 28", military intelligence forces and the Judicial Police raided three houses in Guatemala City, capturing a total of 28 Communist Party and trade union leaders. The prisoners included Víctor Manuel Gutiérrez, secretary-general of the Communist Party (*Partido Guatemalteco del Trabajo* or PGT) and most of the PGT's central committee, as well as Leonardo Castillo Flores, the head of Guatemala's proscribed peasant federation, the *Federación Nacional de Campesinos*. None of the 28 were ever seen again and the Peralta government denied all knowledge of the arrests.

This seems to have been the first taste of blood for the reorganized intelligence system. Shortly before, a confidential report from the US Public Safety Program's chief adviser in Guatemala commented that Peralta had been quite successful in controlling "incipient insurgency" partly due to the identification of the Communist Party leadership thanks to "the capture of lists of Communist Party members". Seemingly the arrests might have been made at any time, but were conveniently carried out just before Peralta's exit and the change of government.

Méndez Montenegro: "A Hollow Figurehead"

Julio César Méndez Montenegro took office on 1 July 1966 having already surrendered to the army a great part of the presidential powers. When, after his brother's murder, he accepted the Presidential nomination, he no doubt did so in the honest hope that his university career and liberal credentials would provide the moral authority to conciliate between the army, the political right (who considered him a leftist), and the guerrillas. The army effectively sabotaged any such role, isolating him completely from its sphere of interest, and making its own political alliance with the political parties of the far right to which

Méndez Montenegro was anathema. The new President was thus reduced to a hollow figurehead legitimizing the army's security operations. Méndez Montenegro's ability to fulfil pre-electoral promises of conciliation and amnesty for the guerrillas was nullified first by "the 28" event and then by the publication of the pact signed with the army.

Nevertheless, the first month of Méndez Montenegro's government brought considerable hope that a change was in the offing. As part of the new President's conciliation programme formal newspaper censorship, in operation for three years, was lifted, and pledges made to reform the police system, to take steps to stop torture and to push through an amnesty law for insurgents. On the day of his inauguration Méndez Montenegro told the press that torture by the security services under Peralta would be "definitively eradicated"; and the new chief of the political police, Senor Hermán Zambrano (formerly a high official of the *Policia Judicial* under Peralta), said that "the agents of the Judicial department will be a guarantee for honorable citizens... Neither torture nor abuse of authority will take place, these things are finished." (*El Imparcial*, 4 July 1966.)

In August 1966 the Judicial (political) Police were renamed Detective Corps (*Cuerpo de Detectives*) and the Deputy Minister of Government told the press of his hope that the new force "will in future be a guarantee of rights, and not the constant menace they have always constituted in the past." (*El Imparcial*, 11 August 1966).

Méndez Montenegro himself declared that certain infamous police cells and torture rooms would no longer be used, including the "Tiger Cage" (*La Tigrera*) at Judicial Police headquarters, and the cells known as "The Stables" (*Las Cuadras*) at National Police headquarters. The Minister of the Treasury, responsible for the Treasury Police (*Guardia de Hacienda*), agreed to search their headquarters for "secret dungeons" (*bóvedas secretas*) and declared that Méndez Montenegro had "proscribed the use of the Treasury police for political repression" or any matters not directly concerning its official task of stopping contraband.[104]

But the guerrillas were sceptical and exceedingly wary of all promises of reform and offers of amnesty, particularly in the face of mounting evidence that, even apart from the March 1966 detention and disappearance of "the 28", the process of detention and imprisonment of suspects was giving way to a pattern of "disappearance" and murder throughout the country. During July 1966 the Guatemala City press reported a number of unexplained detentions and "disappearances" or outright killings in rural areas that appear almost as prototypes of incidents that, after October 1966, occurred almost daily. On 11 January 1966 a peasant farmer had been detained, tortured and shot at "Los Achiotes", Izabal, by military commissioners; in early March, 12 peasants detained by military commissioners in La Jagua, Chiquimula, were later found dead, buried in a mass grave; two others were killed by a military commissioner at Llano de Lágrimas, Chiquimula, on 22 March. Two weeks after Méndez Montenegro's inauguration a communiqué from the Rebel Armed Forces indicated the lack of faith in conciliatory noises from the civilian government that were inconsistent with the realities of army policy, and blatantly contradicted by the pre-electoral pledge the army had demanded of presidential candidates:

> It is known that the conditions imposed by the Army concern precisely what they call 'the implacable fight against Communism', which means to say the repression of any popular struggle, and the continuation of action against the guerrillas 'until they are liquidated'. This is what they desire and what they believe they now can attain by means on the one hand of lies and demagogy, and on the other by redoubling their military operations.

Not only the guerrillas were sceptical. Lic. Carlos Castañeda Paz, law professor and University of San Carlos (the national university) administrator, reminded the press of the similar promises to end torture and harness the secret police after the fall of Ubico, Arbenz and Castillo Armas, concluding that "nonetheless, the tortures and abuses have continued to occur, in the same places that have always been used for these abominable practices."[105]

When newspaper censorship was lifted there followed intensive reporting of abuses under the Peralta regime — for a few weeks. Relatives of "the 28" and of others who had been detained and "disappeared" in the Zacapa-Izabal military zone had gone directly to the press with their accounts, and also to the Association of University Students (*Asociación de Estudiantes Universitarios* (AEU)) which, through its legal services department, pressed in court for the application of habeas corpus on behalf of those missing. On 16 July the Méndez Montenegro government was shaken by a detailed report presented by the AEU's legal department documenting the arrest and murder of "the 28" and of others detained by the police and the army in the last months of the Peralta regime.[106] The AEU's report named 35 individual agents and officers as involved in the detentions and killings, including military commissioners and members of the Mobile Military Police, in co-ordination with military intelligence detachments (Section-2 or G-2) at the Zacapa and Retalhuleu military bases. In one case, that of "disappeared" student Ricardo Berganza Bocallettie, detained by the Judicial Police in December 1965, the AEU presented a dossier to the courts that included photographs obtained from his secret police file showing his tortured body. Subsequently, his bound body, tied to weights, was recovered from Lake Amatitlán.

But the most sensational revelations of the AEU's report were the testimonies of two ex-officers of the Judicial Police who had been involved in the detentions of "the 28", and described their torture and execution in detail; all were reportedly killed between 10 and 15 March. These testimonies were indirectly confirmed by both the new and the former Minister of Government. The new Minister told the press his forces would co-operate fully in recovering the bodies of the dead, noting that "... it is shameful that the extreme should have been reached of killing so many people, especially considering the special circumstances of the case." The former Minister, Colonel Luis Serrano Córdova, disclaimed responsibility for the action of the political police, which, he said, were only technically under his control: "in fact, (the police) have always been dependencies of the presidency of the republic ... In some cases, like the case of the disappeared (the 28), acts were denounced as supposedly committed by the police, but my requests for information on these cases were always refused."[107]

In late July the AEU's lawyers requested the courts to undertake an inquiry into the case of "the 28", and to issue an order for the exhumation of an estimated 30 bodies believed to be buried in the orchard of Don Octavio Solís in Izabal. However, there was no exhumation, no investigation, and no prosecution of members of the security services for their actions. In the next years many AEU leaders and member law students were hunted down and killed.

Attacks on the AEU — and on the University of San Carlos itself, long considered a bastion of the left — increased after its expose of the fate of "the 28". Leaders of the right-wing MLN party and army spokesmen denounced the "AEU-FAR", openly equating the AEU leadership with the guerrillas. Anonymous leaflets took the same line, threatening AEU leaders with death unless they immediately left the country. President Méndez Montenegro's eccentric Vice-President, Clemente Marroquín Rojas, even attacked the University community in his daily newspaper column (published in his own paper, *La Hora*) "for being quick to invoke human rights" when their own (presumably leftist) members are the victims, but remaining silent on the crimes of the guerrillas. Marroquín Rojas went on to praise the decision of "secret" organizations "to apply the law of an eye for an eye" ("*aplicar la ley del talión*"). His remarks on the righteousness of "death-squad" attacks on the AEU and the university were reprinted in the army magazine *Ejército* (May 1967, "*Cuando nos hieren en carne propia*").

The Dead and the "Disappeared"

By the end of August 1966 it was clear that change under Méndez Montenegro was to be change for the worse. In the cities and countryside suspects of left-wing sympathies picked up by the army increasingly tended to either turn up dead or remain "disappeared". The army and police consistently denied responsibility, which they ascribed to vigilante "death-squads" led by right-thing civilians. The "disappearances" and killings in rural areas were usually the work of uniformed army patrols or locally known PMA or military commissioners, while in the cities heavily armed plainclothes men operating out of army or police installations or safe-houses on army property, were usually responsible.

October 1966 saw the launching of a new kind of counter-insurgency offensive in the eastern departments of Izabal and Zacapa under the command of Colonel Carlos Arana Osorio, in charge of the Zacapa military zone. Troops and paramilitary irregulars moved through the villages systematically arresting suspected sympathizers or collaborators of the guerrillas; prisoners were either killed on the spot or "disappeared" into rural detention camps for interrogation — followed by murder. The anti-guerrilla campaign in Zacapa was widely known as "the counter-terror", its objective, to liquidate the "subversives" and intimidate everyone else:

> the objective of the "counterterror" was to frighten anyone from collaborating with the guerrilla movement. Blacklists were compiled which included not only those suspected of working with the guerrillas but also those suspected of Communist leanings.[108]

Villages considered to have gone over to the guerrillas were likely to be razed to the ground; bombing raids, including the use of napalm,[109] were reported for the first time. United States contributions to the army's air power in Zacapa included helicopter gunships and fixed-wing aircraft; some of the latter were provided openly through the MAP programme. US assistance reportedly also included the services of aircraft flying in from the Panama Canal Zone for bombing raids on places believed to be guerrilla redoubts and flying back without ever landing in Guatemala. The US's close involvement in the Zacapa campaign through the provision of MTTs and equipment is discussed further below.

On 2 November 1966 a state of siege was declared throughout Guatemala, suspending civil rights — such as the right to habeas corpus —and placing security wholly under military control. By agreeing to the state of siege President Méndez Montenegro yielded up what little authority he might have retained over the civil police structure, as the Minister of Defense took control of all aspects of the security system, from local police to private security guards. The army's enhanced security prerogatives were complemented by controls imposed on the press, serving to keep the Zacapa campaign entirely shrouded from the public eye and, at the same time, to conceal the take-off of a new and unprecedented campaign of secret arrests and executions in the cities. These press controls ensured that the only reports published on the Zacapa campaign would be those handed out by the army's public relations office. Furthermore, the same day the state of siege was imposed a directive was published banning publication of reports on arrests until they had been confirmed and authorized by the military authorities; a convenient device to cloud the fact that the military had no intention of turning most of the newly detained political prisoners over to the courts, or even to acknowledge their arrest. The "disappearance" of prisoners was to become the norm.

The highest death toll from Guatemalan army operations was in the peasant communities of the guerrilla areas of the mountains of Izabal and Zacapa and, indeed throughout the Zacapa military zone. When, in March 1967, the state of siege was reduced to a "state of alarm", up to 8,000 Guatemalans had been killed in that area alone, a slaughter that succeeded in driving the several hundred guerrillas out of the north-east into the cities. The multiple massacres won Colonel Arana Osorio the sobriquet "The Jackal of Zacapa".

While killings first reached massive proportions in the north-east, and, accompanied by scorched earth measures, largely depopulated some areas, a parallel killing machine was being refined in the cities. Counter-terror there required a special effort to ensure that the new terror tactics would not be blamed on the security services. It was necessary to obscure the identity of the forces serving as counter-terror's instrument, and to relegate all such actions to a status of covert action carried out secretly, or attributed to others, or later denied ever to have have happened.

Special service assassination squads (the counterpart of civilian irregulars integrated into the rural military commissioner network) whose very existence could be plausibly denied were organized within the police and army to fulfil this purpose. Enrolment into the special action forces of gunmen drawn from the army's anti-Communist civilian backers (particularly from the MLN party) and right-wing parties' assistance as a vehicle for propaganda, enhanced the army's capacity to deny all responsibility for the new special service forces. The MLN, in particular, by declaring its support for "vigilante" type "death squads", and insinuating its own very real involvement with such forces, effectively drew the fire of public opinion away from the army and the police, which, in fact, used the MLN gunmen for their own purposes.

In June 1966, a full month before Méndez Montenegro took office, the first anonymous leaflets appeared in Guatemala City heralding the creation of anti-Communist "death-squads" and warning that subversives would be struck down pitilessly, "with the same violence used by the communists", the classic slogan justifying counter-terror. The earliest, dated 3 June 1966, announced the impending creation of the MANO BLANCA or "White Hand", "the hand that will eradicate national renegades and traitors to the fatherland";[110] the acronym MANO standing for *Movimiento de Acción Nacionalista Organizada* (National Movement for Organized Action).

In August 1966 MANO leaflets were distributed over Guatemala City from light aircraft openly landing in the Air Force section of La Aurora airport. Their main message was that all patriotic citizens should unstintingly support the army's counter-insurgency effort; the army was "the institution of the greatest importance at any latitude, representative of Authority, of Order, and of Respect." In sentiments echoing those then appearing in the army *Revista Militar*'s editorials the army is declared to have a central role in fighting subversion and "Consequently to attack it, divide it, or to wish its destruction is indisputedly treason to the fatherland".[111] Later that year leaflets along similar lines announced the formation of another supposedly independent "vigilante" group, the CADEG or *Consejo Anticomunista de Guatemala* (Guatemalan Anti-communist Council) and, in February 1967, a new flurry of leaflets announced the birth of the NOA, or *Nueva Organización Anticomunista* (New Anticommunist Organization). In 1967 a total of some 20 "death-squads" were supposedly operating in Guatemala City under the state of siege, and their leaflets began to publish lists of people "sentenced to death", in some cases running mug shots taken from police files or the Ministry of Interior's passport photographs.[112] In 1967 alone, over 500 names appeared on death lists.

The MLN's contribution to the "death-squad" system was hardly clandestine. In August 1966, statements by MLN spokesmen run as paid advertisements in the Guatemalan press warned of impending "vigilante" action: "... the MLN cannot prevent the people from acting in self defense" (*El Imparcial*, 26 August 1966); "the government should not be surprised that . . . the citizenry organize themselves for self-defense, or take justice into their own hands" (*El Imparcial*, 27 August 1966). The document circulated secretly within the army and the MLN in August 1966, variously attributed to the US Military Group or the CIA, (already discussed on pp. 153–4) places these references to impending "vigilante" action squarely inside the army's new counter-insurgency programme, not as spontaneous or independent self-defence initiatives, but as a boost for the army's own effort to organize civilian paramilitary forces. The MLN's public statements, however, continued to proclaim the "vigilante" character of the death-squad actions that began to be reported in late 1966.

Ten months later in a paid advertisement in *El Gráfico* (4 May 1967) the MLN proclaimed that

> the government, the people, and the Army have amalgamated into a single fighting force, with the object of destroying [the guerrilla] definitively [in] a political and armed struggle without quarter, which will be a true 'national crusade'!

Citizens' groups were described as having begun to act in "self-defense" and to "respond to the enemy with their own arms and tactics".

This 4 May 1967 MLN statement was taken from a much longer, secret document, circulated by the MLN but attributable to the Guatemalan Army or the United States advisory programme.[113] Seemingly a progress report, this document, described the network of civilian irregulars working with the army as "an effective anti-guerrilla movement... fighting the guerrillas with their own tactics and systems." The description of civil-military co-operation — on terms laid down by the army — appears nearly identical to contemporary writing on paramilitary organization in El Salvador which discusses the relation of ORDEN's paramilitary forces to the Salvadorean army, and in every way consistent with the ideal implementation of US counter-insurgency doctrine. Referring in particular to the rural areas the 1967 document states that:

> ... the action of the Army in the northeast found decided and unlimited support from the civil population . . . the Army, arm in arm with revolutionary civilians, received valuable military information, has excellent guides and dedicated and brave peasants who know the terrain.

The document dates to October 1966 "the decision of the National Army to act . . . with certain liberty of action" in the main activity of counter-insurgency, the liquidation of "subversives". Success is claimed for this policy:

> The Army, with its armed civilian units passed from the defensive to the attack [and] in a few short months the anti-guerrilla movement brought peace and order to the greater part of the eastern zone of Guatemala.

The extension of this campaign to the cities, where the anti-guerrilla offensive began with "psychological warfare, from the printing and distribution of leaflets, to the sending of anonymous threats...", is also described in the document. In mid-January, 1967,

> the first civic-military commandos for repression in the capital, and the first operations in which the capital's anti-guerrillas employed the tactics that had been successful for the FAR: They pursued, kidnapped and liquidated the principal guerrilla elements . . . The action of the anti-guerrilla is implacable and unlimited . . .

The 1967 document suggests that public support for the army (and not necessarily the government) was also provided by the paramilitary network by means of packaged demonstrations:

> For the first time, popular demonstrations are organized in the very zones of the guerrilla, in which support for the National Army and repudiation of Castro-Communism is demonstrated.

Set piece demonstrations in the north-east tended, however, to be held in the confines of the army's special counter-insurgency bases, such as Rio Hondo, Zacapa. In November 1966, capital city journalists were invited by the army's chief of "Civic Action and Public Relations" to attend a "spontaneous peasant demonstration" at Río Hondo. On 25 November, the press (see, for example, *El Imparcial*) reported the presence of some 800 to 1,000 farmers enthusiastically shouting "Long Live the Army" and "Down with the Guerrillas", and carrying neatly printed placards with such slogans as "We don't want to be another Cuba", "FAR Surrender", and "We are peaceful peasants. We want to continue being so". (At the time US news agencies accepted at face value the army's press release on the demonstration reporting mass peasant support for the campaign in Zacapa.)

MLN Secretary General Mario Sandoval Alarcón later praised the government's "plan of complete illegality" which, by March 1967, had already achieved spectacular results in the countryside: "the guerrillas have been almost completely eliminated from the Guatemala Oriente".[114] In the cities the escalation of the terror was just as illegal but considerably less successful in rooting out the guerrillas. Its principal effect appears to have been to create a climate of fear, and to intimidate prospective sympathizers of the insurgents.

If the attribution of the murders in the cities to "death-squads" advertising themselves by anonymous leaflets, and by pinning notes claiming credit for killings on the tortured and mutilated bodies of their victims was primarily a device by which the security services could evade accountability, it also served to contribute to the climate of terror. "Disappearance" and murder by phantoms — phantoms with police protection, or by the police or army itself masquerading as phantoms — was especially terrifying as there was no one to turn to for protection. If the army dragged someone away and then blamed "NOA" or "MANO", that was that; unless the victim was from a family with connections very high up in the army hierarchy. Some of the more detailed testimonies on security operations carried out in 1967 under the names of "MANO" and "NOA", however, are from "disappearance" survivors plucked almost literally from the jaws of death by last minute interventions by their families.

Julio Vázquez Alvarado, a 19 year old law student at the national University of San Carlos, had been a student leader in a secondary school and worked as an assistant to left-wing lawyer Edmundo Guerra Theilheimer (himself machine-gunned to death some years later). In mid-January 1967 his law office was raided at noon by a group of some 20 uniformed army troops. Vázquez was taken at gunpoint from the building, and in an army truck escorted by jeeps taken to an isolated area in the outskirts of the capital and turned over to a group of ten plainclothes agents. Hooded, gagged and forced to lie prone on the floor of an unmarked sedan, he was taken to a house at the end of La Aurora airport's runways and interrogated under torture. Reports from opposition groups at the time had already identified an army "safe house" in a new housing development for army widows, next to the airport; its bricked up windows made it easily distinguishable. After several days he and other prisoners were taken to Fort Matamoros, the army's headquarters, and held in a large underground storeroom or tunnel, lit only by a single barred window close to the ceiling, the stone walls pockmarked by bullets. For 15 days army spokesmen denied Vázquez' detention, and attributed his "kidnapping" to "NOA". Steps taken by his family, however, to go straight to Defense Minister Arriaga Bosque apparently saved his life; in an unmarked sedan, again hooded and prone, he was again transferred to a cell at the Judicial Police headquarters where his arrest was "discovered". Five days later, he was released on condition that he immediately left the country (he did, for Mexico).[115] His account is corroborated by press reports and 1980-81 accounts of subterranean torture rooms at Fort Matamoros.

Eduardo Galeano, in his astonishingly early *Guatemala: País Ocupado*, (1967) gives similar accounts of "survivors" of death-squad style detentions. Galeano recounts how the family of PR leader Rodolfo Gutiérrez of El Jícaro, Zacapa —"disappeared" by the army — went straight to Defense Minister Arriaga Bosque. He reportedly gave them a safe-conduct pass and a note for Colonel Arana at the Zacapa base who assigned an army captain to take them to a secret detention camp in the hamlet of La Palma, near Rio Hondo. Gutiérrez was one of the few to leave it alive.[116]

Killings of local leaders of the President's own *Partido Revolucionario* (PR) led to some protests by parliamentarians, but a resounding silence from President Méndez. In February 1967 PR representative Edmundo López Durán spoke out in congress

> . . . the situation of the state of siege has been taken advantage of by the terrorist organization "Mano Blanca" . . . and of the military commissioners, to persecute and kill well-known members of the *Partido Revolucionario*.[117]

Lawyer López Durán's own name was promptly put on a "death list" circulated in the name of CADEG, accused of being a "communist and a traitor", and the *Partido Revolucionario* expelled him from the party.

The May 1967 document ascribed to the MLN and the army, outlined the rationale of the "death-squad" killing campaign, and made particular reference to the local *Partido Revolucionario* leaders as "agents of the guerrillas" to be eliminated. Figurehead Méndez Montenegro is not mentioned in the document:

> Many times there is some difficulty in that a majority of the agents of the

guerrilla movement belong to the official party and occupy municipal posts . . . but that is not an obstacle to pursuing the work of clearing them out . . . Violence is now fought with violence and terror with terror. Today, as we know who the collaborators of the guerrillas are, they are sought out directly and implacably liquidated.[118]

Only in August 1967, after a rash of killings of their leadership, did the *Partido Revolucionario* — without the backing of President Méndez — dare to issue a statement requesting protection for their membership, and protesting against "the sowing of terror and death" by the army and its civilian auxiliaries "under the pretext of fighting the guerrillas", although acknowledging that "At the beginning we were aware that these groups of civilians were part of the cooperation needed by the Army to fight against the subversive groups."[119]

The Death Lists

An important part of the psychological "counter-terror" campaign were the widely circulated "death lists". In January 1968, a booklet containing 85 photographs, was distributed throughout the country entitled "People of Guatemala, Know the Traitors, the Guerrillas of the FAR". Full-size "Wanted" type posters were sometimes prominently displayed on walls in the cities. Selected targets could be terrorized into leaving the country by warning specific groups or individuals; for example, the CADEG leaflet addressed to the leaders of the labour federation FECETRAG: "Your hour has come, Communists at the service of Fidel Castro, Russia and Communist China. You have until the last day of March to leave the country."[120]

The psychological effect was enhanced as special notes of horror were added to the killings: nude and mutilated bodies were placed where numerous passers-by could not fail to see them, particularly in the Guatemala City slum areas; or left on the doorstep of the victims' family; or posted with notes explicitly describing how the victim was slowly cut to pieces, castrated, strangled, burned, drowned or smothered:[121]

> With few exceptions, the corpses tended to show signs of torture, especially mutilation (the severing of one or both hands, of arms or legs, of the nose, the tongue, the ears, eyes, genital organs, the breasts of the women), burns, flagelation, slashes with knives, or they were found totally dismembered . . . One can conclude that leaving the corpses in places where their discovery was certain, and with signs of torture, was the most effective means of disseminating the terror; indeed, it not only proved the seriousness of the threats . . . but also added to the fear of death the risk of prior torment, taking to the maximum the intimidation exercized over the targets . . .

Some threats were couched in crude sexual slang. A MANO circular dated 11 November 1967, posted to trade unionists, students, journalists and politicians on the latest "death list" and flyposted on the walls of the capital, warned them "... you'll be wearing your balls for a neck-tie...". But sexual mutilation of "death-squad" victims was only a small part of the daily diet of news reports and photographs served to Guatemalan newspaper readers after the launching of counter-terror. After December 1966 there were almost daily reports of mutilated bodies found at roadsides, down wells, in ravines, or in "clandestine cemeteries", the usual term for the mass graves that began to be found in the sandpits in the capital's outskirts or in rural areas. Aguilera cites an early example of the latter from Ipala, Chiquimula, reported in the press on 4 February 1967, where a dog uncovered a mass grave with 18 bodies near the railway line.

The press, indeed, served as a useful vehicle to give resonance to the terror, and, subject to the restrictions referred to, was apparently encouraged to report grisly details of the killings, and allowed to publish photographs illustrating the discovery of the victims' bodies and their mutilated condition. Speculation on the responsibility of the police or army for the detentions and killings, or comments on the indifference of the security forces to these crimes were not permitted. By mid-1967 police reports on the discovery of tortured bodies settled into a routine pattern: the press was informed of measures to identify the *bodies* — not the murderers — or newsmen were provided with data from police files indicating that the victim was a recidivist criminal or a dangerous Communist suspect.

The very arbitrariness of the new violence enhanced its psychological impact, if not effectiveness. In colonial times, the spectacle of executions in a market square or heads displayed on pikes was at least nominally carried out in the name of the law, and not an everyday occurrence. The new terror could only undermine the law and traumatize the society.

Only the Guatemalans themselves have been exposed to the full impact and graphic horror of the "counter-terror" either through their own, or their friends' personal experiences, or by means of the daily bombardment of new incidents reported in their news media. Cutting files compiled from Guatemalan newspapers since 1966 are littered with photographs of jumbled heaps of human bones, severed heads, headless bodies, rotting heaps of clothing and discarded shoes: press records of human dumping grounds discovered littering ravines and mountainsides throughout the country.

Nearly ten years elapsed before the Guatemalan terror became fully known in the outside world.

Although the US had a great many military advisers and police trainers on the ground in Guatemala during the 1966-68 carnage, little official documentation describing the Zacapa counter-insurgency offensive has been declassified, and none is available in which the relation of US assistance to the new tactics and organization of forces is discussed. The Department of the Army's records are a particular blank spot; Freedom of Information Act requests for records on US Army MTTs present in Guatemala between 1966 and 1974 were rejected on the grounds that such records "probably do not exist".[122]

One of the few overviews to appear in a declassified document from within the US security assistance establishment was the 1967 survey report produced for the Public Safety Program that has already been cited. Unlike the authors of other Public Safety reports on Central America, former Ambassador C. Allan Stewart was neither assessing his own work, nor involved in the operational side of security assistance. Perhaps as a consequence his report was less guarded than those of other US officials who had actually served in Guatemala. The report praises the army's counter-insurgency strategy, and attributes its success largely to US training:

> Well trained units of the armed forces have been entrusted with control of rural guerrilla campaigns and by energetic methods have blunted the efforts of the procommunist forces... The armed forces, fortified with US-directed counter-insurgency training have had great success in halting guerrilla groups, working principally in the Northeast part of the country, principally in the Sierra de las Minas mountains.[123]

A key part of the army's forces described in the report were the "about 9,000 military commissioners and associates in the rural areas", and "urban extra-legal groups". The author also expresses some minor disquiet at the potential hazards of paramilitary organization:

> These commissioners, made up of ex-military men, rightist landowners, etc., are becoming more aggressive as the guerrilla movement weakens, and it is feared they may turn to political reprisals as the need for their anti-guerrilla efforts diminishes. Urban extra-legal groups, it is reported link right-wing elements with Army officers. This might well have an inhibiting effect on the inauguration of the social reforms people are asking.

The 1967 report also acknowledged the use of summary execution in the counter-insurgency campaign, and implies that while unsavoury, terror tactics served a justifiable end:

> The methods used to discourage guerrillesque activity are patterned after US far west frontier justice of the days when courtrooms were few and far between. Occasional articles appear in the press reporting that bullet-riddled bodies were found in areas where guerrillas were said to be operating... It is believed by informed Guatemalans that the bodies are those of guerrillas who were captured, summarily executed, their bodies

removed from the immediate area and left to be discovered by the peasants.

The author of the 1967 report rationalizes the turn to outright killing of suspected guerrillas as a response to the inadequacy of the court system; summary executions are described as actions that "by-passed the courts in impressing suspected guerrillas and supporters of the error of their ways". This is described in part as a response to a "morale" problem:

> In discussing guerrilla warfare, Guatemalan Army officers significantly remark that the first suspects captured were turned over to the courts but several weeks later obtained their freedom, a development that the officers described as bad for their forces' morale. Thereafter the number of guerrillas turned over to the courts seemed to diminish somewhat.

This argument that the courts are an obstacle to counter-insurgency or crime control is hardly new; a US Defense Department study from 1965 described as one of the major "handicaps" to counter-insurgency "the fact that many of the [Latin American] legal systems require courts to free prisoners, even notorious guerrillas . . . unless witnesses can testify they actually saw the accused commit the crime with which he is charged".[124]

Although the Stewart report presents a probably accurate reflection of the Guatemalan military's and their US colleagues' rationale for counter-terror, it illustrates the departure in practice that has distinguished US counter-insurgency doctrine from the doctrine of other Western powers. In Sir Robert Thompson's classic *Defeating Communist Insurgency* the author warns that the appeal to the easy solution in counter-insurgency may lead directly to policy failure, and refers specifically to the "temptation" to bypass the courts:

> There is a very strong temptation in dealing both with terrorists and with guerrilla actions for government forces to act outside the law, the excuses being that the processes of law are too cumbersome, that the normal safeguards in the law for the individual are not designed for an insurgency, and that a terrorist deserves to be treated as an outlaw anyway.[125]

Thompson warns that the effects of extra-legal actions are not easily gauged, and insists that such action is not only in itself

> morally wrong, but over a period . . . will create more practical difficulties for a government than it solves. A government which does not act in accordance with the law forfeits the right to be called a government and cannot expect its people to obey the law.[126]

In the Guatemalan case the counter-insurgents gave in to the temptation to do a quick fix with counter-terror; counter-terror was introduced in accordance with counter-insurgency doctrine's prescription of extraordinary extra-legal means to rapidly crush insurgency. That already by early 1967 this tactic was perceived to have been to some degree effective is noted in the Stewart report. Ambassador Stewart is uneasy about the tactics for much the same reasons enunciated by Robert Thompson. But the ends are ultimately seen to justify the means, distaste is overcome by misplaced realism:

> These tactics, if carried out, present a problem for a democratic government, especially if there turn out to be innocent victims, or if personal vengeance is carried out under the guise of ridding the country of anti-government fighters. On the other hand, while I was in Guatèmala from June 8-11 it was reported that numerous students of univesity and high school age had returned to their homes from the hills, convinced that the glamorous life of a guerrilla was becoming too risky to continue.

But counter-terror was to continue without interruption, even after the guerrillas had been largely defeated in the mountains of the north-east.

"The Killing Has Never Stopped"

During that first counter-insurgency offensive in 1966 and 1967, Guatemala's security system crystallized into what became its permanent form; the army never looked back; the killing has never stopped. By the end of 1967 the guerrillas had been cleared from the mountains of Zacapa and Izabal and survivors were believed to be licking their wounds in Guatemala City hideouts, a spent force. President Méndez Montenegro in his annual message to congress in 1967 suggested the guerrillas were defeated, and begged the question of continuing governmental violence: "Satisfactory results have been obtained . . . in the campaign of pacification . . . public tranquility is returning rapidly to all sectors of the nation". The apparent defeat of the insurgents did not, however, halt the increasingly unjustifiable counter-insurgent killings in the north-east and throughout the country.

In the cities one particular case outraged important sectors of public opinion. In December 1967, 26 year old Rogelia Cruz Martínez, former "Miss Guatemala" of 1959, a girl of good family but known for her left-wing sympathies, was picked up and later found dead, having been tortured, raped and mutilated. On 16 January 1968, before the outcry had died down, a guerrilla attack on a carload of United States military advisers was widely seen as a "reprisal" for this murder. The victims of the guerrilla attack were fired upon, some ten blocks from the US

Embassy in Guatemala City, from a passing car. The chief of the US military mission, Colonel John D. Webber, and Naval Attaché Lieutenant Commander Ernest A. Munro, were killed instantly by submachine-gun fire; two others were wounded. The FAR issued a statement which made no specific reference to the murder of Rogelia Cruz Martínez, but said the killings were in vengeance against the Americans who had created the "genocidal forces" that had "resulted in the death of nearly 4,000 Guatemalans" during the previous two years.

The incident that stirred even timid President Méndez Montenegro from his complacence, was, however, more ludicrous than horrible. The abduction of Guatemala's Roman Catholic Archbishop Mario Casariego on 16 March 1968 was initially denounced by the right-wing parties and the army as an outrage committed by the FAR. Picked up within 100 yards of the National Palace in the presence of heavily armed troops and police, the Archbishop's kidnap was widely believed by people on the left to have been an "*auto-secuestro*" or self-kidnapping meant to embarrass the left. The Archbishop was well known for his extremely conservative views, and critics considered it just possible that he would co-operate in his own kidnapping in order to blacken the reputation of the guerrillas. In the event, he refused to go along with the scheme and the kidnappers' plan "to create a national crisis by appealing to the anticommunism of the Catholic population" backfired.[127] Even Méndez Montenegro could not overlook the Archbishop's kidnapping and evidence that the army high command had orchestrated the affair forced a confrontation. The upshot was that the Archbishop went home unscathed and two civilians involved in the operation, potentially embarrassing to the army — Raúl Estuardo Lorenzana and Inés Mufio Padilla — served as scapegoats. They were arrested and taken off in a police patrol car. In transit the patrol car stopped and the police guards got out as gunmen shredded the rear of the car with submachine-gun fire, killing the two handcuffed prisoners. One press report said Lorenzana's body had 27 bullet wounds and Padilla's 22. The police escort was unhurt.[128]

The army did not emerge unscathed from the scandal, and its three top counter-insurgents, those most publicly linked to the "death-squad" policies, were replaced. Defense Minister Colonel Rafael Arriaga Bosque was sent to Miami, Florida, to become Consul General; the Director of the National Police, Colonel Manuel Francisco Sosa Avila, to Spain as Military Attaché; and the head of the counter-insurgency offensive in the north-east, Colonel Carlos Arana Osorio, was named Ambassador to Nicaragua.

The new Defense Minister, Colonel Rolando Chinchilla Aguilar, continued the army's counter-insurgency operations with little concession to public opinion; but the months following the Archbishop Casariego affair marked perhaps the lowest point of death-squad activity in Guatemala after 1966.

In August 1968, however, the lull ended. US Ambassador John Gordon Mein was shot dead in his car, apparently while resisting a kidnap attempt; the FAR guerrilla group was credited with the killing. The affair was unusual in that the Guatemalan security authorities claimed to have "solved" the crime almost immediately. Police said they had located one of the plotters later the same day: "Michele Firk, a French socialist who had rented the car used to kidnap Mein". However, "when the police came to interrogate her, she shot herself".[129]

The case assumed further, considerably more mysterious aspects ten years later, when a Guatemalan, reputedly a former bodyguard of Colonel Carlos Arana Osorio, told US government investigators that high army officers were involved in Mein's murder.[130] The source of the allegations was Jorge Zimeri Saffie, the son of a business partner of Colonel Arana, who fled Guatemala in 1976 after apparently falling out with Colonel Kjell Laugerud García's incoming military government; articles on Zimeri appeared in the *New York Times* and the *Washington Post* a year after his arrest in Miami on federal fire-arms charges in December 1977, when threats were made to extradite him to Guatemala where he might have been killed. On 18 October 1978, the *Washington Post* cited "sources familiar with the case" in reporting:

> Zimeri has implicated in conversations with US investigators, one high official in the current military government of Gen. Romeo Lucas García and two officials in a previous Guatemalan government in connection with the 1968 assassination of John Gordon Mein, then the US Ambassador to Guatemala. "I came across a lot of information" about the killing of Mein and others, Zimeri said in an interview yesterday. [His lawyer] declined to let his client divulge the information.

On the same day, the *New York Times* described Zimeri as possibly "the key informant regarding the 1968 assassination of John Gordon Mein."

Little more was heard about Sr. Zimeri's case in the US press, and nothing more about the alleged involvement of army officers in killing Mein, or setting him up to be killed, perhaps by leaking his movements to the guerrillas, or withdrawing his police guard without warning. Although the guerrillas apparently never denied having been responsible for the kidnap attempt it is not inconceivable that top army officers were in some way involved. The Mein affair occurred at a momentary lull in guerrilla activity in Guatemala, when Méndez Montenegro was claiming the guerrillas had been annihilated (a claim then not far from the truth) and the state of siege had been lifted. More important, there had been a significant national and international backlash in public opinion to the more atrocious methods of counter-insurgency, culminating with the March 1968 "kidnap" of Archbishop Mario Casariego. The gentle exile of three of the army's top officers after the Casariego affair was widely represented as a move by Méndez Montenegro to rein in the lawless elements of the counter-insurgency campaign, and may have been a sincere effort to that end. The murder of the American Ambassador, however, provoked renewed public calls for more, tough counter-insurgency measures, ensured a reinvigorated flow of US security assistance, and triggered a rash of "death-squad" killings under the aegis of the new Defense Minister, Colonel Rolando Chinchilla Aguilar and army chief of staff Colonel Doroteo Reyes.[131]

Before the Mein killing there is some record of terrorist assaults and bombings attributed to the FAR having been carried out by Guatemalan security services as a deliberate means to discredit the guerrilla movement, and to justify to the public extraordinary counter-insurgency measures. These were particularly frequent in the first months of 1966. United States counter-insurgency doctrine, moreover, provides for the legitimate use of such tactics to induce the public to accept subsequent harsh measures. That such actions might be extended to include clandestine actions against US personnel or property is conceivable in so far as the perpetrators could be assured that blame would be placed squarely on the leftist insurgents.

In June 1966 National Security Advisor Walt Rostow brought to the attention of President Lyndon Johnson a cable from John Gordon Mein (dated 15 June) which advised the Department of State that he had learned of impending assassination attempts against both himself and German Ambassador Count Karl Von Spreti.[132] Ambassador Mein downplayed the urgency of the threat, although he said he had no doubts of its authenticity. What is important, in the light of subsequent events, is that Mein insisted the threat probably came from the *right* not the *left*. The matter was taken extremely seriously in Washington: Rostow's memorandum to Johnson, with the cable attached, was on the President's desk the same day it left Guatemala City.[133]

On 31 March 1970 Count Karl Von Spreti was kidnapped when his car was intercepted by armed men. A ransom demand was made in the name of the FAR, the group to which responsibility for John Gordon Mein's murder had been attributed. The kidnappers demanded the release first of 17, then 25 political prisoners (whose names were never made public) and $700,000 ransom. The government outraged the diplomatic corps, and the German government, by refusing to negotiate. On 9 April an anonymous telephone call informed the Papal Nuncio that Count Von Spreti had been shot, and his body could be found at kilometre 17 on the road to San Pedro.[134] Von Spreti was found shot once in the head. Unlike the killing of the American Ambassador, there were no claims that anyone apart from the FAR guerrillas themselves was involved. This, moreover, was the third in a series of spectacular kidnappings, indisputably laid to the FAR, within the space of little more than a month. On 27 February Foreign Minister Alberto Fuentes

Mohr was kidnapped and exchanged unharmed after negotiations had won the release of prisoner José Vincente Calvillo (one of the "disappeared" prisoners of the time); on 6 March Sean Holly, second secretary of the US Embassy was kidnapped and released in exchange for four prisoners also held in secret detention.[135]

Arana Osorio's Continued "Pacification"

In Presidential elections on 1 March 1970, Colonel Carlos Arana Osorio, back from his brief stint in Nicaragua, ran as the candidate of the MLN and the Institutional Democratic Party (PID), his platform a promise of continued "pacification". Although press reports tended to describe his victory at the polls as a tribute to his personal popularity, and ratification of his pacification programme, there were other explanations to the election outcome, not least the absence of an opposition candidate with any popular following to speak of. More significant, perhaps was the delivery of packaged votes to Arana from the rural areas through the army's military commission network. Norman Gall, writing in the *New York Review of Books*, commented that part of Arana's support was attributable to the commissioners, who in the eastern part of the country "threatened to burn down villages that did not vote overwhelmingly for MLN candidates".[136] Although Arana did not achieve an absolute majority over the Revolutionary Party and Christian Democratic Party candidates, congress confirmed him as the victor.[137] Arana's influence was apparent from the day of the election, however, and particularly in the aftermath of the Von Spreti killing, when Zacapa tactics were brought to Guatemala City with a vengeance. In the two months following Count Von Spreti's murder, "death-squad" killings escalated in what Guatemalan social scientist Gabriel Aguilera termed the second great "wave of terror". The killings, attributed to a backlash against the guerrillas, claimed the lives of several leading citizens who had had the temerity to criticize illegal counter-insurgent violence, including that of poet and journalist Julio Cesar de la Roca, and national university professor Justo Rufino Cabrera, both abducted, tortured and murdered in June.[138]

With the inauguration of ex-Zacapa commander Arana Osorio, who returned in triumph from his temporary political "exile" as Ambassador to Nicaragua, a third, much more extensive wave of terror began.

Arana had been in charge of orchestrating counter-terror in the countryside during the Zacapa campaign and, even before assuming the Presidency, in July 1970, warned that he would utterly destroy the guerrilla movement during his term of office. He made his methods clear too. When asked, shortly after Count Von Spreti's killing, how he would deal with guerrilla kidnappings, Arana told a reporter: "I will set a deadline for [the captive's] release at four o'clock in the afternoon, and for each hour that passes I will shoot one *Fuerzas Armadas Revolucionarias* criminal in our prisons."[139] This was, of course, already a time when the government denied holding any political prisoners.

As in the case of the previous administration, the government waited several months before launching another intensive counter-insurgency campaign. Killings and disappearances never really ceased (the press reported 107 "death-squad" murders and disappearances between July and October 1970, almost one a day).[140] Four months after taking office, on 13 November, Arana followed the lead of Méndez Montenegro's Defense Minister, Colonel Rafael Arriaga Bosque, and imposed a state of siege.[141] Some days later, on 19 November, Arana made a speech in which he declared that:

> ... You have elected Arana and Cáceres Lenhoff [the new vice-president] and given them a mandate: pacify the country and end the wave of violence and crimes. You did not give them conditions or tell them how to do this ... The government you elected made a promise and is going to keep it no matter what the cost, even though it must resort to very drastic measures to save the country.[142]

The state of siege included a 9 pm to 5 am curfew during which anyone abroad could be — and was — shot on sight; even ambulances and firetrucks were forbidden to be out at night. During the first 15 days, according to press reports, house to house searches led to 1,600 detentions in the capital. Some 700 prisoners were later reported executed in the first two months of the state of siege alone.

Some of the first of Arana's siege victims were his harshest critics in the press and in the University. Guatemala City journalists Enrique Salazar Solórzano and Luis Pérez Díaz were taken and "disappeared" on 26 November, apparently in direct reprisal for having written newspaper stories denouncing repression. National University law professor Julio Camey Herrera — an active critic of the Arana government — was murdered on 27 November.[143] And on 28 November, radio station owner and broadcaster (*Radio Nuevo Mundo* and *Radio Sensación*) Humberto González Juárez together with his business partner, Armando Bran Valle, and a secretary were victims of a classical "death-squad" operation: initial press reports said they were stopped by police on the way to a Pacific beach; the police denied having had anything to do with the case; the three bodies were subsequently found in a ravine near the highway to the sea. Much later, in 1975, Lauro Alvarado y Alvarado a former member of the Detective Corps jailed for a non-political offence, told reporters he had carried out many political murders on the orders of superior officers, including the detention and murder of González Juárez and his companions on 28 November 1970.[144]

Christian Democratic Party leader René Schlotter de León made one of the few efforts to publicly denounce the new murder campaign. Though a member of congress he had been refused the right to address it on the subject of repression. A statement of his was to have been published in the press as a paid advertisement on 6 October 1972. Not one paper printed it. Eventually published privately, the statement demanded of the Minister of Government an explanation concerning "clear cases of the participation of the police in criminal activities".

> How can one explain that in the last five months the number of dead at the hands of unidentified armed groups has tripled? And that the number of disappeared has quadrupled? . . . What is the response of the government about the responsibility of members of the police for these acts?[145]

Predictably, no explanation was forthcoming. Equally predictably, Schlotter began to receive threats, and attempts were made against his life, but he gamely stayed on in Guatemala until 1976 when he left after being wounded in the arm by a bullet in a final attack.

In September 1972 President Arana's security forces duplicated the famous case of "the 28" by capturing half of the PGT's Central Committee, including Secretary General Bernardo Alvarado Monzón. He and Mario Silva Jonama, Hugo Barrios Klee, Carlos René Valle, Carlos Alvarado Jerez, Miguel Angel Hernández, Fátima Rodríguez and her servant, Natividad Franco Santos, were captured during a meeting in a Guatemala City home and taken to the headquarters of the Detective Corps. Like "the 28", they were never seen again. In November 1972, Guatemala City newspapers reported a statement by Detective Abel Juárez Villatoro affirming that the eight prisoners had been captured by detectives and then turned over to the Fourth Corps of the National Police and presumably murdered:

> At about 10 that night, Don Arnoldo Argueta, Second chief of the Detective Corps, Don Luis Ocaña, now Third Chief . . . and Inspector Abel Martínez García turned the eight prisoners over to a squad chief of the Fourth Corps known as 'Chino Lima'.

Juárez Villatoro's statement was not entirely voluntary: he himself had been kidnapped by FAR guerrillas, and several newspaper reporters were brought in to witness his account of the affair. Juárez Villatoro was released by the guerrillas, but his fate at the hands of his own colleagues is unknown. Minister of Government Roberto Herrera Ibarguen declared the press statements to be fabrications, and repeated that both he and the President had already denied the eight had ever been arrested, and that was that. No one in Guatemala, however, has any serious doubts the eight were murdered, or about who murdered them.[146]

It was under the overtly military regime of Arana and not the civilian government of Méndez Montenegro that international organizations and important sectors of the foreign press first began to take serious notice of the slaughter in Guatemala. Amnesty International, for instance, first raised the subject of "arrests, disappearances and murders of the opposition" by the Arana government with the Inter-American Commission on Human Rights in February 1971, backing its submission with hundreds of documented cases confirming that units of the security forces carried out "extralegal detention and disappearance".

United States organizations paid particular interest to US involvement in the Guatemalan government's recourse to terrorism. In December 1971, the Latin American Studies Association (the principal professional organization of US Latin Americanists) resolved to condemn "semi-official and official rightist terror in Guatemala"; and noted that "it is impossible to ignore the complicity of the US in this repression, through its support of the Arana regime, and most particularly through its police and military programs."[147] LASA initiated its own investigation through an Ad Hoc Committee and published a report in 1973 detailing both the particular excesses of the 1970-71 state of siege, and the institutionalization of state terror:

> One measure of the degree to which political violence and repression has become a system or way of life is that during the nine years from 1963 through 1971 (108 months), Guatemala spent 48 months, or nearly half, under a state of siege. A state of siege has always meant the abrogation of constitutional guarantees and political rights, the prohibition of regular political activity even by legal parties, and strict censorship of the press and radio ... In short, it should be clear that the situation in Guatemala in 1971 was not a temporary aberration or excess in a generally democratic system. Rather, it was part of a system of official terror and repression . . .[148]

US congressional investigations also criticized US involvement in Guatemalan state terrorism. A staff report on Guatemala and the Dominican Republic prepared for the Senate Foreign Relations Committee in 1971 may have considerably influenced subsequent legislation placing human rights restrictions on security assistance. In its evaluation of the security assistance programme, the report warned of the political price paid for involvement in "police terrorism".

> The argument in favor of the public safety program in Guatemala is that if we don't teach the cops to be good, who will? The argument against is that after 14 years, on all evidence, the teaching hasn't been absorbed. Furthermore, the US is politically identified with police terrorism.[149]

On leaving office in July 1974, Colonel Arana Osorio turned over control of a security system that had been in smooth operation since 1966. Throughout those eight years the Guatemalan military had worked closely with US military and civilian security advisers, and applied US funds and material in putting the doctrine of counter-insurgency into practice. The US's role in regearing the security system for counter-insurgency between 1963 and 1966 has already been discussed; the US security assistance programme's responsibility in subsequent developments was no less broad and direct.

1966-74: Intensification of US Security Assistance

In the 1966-74 period the US placed the largest number of security assistance personnel in Guatemala, and security assistance packages reached the highest dollar values. After 1974 there would be no overt police training programme for Guatemala, and the military group there would be progressively downgraded in strength. Human rights restrictions on security assistance under the Carter administration would, after 1977, significantly reduce assistance through normal channels to Guatemala. In an overview of US security assistance, the Méndez Montenegro and Arana governments stand out as periods when US security personnel were most frequently reported to have had a direct involvement in waging Guatemalan counter-insurgency, and when states of siege and waves of mass counter-terror coincided with massive infusions of US assistance.

Reports that US military advisers were in the field, helping their Guatemalan counterparts implement counter-insurgency, began to reach the press almost as soon as the Zacapa offensive was launched in October 1966. In December 1966, *Chicago Daily News* reporter Georgie Ann Geyer filed some of the earliest stories on the US presence in Zacapa, and reported guerrilla estimates that up to 1,000 US Army Special Forces Green Berets were in the country; actual numbers were unknown, but Geyer and others such as North American priest Blase Bonpane (who would subsequently be expelled) were convinced that large numbers of 'Green Berets' were indeed in the Zacapa combat zone.[150] Minister of Defense Arriaga Bosque denied the Geyer allegations, and said there was "no need" for foreign troops. The US Embassy issued a statement that Geyer's reporting was "completely unfounded" and "absurd"; there were "no [Green Beret] forces serving or present in the country".[151] The Department of State gainsaid the Embassy, however, by telling the wire services that yes, in fact members of the Special Forces were in Guatemala "on a temporary training mission ...and not as a unit of the Special Forces". The Special Forces were participating in "programs of civic action, vehicle maintenance and vocational education".[152]

Precise statistics on MTTs movements in and out of Guatemala are, as noted, unavailable, although declassified documents do register the sending of "counter-insurgency MTT's" to Guatemala in 1966 at the request of new Defense Minister Arriaga Bosque. A 1974 NACLA report on Guatemala summarized reports on a US presence in the north-east, and concluded that "a significant number of US advisers" were working there with Guatemalan army units:

> It was no secret . . . that a US Army Mobile Training Team (MTT) was operating in Guatemala's northeast. As one US adviser admitted privately, 'there were a lot of guys running around in fatigues up there.' In addition, a Guatemalan military source reported that during his assignment to the Zacapa base in 1966-67 Special Forces advisers accompanied Guatemalan army patrols into combat areas. This seems to have been a frequent practice. Moreover, the line separating advisory and combative activity in a combat zone remains exceedingly thin.[153]

A March 1974 paper prepared by defense analysts Luigi Einaudi, Brian Jenkins and Cesar Sereseres drew similar conclusions, distinguishing "official" US postures from reported practice:

> Officially, US participation in the counterinsurgency campaign was limited to the provision of equipment and advice and the training of Guatemalan officers in US military schools . . . There are, however, persistent rumors that the United States participated more directly in the campaign, and that US officers had greater knowledge than is officially admitted of the terrorist campaign which accompanied the counter-insurgency effort (. . .) There may be a small grain of truth in each one of the allegations. Armed US advisors sometimes did accompany Guatemalan officers in the countryside, though supposedly not on planned military operations (. . .) American pilots sometimes did fly Guatemalan aircraft — one was killed in a crash in 1967 — for the purposes of testing the aircraft and in order to maintain their flying status, though some charge that 'testing' included strafing runs in Zacapa. There were Special Forces (Mobile Training Teams) in Guatemala which the US Embassy publicly acknowledged . . .[153]

Official, public policy in the 1960s was clear: advisers did not go into combat; but there is some evidence that this public policy overlay a quite different set of operational guidelines followed by advisers in Latin America. Declassified documents from the period suggest it was both accepted and expected practice for US military mission members or advisers to accompany foreign troops in combat operations. In Peru, for example, US Ambassador Jones cabled General Maxwell Taylor (then head of the Special Group/Counterinsurgency) to complain that while good relations were maintained with the Peruvian military, "They have been unusually secretive about their anti-guerrilla actions in the field and have not allowed our attaches to visit operational units".[155] The Peruvian army's nationalist reluctance to comply with what appears to have been standard operation procedure for US military missions in situations of counter-insurgency was clearly resented.

In the 1960s, public information on the US military presence in Guatemala was largely limited to occasional press coverage by intrepid reporters like Geyer (who went into the hills to interview guerrilla leader César Montes) and reports that could not be hushed up, like the death of members of the military mission (deaths of temporary duty MTT members, may, in contrast have been hushed up; none were acknowledged). It was only after the assassination of Colonel John Webber and Commander E.A. Munro, for example, that Webber's earlier statements about the counter-insurgency war were published by *Time*. There was little publicity, however, after the death of Air Force Captain Bernard Westfall in September 1967. Westfall, a part of the permanent military mission, was killed when his Guatemalan airforce T-33 crashed into a hillside while, according to the Embassy, testing the aircraft. The Guatemalan army magazine *Ejército* eulogized Westfall and described him as having been an "operations adviser".[156] Claims that he had taken helicopters and fixed wing aircraft into combat zones received little consideration in the US; a 1971 book noted that:

> It was common and public topic of conversation at Guatemala's Aurora Air Base that (Westfall) often tested Guatemalan aircraft in strafing and bombing runs against guerrilla encampments in the northeastern territory.[157]

A second member of the Military Group, Colonel Robert Mundinger, died in a helicopter crash in 1972 "while en route to visit a Guatemalan Army unit".[158] An obituary published in the *Review of the Inter-American Defense College* (August 1972) described an officer at the top of a very exotic and elite branch of his profession. Born in 1923 in Argentina, Mundinger was bilingual in English and Spanish, a graduate of Princeton University with a law degree from Louisana State, and trained in intelligence and command operations in service with the Office of Strategic Services in France and China during World War II. Colonel Mundinger subsequently studied in the *Ecole Supérieure de Guerre* in France at the height of the Algerian insurgency. Although postings to South-East Asia are not enumerated,[159] available information suggests Mundinger was a specialist in waging the irregular, clandestine warfare then in progress in north-eastern Guatemala; such a man would not be wasted in combat, but would be in the thick of operational planning and implementation.

A systematic attempt to find answers to questions regarding the scale and substance of the US advisory presence in Guatemala between 1966 and 1974 was made in congressional hearings in 1976 by congressman

Michael J. Harrington. Harrington raised questions with the Department of State regarding actions of the conventional Military Group, and by forces working with it and the CIA in counter-insurgency warfare. Harrington cited reports from three sources, and requested the response of State Department official Hewson Ryan, a witness at the hearings:

> 1) The CIA Director, testifying before the Intelligence Subcommittee of the Armed Services in April 1974, when asked by the chairman in what areas of the world besides Cuba we might be engaging in operations similar to those taken in Chile, answered Guatemala; 2) An employee of the House of Representatives who was an Air Force intelligence officer in the later part of the 1960's through 1970, told me from his direct knowledge that paramilitary units were flown from Florida Air Force bases and used directly in Guatemala to suppress the insurgent activities during this period. Finally, Georgie Anne Geyer indicated in the course of a conversation about her experience in Guatemala and about her later contact with an American colonel who was in charge of these groups, that she firmly believes that Americans were militarily involved there during this period. I would like you, Mr. Ryan, to comment on the scope of the activities that this country was engaged in, not a generation ago, but as recently as I can document it, in 1974.[160]

The State Department representative denied ever having heard such allegations before.[161]

Congressman Harrington subsequently submitted nine questions for written response to the State Department to pursue the matter:

> It has been alleged that US Special Forces ... advised the Guatemalan military throughout the counterinsurgency campaign. Where were these stationed? Under what legal authority were they sent? When did they arrive in Guatemala? What was the total number of US Special Forces and/or contractees for each year after their arrival? Were there any Cuban nationals included in these forces?[162]

The response answered almost none of Harrington's questions about the members of Special Forces in Guatemala at any one time during the period in question, or their specific locations or tasks. In contrast Harrington was given a statement of public policy:

> Under the terms of the Foreign Assistance Act and the Security Assistance program carried out under its authority, Mobile Training Teams (MTTs) are regularly sent to Guatemala for training assignments.
>
> This training is normally of short duration and is carried out in accordance with approved Department of Defense procedures. Training is given only for specific tasks such as communications maintenance and repair, equipment operations and logistical control. The teams are

generally small in numbers of personnel and may include individuals who have had Ranger or Green Beret training in their military careers. However, such teams have never been assigned to Guatemala in an operational (i.e. combat) role, nor have they ever participated in combat operations.[163]

Representative Harrington also requested a response to reports that between 1966 and 1972 a total of 28 Americans died while serving in an advisory or combat capacity, and asked to receive a list of "US deaths in Guatemala from 1966 to 1972 that resulted from actual combat, training exercises or any other operation of a military or paramilitary nature." The response does not refer to the figure of 28 deaths, and describes only the deaths of Ambassador Mein, Colonel Webber, Commander Munro, and the two officers killed in aircraft incidents (both of whom were assigned to the Military Group, and not to an MTT). When asked to account for the times in which US personnel found themselves in combat situations, the response was equally uninformative, a statement of policy not practice:

> It has been US Government policy throughout the counterinsurgency period that no US military personnel be either ordered, or permitted, to participate in combat operations in Guatemala. Also, there is no evidence to indicate that any US military personnel ever engaged in combat on their own initiative.[164]

It may be many more years before even congressmen determine precisely how many US military advisers and irregular warfare specialists were involved in the first years of Guatemala's shift to "counter-terror" as a way of life, and more years still before their precise activities there are known. The experience of looking for these answers in the early 1970s, however, may have influenced the subsequent congressional posture toward human rights as an element in foreign policy generally, and specifically its close watch on the emerging Salvadorean conflict in the late 1970s.

US military or paramilitary personnel's involvement in combat, or combat situations, in Guatemala, particularly if associated with piloting helicopter gunships or aircraft on strafing or bombing runs, may have been a significant part of the US contribution to counter-insurgency operations in Guatemala. It is, however, hardly necessary to further document that particular covert aspect of the assistance programme in order to tie the US intimately to the introduction and implementation of counter-insurgency doctrine in Guatemala. The ties of doctrine, advisory and material assistance have been amply documented. It only remains to provide a quantitative overview of security assistance in the 1960s and through the end of the Arana government in 1974. While a considerable assistance effort may have been channelled through covert training or operations programmes, and funded as part of the regular budgets of the armed forces or intelligence agencies, published budgets for the varying elements of the overt assistance programmes must suffice as a guide to the programmes' changes over time.

Summaries of security assistance to Latin America generally give published figures for the Military Assistance Program, credits granted under the Foreign Military Sales programme, and before 1974, annual budgets for the Public Safety Program. An overall annual figure for security assistance, however, should include figures for FMS sales, that is, credits taken up, allocations under the IMET (International Military Education and Training) programme, and grants under the EDA (Excess Defense Articles) programme. Figures published for EDA programme grants are defined as "acquisition costs", and do not necessarily reflect the full value of the articles provided.

Between 1957 and 1980, budgets for training programmes under IMET totalled $7.494 million, with major budget rises following the emergence of the first guerrilla groups in 1960, and in 1963 after Peralta Azurdia overthrew General Ydígoras. After 1964, however, IMET budgets did not fluctuate widely, but until 1977 remained at between $300,000 and $500,000 annually.[165]

Public Safety Program funding levels fluctuated dramatically after the 1960 and 1963 events, and before major changes in Guatemala's counter-insurgency programme in the late 1960s and early 1970s. Major rises in 1963 (Peralta's coup), in 1967 (the Zacapa campaign), and in 1970 (Arana's state of siege) coincided with key periods in the development and deployment of the counter-insurgency apparatus, and were provided largely through emergency contingency funds outside the programmed budget. The major boost in assistance after the Peralta coup, moreover, appears to have been deliberately concealed in reports on Public Safety funding to the US congress in the 1960s. The rise from $71,000 in 1962 to $382,000 after the March 1963 coup was not registered in 1960s documents. In the 1974 Termination Phase Out report on the Public Safety Program in Guatemala,[166] however, the full figure is given with a notation that it included $216,000 from contingency funds. In contrast, the official figure published for 1963 throughout the 1960s was $166,000, suggesting that only a modest increase — budgetted before the coup — had followed the overthrow of President Ydígoras Fuentes. Extra funds provided in 1963, 1967 and 1970 went largely toward commodities grants. The 1963 grants may have been concealed because of congressional unease over assistance to governments that attained power through *coups d'etat*. The 1966 report on "US Internal Security Programs in Latin America", for example, reported the concern in 1963 of the US "Country Team" in Guatemala over the possible effect of congressional moves to restrict aid to such governments ("uncertainties about the Foreign Aid Bill arising out of the proposed Morse Amendment which would have stopped assistance to countries whose governments had been taken over by military coups").[167] The obvious implication is that if funds could not be provided one way, they would come through a back door to avoid unreasonable interference from congress.

A chart from the 1974 Termination Phase Out report of Public Safety in Guatemala — the "Public Safety Funding Digest" — reproduced in Table 4.2, illustrates changing patterns of emergency and supplemental assistance.[168] The rise in Public Safety funding from $411,000 in 1969 to $1,129,000 in Arana's first year of government, as for previous rises, was paralleled by rising military assistance levels. Military assistance statistics show major rises were registered between financial years 1970 and 1971, with MAP funding increasing from $907,000 to $1,490,000 in 1971. The most enormous rises, however, were in grants of commodities under the Excess Defense Articles programme, and credits extended under the FMS programme. Although MAP grants in 1970 and 1971 included one UH1H helicopter and one C-47 transport, credits under FMS went toward a further UH1H and eight A-37 attack aircraft (at a total cost of about $5.4 million) and ammunition valued at about $700,000.[170] The overall picture of military assistance budgets between 1966 and 1975 is chartered in Table 4.3

Table 4.1
Military Assistance Budgets, 1974–82* (in US$ thousands)

	MAP	IMET	FMS (sales)	EDA	Totals
1974	430	497	852	1,021	2,800
1975	162	393	892	788	2,235
1976	134	487	3,041	42	3,704
1977	6	490	2,169	67	2,732
1978	1	—	2,410 (delivered)	—	2,510
1979	6	—	3,327 (delivered)	—	3,333
1980	—	—	2,254 (delivered)	—	2,254
1981	—	—	—	—	—
1982	—	—	—	—	—

From tables in Hearings, "Human Rights in Guatemala", pp. 38-40.

Table 4.2
Annual Budgets of the Public Safety Program, Guatemala[168]

Past (1957–72) Fiscal Years (FY) Obligations (US thousands)

FY	TOTAL	TECH	PART	COMMOD	OTHER	REMARKS
57	280	38	0	242	0	
58	158	58	37	58	5	
59	72	53	13	0	6	
60	71	46	4	9	12	
61	267	37	1	219	10	
62	71	24	20	15	12	
63	382	44	17	304	17	Includes $216 CF
64	128	90	21	14	3	
65	270	96	100	69	5	
66	249	121	57	61	10	
67	644	118	80	438	8	Incl. $324 CF
68	218	125	52	36	5	
69	411	133	90	182	6	Incl. $295 SA
70	1129	209	95	401	424	Incl. $410 SA; $378 CF
71	413	239	105	54	15	
72	456	274	64	111	7	
73	490	230	69	189	2	

Table 4.3
Annual Military Assistance Budgets, Guatemala, 1966–75 (in US$ thousands)[171]

	MAP	IMET	FMS (sales)	EDA	Totals
1966	994	270	391	113	*1,768*
1967	1,745	320	207	334	*2,606*
1968	730	300	366	371	*1,767*
1969	1,609	228	144	44	*2,025*
1970	907	271	464	264	*1,906*
1971	1,490	392	7,586	354	*9,822*
1972	1,305	25	2,065	721	*4,342*
1973	322	497	3,621	500	*4,940*
1974	430	497	852	1,021	*2,800*
1975	162	393	892	788	*2,235*

Notes to Part 2

Chapter 3

1. Richard Adams, *Crucifixion by Power, Essays on Guatemalan National Social Structure, 1944-1966*, University of Texas Press, Austin, Texas (1973) p. 261. Roberto Alejo's brother, Carlos, was then Guatemalan Ambassador in Washington, D.C.

2. Jerrold Buttrey, in "The Guatemalan Military, 1944-1963: An Interpretative Essay", University of Texas, at Austin, 1967 (unpublished manuscript), enters into the factors involved in upsetting the military.

3. US Embassy cable to the Department of State No. 226, 14 November 1960, 7 pm (Carrollton Press), describes Ydígoras as "Vociferously castigating Fidel Castro as responsible for the uprising", a claim the Embassy wholly discounted and described as coming after "GOG [Government of Guatemala]'s cries of wolf over past months."

4. Estimates on the strength of the revolt are from Alvaro López, "La Crisis Política y la Violencia en Guatemala", in *Diez años de insurrección en América Latina*, Santiago: Ediciones Pressa Latinoamericana (1971) p. 91; the account of the 800 peasants in Zacapa, from Adolfo Gilly, "The Guerrilla Movement in Guatemala, Part I",*Monthly Review*, May 1965, p. 14; both cited in NACLA,*Guatemala*, Berkeley and New York (1974), p. 179.

5. Ibid.

6. Cited in Richard Gott, *Guerrilla Movements in Latin America*, London, Nelson and Sons (1970), p. 39, from Alan Howard, *New York Times Magazine*, 26 June 1966.

7. Accounts of the affair by writers from quite opposite political perspectives insist on referring to "CIA B-26 bombers" specifying the pilots were mercenaries or Cuban exiles. But the important point is that they were US government aircraft, flown by personnel employed and paid by the US government, and acting on the US government's explicit instructions. Continual reference to such activities as CIA exploits tends to blur accountability and minimalize the significance of such events. To the rebel army officers the technicalities of which US agency was bombing and strafing their positions was immaterial. It is impossible to rule out the participation of the Special Air Warfare Squadron based in the Canal Zone (under the control of the regular US armed forces) in the 1960 intervention, at least until documents on the affair are declassified.

8. Brian Jenkins, Cesar Sereseres, Luigi Einaudi "US Military Aid and Guatemalan Politics", California Arms Control and Policy Seminar, March 1974. The authors state quite clearly that intervention was taken to safeguard the invasion plot, and planes were flown by Cuban exile pilots. Richard Adams adds that Ydígoras flew to Quetzaltenango during the revolt, and there was widespread speculation "that he felt he could rely on the foreign forces at Helvetia to protect him should the revolt prove difficult to contain" (in *Crucifixion by Power*, p. 261).

9. Richard Gott, op. cit., p. 42. His account of the development of Guatemala's various guerrilla organizations, their actions and ideological orientation is well documented, highly readable, and the best comprehensive source available on the subject. In the present study I deliberately avoided attempting to go into detail on the guerrilla opposition groups, since excellent source material already exists in important published works.

10. Ibid., p. 43.

11. To place Guatemalan events in a broader time frame it should be recalled that in August 1963 a decision was taken in Washington to support an army coup against another allied leader who was becoming an embarrassment and a security problem, South Vietnam's President Ngo Dinh Diem (see Frances Fitzgerald,*Fire in the Lake*, New York, Vintage Books (1973), pp. 180-4; but Diem was made of sterner stuff and the political climate more lethal. He held out against moves against him until his detention and murder, with his family, in Saigon on 2 November 1963.

12. *Ejército* (Guatemalan army magazine),April 1963, pp. 2-3.

13. CIA, "Survey of Latin America", 1 April 1964 (Johnson Presidential Library), p. 119.

14. That the 1963 coup obeyed specific institutional interests of the army and was not merely a power play by Peralta is supported by the record of social welfare and other measures benefiting the military as a whole, and particularly the officer

110

corps, under the Peralta administration. The principal academic authority on the period, Jerry Weaver (see "The Military Elite and Political Control in Guatemala, 1963-66", *Social Science Quarterly*, Vol. 50, No. 1, June 1969, p. 135) writes of the political resources available to the military in the 1963-66 period for attaining and holding political power, and of the interests it defended in doing so. Weaver also (p. 135) notes a probability that the military once having claimed power under Peralta would tend to wish to retain it.

15. "G-2 Report", 25 September 1940, Lt. Col. Glass, Director, Escuela Politecnica de Guatemala: "Resume of Lt. Col. Enrique Peralta Azurdia who served Glass as his executive officer". Other basic biographical data is from *Ejército*, April 1963, p. 3.

16. *Ejército* (October 1963) cited a speech by Deputy Secretary of State Edwin Martin (slightly out of context) as evidence of US support for the Guatemalan army's seizure of power. Martin is quoted as having said that recent coups should be seen "not with alarm", but with the "confidence that these military bodies will voluntarily evolve... Armies have not always supported antidemocratic causes... look at Ecuador and Guatemala which have announced programs of socil reform." Guatemala's coup was presented as a good example for the hemisphere.

17. Most studies of the Peralta administration have emphasized his *resistance* to US efforts to flood the country with funds for economic development, and even US security assistance. Despite some authentic evidence that US agencies *felt* Peralta overly resisted American security assistance plans, while a nationalist, he cannot be considered in any way anti-American as some writers have suggested: the evidence is in the expansion of security assistance and Peralta's wholehearted regearing of the security system in line with American counter-insurgency doctrine.

18. Political scientist Ross Baker produced one of the only studies to deal with the perceptions of Latin American army officers, with Guatemala as one of his case studies, and discussed the significance of "anti-Communism" within the Latin American armies. Baker links the extreme intensity of anti-Communism partly to deliberately induced fears that Communism would mean the destruction of the armed forces; anti-Communism is, as a consequence, seen as both "correct" (it is a large component of the teachings of allied military establishments) and an institutional necessity for survival. Articles and speeches in Guatemalan army magazines under Peralta and afterward, particularly those reprinted from US army publications, stress danger to the army's continued existence as a primary element of the menace of subversion (the disbanding of the Cuban army was a ready example). Baker adds that "the reluctance of North American scholars to accept the military fear of communism as a bona fide issue in intervention is surprising". (See "A Study of Military Status and Status Deprivation in Three Latin American Armies", American University, Center for Research in Social Systems; Washington, D.C., 1966, pp. 5-6.)

19. Speech by Peralta Azurdia to the "First Central American Meeting on Civic Action", from *Ejército*, August 1963.

20. *Prensa Libre*, 18 July 1963.

21. Jerry Weaver, "The Political Style of the Guatemalan Military Elite", *Studies in Comparative International Development*, Vol. V, 1969-1970, p. 70, footnote 13.

22. Ibid.

23. Guatemala City newspapers; *El Imparcial*, 4 and 5 July 1966. The new President seemingly overestimated his powers; he may have authentically intended to clean up the *judiciales*.

24. *Ejército*, August 1963, "El Ejército cuenta con elementos para frenar la subversion comunista", speech by Peralta Azurdia to open the "First Central American Conference on Civic Action".

25. *Ejército*, December 1963; this agreement was a precondition to the organization by technicians of the US Public Safety Program of the Central America and Panama

Telecommunications Security Network which linked the top intelligence agencies of each country and the Panama Canal Zone, a matter discussed below.

26. As described in *Ejército*, September 1965, "Clausura de Operación Halcón Vista", an account of the first joint manoeuvres of CONDECA, in and around the Guatemalan port Puerto Natías de Gálvez. General Robert W. Porter, commander of the US Army Southern Command at the Canal Zone was present and in a ceremony at the conclusion of the manoeuvres was presented with the CONDECA flag.

27. The creation of CONDECA required a revision of the charter of ODECA agreed by a meeting of Foreign Ministers in Panama in 1962; members of CONDECA's policy meetings were to be the respective Ministers of Defense. CONDECA headquarters was to be an office with a separate acronym, COPECONDECA; Permanent Council of CONDECA, based in Guatemala which opened in late 1964 (see John Childs, op. cit., p. 395). The treaty of 14 December 1963 was initially ratified only by Guatemala, Nicaragua and Honduras; El Salvador subsequently became an active participant.

28. Department of State, "US Internal Security Programs in Latin America", Volume II, Guatemala, Internal Security Programs Evaluation Group, 30 November 1966, p. 7 (Freedom of Information Act request by the author, declassified 1980).

29. Ibid., p. 8. The same source indicates the relative increase in security assistance after 1961: "The relative size of the old and the new programs can be appreciated from a comparison of cumulative MAP grant aid for the two periods, 1956 thru 1961 ($1,796,000) and 1962 thru 1967 ($10,716,249)." (p. 6).

30. Ibid., p. 8.

31. Ibid., pp. 10, 39; $220,000 of the AID funds were disbursed as commodities, primarily army transport equipment, including trucks for troop transport and aircraft adaptable either for special air warfare or for transport of "civic action" teams, including H-19 aircraft.

32. Ibid., p. 11.

33. Ibid., pp. 11, 17.

34. Ibid., pp. 11-12.

35. Ibid., pp. 11-13; and Cesar Sereseres, "Military Development and the US Military Assistance Program for Latin America: The case of Guatemala, 1961-1969". Dissertation (1971) University of California, Riverside, p. 113.

36. Ibid., p. 119. Wherever the US has helped armies create "Special Forces" counter-insurgency units in Latin America, they have been given dramatic names, often drawing on pre-Colombian traditions. "Kaibiles" in Kekchi means strong man, or warrior. In Peru, in the 1960s, a special counter-insurgency battalion was formed in the Civil Guard called the "Sinchis" — Quechua for valiant man or warrior. The most recent such creation is the Salvadorean army's Atlácatl Battalion, created in 1980 for counter-insurgency by US advisers.

37. The MAP budget for 1964 had included $600,000 earmarked for "Civic Action", with $492,000 for the grant of material. The ambiguity of the destination of "Civic Action" funds is reinforced by the explanation in the 1966 report cited above that the destination of particular funds cannot be broken down, as the objective was to encourage "Civic Action" in all parts of the armed forces: "[funds cannot be] associated directly with specific projects . . . since MAP funds are used to build a capability for civic action into all units." ("Internal Security Programs in Latin America, 1966, p. 40.) The same source (p. 14) adds that the training emphasis for all air units was placed on "counterguerrilla operations, small unit tactics, and patrol and search units. During 1964, 1965, and 1966 these units participated in joint exercizes . . . [with US forces]".

38. Ibid., p. 19; the same report refers to the 1960s opening of "Guatemala's first combat operations center at the Naval Headquarters in Matias de Galvez." A report by the Chief Public Safety Advisor in Guatemala from 1961 to 1965 gives a similar assessment of the scope of the guerrilla threat to that given in the 1966

interdepartmental report "Internal Security Programs in Latin America": "The primary threat is offered by the small Communist and Castro-backed guerrilla and terrorist movement... engaged in sporadic subversive activity such as bombings in the capital and the assassination of several military officers and ranch owners in the Izabal and Zacapa areas. While the movement offers no serious threat to the [Government's] stability . . . under the present circumstances, the GOG will probably be unable to eliminate the guerrillas completely . . . the movement could represent a dangerous subversive nucleus". (Crisostomo, "Briefing Report", October 1964). Here, as elsewhere, the intent of counter-insurgency advisers appears to have been the total extirpation of the "subversive nucleus", in the apparent belief that wiping out the guerrillas today will bring long term peace and quiet.

    An unconfirmed Guatemalan press report also claimed the setting up of a secret training camp in May 1962 in Mariscos, Izabal, by the US military mission, staffed by a Special Forces unit of five men of Hispanic origin, all veterans of covert operations in Laos. They were reportedly assisted by 15 Guatemalan officers, all graduates of counter-insurgency training at Fort Gulick in the Canal Zone (see NACLA, *Guatemala*, op. cit., 1974, p. 194, citing *El Imparcial*, 17 May 1962).

39. CIA, "Survey of Latin America", 1 April 1964; and attached memorandum, Robert M. Sayre to Bundy (McGeorge), 12 June 1965, "Task Force Report: Guatemala" (Johnson Presidential Library).

40. The 1974 "Phase Out Report" ("Termination Phase-Out Study: Public Safety Project, Guatemala", July 1974, AID, Office of Public Safety) gives the following figures for Public Safety funds disbursed up until 1966:

	1960	1961	1962	1963	1964	1965	1966
			(in $ thousand)				
Advisers	46	37	24	44	90	96	121
Training	4	1	20	17	21	100	57
Commodities	9	219	15	304	14	69	61
Other	NIL	NIL	NIL	17	17	5	10
Total:	71	267	71	382	128	270	249

The Public Safety assistance figures presented to the US congress in 1974, when the programme was being shut down, and those given in the 1960s differ considerably. The dramatic increase in funds from $71,000 in 1962, to $382,000 after the March 1963 coup put Peralta at the head of a military government was not reported at the time, neither did it appear in the 1966 report on "US Internal Security Programs in Latin America" (classified "Secret"), nor in routine reports to congress. The full figure is given only in the 1974 report with a notation that it included "$216,000. CF": CF is probably "Contingency Funding". The published figures produced in the 1960s, gave a total of $166,000 for 1963, suggesting that only a modest increase had followed Ydígoras Fuentes' overthrow and that it had been budgetted before the coup. The incrase of "CF" funds went to increase the commodities budget. The published budget in 1966 indicated commodities worth $88,000 were provided in 1963: $88,000 budgetted funds plus $216,000 "CF" funds, totalling $304,000 for commodities. The statistics on Public Safety assistance may or may not have been juggled intentionally, but they contributed to a polite fiction of Peralta Azurdia as actively resisting United States assistance.

41. "US Internal Security Programs in Latin America", op. cit., p. 45.

42. Ibid. The report continues with a rather wistful remark on the futility of promoting the "civilian police concept" with one hand, while insisting on military predominance on the other. The figures cited in the report for assistance in fiscal years 1963 through 1966 were: MAP, $6,920,817; AID, $813,000 for Public Safety assistance (p. 47).

43. Ibid., p. 27.

44. International Cooperation Administration (ICA), US Department of State, "Report on the National Police of Guatemala", 1956, Appendix p. 1 on 'Implementation".

45. "US Internal Security Programs in Latin America", op. cit., p. 38. Subordination of civil police to the military, and turning the military to police functions occasioned some apparently acrimonious debate within the US security establishment in Vietnam in the 1960s. A declassified CIA "Intelligence Report" (31 July 1967) reported that "some American police advisors" were critical of the trend which they said "has destroyed the concept of a civil police organization". The report points out that the militarization of the police for more effective counter-insurgency action (if not better conventional law enforcement) had been in line with American doctrine; doctrine some police specialists were unhappy with: "The US advisory effort itself . . . has encouraged increased paramilitary activities by the police, including the formation of the Police Field Forces in support of Revolutionary Development, [and] more clandestine operations directed at ferreting out the Communist covert apparatus." CIA, "Intelligence Report: Situation in South Vietnam (weekly)", 31 July 1967, declassified 20 February 1976.

46. Cesar Sereseres, paper presented to the Latin American Studies Association, "The Guatemalan Armed Forces: Military Development and National Politics", March 1976, p. 37.

47. Prof. David D. Burk, "Insurgency in Latin America", 15 January 1968, included in Senate Committee on Foreign Relations, Subcommittee on American Republics Affairs, 91st Congress, 1st Session, "Survey of the Alliance for Progress", 29 April 1969, pp. 226-7.

48. Vicente Collazo-Davila, Major, US Air Force "The Guatemalan Insurrection", in Bard E. O'Neill et al., (editors) *Insurgency in the Modern World*, Boulder, Colorado: Westview Press (1980), pp. 115-6.

49. Elsewhere Major Collazo-Davila notes ". . . a good deal of evidence that MANO and NOA were controlled by the army and that many of the actual gunmen were off duty policemen and army officers." (p. 117). To what extent police or army personnel working under the control of the army could under any circumstances be considered "off duty" is difficult to understand; perhaps the distinction would be better made as one between overt, officially acknowledged duties, and covert action.

50. Ibid., p. 120.

51. *Time* magazine, 26 January 1968, as cited in op. cit., NACLA, *Guatemala*, p. 202.

52. Ibid.

53. "El Patron de la Guerra de Guerrillas", Gen. Michael Calvert, *Revista Militar de Guatemala*, October-December 1966, pp. 50-58. General Calvert was writing from his experience in the British armed forces.

54. US Army, School of Special Warfare, "*Guia para el planeamiento de la contrain-surgencia*", Texto Especial 31/176, undated, reproduced in Alejandro de Corro, *Guatemala, la violencia*, CIDOC Dossier 19, three volumes, 1968. The authenticity of the document as US army material would be difficult to dispute as much of its text is virtually identical to material recently declassified, such as the 1965 "Employ-ment of a Special Forces Group" cited above. Everything in the document can also be found in other declassified material and there is no question but that it was circulated in Spanish within the Guatemalan military in the mid-1960s. It is unique in that it was acquired from Guatemalan army sources, in Guatemala, at the very time counter-insurgency offensives were taking shape.

55. Ibid., Alejandro de Corro, pp. 180-184; a copy of the document dated 4 August 1966 was widely circulated within the MLN party.

56. Guatemala specialist Cesar Sereseres Dissertation, op. cit., p. 113 described the PMA (in 1971) as consisting solely of the 800 man strike force. Later Sereseres refers to the penetration of rural areas by the military: "Military ruralization has been a function of the institutionalization of the doctrines of counterinsurgency and civic

action as well as a consequence of the injection of material resources from the MAP [Military Assistance Program]." (p. 242). The need for a means for government forces to respond to rural insurgency threats was commented upon in virtually all material produced in the period on proposals for counter-insurgency in Guatemala. Even considerably after the Mobile Military Police became operational, specialists in the Public Safety Program urged the intensification of rural "police" services: "as a means for the prevention and early detection of guerrilla activity and other related security problems ... [including] development of small reserve-type ready reaction rural police units for checking low-level organized violence in the incipient stages." (from "Report on a Visit to Central America and Panama (CAP) to study AID Public Safety Programs, 18 May-14 June 1967", Office of Public Safety, Ambassador C. Allan Stewart (ret.), AID/OPS consultant; AID/OPS, Freedom of Information Act request, declassified 2 April 1980.)

57.   *Diario Oficial*, 9 July 1938, "Establece el cargo de Comisionado Militar"; *Diario Oficial*, 19 March 1946, "Reglamento de Delegados y Comisionados Militares", reaffirmed their duties as agents for recruitment, but did not refer to law enforcement functions; Decree 79 of 10 September 1954 placed the military commissioners under the departmental military reserve commanders' authority. Dates given for legislation are those of publication in the official government gazette, when they became law.

58.   Jerry Weaver, "The Political Style ... ", p. 74. The potential for the commissioners to expand their local role as a security resource was already a consideration under the reformist Arbenz government, when labour organizations raised, with the Minister of Defense, the case of commissioners accused of obstructing rural reform projects and demanded their dismissal. This is discussed in Ross Baker ("Status Deprivation ...", p. 45); he reviewed microfilmed documents acquired in 1954 (with the overthrow of Arbenz) now in the Manuscript Division of the Library of Congress, and cites some two dozen cases in which the head of the *Confederación Nacional de Campesinos* called for particular commissioners to be dismissed for abuse of authority.

59.   Responsible for the commissioners' system in the first year of the regime was Col. Armando Joel Alons, appointed to head the *Servicio de Reservas Militares* in April 1963 upon his return from a five month study course at the Inter-American Defense College, Fort McNair, Washington, D.C. (*Ejército*, April 1963).
   Service as head of the military reserve system, particularly after the military commissioners became an active part of the counter-insurgency apparatus, may have been a prestigious and useful part of senior officers' careers. Perhaps significantly, Col. Rafael Arriaga Bosque, the Minister of Defense who presided over the launching of the 1966-67 counter-insurgency offensive in which the commissioners were "turned loose" against the guerrillas, had previously served as commander of the *Servicio de Reservas Militares*, and so had personal knowledge of the network's potential. See *Revista Militar de Guatemala*, "Reservas Militares cumplen 15 años", July-September 1969.

60.   John Durston, "Power Structure in a Rural Region of Guatemala: The Department of Jutiapa", MA thesis, University of Texas at Austin (1966), p. 84.

61.   AID, "Termination Phase-Out Study" (1974), p. 48.

62.   Jerry Weaver, "Political Style . . .", p. 74.

63.   Cesar Sereseres, dissertation, p. 111. The 1965 army law distinguishes between "permanent" active service (the standing army) and "available" active force (the commissioners). Commissioners were authorized to wear army uniforms with a shoulder patch, "*Comisionado Militar*". They were also permitted to wear civilian clothes — and generally did so — and so enhance their intelligence capabilities.

64.   Jerry Weaver, "Political Style ...", p. 74; see also Cesar Sereseres, dissertation, p. 112. The duties of commissioners who were not occupied full-time in counter-insurgency were balanced between assisting the army, and service to local elites

that supplemented their income. Weaver reports that military commissioners commonly served as labour contractors for cotton and coffee planters "forcibly persuading Indians to climb aboard trucks destined for the fields"; in this role commissioners wielded the double threat of physical violence or instant, unappealable conscription. In the 1980s, military commissioners reportedly continue holding labour contractor jobs.

Richard Adams elaborates on the intelligence role of the new commissioner network in *Crucifixion by Power* (pp. 199-200): "Under the military government [1963-66] the comisionado in the south coast, and especially in the oriente, became a local listening post for the military government . . . Its use by the military as local 'spies' provided the military, for the first time, with a communication channel down to the lowest level of the population. Whereas before the *comisionado* was restricted to information derived from strictly military sources, they now had a network that cut into every civilian community. The purposes for which this information was used during the military government was obviously determined by the then current perception of what constituted danger to the country as a whole."

65. Cesar Sereseres, dissertation, p. 111.
66. Richard Adams (*Crucifixion by Power*, p. 272) notes further that such commissioners "were occupied full time [with counter-insurgency] and were paid for it."
67. Cesar Sereseres, Brian Jenkins, Luigi Einaudi, "US Military Aid and Guatemalan Politics", March 1974, paper presented to the California Arms Control and Foreign Policy Seminar, p. 10. In this and other papers on Guatemala these authors insist on describing the commissioner network as composed of "civilian vigilantes", *and* as an official government force, organized, issued with weapons and credentials, and deployed by the Army: seemingly a contradiction in terms. The same authors in this and other papers suggest, at considerable length, that US military assistance (doctrine and material) was virtually unconnected with Guatemalan counter-insurgency, which, they maintain, has been influenced primarily by internal political factors.
68. Howard Blutstein, et. al., *Area Handbook for Guatemala*, Washington, D.C., US Government Printing Office (1973), p. 320.
69. Sereseres, Jenkins and Einaudi, op. cit., March 1974, noted the overlap between government and elite control of the military commissioners ("While the Comisionados were formally under military control, in reality many of them took orders from local landowners and politicians".) The army was (and is), however, the final authority, and local landowners and politicians were rarely induced to buck its authority; apparently army policies in the 1960s were in the best interests of the rural elites. Conversely, the army established as a basic operational policy that the commissioners and their local elite clients could exercise immense discretionary power in the exercise of lethal, illegal violence toward broadly defined security goals.
70. See, for example, Sereseres, Einaudi, Jenkins, op. cit., March 1974, p. 10.
71. In another paper (1976) Jenkins and Sereseres describe the MLN's usefulness to the army in organizing its irregular support organizations; as in their earlier work, however, they persist in referring to these irregular forces as "vigilantes", the MLN tail wagging the army dog, as it were. ("United States Military Assistance and the Guatemalan Armed Forces: The limits of military involvement in Latin America", manuscript, June 1976.) See also Brian Jenkins and Cesar D. Sereseres, "US Military Assistance and the Guatemalan Armed Forces", in *Armed Forces and Society*, Vol. 3, No. 4, 1977.
72. Sereseres, Jenkins and Einaudi, op. cit., March 1974, p. 10.
73. Jerry Weaver ("Political Style . . .", p. 66) distinguishes these traditional economic sectors from modernizing elites who provided Peralta with political support, and benefited from protective tariffs, new credit institutions and policies. In contrast to the traditional elites, these newer elites saw government "as a positive instrument to be used for their personal advantage . . ."

74. Ibid.
75. Here the major sources are Jerry Weaver, "The Political Style…" and "The Military Elite and …".
76. US Department of State, "US Internal Security Programs in Latin America", November 1966, p. 13.
77. AID, Office of Public Safety, "Termination Phase-Out Report …", p. 73.
78. "End of Tour Report", 13 October 1966 (tour began 27 June 1964), Alfred Naurocki, Office of Public Safety, AID.
79. "Termination Phase-Out Report …", pp. 73, 81. The same source outlines the general thrust of the communications assistance programme as follows: "The overall communications program effort in Guatemala has been to develop an effective communications system to support civil police/security functions in metropolitan and rural areas … the need for security-type communications to enable an interchange of timely information and appropriate responses to urban and rural security problems is critically underscored for this country due to its greater than average share of such problems."
80. "Termination Phase-Out Report…", p. 81; the creation of the "*Agencia presidencial de Inteligencia*" in 1964 was the subject of remarks in Peralta's last speech before leaving office in 1966, which confirmed it maintained close contact with other top intelligence agencies in Central America. The Chief Public Safety Advisor in 1964, D.L. Crisostomo, reported the station was then termed the "Presidential Radio Group", and fully operational by October 1964; the intelligence agency operating the station was described as "a separate and relatively new security agency within the country" ("Briefing Report for the OPS/Washington Evaluation Team on the Public Safety Program in Guatemala", 23 October 1964, D.L. Crisostomo, p. 14).

    The "Stewart Report" ("Report on visit to Central America and Panama", 1967) cited previously said the following on the regional scope of the new security network: "The Central American radio teletype network … was installed by AID and completely operational within seven months after a formal recommendation by the Second Meeting of Ministers of Government, Interior and Security of CAP (Central America and Panama) in January 1964 … It is a highly successful project, with all stations (in the six countries) manned on a 24 hour basis … I glanced at the message files in each station and noted they covered a wide variety of subjects, including suspected subversives … The network in each country is tied into the local police, border patrol, customs and military systems …" (p. 8).
81. Ibid., p. 81.
82. Department of State, "US Internal Security Programs in Latin America", Volume II, Guatemala.
83. AID, Office of Public Safety, "Termination Phase-Out Report …".
84. See, for example, reference to "La Regional" in Comite de Defensa de los Derechos Humanos, *La Violencia en Guatemala*, (Mexico: Fondo de Cultura Popular, 1969).
85. The 1974 "Termination Phase-Out Report" gives what purports to be a complete list of Public Safety Advisors to Guatemala during the programme's history, but does not list an Investigations Advisor for the period July 1966 to November 1967. But the Stewart Report refers to Ambassador Stewart's interview with Investigation Advisor Dave Wright in mid-1967. The Investigations Advisors listed in the Phase-Out Report were John Popa (1956-62); J. Andy Rogers (4 June 1964-July 1966); Richard D. Van Winkle (1967-70) and Dudley Burris (July 1969-June 1971). Why Dave Wright's name is excluded from the regular reports of the Public Safety Program remains to be seen.

Chapter 4
86. As previously noted, the publication of the "Pentagon Papers" revealed that

the acronym "CAS" was widely used even in classified documents as a euphemism for CIA.

87. Stewart Report, pp. 5 and 31.
88. NACLA, *Guatemala*, pp. 200-201.
89. Ibid.
90. Memo from Robert M. Sayre to McGeorge Bundy, 12 June 1965.
91. Ibid., and Peter Crisostomo, "Report on Police Progress and Development in Guatemala" (January 1961 to end 1965). This was later termed "*Comando Seis*" and reportedly the most brutal of the specialty squads fielded by the National Police.
92. Memo Sayre to Bundy, 12 June 1965.
93. The candidates were initially Mario Mendez Montenegro, leader of the *Partido Revolucionario* (PR), a relatively conservative, but progressive party; former Army Chief of Staff Col. Miguel Angel Ponciano Samayoa, for the MLN party; and Col. Juan de Dios Aguilar de Leon, considered closest ideologically to Col. Peralta Azurdia. Mario Méndez Montenegro was assassinated on 31 October 1965 in a killing which has never been explained, and the PR subsequently nominated his brother, Julio César Méndez Montenegro, the popular former dean of the law school at the National University of San Carlos.
94. Department of State, "US Internal Security Programs in Latin America", p. 55.
95. Ibid.
96. From *El Grafico*, 24 December 1965, "Los Guerrilleros: Dialogo Marroquin-Ponciano II", cited in Alejandro de Corro, *Guatemala, la violencia*, CIDOC Dossier 19, Vol. I, 1968.
97. All citations are from the text as reproduced in Mario Monteforte Toledo, *Centro America: Subdesarrollo y dependencia*, Mexico, D.F.: UNAM (1972).
98. Department of State, "US Internal Security Programs in Latin America", pp. 5, 56.
99. For Arriaga Bosque's biography see *Ejército*, July 1966; prior to his appointment as Minister of Defense he served as head of Army Public Relations, head of the national military reserve system (*Jefe del Departamento de Reservas Militares de la República* (a key post during the reorganization of the military commissioner system in the early 1960s) and as commander of the *Cuartel General* of the *Zona Militar Rufino Barrios* in the capital. For Arana's biography see *Revista Militar*, July-September 1970. Born in 1918 in the department of Santa Rosa, Arana served as military attaché in Washington from 1958 to 1959 and 1965 to 1966; and in 1959 as head of the Guatemalan delegation to the Inter-American Defense Board.
100. Some studies of military assistance have included IMET funds as a part of the general Military Assistance Program budget. Statistics cited here are from Hearings on "Human Rights in Guatemala", 1981, pp. 38-40, in which the Department of State provided a detailed breakdown of military assistance under specific budget headings.
101. IAD, Office of Public Safety, Termination Phase-Out Report, p. 53.
102. Ibid., pp. 63-4, and Stewart Report, p. 25; on ammunition, Office of Public Safety, Termination Phase-Out Report.
103. For a detailed examination of the fluctuating position of the PGT toward the various guerrilla organizations see Richard Gott, op. cit., or Eduardo Galeano, *Gutatemala, Pais Ocupado* (1967). The US government source cited is D.L. Crisostomo, op. cit., 1965.
104. *El Imparcial*, 5 July 1966.
105. Having denounced such methods appears to have been one of the factors contributing to Lic. Castaneda Paz' own rearrest and "disappearance" in December 1970.

The 1976 Amnesty International report, *Guatemala*, cited cases of jailed trade unionists tortured with rubber hoods and gamezan insecticide; their 1981 report cited the March 1980 National Police's detention of student leader Alejandro Coti Lopez — subsequently found tortured and murdered, his hair impregnated with gamezan. Hooding of a similar nature was also reported used by Anastasio Somoza's secret police, the Office of National Security. See Amnesty International, *The Republic of Nicaragua* (1977).

106. *El Imparcial*, 16 July 1966.

107. Ibid., reported the essence of the account given by the former secret policemen, as did the *New York Times*, 18 July 1966. The 1967 study by Guatemalans, *La violencia en Guatemala* adds details consistent with other facts, such as the murder of some prisoners in the basement of the *Cuartel General del Ejército* (the *Cuartel de Matamoros*). Amnesty International's 1981 report on Guatemala confirms the existence of cells used for torture in the basement of the *Cuartel General*, and still in use in 1980. Most of the bodies of the "28" were reported to have been jettisoned from aircraft over the Pacific. Richard Gott's *Guerrilla Movements in Latin America* (pp. 69-71) provides a good account of the affair and of the efforts within the country first for the release of the "28", and subsequently for their fate to be acknowledged.

108. Brian Jenkins, Cesar D. Sereseres, "US Military Assistance and the Guatemalan Armed Forces: The limits of military involvement in Latin America", June 1976 (manuscript).

109. The use of napalm is alleged by guerrillas interviewed in the 1960s. There is no doubt some villages were destroyed from the air by fire; that it was napalm dropped from US aircraft is reportedly substantiated by Vice-President Marroquin Rojas (renowned for his indiscretions) in an interview with Uruguayan journalist Eduardo Galeano in 1967. Marroquin Rojas, according to Galeano, was disgusted not by the use of napalm, but because, he said, the squadron of US aircraft up from the Canal Zone had gone straight to their targets — a guerrilla redoubt in the Sierra de las Minas — and back again without the expected landing for a courtesy call (p. 56, Galeano). Marroquin Rojas was quoted along the same lines by a correspondent of Interpress citing a September 1967 interview in an article in *Latin America*, 15 September 1967.

110. Eduardo Galeano, op. cit., p. 49.

111. Cited in *La violencia en Guatemala*, p. 38.

112. Gabriel Aguilera, "El Proceso del Terror en Guatemala", September 1970 (mimeograph) produced a glossary of the acronyms of the more obscure "death-squads", some of which he notes existed only for the time it took to prepare and distribute one or more anonymous leaflets. Apart from the most popular acronyms already cited (MANO, NOA, CADEG), some of those listed by Aguilera were APRI (*Accion Patriotica de Recuperacion Institutional*), 1967; APA (*Agrupacion Patriotica de Anticomunistas*), 1967; CRAG (*Comite de Resistencia Anticomunista de Guatemala*), 1967-1968; FUNA (*Frente Unido Anticomunista*), 1967; FRN (*Frente de Resistencia Nacional*), 1967; MPMMM (*Movimiento por la Memoria de Mario Mendez Montenegro*), 1967; MAG (*Movimiento Anticomunista de Guatemala*), 1967.

While MANO, NOA and CADEG appear to have been a facade for very real actions by the security services, coordinated by the "*Centro Regional de Telecomunicaciones*" and incorporating MLN personnel, others of the "groups" listed above apparently never existed in any form: most faded from view entirely after 1968; some announced their "existence" only in a single round of threatening leaflets.

113. Reproduced in Alejandro de Corro, *Guatemala, la violencia*: the mimeographed "Guerrilla y Anti-Guerrilla en Guatemala", 4 May 1967, was circulated within the MLN party; Gabriel Aguilera ("El Proceso del Terror . . .", September 1970) describes it simply as an anonymous mimeographed document; the document published in the press of 4 May 1967 by the MLN includes chunks of the same text.

114. Norman Gall, "Guatemalan Slaughter", *New York Review of Books*, 20 May 1971,

p. 13. Mario Sandoval Alarcon has also been credited with the MLN's slogan that it is "The Party of Organized Violence" (*El Partido de la Violencia Organizada*).

115. Cited in Carlos Caceres, *Aproximación a Guatemala* (Culiacan, Mexico: Universidad Autónoma de Sinaloa), 1980, pp. 119-129.
116. Eduardo Galeano, op. cit., pp. 50-51.
117. Gabriel Aguilera, op. cit., p. 13, citing *El Imparcial*, 1 February 1967.
118. MLN document, 4 May 1967.
119. Press statement of the *Partido Revolucionario*, August 1968, reproduced in *La Violencia en Guatemala*, pp. 199-200.
120. Gabriel Aguilera, op. cit., (September 1970), p. 9. Aguilera in this first of his several studies of the process of terror in Guatemala cites a large variety of "death-squad" literature from 1966 to 1970, printed and produced by mimeograph and offset, principally distributed under the logos of CADEG or MANO. A "CADEG" printed circular dated 26 July 1967 entitled "Communists of the Department of Izabal" included a long list of "Communists" declared to be sentenced to death. See also Gabriel Aguilera, "La Violencia en Guatemala como fenomeno politico", CIDOC Cuaderno No. 61, 1971.
121. Gabriel Aguilera, September 1970, citing *El Grafico*, 4 February 1968.
122. In 1979 a request was filed by the author under the Freedom of Information Act for copies of reports filed by MTT leaders on completion of duties in Central America; the request referred to one such declassified report prepared in 1962 by an MTT detailed to Colombia. The request was transferred from the Pentagon, to Fort Benning, Georgia, and, finally, to Fort Bragg, North Carolina which gave the above reply.
123. Stewart Report, pp. 27-8.
124. Office of the Assistant Secretary of Defense for National Security Affairs, "US Policies toward Latin American Military Forces", 25 February 1963, p. 43. The same refrain has been heard frequently from the Guatemalan military itself; Ydígoras Fuentes, in his last address to congress (May 1963), condemned the courts in the same terms as his US military colleagues: "The Police have hardly turned a criminal over to the courts of justice, before they suddenly see him again on a street corner, free and bolder than ever. The police now have a complex, a complex of impotency and defeat. They are given a club and a gun so they have greater force than the outlaw. They overcome him and turn him in. And when the criminal is released, he brings an instinct of vengeance toward the person who sent him to jail."
125. David G. Epstein, "The Police Role in Counterinsurgency Efforts", *Journal of Criminal Law, Criminology and Police Sciences*, Vol. 59, No. 1, March 1968, p. 149, citing Robert Thompson, *Defeating Communist Insurgency*.
126. Ibid.
127. NACLA, *Guatemala*, p. 186.
128. Lorenzana was more or less a "front man" for MANO, and signed one of its mimeographed documents entitled "Ideology of MANO" ("*Ideologia de la MANO*") (8 November 1967) describing the "energetic measures" necessary to deal with political "immorality": "Gangrene demands the amputation of the affected limbs, and cancer the extirpation of its roots . . . We will impose order, organization, discipline, fulfillment of duty, honor and labour. No country can survive when dominated by anarchy disguised as democracy . . ." Lorenzana was not just a freelance madman, or independent patriot, but worked out of headquarters in the army *Cuartel de Matamoros* and the "safe house" at La Aurora airport already described.
129. NACLA, *Guatemala*, p. 186.
130. *Washington Post*, 18 October 1978 and *New York Times*, 18 October 1978.
131. Both were promoted to General in September 1968.
132. Guatemala Country File, National Security File, C096, Walt Rostow to President, with John Gordon Mein's cable (15 June 1966) in Lyndon Baines Johnson

Presidential Library. See Volume I for reference to similar threats received by US
diplomats in El Salvador.

134. *The Times* (London), 7 April 1970.
135. *Sunday Times* (London), "Why the Ambassador Died", 12 April 1970.
136. Norman Gall, "Guatemalan Slaughter", in *New York Review of Books*, Vol. XVII,
No. 9, 20 May 1971.
137. NACLA, *Guatemala*, New York, 1974, pp. 186-7.
138. Their killings were attributed to a "new" group calling itself *Ojo por Ojo*, "Eye for an
Eye"; see Gabriel Aguilera, op. cit., 1970, p. 15; Aguilera reports 27 confirmed cases
attributed to "Eye for an Eye" after the Von Spreti killing but before the
inauguration of Arana on 1 July 1970.
139. *Miami Herald*, 28 June 1970.
140. Gabriel Aguilera, op. cit., 1970, p. 16.
141. *El Imparcial*, 20 November 1970. The state of siege was declared on 1 November
1970; the previous state of siege had been declared on 2 November 1966.
142. Amnesty International, *Guatemala*, 1976, p. 5.
143. See Aguilera, op. cit., CIDOC Cuaderno No. 61, 1971, on the state of siege. Prof.
Camey Herrera in particular had opposed Arana's signing of a contract with the
International Nickel Corporation (INCO) for mining rights in Izabal, and served
as a member of an "Ad Hoc Commission" opposing the deal; another chief
opponent on the Commission, a lawyer and recently elected member of congress,
Adolfo Mijangos, a paraplegic, was machine-gunned to death as he left his office in
a wheelchair in January 1971. A third lawyer, Alfonso Bauer Paiz, was badly
wounded, but survived an identical attack (also linked to his opposition to the
INCO contract) in November 1970. The agreement was signed with INCO in
February 1971 (see NACLA, *Guatemala*, pp. 160-1, 188).
144. The case of Alvarado y Alvarado appears in the 1976 Amnesty International report,
Guatemala, p. 15. Gonzalez Juarez had served as the private secretary of President
Col. Jacobo Arbenz and as the Minister of Information of the equally tainted
President Arevalo. Arana left few stones unturned in rooting out "Communists".
145. From *Correo de Guatemala*, No. 24, October-December 1972, an opposition
newspaper published in Mexico.
146. Ibid.
147. Latin American Studies Association, Ad Hoc Committee on Guatemala (Seymour
Menton, James Nelson Goodsell, Susanne Jonas), *Report*, 15 April 1973, p. 1.
148. Ibid.
149. US Congress, Senate Committee on Foreign Relations, Subcommittee on Western
Hemisphere Affairs, *Guatemala and the Dominican Republic*, Staff Memorandum,
Pat Holt, Government Printing Office, Washington, D.C., 1971.
150. See Geyer, cited in *El Imparcial*, 13 December 1966 (UPI cable); Blase Bonpane
cited in NACLA, *Guatemala*, p. 199.
151. *El Imparcial*, 14 December 1966.
152. Ibid.
153. NACLA, *Guatemala*, p. 199, citing interview with Guatemalan army officer, and
Latin America, 15 September 1967.
154. Jenkins, Sereseres, and Einaudi, op. cit., p. 24.
155. See cable, American Embassy, Lima, to Secretary of State for General Taylor, 3
November 1965, National Security File, Peru, Lyndon B. Johnson Library,
Declassified 1977. Several books and articles published in 1967 and 1968 made
rather specific allegations on the background and activities of individual members
of the Military Group. Donn Munson, in *Zacapa*, (Canoga Park, Cal., Challenge
(1967), pp. 62-3) reported an interview with Col. John Webber, head of the Military
Group, and said Webber had introduced Col. Lunsford Thying, deputy head of the
MILGRP as "our counterinsurgency expert"; Munson added that Thying had
taught at the US Army School of Special Warfare at Fort Bragg, had "fought
Communist guerrillas in Colombia", and that he denied ever having gone into

combat in Guatemala. Norman Diamond ("Why they shoot Americans", *The Nation*, 5 February 1968) reported an interview with Thying in which he is said to have admitted to having supervised "mopping up" operations in Colombia but said little on his duties in Guatemala. Both sources are cited in NACLA, *Guatemala*, p. 198.

156. *Ejército*, September 1967.
157. NACLA, *Guatemala*, citing Tom and Marjorie Melville, *Guatemala: The Politics of Land Ownership*, Free Press, New York (1971), p. 170.
158. US Congress, Hearings on "Human Rights in Nicaragua, Guatemala and El Salvador: Implications for US Policy", 1976, p. 217, Statement of Department of State.
159. *Review of the Inter-American Defense College*, August 1972.
160. US Congress, Hearings on "Human Rights in Nicaragua, Guatemala and El Salvador . . .", p. 118.
161. Ibid.
162. Ibid., p. 216.
163. Ibid., pp. 216-7.
164. Ibid., p. 217.
165. Ibid., pp. 38-40.
166. OPS, "Termination Phase-Out Study . . .".
167. Department of State, "US Internal Security Programs in Latin America", p. 32.
168. OPS, "Termination Phase-Out Study . . .".
169. See Hearings, 1981, "Human Rights in Guatemala", pp. 3-40.
170. Figures from ibid., and Hearings, 1976, "Human Rights in Nicaragua, Guatemala and El Salvador: Implications for US Policy".
171. Figures from ibid.

Part 3: Guatemala: 1970s to 1980s

5. Organization for Resistance

In mid-1973 President Arana chose his successor from the top officers in the army hierarchy: General Kjell Laugerud García, Minister of Defense when nominated as candidate. He had worked with Arana both when Arana was commander of the Zacapa military zone (and as such director of the 1966–68 counter-terror campaign there) and, later, when he was President. Laugerud, who ran as candidate of the PID and MLN parties, was the second President selected from officers directly involved in the Zacapa campaign, known as the "Zacapa Group". Like Arana, Laugerud had previously served as military attaché in Washington, and head of delegation to the Inter-American Defense Board.[1] Born in 1930, Laugerud entered the *Politécnica* military academy in 1945 and graduated with the class of 1947. He received basic and advanced infantry officers' courses at Fort Benning, Georgia; attended Command and General Staff College at Fort Leavenworth, Kansas, and, between 1961 and 1965, took two refresher courses there. In 1966 he was appointed army deputy chief of staff, and was reportedly responsible for liaison with Arana on the Zacapa offensive. When Arana assumed the Presidency, Laugerud was promoted to chief of the army general staff, the top of the hierarchy; the Defense Ministry went to Arana's executive officer in Zacapa, Colonel Leonel Vassaux Martínez, like Laugerud a graduate of the *Politécnica*'s class of 1947.[2] In 1972 Laugerud replaced Vassaux as Minister of Defense.

Laugerud's own successor in 1978, Colonel Romeo Lucas García, was another close associate of Colonel Arana Osorios, and had served under him as chief of staff for the Zacapa military zone during the 1966–68 period. In the 1970s Arana's garrison intelligence chief in Zacapa, Colonel Germán Chupina, served first as director of the Mobile Military Police and, under Lucas García, as head of the National Police.

In 1973, the year before the change of government, there was no major wave of terror comparable to the slaughter of the 1970–71 state of siege period, but counter-terror "disappearances" and killings — of peasant organizers, trade unionists, students and professionals, and virtually anyone suspected of subversive sentiments — had apparently become an institutional routine. Although trade unionists were a principal target of Arana's counter-terror programme, summer and autumn 1973 were marked not by a decline, but by an unprecedented surge of labour organization and activity and the mobilization of broad public sectors in protests against enormous rises in the cost of living under the Arana regime. The catalyst of mass mobilization in late 1973 was a national teachers' strike which, perhaps because of the pre-electoral need to restore a respectable public image to the regime, was not crushed by the Zacapa-type methods of the first two years of Arana's government. The strike — organized by the National Teachers' Front — was a prelude to the unification of all public sector employees, and of a unified trade union movement under the next government;[3] a first step was the creation of the National Trade Union Advisory Council (*Consejo Nacional de Consulta Sindical, (CNCS)*).[4]

The 1974 pre-election period brought one of the few lulls in government killings after 1966, although Arana warned of harsh measures in store for those behind an alleged conspiracy to disrupt the elections.[5] In a January 1974 speech, Arana denounced a "plot" by "remnants of the guerrilla and the PGT, extremists infiltrated into the city government of the capital, the University, autonomous professional and trade union entities", and warned that while opposition parties could campaign freely within the law, "the instigators of illegal strikes and demonstrations ... will suffer the consequences of their actions", as the government would use "whatever force is necessary to smash subversion".[6]

The final weeks before the 1 March elections saw considerable press coverage of efforts by several organizations to open a public dialogue on violence in the country. In February the Committee of Relatives of Disappeared Persons (formed in 1967 and the first of its kind) proposed a forum on violence and invited the three presidential candidates to participate. The forum was to discuss the institutionalization of violence, the fate of the "disappeared", and the army's role in the violence. Candidates Ríos Montt and Páez Novales initially agreed to attend but then backed out, declaring that the forum was "organized by Communists".[7] The organizer, lawyer Edmundo Guerra Theilheimer, director of the National University's legal aid centre (*Bufete Popular*) and adviser to the Committee of Relatives, was perhaps marked for death then and there. The day after the elections Theilheimer seems to have sealed his fate by publishing an open letter in the press denouncing, and detailing, the evidence of electoral fraud in Laugerud's favour. On 10 March plainclothes gunmen strolled into the legal aid centre and killed him at his desk.[8]

Theilheimer was one of the better known Guatemalans to be murdered in a spate of killings between election day and the 1 July inauguration of the victor. Another key critic of Arana and the electoral fraud, radio broadcaster Mario Monterroso Armas, was gunned down on 22 March.[9]

Initially, the elections had reportedly swung in favour of the Christian Democrat candidate, General Efraín Ríos Montt, but the army high command's choice was victorious; Kjell Laugerud García became President, with Mario Sandoval Alarcón his Vice-President. The *New York Times* cited a series of sources to support claims that "the authorities resorted to extensive fraud" to ensure Laugerud's victory.[10] Ríos Montt, who protested against the fraud, was unceremoniously hustled to the airport, restored to "active" status in the armed forces, and ordered to take up a post as military attaché in Madrid. He remained there for several years, returning to public life in 1982.

Perhaps because the 1974 election campaign took place while major labour conflicts shook the Arana government, and further massive labour unrest was threatened, Kjell Laugerud in his election campaign, moderated the army's past harsh characterization of trade unionism as an aspect of insurgency. In a speech in February 1974 Laugerud pledged to improve the government's relations with the trade union movement:

> ... my government will respect trade union freedoms and the organization of labour guilds. Trade unions are legitimate instruments for action on behalf of the worker's interests. My government will maintain friendly relations with the unions.[11]

For most of the first two years of Laugerud's government there appeared to be some improvement in labour's lot. Many small unions that had sought legal recognition for years were registered under the new government, and not every strike was declared illegal.[12] The expansion of organized labour, legally recognized or not, was to some extent an inevitable consequence of the 1960s expansion of light industry, commerce and the public sector, itself influenced by the lifting of trade barriers within the Central American Common Market. By the time of the 1973 census some 14% of the economically active population of 1.547 million were classified as manufacturing workers (212,780); and 7% (113,800) were in commercial and financial services; agricultural workers still made up 57% of the working population (881,420).[13]

In the early 1970s only a minority of urban workers, and a tiny fraction of the total agricultural workforce (concentrated primarily in the sugar industry) were trade union members. By 1975 union membership in the three major legal labour federations was estimated at around 85,000.[14] On paper the largest was the Confederation of Federated Workers (CTF), which claimed some 50,000 members; the CTF was the only major federation to give its support to the government, and was relatively inactive.[15]

An estimated 17,000 urban and rural members were grouped in the National Workers Confederation (*Central Nacional de Trabajadores*, (CNT)) by the 1970s. Created as a Christian Democratic trade union federation,[16] the CNT was affiliated to the World Confederation of Labour and its regional organization, the Latin-American Confederation of Labour (*Confederación Latinamericana de Trabajadores*, (CLAT)), and has been known under its present name since 1968.[17] The third major federation, the Autonomous Trade Union Federation of Guatemala (*Federación Autónoma Sindical de Guatemala*, (FASGUA)), created in 1955, was, by the 1970s, somewhat to the left of the CNT and relatively strong in some rural areas.[18]

Although both the Christian Democratic oriented CNT and FASGUA had rural affiliates (155 peasant leagues were CNT members by 1979 [19]) organization in the countryside had moved slowly until the mid 1970s, obstructed, since 1954, both by systematic repression and the social structures of the peasantry itself. In the western highlands most of the population lived and worked in isolated traditional indigenous communities, their isolation in some cases compounded by the mutually incomprehensible languages of the many highland ethnic groups. Seasonal labour in the highland coffee estates (*fincas*) apparently did little to break through this isolation, and, until the 1970s, labour organization was limited almost exclusively to permanent employees of large farms and plantations and to associations of small independent landowners in the primarily *ladino* (non-Indian) areas of the country, clustered in the eastern regions.

Even during the 1944–54 period peasant organization had been largely restricted to the permanent workforce of the larger farms and plantations. The first true unions were created in 1944 at the United Fruit Company's Pacific Coast plantation in Tiquisate, Escuintla, and in its Atlantic Coast establishment at Bananera, although a legal basis for peasant organizations was not established until the 1947 Labour Code (*Código Laboral*) came into force. A total of 96 *sindicatos campesinos* (peasant labour unions) were registered by February 1950; under the Arbenz government (1950–54) 249 more were recognized. When the clock was turned back in May 1954, 319 of the 345 organizations recognized as peasant labour unions were organizations of workers on large farms, 26 were groupings of "independent agriculturalists".[20] The peasants of the Indian communities in the highlands, however, remained largely untouched by the process of intensive organization of labour in the countryside under Arbenz. Anthropologists have stressed the compartmentalization of the Indian population in traditional communities as a barrier to mass organization and mobilization, one test having been highland Indians' failure to affiliate to the mass organizations created by the central government during the revolutionary period. Even in the 1970s the Indian peasantry was characterized as being entirely local in outlook, and without prospects of uniting in any common cause. As Richard Adams puts it:

The domain structure of the western highlands is comprised primarily of a series of separate communities under the complementary controls of Indian civic and religious leaders and Ladino commercial interests... The communities have no serious confrontations (except for occasional squabbles over the allocation of woodland resources and similar problems) but maintain rather a high degree of sociocultural isolation from each other... In short, the Indian has developed no basis for unity beyond the local community.[21]

In the 1960s and 1970s many factors contributed toward the eventual rupture of the isolation of the highland Indians. It is difficult to assess the influence on mass organization of counter-insurgency violence, that moved west to affect all the country in the early 1970s. Seemingly the most influential factors were major changes in land use and labour requirements for agriculture introduced in the early 1960s, which, combined with state terror, appear to have created the preconditions for the new peasant organizations that were to blossom in the late 1970s. Incorporation of the Indian peasantry of the highlands into mass labour organizations was, in turn, a precondition for the development of the Indian-based guerrilla organizations that emerged in force in the 1980s.

By the 1970s the development of industrial agriculture on Guatemala's Pacific coast required the annual migration of some 200,000 to 300,000 Indian peasants from their highland villages. Political mobilization of the highland peasantry in the 1970s may not have occurred if virtually all the nearly landless peasants of the highlands had not experienced this seasonal migration. Although seasonal work in highland coffee farms had been a feature of highland Indian life since the late 19th Century, coastal agricultural development and agro-industrial employment patterns came much later. As in El Salvador, major changes in land use on Guatemala's coast came in the late 1950s and the 1960s, as large landowners diversified into the production of export crops on land previously dedicated to cattle-ranching and share-cropping. Again, as in El Salvador, the Pacific coastal areas were converted into enormous cotton and sugar plantations providing relatively little permanent employment, but requiring large scale seasonal migrant labour. Sharecroppers and subsistence farmers were driven from the area. The expansion into cotton was the most dramatic shift, turning much of the southern coast into an enormous factory farm owned by a very few individuals, even though in the late 1960s much of the coast was still considered an area for colonization.[22] From a cultivated area of 11,712 *manzanas* (one *manzana* = 1.72 acres) in crop year 1951–52, and 33,151 in 1960–61,[23] cotton culture in 1965–66 grew to cover 134,201 *manzanas* [24] and continued expanding until the mid-1970s. In 1975, top agricultural exports by value were: coffee ($158 million), sugar ($116 million) and cotton ($77 million). Expansion of the coastal sugar estates too was promoted, in part due to the market gap brought about by the Cuban revolution and ensuing blockade.[25]

Peasant Labour and Agro-Industry

Agro-industrial development was a major influence on the quarter of a million or so peasant labourers brought in seasonally from the Indian highlands as a temporary work force. Previously the highland Indian population provided seasonal migratory labour in coffee areas in the arc of highlands flanking the Pacific coast known as the southern piedmont, and in the northern highlands of Alta Verapaz and El Quiché department.[26] The south coast plantations took advantage of population pressure in the highlands, and, in many cases, used coercive means to recruit seasonal labourers.[27] Statistics on the numbers of seasonal migrant labourers to highlands coffee plantations and to coastal agro-industrial estates are incomplete, partly because many worked without contracts and for periods of varying length. Estimates from the late 1960s and early 1970s put the figure at between 150,000 and 240,000 for the coffee plantations.[28] One study cited the official figures for the 1965–66 harvest period as a basis to estimate the total numbers of migrant labourers for the different crops at "between 118,000 and 150,000 in cotton, 167,000 and 237,000 in coffee, and 17,500 to 21,000 in sugar cane. In addition to this there are an estimated 4,700 permanent employees and labourers in the cotton farms".[29] Studies in the mid-1970s indicate that at that time well over 200,000 workers migrated to the coastal plantations.[30]

The relatively new migratory pattern involved a large proportion of Guatemala's landless and nearly landless Indians in previously unfamiliar forms of work on large agro-industrial estates (as contrasted with the smaller units and traditional forms of cultivation on the coffee estates).

Much has been written on the immediate social costs of cotton culture on the south coast:[31] lack of food, medical attention, sanitation; primitive shelter in enormous communal sheds; working conditions that routinely exposed child and adult labourers to lethal insecticides (including DDT, banned in its country of manufacture); and a system that paid workers by the task and regularly cheated them of their wages. Meanwhile, the cotton and sugar planter enjoyed a combination of near-absolute feudal power and modern, cosmopolitan, conspicuous consumption, with many great landed families owning dozens of coastal and highland farms.

Economic criticism of the rush into cotton culture centred on the long-term damage to the land caused by intensive, short-term profit cultivation methods and the dependence on high-technology imports in order to keep the land in cotton at all. Although in the late 1950s and 1960s the Guatemalan government actively promoted cotton culture as a means of bringing in foreign exchange, a good proportion of the foreign exchange coming in went out again to pay agricultural fertilizer, insecticide and equipment suppliers in the United States. A figure of slightly over $150 million is given as total foreign exchange earnings from cotton exports between 1954 and 1965, but one authority estimates that input costs consumed over half these earnings.[32]

Many cotton growers, particularly those who leased large tracts on a yearly basis, were out to make the maximum profit in the short term as possible, with no concern for the future. According to Richard Adams the cotton lands were "perhaps the most promising for general agricultural development in Guatemala and . . . should be treated rationally for long-term production. . ."; he pointed out that, in fact, the land was undergoing "systematic destruction" expected to continue "as long as there is a satisfactory international cotton market and there is still land left to destroy" with little benefit to more than between 1,000 and 2,000 Guatemalans, "the cotton growers, the land owners who rent to them, and the agricultural suppliers who get the actual profits from this cultivation."[33]

In the late 1970s, much as had been predicted by outside observers, soil exhaustion, the rising cost of imports necessary to maintain production, and market forces, all combined to bring about the near collapse of the Guatemalan cotton industry. Cotton earnings peaked in 1979 at some $200 million (with the People's Republic of China buying almost one-third of the crop) and then began a steady decline.[34] Commodities reports in 1982 attributed the decline to high costs, low world prices and "disruption of production by the guerrillas". Between 1979 and 1982 production declined by 66% with a fall in both production and earnings expected to continue.[35] While landowners can be expected to survive comfortably, as most of them still hold profitable coffee and sugar estates, the impact on migrants workers from the highlands exacerbated an already desperate situation.

> Declining production is also increasing rural unemployment. In Guatemala the structures of the rural economy are being disrupted. Traditionally, the Indian families in the highlands have subsisted on food grown on small-holdings, supplementing this with money earned from seasonal work on the sugar and cotton plantations on the Pacific coast. The decline in production of both crops, together with the introduction of mechanical cutters, has greatly reduced the demand for labour, and the migration has virtually stopped.[36]

During the period of somewhat more than 20 years in which highland Indians were coerced by design or circumstances to travel to the coast they became familiar with new forms of production — the factory farms they dreaded — and of labour organization. The vast scale of the coastal plantations threw together seasonal labourers from different areas and with different backgrounds, and provided the basis for labour organizations not circumscribed by the geographic or cultural limits of the peasant's own community or region.

Development of Peasant Co-operatives

The destruction of most of Guatemala's existing peasant organizations in 1954 was followed by the introduction of an innovative alternative to traditional peasant unions: the development of peasant co-operatives. The promotion of a rural co-operative movement, seen as a lesser evil than the peasant leagues and unions of the "revolutionary" period, was undertaken by the Roman Catholic Church in the immediate aftermath of Castillo Armas' assumption of power.[37] Archbishop Rossell pressured the new government to permit foreign missionary orders to work in Indian parishes, build church schools and promote agricultural, consumer and credit co-operatives "as a way to protect the country's poor from 'the evils of international communism' ".[38] But the foreign missionaries involved in implementing the programmes themselves underwent a change:

> as they became more acquainted with rural peoples and their problems, they began to seek out methods for improving the social and economic conditions of their parishioners.[39]

The co-operative movement served admirably to overcome the economic and social isolation of some Indian communities and, when successful, to bring economic self-sufficiency by the use of community resources which permitted members to cease their seasonal migration to the coffee *fincas* or the coastal plantations.

In the 1960s the Catholic Action organization and the Christian Democratic party openly worked to build rural co-operatives, and the movement became the focus of most church rural development programmes. Co-operatives set up with the assistance of progressive clergy in the isolated lowland areas of northern Huehuetenango and El Quiché, only recently colonized by Indian migrants from the highlands, became relatively prosperous and independent of local elites for marketing their produce and bringing in goods from the outside. Church-owned light aircraft provided the principal link between the co-operatives in these roadless areas and the national market-place.[40]

Although during the 1960s periodically under attack as centres of subversion, by 1967 there were 145 registered co-operatives in Guatemala; and by March 1976 510, with a total membership of 132,116. More than half were in predominantly Indian areas of El Quiché. Huehuetenango, Sololá and San Marcos.[41] although previous governments had to some extent tolerated the co-operative movement, its most significant growth occurred in the first two years of the Laugerud government, apparently at US prompting. Unlike his predecessor, Arana, who publicly equated the co-operatives with "communism", Laugerud seemed to give them his support, and so could take advantage of the political and financial incentives offered by the US government, which supported them as a mechanism for controlled economic self-help. The US Agency for International Development (AID) responded to Laugerud's overtures to the co-operativists by providing a $4.5 million loan to finance purchases of fertilizers and other supplies, and the Inter-American Development Bank, in early 1976, approved a loan of over $15 million for "cooperative development".[42] Laugerud's support is somewhat suspect, however, if only because he was on the record in his election campaign speeches as having strong and unfavourable views on co-operatives, differing little from those of his predecessor, General Arana. In a 27 February 1974 speech Laugerud had attacked the Christian Democrats for having supported the co-operative movement and characterized it as a facade "under which the Soviet Communist system is disguised".[43] In addition, at the same time as he was winning international praise for supporting co-operatives, some co-operative leaders were being killed and others threatened with death in the name of the "death squads".

In 1975, guerrilla operations in the department of El Quiché, (during which the Guerrilla Army of the Poor (*Ejército Guerrillero de los Pobres*, (EGP), killed landowner Luis Reina — "the Tiger of Ixcán" — virtual lord of large tracts of land in the area) were followed by army operations in which co-operative leaders in the Ixcán area were systematically taken and killed.[44] Luis Reina was killed in June 1975: on 7 July a contingent of army paratroopers lined up the men of the Xalbal co-operative in Ixcán Grande in the market-place, picked out 30 and took them away in helicopters. The 30 co-operativists — who were never seen again — and seven others detained and "disappeared"were named in a sworn statement delivered by 25 surviving members of the co-operative to President Laugerud in November 1975; the statement requested the missing men be accounted for; the only response was a denial by the Ministry of the Interior that they had ever been arrested.

In retrospect, foreign development experts who worked with co-operatives during the Laugerud period see a dual nature to the official support; potential leaders among the peasantry were encouraged to show themselves in the mid-1970s so they could later be killed off:

> People are fearful of holding meetings, particularly of cooperatives, which President Laugerud ... appeared to promote. Many leaders became known and very visible and many of them are dead today.
> (. . .)
> My work was basically in a northern province. Between 1975 and 1977, 46 project leaders were assassinated or disappeared. One returned. He suffered torture and witnessed the murder of some 30 members of his community.[46]

Co-operatives in the cities and towns were also under threat. Press reports in July 1975 published the text of a mimeographed letter sent to leaders of photographers' and other co-operatives in the name of the "death squad" MANO:

> We know of your PROCOMMUNIST attitude... We know by experience that all labour organizations and cooperatives always eventually fall into the power of the Communist Leaders infiltrated into them. We have the organization and the force to prevent this from occurring again. . . As evidence we speak the truth: there are THIRTY THOUSAND CLAN-DESTINE PEASANT GRAVES TO BEAR WITNESS. For your own good and thinking of your family we urge you to remember this. . . Whether the brutal repression we have unleashed in the departments against the COMMUNISTS HIDDEN BEHIND THE FLAG OF COOPERATIVISM should catch up with *YOU* here in the capital depends on your future conduct.[47]

Simultaneous to the mid-1970s high point of the co-operative movement and conversion of the south coast into vast agro-industrial estates was the closure of the northern border areas to the highland Indian peasants. These previously totally isolated areas, lacking means of communication or transport, had served as population "escape valves" where highland Indians, no longer able to survive in their traditional homelands, and unwilling to depend on seasonal plantation labour, could go and clear unclaimed land. The Petén, a vast, underpopulated lowland province in the north-east of the country, almost entirely owned by the State, had been officially designated a "colonization" zone in the 1960s. In practice, however, it had been broken up into vast cattle ranches, many of them appropriated by army officers. Some small Kekchi Indian groups had filtered into the department from the highlands of Alta Verapaz, but spontaneous colonization by highland Indians was far more significant in the lowland areas of the belt of land reaching across the northern parts of El Quiché. Huehuetenango and Alta Verapaz departments along the Mexican border. This area, and, especially, the so-called "Reina Zone" (the Reina family were the principal landowners) had been gradually settled by Indian colonists since the 1950s, and, with the assistance of progressive Roman Catholic priests, many of them had joined to form co-operatives.[48]

In the mid-1970s, however, when the northern zone was closed to highland Indian immigration and many peasant communities and co-operatives already established were expelled, this all ended; at the same time, a project to build a great east-west highway across the north, linking Huehuetenango and Izabal began. The highway was the keystone of a development project which would open up what was thenceforth known as the *Franja Transversal del Norte* (Transversal Northern Strip).[49] Though billed as a "resettlement" or "colonization" project, its object was hardly that of helping Indian peasants find new land and get their crops to market; the ambitious new development programme responded to the discovery of vast oil reserves in areas near to the Mexican border — oil which might eventually provide the massive export earnings and cheap fuel necessary to make Guatemala's nickel mine and refinery complex at Izabal productive. (The EXMIBAL nickel complex, built in the 1960s before the Arab oil embargo led to sky-rocketting fuel prices, has never gone into production.) Funding for the new road came through the National Institute for Agrarian Transformation and, according to press sources, the Shenandoah Oil Company.[50]

The dramatic increase in land value brought by the new road, and the oil prospects, provided strong incentives to throw the peasants off the land and destroy the existing co-operatives and communities. By 1976 there was already significant evidence of a great land-grab throughout the northern region, coinciding with a fresh, intensified wave of terror against the church-backed co-operatives and the traditional peasant communities there.

In July 1976 the Conference of Guatemalan Bishops published a 58 page document entitled "United in Hope" ("*Unidos en la Esperanza*"), sternly criticising the violence and injustice in Guatemala, condemning the concentration of land rights in the hands of a tiny privileged minority, and expressing the church's concern that a new wave of violence was occurring precisely in areas being opened up for development:

> But this situation, far from being resolved, is becoming more and more critical every day. A proof of this is the tensions that have arisen in the so-called Development Zones (Izabal, El Petén, Alta Verapaz and Quiché) where continuous turmoil prevails . . . because large landowners want to possess ever greater amounts and take over lands which have been acquired legitimately by those who have worked them for many years. *Perhaps the expectation of discovering oil in these regions has awakened immoderate ambitions and has sparked off an unjustified violence that we cannot refrain from denouncing.* Chisec, Morán, Nebaj and others are . . . places where peasants have died for the 'crime' of defending the land that they have possessed for a long time. . .[51]

An important factor in the wave of violence was the emergence of the Guerrilla Army of the Poor (*Ejército Guerrillero de los Pobres*, EGP) in a series of spectacular attacks in northern El Quiché, but massive counter-insurgency operations in the area were followed by the expulsion of many long-standing settlers, the closure of cooperatives and the takeover of large tracts of land by army officers, oil companies, and the already landed elite.[52] The editor of the Guatemalan daily *El Gráfico* publicly questioned the government's claims that opening up the Transversal Northern Strip would help the peasantry, observing that individual landowners had already taken advantage of the project to grab, with INTA and army assistance, properties of up to 30 *caballerías* (some 25,000 hectares) from which they expelled former peasant occupants.[53]

By 1979 the entire region bordering the new road connecting Izabal and El Quiché was known as the "Zone of the Generals", although land grabs were also successfully carried out by civilian members of the 1970s governments and the landed elites identified with these governments.[54] According to opposition sources those profiting from this development project included Laugerud's Defense Minister, General Spiegler Noriega, as well as former, present and future presidents Generals Carlos Arana Osorio, Kjell Laugerud, and Romer Lucas García.[55]

1976: Earthquake and After: State Repression and Violence

An earthquake registering 7.5 on the Richter scale struck Guatemala City and vast rural areas on the morning of 4 February 1976. The wealthy suburban areas of the capital were relatively unscathed, but in the city's slums, where shanty-homes were perched precariously on the slopes of ravines, and rural areas of the 16 (out of 22) departments affected more than 22,000 people were killed.[56] Most of the deaths in the urban slums and peasant villages occurred when massive adobe walls and heavy tile roofs crashed in upon sleeping families. Dubbed a "class quake" by reporters astonished at its failure to affect the wealthy,[57] the earthquake rendered one million Guatemalans homeless and injured more than 77,000.[58] In the central highland department of Chimaltenango, a densely populated Indian area, 41,677 out of 42,794 homes were reportedly destroyed.[59]

This disaster prompted an immediate flood of international aid to Guatemala. The US congress voted $25 million in emergency funds for relief and reconstruction, to be channelled through AID. The Inter-American Development Bank and the Central American Bank for Economic Integration allocated $38.9 million, and the World Bank $20 million, all within a matter of weeks.[60] Meanwhile, the Guatemalan authorities took advantage of the confusion to carry out a wave of political killings in the capital. Amnesty International reported the "death-squad" killing of at least 200 people in Guatemala City in the immediate aftermath of the earthquake.[61]

The beginning of an offensive in the rural areas of the north followed the earthquake, and though provoked by guerrilla actions most victims of this offensive were from among the rural co-operative leadership. An Oxfam-America report based on testimonies from development workers close to the co-operative movement noted that counter-insurgency operations launched immediately after the earthquake had decimated the co-operatives of El Quiché:

> Just two weeks after the earthquake, the Army began its 'counterinsurgency' program in El Quiché. Members of Catholic Action and the cooperative movement especially felt the blows of the government's terror campaign. Between February 1976 and the end of 1977, 68 cooperative leaders were killed in the Ixcan, 40 in Chajul, 28 in Cotzal, and 32 in Nebaj.
>
> Several of the survey respondents indicate that the chaos created by the earthquake seemed to serve as a pretext for the increasing militarization of the rural areas.[62]

The earthquake also gave the authorities an opportunity to break trade unions in several sectors. The Chambers of Commerce and Industry announced only days after the event that Guatemala City's industrial base had not been seriously harmed, and production would not be interrupted (once electricity, cut for two days, was restored). In the following weeks, however, hundreds of industrial trade union members were dismissed arbitrarily, or on the grounds that they had failed to show up for work the day after the earthquake. In one textile factory (which remained in production) 120 members of an unrecognized union were dismissed the week after the earthquake on these grounds. Some 150 employees of the *Embotelladora Guatemalteca*, SA (the Coca-Cola bottling plant) who had been seeking legal recognition for their union since August 1975, were dismissed on the grounds that they had "damaged the factory premises" and "attempted to form a subversive movement."[63] Similar mass dismissals of unionized workers on the pretext of the earthquake occurred in provincial food processing plants and sugar mills. The impact of union smashing and the general suffering of the urban working people occasioned by the earthquake itself was seen by some observers as significantly influencing the subsequent growth and direction of the union movement.[64]

Two months after the earthquake eight of Guatemala's largest unions and federations joined to form an umbrella labour organization linking unions and peasant leagues, including the CNT and FASGUA, the sugar workers' union on the coast, the Municipal Workers Union and the National Teachers' Front.[65] In the next two years this broad union front, called National Committee of Trade Union Unity (*Comité Nacional de Unidad Sindical*, (CNUS)) also gained the support of a new federation linking the many organizations of public employees in the Council of State Employees' Organizations (*Consejo de Entidades de Trabajadores del Estado*, (CETE)).

The birth of CNUS was directly related to both the immediate consequences of the earthquake and the dismissals at the Coca-Cola bottling plant, where the unrecognized union (some 80% of the workforce) was headed by top CNT leaders. The Coca-Cola industrial conflict became a test case for inter-federation labour co-operation when dismissed workers sat in at the factory, to be evicted by National Police and Mobile Military Police with considerable violence, with 12 subsequently imprisoned at El Pavón prison farm. Protests against the dismissals and arrests united most sectors of the labour movement, and on 31 March FASGUA, CNT, the sugar workers' unions, unions of municipal workers in Guatemala City and Escuintla, and representatives of peasant leagues, held a general meeting to discuss joint action in solidarity with the Coca-Cola workers; the bottling plant agreed to reinstate the 150 dismissed workers when some 50 unions threatened to strike. Representatives of the principal labour federations decided to create CNUS at the general meeting on 31 March called to organize strike action in support of the Coca Cola workers.[66]

Although support for the Coca Cola workers was the CNUS' first initiative, its programme of action's major emphasis was on a platform of demands for assistance to victims of the earthquake in Guatemala City, and protest against the wave of organized violence launched in its wake.[67] Laugerud's ostensible tolerance of trade unionism evaporated in the face of CNUS' unification of the labour movement and its threat to bring together mass organizations of the urban poor in the aftermath of the earthquake. In his speech to congress on 1 July 1976 Laugerud attacked the CNUS leaders as "enemies of national reconstruction" and accused them of "fabricating strikes to weaken national production and foster anarchy and violence."[68] After 1976 Laugerud would grow closer in word and deed to his predecessor Arana, and return to the political philosophy he had voiced prior to his Presidential bid; as director of the military academy in 1969, for example, he declared that Guatemala was in a permanent state of war, "under continuous aggression from extremists", that war was not "an instrument of politics", but "politics itself".[69]

Many CNUS demands coincided with those of leaders of the small United Front of the Revolution (*Frente Unido de la Revolución*, (FUR)), a political party whose founder, Manuel Colóm Argueta, had been mayor of Guatemala City from 1970 to 1974. The FUR, which later affiliated to the Socialist International, gained significant support during the Laugerud regime, and was particularly influential in the capital. As it was not recognized as a national political party, it could run candidates only at the municipal level. The municipal government's efforts to temporarily rehouse the tens of thousands of poor Guatemalans whose homes had crumbled into the canyons and ravines of the city's slum areas placed FUR municipal officials in conflict with private landowners. There was insufficient publicly owned land available in the capital for all those made homeless by the earthquake; some were forced to improvise shelters on privately owned land — with the municipal government's support. The first major assassination attributed to Laugerud's security services in the wake of the earthquake, one which provoked mass protests and demonstrations, was the murder of Rolando Andrade Peña, FUR leader and municipal government official, who had tried to arrange emergency tent housing on privately owned land.[70]

The Christian Democratic party was also hit by a wave of post-earthquake violence. In a 23 March 1976 statement, the party protested that all its executive committee members had received death threats and that three party members in El Quiché department had been arrested by the Detective Corps and "disappeared"; two executive committee members, Enrique Guillén Funes and Alfonso Alonso, survived an assassination attempt in May, but in subsequent months other Christian Democrats were gunned down in rural areas.[71]

A strike, launched on 18 May, at the country's largest sugar refinery complex, the *Ingenio Pantaleón*, backed by the Sugar Worker's Federation and CNUS, was the first test of co-operation between urban and rural labour organizations under the CNUS umbrella.[72] The sugar workers' strike reflected CNUS' own heterogenous make up, involving both permanent and migrant seasonal workers, mostly of Indian origin, who combined the tasks and low wages of peasants with the responsibilities and organization typical of industrial workers. The strike was to protest against the brutality of Mobile Military Police guards and armed plain-clothes police stationed at the complex, and the failure of the managers to pay the workforce the national minimum wage established for sugar workers (the union claimed they were paid only 90 cents a day in many cases, whereas the minimum wage was $1.12).[73] The main demand was for both permanent and seasonal workers to be granted a 40 cents a day raise, and that a previous collective agreement on working conditions be respected.[74] Two other sugar refineries on the coast were shut down by simultaneous strike actions. Under the terms of the Labour Code, which forbids strikes or stoppages by agricultural workers at harvest time, the strikes were declared illegal and fought by arrests and dismissals. Although 80 union members at the *Ingenio Pantaleón*, including its secretary general, were dismissed, and the strike never fully achieved its objectives, in the next three years, sugar workers there and in other refineries provided a strong basis of support for the organization of seasonal migrant workers and for combined, national strike action.

The Laugerud regime's last two years saw continued efforts at joint urban and rural labour organization and a further mobilization of the urban poor. In turn, the government's response became increasingly violent, and virtually any member of a grass-roots organization, in the countryside or the city slums, was put at risk of torture and death. There were also several high-profile assassinations and "disappearances" of key figures in the strike movement. On 8 June 1977, labour lawyer Mario López Lárrave, a driving force behind CNUS, was shot down by submachine-gun fire in front of his home; as lawyer and adviser to the main labour federations he had played perhaps the greatest part in bringing them together in CNUS.[75] After this murder, CNUS began a phase of increased militancy, and, accelerated by mass killings of its affiliates' leaders in 1978 and 1979, became increasingly clandestine. Mario López Lárrave's murder was followed by what became a regular feature of Guatemalan political life: the funeral procession become a mass demonstration against the government.[76] Selective assassination after the death of López Lárrave brought increasingly large numbers of Guatemalans into the streets.[77] In June, students Leonel Caballeros and Robin García, leaders of the Association of Secondary School Students, were detained and "disappeared"; university and secondary school students marched repeatedly in the streets to demand their release. In August the bodies of the two boys were found, mutilated by torture. Robin García's funeral turned into a demonstration by an estimated 50,000 Guatemalans.[78]

It was a massacre of over 100 Kekchi Indian peasants at Panzós, Cobán, in the Department of Alta Verapaz on 29 May 1978 that provoked the last great demonstrations in the final months of the Laugerud regime, and illustrated the growth of rural-urban unity in what had become a broad opposition movement combining urban and rural trade unions and "popular" grass-roots organizations with such opposition parties as the FUR.

The Kekchi Indians, protesting against land grabs from their ancestral communities, had converged on Panzós, where their leaders intended to meet with municipal authorities. Once in the small village square the crowd was machine-gunned by strategically placed soldiers. The true number of deaths has never been determined, but the incident acquired international notoriety when photographs of municipal dump trucks heaped full of Indian bodies were published in foreign news media. Preparations for the massacre had been made at least a day in advance: machine-gun emplacements were set up on roof-tops around the square and, the day *before* the slaughter, two mass graves were excavated with bulldozers.[79]

The Panzós massacre differed little from other massacres in Guatemala, either in scale or brutality. It did differ in that it rapidly became known throughout the country, bringing together rural and urban sectors in protest against governmental repression. On 1 June tens of thousands of urban Guatemalans marched in the capital in an unprecedented display of solidarity with Indian peasants. On 8 June some 60,000 to 80,000 demonstrators marched through Guatemala City to protest against the Panzós massacre and the selective murder of trade union leaders; the date chosen was the anniversary of Mario López Lárrave's assassination.[80] Urban trade unionists, university and secondary school students, and members of a new kind of peasant organization to be discussed below, united in a common cause. When General Romeo Lucas García assumed the Presidency in July 1978 mass organization in town and country threatened the military government with new kinds of opposition, less manageable than either the traditional political parties or the guerrilla movements of the 1960s.

Lucas García's Presidency: the Violence Continues

Outgoing President Laugerud had backed his Defense Minister and fellow member of the "Zacapa Group" to succeed him in 1978; as in his own case, there was little doubt about the outcome of the elections. General Lucas García ran as candidate of the PID, the CAO (*Central Aranista Organizada*, comprising Arana's supporters) and the Revolutionary Party, and won a majority.[81] His election was confirmed by congress and he took office on 1 July 1978. Unlike the pre-election period in 1974, there was no pause in governmental violence, either before or after the change of government.

The first joint effort of the trade unions organized in CNUS, the public sector workers, and organized sectors of the capital's students and urban poor to make demands of the new government followed the doubling of bus fares from five to ten cents in late September 1978; fare rises are a traditional flash-point for popular mobilization in Latin America, and in Guatemala fares already cost the average urban worker between 10 and 20% of his income.[82] Strike action and demonstrations demanding a reversal of the measure linked CNUS and the state employees federation CETE, the students of the AEU and a new, more radical organization named after student leader Robin García, the *Frente Estudiantil Revolucionario Robin García*, (FERG) (a new form of semi-clandestine student organization without formal status or a visible leadership) and new organizations of the residents of Guatemala's poor neighbourhoods.[83] After 2 October demonstrations were attacked by police gunfire, and by 9 October there were over 50 recorded deaths and 400 wounded.[84] The killings provoked further, larger demonstrations and a strike, which within a week became a general strike paralysing the capital's industry and commerce.[85]

In a televised address to the nation on 9 October, President Lucas García announced that the government would rescind approval for the fare rise, and restore the previous five cent fare by means of a government subsidy.[86]

The October general strike ended in victory for the strikers, but marked a watershed for mass mobilization in Guatemala; an intensive campaign of governmental murder followed that beheaded many of the labour and other organizations involved in the strike, forcing the survivors underground. In the course of the strike itself the first anonymous manifestos were circulated in the name of a new "death-squad", calling itself the "Secret Anti-Communist Army" (*Ejército Secreto Anticomunista*, (ESA)), pledged to liquidate ideological enemies of the government. Many of the assassinations and executions subsequently carried out by government forces under Lucas García were attributed to the ESA.

Selective murder was first directed to the student sector. On 20 October, after addressing a demonstration to commemorate Ubico's overthrow in 1944, AEU president Oliverio Castañeda de León was submachine-gunned less than a block from the National Palace and in plain view of dozens of impassively watching armed, uniformed policemen.

Castañeda's successor as president of the AEU, Antonio Ciani García de León, was arrested on 6 November, and never seen again. President Lucas García responded to the clamour for Ciani's release by stating that he would have no dealings with the AEU because the university was a centre of subversion aimed at overthrowing his government.[87]

Both Ciani and Castañeda had been named on a first "death-list" issued on 18 October in the name of ESA, which included 38 people said to have been "tried and sentenced to death", among them student, trade union, peasant and church leaders. A second "ESA" "death-list", issued on 9 December, named nine top leaders of the CNUS and the CNT (National Workers' Central), and a third, issued on 3 January 1979, named 23 trade unionists and academics, all "sentenced to death".[88]

Attacks on student leaders coincided with actions against CNUS leaders, particularly those from the CNT and its affiliate at EGSA, the Coca-Cola bottling plant. Israel Márquez, an EGSA union leader and member of the CNUS executive committee, survived an assassination attempt on 16 October; on 12 December, Antonio Quevedo y Quevedo, former Secretary General of the EGSA union, was murdered; on 24 January 1979 gunmen attacked Israel Márquez' home and murdered Manuel Antonio Moscoso, a lodger, apparently as a result of mistaken identity.[89] Márquez sought asylum in the Venezuelan Embassy and was flown into exile. His successor as the union's Secretary General, Manuel López Balam, had his throat cut on 5 April 1979; López Balam's successor, Marlon Mendizábal García, was shot to death on 27 May 1980; Edgar René Aldana, a member of the union's executive committee, was seized on 20 June 1980 and later found shot dead.[90]

On Sunday 27 June 1980 27 top CNT leaders met at the union's headquarters, one block from the Presidential Guard building at the rear of the presidential palace complex, to discuss plans for recently murdered Coca-Cola union leader Edgar René Aldana's funeral. Uniformed police closed the street to traffic while the union offices were raided and all 27 leaders detained and driven off to places unknown. Authorities denied that they had been arrested, saying they had been "kidnapped" by unknown assailants.[91] On 24 August another 17 CNT leaders, meeting at the Roman Catholic retreat and conference centre *Centro Emaús*, in Palín, Escuintla, were arrested by combined army and police forces: they too disappeared permanently.[92] After the two mass arrests and "disappearances" in 1980, the selective murder of CNT leaders and leaders of other CNUS affiliates continued throughout the Lucas García government. But from mid.1980 the CNT and CNUS ceased to act publicly and became semi-clandestine.

Other victims of the Lucas García government's first years were leaders of small opposition parties based in the capital that had been seeking registration to run candidates for the presidency and congress. In 1979, economist and former minister under Méndez Montenegro, Congressman Alberto Fuentes Mohr, then leader of the small Social Democratic Party, was gunned down on the steps of the congress building the day his party submitted its petition for legal recognition.[93] On 22 March the charismatic former mayor of Guatemala City, Manuel Colom Argueta, was pursued by three car-loads of armed men and two motorcycles as a police helicopter hovered overhead; he was killed in a hail of bullets in the heart of Guatemala's fashionable and heavily patrolled embassy district in an operation his family blamed on the government and the army.[94] Colom Argueta's murder came only a few days after the moderate FUR party he had founded was legally recognized as a national party, a measure he told an interviewer "might have to be paid for with his own head".[95] Colom Argueta and Fuentes Mohr were seen as potential alternatives to the succession of army officers in the Presidency. Both were close to the Socialist International which, in a statement condemning the murder of Fuentes Mohr, had demanded guarantees of the personal safety of Colom Argueta.[96]

While the most widely reported killings were those affecting urban sectors, the largest group of victims were the peasantry and those who worked with them. Among these last the killing or arrest and "disappearance" of Roman Catholic priests and lay church workers was one feature of Lucas García's move against rural organization; three priests were killed and one "disappeared" in 1980 alone.[97] The main targets among the peasants themselves were those who had emerged as community leaders either in the rural co-operatives, or in post-earthquake reconstruction committees set up throughout the country. A 1982 Oxfam-America report quotes several former development workers who described the earthquake as having united the rural population in adversity. Where people were effectively united in reconstruction efforts by means of ad hoc committees or through their co-operatives, these local organizations acquired fresh potential as centres of independent action and/or opposition to government control.[98]

Under Lucas García the army moved to eliminate "any campesino involved in the organization of other campesinos";[99] one former development worker said:

> Everyone who participated in these [community development] courses since the beginning of the 1970's has been killed or forced to leave the country. I know of 82 Indian leaders who have been killed from 1979 to 1982.[100]

Another former development worker described the savage nature of the destruction of the co-operative movement:

> ... In March 1981, 15 members of our coop were dragged from their homes and murdered by the military. In December 1981, assassins in army uniforms and with government trucks entered a remote village and assassinated several coop leaders. Five others were found later, crucified with sharp sticks to the ground and tortured to death. The local priest barely escaped assassination and went to Mexico.[101]

Army counter-insurgent operations in the northern departments of El Quiché and Huehuetenango had, since 1976, made peasant organizations and co-operatives a target of mass killings. El Quiché's situation in particular, was brought home to Guatemala City and international public opinion when successive delegations of Indian peasants from the department of El Quiché travelled to the capital seeking (unsuccessfully) audience with President Lucas García, to request an investigation of the army's action in the area — including almost 60 murders and "disappearances" — and withdrawal of troops.[102] On 31 January 1980, 22 members of the delegation went to the Spanish Embassy, intending to stage a sit-in in order to gain the Ambassador's help in getting a hearing with Guatemalan authorities, and to make their case known internationally. Amnesty International described the subsequent events.

> Informed of the peasants' presence, the police surrounded the building. When the delegates saw the police outside, they at first refused to leave. Despite a demand by Ambassador Maximo Cajal y López that police stay out of the embassy and the agreement of the delegation to withdraw peacefully, police stormed the embassy. Thirty-eight people died, some from shot wounds and others in an ensuing fire.[103]

The demonstrators who died, mainly Indian peasants from the Uspantán area of El Quiché, were almost all relatives of previous victims of "disappearance" and execution by the army. They were also members of a new, semi-clandestine peasant organization — the Committee of Peasant Unity — that was to play a major role in the mobilization of the Indian peasantry of the highlands in the coming years.

The Committee for Peasant Unity: A New Solidarity

In the two years after the creation of CNUS in 1976, a new kind of peasant organization took shape, outside the formal structures of traditional labour organizations or regional peasant leagues. Its constituency was in the mountainous areas of the western and northern highlands, among landless or nearly landless Indians, and a minority of poor *ladino campesinos*. This organisation — the Committee for Peasant Unity (*Comité de Unidad Campesina*, (CUC)) — united peasants from the poorest and most isolated areas of the country; most of its members, however, had experienced working on the agro-industrial plantations of the coast or the highland coffee estates. Many had been involved in co-operatives which, for a time, had seemed to offer them a secure future. The coast and the co-operatives provided experience of forms of organization and collective action previously unknown to the tight-knit, isolated Indian communities.

Although the CUC incorporated non-Indian peasants and promoted co-operation between its own membership and other sectors of organized labour, this was the first time Guatemala's largely Indian population, including people speaking different Indian languages from widely differing areas, came together in an organization dominated by Indians who determined both its political and its economic objectives. The means used to achieve the CUC's high level of organization remain largely a mystery. CNUS, which made a point of providing support for peasant "leagues", organized communities engaged in land or labour conflicts, and regularly published information on rural disputes, played a significant role in launching CUC, but other factors were involved. By 1978 the common Indian experience of repression at home and oppression on the coastal plantations had put an end to the traditional isolation of the Indian communities. Progressively worsening conditions on the coast, expulsion of Indians from the lands of the frontier area of the north, growing pressure on the land in the highlands, destruction of the co-operatives, and the savage everyday persecution of the peasantry in general were incentives enough to unite and resist.

As a mass organization the CUC was unique in Guatemala in that it was largely clandestine: it had no visible leadership, did not advertise the names of affiliated communities, organizations, or co-operatives, and did not aspire to legal recognition. The relative opacity of CUC's organization structure may have been facilitated by its largely Indian membership; few army intelligence officers speak or understand Kekchi, Mam or Quiche. Though not a guerrilla organization, CUC advocated both the conventional strategies of traditional labour organizations, strikes and sit-ins, and more vigorous forms of direct action to achieve political and economic ends, and to exercise self-defence.

CUC was first heard of when a large contingent of its members participated along with CNUS in the 1978 May Day demonstration in Guatemala City. At the same time it put out a leaflet which circulated in the capital and elsewhere; dated 1 May and entitled *The Committee for Peasant Unity to the People of Guatemala*, it accurately and dramatically describes the peasants' plight:

> The workers of the countryside ... together with the labourers are the ones that maintain life in Guatemala and produce its wealth. But nevertheless it is us whose lives are taken and destroyed by the rich of Guatemala, the powerful foreigners, and the authorities that are at their service. Our labour is every day more harshly exploited in the coffee farms, the cotton plantations and the sugar estates. We need land to sow. In other places they threaten us, and they expel us from land won through the sweat of our brows... They even take from us the water, to make a profit from it. They exploit our forests, leaving our lands dry like deserts. For the workers of the countryside there are no roads, no medicines, no decent housing, no possibility of education, nor rest. The wealth we produce serves to fatten our own enemies, to build a new military academy, to buy new and murderous arms. for us the repression is abundant. They kidnap our sons to take them as soldiers. We we demand our rights, when we demand part of all this wealth we produce they pursue us, torture us, and murder us. Not even in our own communities can we walk freely, but we must defend ourselves from the police, the army, the detectives, the Treasury Guard, and the bands of gunmen of the estate owners who have us in a constant state of siege.[104]

The leaflet proposed that the CUC work to organize the people of the countryside to collaborate with "the urban labourers and other popular sectors to bring an end to this system of exploitation".[105]

Press reports in September 1979 suggest the peasantry, whether or not associated with the CUC, was reaching boiling point. On 29 September the press reported an attack on a National Police patrol by "women wood-gatherers" in Sesac, Alta Verapaz, to prevent the detention of Mariano Cruz; the near-lynching of a detective in San Pedro Solomá, Huehuetenango; and an incident in the San Martín Jilotepeque, Chimaltenango, hamlet of Chalva, following the arrest of two young men for distributing "subversive propaganda": some 300 residents surrounded the police post and threatened to burn it down unless the two were released — they were.[106]

In October 1979, peasants of the "El Izotal" plantation in Rafael Dueñas, Sacatepéquez, affiliated to the CNT and CNUS, reinforced by contingents from local peasant leagues and workers from a large textile factory marched for the right to "Life, Labour and Organization". Attacked by police in Chimaltenango, peasants and factory workers travelled to Guatemala City and occupied the centrally located "El Calvario" church, protesting against poor labour conditions and violence in their home departments. Armed police broke up the sit-in on 12 October, dragging protestors from the church and systematically beating them; large numbers of Guatemala City residents gathered around the church in solidarity with the sit-in and had to be driven off with tear gas. The "disappearance" of one protestor dragged from the church and detained, "El Izotal" farmworker Miguel Angel Najarro Archila, became the focus of further protests. When Najarro's body was reported found with a bullet in the back in the countryside miles from the capital, further protests were organized by labour and student groups. On 20 October, the traditional day of demonstrations in commemoration of the 1944 overthrow of the Ubico regime, trade union, peasant, student and slum-dweller organizations joined in mass demonstrations protesting against rural repression and the fate of the "El Izotal" protestors.[107]

In 1979, the advance of peasant organization was countered by increasing violence in most parts of the country. Plans for a general strike of plantation workers on the South Coast, set for the key harvest months of February to April 1980 — the first important mass action organized by the CUC — were known to the authorities and led to a rash of "disappearances" and killings of members of peasant leagues in the western part of the country. A classic instance occurred in the community "El Naranjo" in Santa Lucía Cotzumalguapa, Escuintla, on 18 and 19 October 1979. Plain-clothesmen armed with submachine-guns moved into El Naranjo, broke down the doors of the local peasant league leaders, Pablo Almira, Francisco Almira Skrec, José Luis Tejada Guzmán and Demesio Sutuj, and took them away in official police vehicles. In the following weeks their bodies were found on neighbouring cotton plantations.[108]

Despite the crackdown on rural organizers the South Coast strike for higher wages went ahead in April 1980. It would subsequently be seen as a major victory for the CUC, in spite of the very high costs. CUC leaflets distributed in the last months of 1979 outlined in words and cartoons the wage demands to be made: 5 *quetzales* (equivalent to US$5) for every ton of cane cut, and every *quintal* (equivalent to 100 pounds) of cotton picked. These demands were justified by reference to the high prices paid on the international market for Guatemalan cotton and sugar — compared to derisory wages — the rising cost of food, and, in some leaflets, the Salvadorean farmworkers' victory in obtaining in November 1979 what the CUC described as a "minimum wage of 6 *quetzales* a day".[109]

> The majority of the peasants of our country are now cutting the cane and cotton of the planters. We bring our wives and our children so that they also work to help us to earn a few centavos more. We Indian peasants came once more to the heat of the coast where exploitation and disrespect awaited us. With the miserable salary that the rich man gives us we cannot

feed our families well, or give them clothing, medicines or a house.

Although the CUC pamphlets provide an excellent illustrated briefing on the exploitation of both permanent and seasonal plantation workers and raise such issues as the impact of mechanization on the day labourers, in retrospect, they appear even more remarkable for the manner in which they recognize the risks facing striking agricultural workers in Guatemala, and propose self-defence measures to reduce them:

> In this leaflet we are going to say that it is possible that the planters raise our salary. Read this leaflet slowly, talk about it with your compañeros and let's try to bring ourselves together to achieve our just demands.[110]

> We know that the exploiters will respond to our struggle by increasing still more the repression we already suffer daily. There will be more soldiers, more arms, more spies, more detectives. The repression is the other face of exploitation and it will continue to fall upon us whether we fight or not. So we must improve our means to defend our Organization, our leaders and our struggle. We cannot permit any of our companeros to be grabbed by them while alone. With our own intelligence, with our own strength and all of the means at our disposal we will defend ourselves against those who threaten our lives and the lives of our people.[111]

Repression of peasants associated with peasant leagues acclerated after November 1979, affecting both those already at work on the plantations and peasant communities of the coastal departments of Escuintla, Retalhuleu and San Marcos. To some extent repression was matched by guerrilla actions against the coastal plantations: crop duster aircraft were attacked and destroyed on the ground, cane fields burned, and attacks on military commissioners working as labour contractors increased.[112] CUC members interviewed after the strike expressed appreciation for the guerrilla actions as having drawn the security forces' fire away from the farmworkers.

An account published in the Guerrilla Army of the Poor's monthly magazine *Compañero* said the strike began on an afternoon in February 1980 at the "Tehuantepec" plantation in Santa Lucía Cotzumalguapa, Escuintla when 20 year old CUC leader Pablo Bautista "jumped on a loaded cart and called on his fellow workers to begin a work stoppage until they were granted the following demands: that the overseer be fired, fair weighing of cane on the plantation's scales, and a wage increase.[113] The strike then rapidly spread up and down the coast. An attempt to kidnap Pablo Bautista was thwarted by CUC self-defence action and, though wounded, he managed to escape through the cane fields. The assassination attempt infuriated the workers and increased their determination. The call for a work stoppage spread to the entire region.

> Machetes in hand, thousands of peasants occupied farms and intercepted tractors, buses and trucks on highways. They forced them to drive to the nearest service station and fill up with gas which was later used to burn the residential areas of several plantations. The strikers blocked the highways with carts and trailers loaded with sugar cane, and came close to occupying the heart of sugar cane production: Santa Lucía Cotzumalguapa. . .
>
> The sugar cane cutters' strike involved more than a hundred thousand workers. It was a violent mass action which, aside from achieving economic gains, increased the class consciousness of the workers involved.[114]

The same report points out that the strike was by no means spontaneous; it had been preceded by a series of partial work stoppages on several plantations, called by the CUC, which had served as practice for the great February-April strike.

The strike lasted somewhat more than a month and stopped harvesting on much of the South Coast; tens of thousands of peasant workers supported the strike, while the estimated number of CUC members involved range from 4,000 to 17,000.[115] A government and growers' associations publicity campaign characterized the strike as insurrection and at least 100 supposed strike leaders were assassinated or "disappeared" in its course. The threat it posed to the harvest, however, forced a partial surrender to the CUC's demands: a rise in the average daily agricultural wage to 3.20 *quetzales* — more than three times the previous wage. Although not all the growers would *pay* this minimum in the future, the strike did represent an unprecedented economic and political victory for an organization which for the first time had sought to unite peasants from different regions and diverse ethnic origin in a common cause.

A CUC member interviewed in November 1980 by Guatemalan poet and art critic Alaíde Foppa (who was detained and "disappeared" in Guatemala shortly afterward) described the coastal strike as CUC's first major action, and illustrated its concept of active self-defence: actions to prevent the killing or abduction of its members and supporters.[116] She also makes clear that although the CUC stopped short of armed guerrilla actions, it sympathized with the guerrillas and considered them brothers pursuing the same aims by different means:[117]

> Q. . . . there are not only verbally expressed demands, but also self-defense? In what form?
>
> A. Well, for example, we work mostly in sabotage, scattering small tacks in the road, making ditches or tunnels, or destroying bridges so that it is

149

not so easy for the enemy to advance. We also defend ourselves with our machetes and everything we have at hand.

Q. How or in what way do peasant groups, or more concretely, the CUC, feel supported by the armed struggle, or in what way do you feel you are helping the guerrillas from your position?

A. As an organization we feel it by means of the actions they have done. They have also done sabotage. When there are armed encounters, the enemy pays attention to them and leaves us in peace. Also, the distribution of pamphlets by the guerrillas helps us in that we can feel as brothers in the struggle. It is not only we who suffer and struggle. If the enemy does not sleep, we do not sleep either.[117]

In the aftermath of the South Coast strike Indians in many communities were faced with a series of undesirable options. They could remain in their communities, despite insufficient land to produce a livelihood, and the real risk of murder at the hand of the army's counter-insurgency forces; they could travel to the coast and risk murder there, since their very clothing identified them as coming from Indian communities classified as "subversive", or they could flee to the cities.

With the destruction of the co-operative movement in the highlands, the closure of the north to colonization, the militarization of the highlands by counter-insurgency forces, and the suspension of migrant labour on the coast, the highland peasantry was caught between murder and starvation.[118] It was in this period that the Indian-based guerrilla movements of the Guerrilla Army of the Poor (*Ejercito Guerrillero de los Pobres*, (EGP)) and the Revolutionary Organization of the People in Arms (*Organización Revolucionaria del Pueblo en Armas*, (ORPA)) took on major importance.

The escalation of repression against the highland Indian communities and co-operatives forced whole communities to either leave their homes and lands, or develop what they called means of "self-defence"; in practice this meant watching out for army patrols and, whenever they posed a threat to the community, attempting to block their passage, or co-ordinating mass flight into the mountains until the threat was gone. Rigoberta Menchú, daughter of Vicente Menchú, one of the leaders of the Indian delegation burnt to death in the Spanish Embassy in January 1980, has described the process or organization in the Indian highlands of El Quiché in a series of interviews which took place in 1982 when she was 25 years old. She describes going with her family to South Coast plantations each year, because their own land could not support them for more than four or five months in the year, how her father, a community leader, was once jailed, and once kidnapped, tortured and left for dead, and tells how she herself became a *catequista* (a lay catechist) and worked with the Catholic Action organization in her community. According to her, after 1977, the people of the area began to organize for self-defence against the army — largely through flight — with the *catequistas* very much at the centre of community organization:

> From then on we knew we had to organize ourselves. As I said before, I was and am an ardent Catequista. In the community we began to reflect together about what the Bible told us. The story of Judith, for example, impressed me a great deal; she cut off the head of the king in order to save her people. We also understood that, faced by the violence of the rich, we had to respond with our own violence, the violence of justice. Also the example of Moses helped us a great deal: Moses who led his people across the world in order to save them. We began to build camps in the mountains where we would spend the night, with the aim of preventing the troops from killing us while we slept. In the daytime, we had taught the children to keep watch over the roads so they could warn us whenever the soldiers arrived in town. This was the beginning of our self defense. And it's through the Bible that we organized our struggle. On the other hand, we also had the example of our ancestors, among whom were many martyrs and great heroes. . . In this way we organized ourselves, and the response was an enormous repression and, above all, the persecution of the Catequistas. . .[119]

Vicente Menchú and other Indian community leaders subsequently joined the CUC, as at that time, according to Rigoberta Menchú, they saw their problems as "political", and amenable to peaceful, political (not military) solutions.

It was after the death of Vicente Menchú and the other delegates from the Quiché, Ixil, Achi and Pocomchi at the Spanish Embassy that some former CUC members of El Quiché created an organization called Revolutionary Christians "Vicente Menchú" (*Cristianos Revolucionarios Vicente Menchú*, (CRVM)). A year after the Embassy fire, in January 1981, the CUC joined the CRVM and organizations of university and secondary students, slum-dwellers, trade-unionists and others in the *Frente Popular 31 de enero* (FP-31) (31 January Popular Front), named in honour of the Spanish Embassy victims.[120] The FP-31 pursued a policy of direct action for both labour and political objectives as well as "self-defence" techniques. Initially sympathetic to the guerrillas, they gradually shifted from friendly approval to whole-hearted support, as more and more of their members were killed, tortured or forced underground. By 1982 the counter-insurgency tactics of mass counter-terror had completely obscured the difference between armed and unarmed struggle, making such distinctions irrelevant as far as the Guatemalans themselves were concerned: by then non-violent resistance led only to death.

The New Guerrillas

The development of mass urban and peasant organizations in the 1970s and their eventual union in broad fronts was related to changing economic conditions and the backruptcy of traditional trade unions and political parties in the face of systematic state terror.

In the rural areas the CUC united the peasants, in the cities the trade-unions, through CNUS, united with student and slum-dwellers' organizations. The escalating repression of Lucas García's first months in government further cemented this union, and generated a new umbrella organization linking both urban, trade-union, and peasant organizations with church groups and political opposition parties in the Democratic Front Against Repression (*Frente Democrático Contra la Represión*, (FDCR)). Founded by a General Assembly of representatives of 140 organizations called by CNUS in February 1979, the *Frente* included all the CNUS affiliates, the CUC, the student organizations AEU, FERG and others, the Roman Catholic Committee for Justice and Peace, the Democratic socialist Party and, subsequently, Manuel Colom Argueta's party, the FUR. Firmly pluralistic from the beginning, the FDCR's declaration of principles included:

> The commitment to fight permanently against repression and for the achievement of the democratic rights of the people;
> The unity and common cause of all sectors of the people of Guatemala affected by the repression and who are prepared to fight against it;
> Respect for the integrity and independence in matters of organization, ideology of philosophy, politics and religion of the participant organizations.[121]

While serving as a medium for denouncing repression through the regular publication of bulletins documenting arrests, torture and murder on a case by case basis, the FDCR, from its inception, served as a central co-ordinating body uniting Guatemalan mass organizations in opposition to the government. While serving as spokesman for virtually the whole opposition, armed opposition was left to guerrilla organizations working independently of, though in sympathy with, the mass organizations united in the *Frente*.

From the mid-1970s, under the Lucas García government, four guerrilla organizations were active in Guatemala, all differing radically in composition and tactics from the guerrilla groups of the 1960s, although influenced by veterans of the 1960s insurgent experience. A difference was that while the guerrillas of the 1960s largely failed to incorporate the Indian peasantry into their movement, those of the 1970s consciously bent their energies toward that end, and, helped by unprecedented massive repression in the rural areas, achieved it to a very significant extent. The changing strategies have been outlined as follows:

The guerrilla groups of the 1960's — young middle class *Ladinos* who refused to be coopted by the regime — had fallen victim to the delusions of the *foco* theory. They offered their lives for the liberation of an oppressed peasantry, but neglected all but the most perfunctory efforts to gain the peasants' support. they felt deeply the immense injustice to which the *Indigenas* had been subjected for centuries — but lacked the knowledge to penetrate their secret world ... the guerrilla groups that have emerged in the mid and late 1970's after a few years of deceptive tranquillity, have learned from the errors of the past. Rejecting a purely military approach, they began by concentrating systematically on the development of a peasant base. Indeed the Ejército Guerrillero de los Pobres — the first of the new guerrilla groups — initiated military action only after three years of secret work among the Indígenas of the Altiplano.[122]

The *Ejército Guerrillero de los Pobres*, (EGP) (Guerrilla Army of the Poor), in its own publications, describes its organizational work as having begun in January 1972, when 15 "founders" entered Guatemala from Mexico through the Ixcán region of El Quiché. Organizers worked both in the northern areas of El Quiché and Huehuetenango, and on the South Coast plantations. In November 1975 the EGP announced its existence and a series of actions in leaflets published in the Guatemalan news media.[123]

A second major guerrilla force organized in the Indian highlands, the Organization of the People in Arms (*Organizació1n del Pueblo en Armas*, (ORPA)) burst on the scene in the late 1970s, seemingly from nowhere. Its origins remain obscure to date. The two other organizations rounding out the guerrilla spectrum were the Rebel Armed Forces (*Fuerzas Armadas Rebeldes*, (FAR)), built on the survivors of the 1960s FAR, and a guerrilla group which originated from a sector of the Communist Party of Guatemala, the PGT (*Núcleo de Dirección Nacional del Partido Guate-malteco del Trabajo*).

While a high degree of grass-roots support for each of the four guerrilla organizations was the major qualitative change from the 1960s, a second was that the four organizations appear to have overcome the ideological divisions that had previously hampered the co-ordination of operations. In 1979 the four guerrilla organizations united under a joint command, the Guatemalan National Revolutionary Union (*Unidad Revolucionaria Nacional Guatemalteca*, (URNG)).

A January 1981 interview by a Mexican journalist with four Guatemalan Indian women, representing the four guerrilla groups linked in the URNG, illustrated both the new unity of the armed opposition and its successful integration of the Indian peasantry. The four women were sent by their respective organizations to a secret rendezvous in Guatemala City, and stated they had joined the guerrillas because there was no alternative:

> What those of us that are in the organization have in common is that we have nothing, and also that since the repression is the same and hits *any* kind of organization, we might as well join together ... the army has had to carry out massacres of entire villages, because now they have no way of knowing who helps the guerrillas and who doesn't.[124]

In the same interview, the guerrilla women described the changing perception of the guerrillas by the Indian people of the highlands from the 1960s to the present:

> In our indigenous languages ... at first we called them a word that means foreigner; then we called them "the gentlemen of the trees'; and now when the guerrilla arrives at a community, now they tell us that 'the brothers' have arrived.[125]

A similar view of the changing relations and increasing identification between the guerrilla movement and the largely Indian rural population appears in a 1982 OXFAM-America publication based on a survey of foreign development workers on their experience in Guatemala; the testimonies help explain the new closeness between the guerrillas and the local population:

> During armed propaganda meetings, the guerrillas wear native dress and speak the Indian languages. Although they destroy property and kill local political bosses, landowners, liquor merchants, and military personnel, they never terrorize the general population. They help organize people for community defense and provide an effective structure for community survival in the face of the collapse of local cooperatives, schools, health clinics, and other institutions. Most important, they provide young people with an alternative to conscription in the national army. The guerrilla organizations, in contrast to the national army, call upon Indian youths to defend their people and to affirm their ethnic identities.[126]

The same report cites excerpts from statements by individual respondents who were asked if members of their communities had co-operated with or joined the guerrillas and why:

> Many people did begin to join the guerrillas, while many more were sympathetic or quietly supportive. The guerrillas are the only remaining source of defense left to a community or family. I know of villages that experienced actual massacres against innocent campesinos, who were not even members of coops. The survivors of these massacres would often turn to the guerrillas. With all their anger about the murders of their kin and neighbors, there was nowhere else to turn.
> . . .

Some of my friends talked about joining the guerrillas in 1980 on the grounds that they would be safer with them than at home.
. . .

[People were joining the guerrilla organizations] because they felt that there was no way they would survive in their communities and outrightly work for change. Their family members had been killed and they had no choice but to go into hiding and join the guerrilla movement.
. . .

One women, a good friend, wrote me that she may join the guerrillas. She stated that her brother had been killed and that she was next. She had worked for the Catholic Church. She said that she had no other choice; it was either death or join the guerrillas.[127]

In considering the growth of the guerrilla movement in the late 1970s credit should go both to the guerrilla organizers' ground work and to the programmed repression by the Laugerud and Lucas García regimes. The Indian peasantry appears to have been both attracted to the guerrilla movement by the nature of its organization and action, and pushed into it by the repression of all other forms of grass-roots organization. These two factors, coupled to the rising desperation of land-hungry peasants, were sufficient to give the guerrilla movement a broad popular base by the late 1970s. Sociologist Gabriel Aguilera Peralta describes it as a process of integration:

These organizations have managed to achieve a high level of integration with the popular sectors, particularly with the poor peasants of indigenous ethnic origin. As a consequence, these organizations have not only been able to resist the waves of terror, but also to grow in rapid fashion. At the end of 1979 it was estimated that there were at least 1,800 armed guerrillas; a year later, the figure could easily have been triple that number.[128]

By mid-1982 guerrilla actions, including ambushes, short-term occupations of large private farms and villages, and others, were regular occurrences in 16 of the country's 22 departments. By then, also, the mass organizations of the late 1970s, united in new broad fronts, had moved from timid toleration or verbal support for the guerrillas' way of struggle, to overt backing, as in the May 1982 manifesto of the FP-31:

The 31 January Popular Front —FP-31— and the Revolutionary Mass Organizations that belong to it reiterate that it continues and will continue to fight with the other patriotic, popular and democratic sectors of our people in the victorious, difficult, and necessary Popular Revolutionary War directed by the Guatemalan National Revolutionary Union formed by the Guerrilla Army of the Poor —EGP—, the Rebel Armed Forces —FAR—, the Organization of the People in Arms —

155

ORPA—, the Guatemalan Party of Labour —PGT— (Núcleo de Dirección Nacional).

The 31 January Popular Front also calls for consolidation of our struggle and efforts by the constitution of a Patriotic Front of National Unity and the installation of a Revolutionary Government, Patriotic, Popular and Democratic, that shall be truly representative of these sectors and that based on the five programmatic points for government stated by the Guatemalan National Revolutionary Union —URNG— in their joint proclamation, setting the basis for putting an end to the exploitation, repression and discrimination that our people now suffer.[129]

6. A Security System for the 1980s

The Civilian Security Services

The functions and force levels of the National Police, its political branch, the Detective Corps, and the Treasury Guard changed little in the course of the 1970s. Fairly accurate statistics on the numbers for each corps in 1974 are available from Public Safety Program documents.[130] The National Police grew from about 3,000 men in 1965 to 5,368 in 1974, including the 324 members of the Detective Corps. By 1980, the National Police was estimated to have grown to a force of about 7,000.[131] In 1974 the Treasury Guard remained at about its 1965 level, at 1,073; no figure on its 1980s strength is available.

Although in the 1970s all sections of the National Police were apparently involved in the extra-legal execution both of common criminals and political suspects, the Detective Corps remained the principal civilian political police agency, working in tandem with the army's own intelligence division. Unlike their military counterparts the detectives did not always remain completely anonymous. In 1976 two cases received enormous publicity when it was denied that students seized by detectives were in detention, despite published evidence to the contrary.[132] José Fernando Lobo Dubón was arrested on 1 June 1976 with four other students and taken to the Detective Corps headquarters for interrogation; the others were released and raised the alarm. An open letter from Lobo Dubón's father to President Laugerud, holding him responsible for the detectives' actions, was published in the news media, and a press campaign waged for Lobo Dubón's release but he was never seen again. The family of another "disappeared" student, Mario René Castellanos de León, also published an open letter denouncing his capture by nine members of the Detective Corps "travelling in vehicles belonging to the Detective Corps. Toyota H-Ace number 117555 and Ford Maverick number 545560 ..." The press campaign waged by the influential Castellanos family eventually prompted a press statement from the Ministery of the Interior in October 1976 in which it "categorically denied that Castellanos de León is held in any of the detention centres ... this is a case of kidnapping which has not been solved ..."[133]

The dismissal of the head of the Detective Corps, Colonel Manuel de Jesús Valiente Téllez (a police, not an army colonel) in August 1980, and a subsequent purge of the corps led to public statements by Valiente Téllez which throw some light on the extra-legal activities of the National Police, and reveal an ongoing vendetta between different security chiefs.

Valiente Téllez was the subject of several assassination attempts after his dismissal, and many of the more than 50 detectives dismissed along with him were killed in "death-squad" attacks. While still serving as head of the Detective Corps in 1978-80 Valiente Téllez had directed a private security agency, known as "*Los Vigilantes*", and possibly conflicts between his private business operations and his official police work had led to his dismissal; in any case after August 1980 the employees of "*Los Vigilantes*" also became targets for "death-squad" murders.

In October 1980 Valiente Téllez went to the Guatemalan press after a submachine-gun attack on his house, which he blamed, along with the previous series of murders, on Colonel Pedro García Arredondo, who had replaced him as Chief of Detectives, and previously had headed "Commando Six", a National Police rapid reaction force in the capital (see below). Valiente Téllez attributed the spate of murders, and attacks on him, to a personal vendetta born of past clashes between "Commando Six" and the Detective Corps, due to incidents in which detectives had stopped unmarked "Commando Six" cars travelling without registration plates on unauthorized operations. He warned that if the attacks did not stop he would go to the public with information on the extra-legal actions of the security services:

> It is right that they pursue and kill criminals, but it is unjust that they harass people who collaborate with the government in fighting crime ... With this attack on my residence I have confirmed that the present chief of the detective corps has personal grievances against me ... We do not want to hurt those who are pursuing us, because it is not their fault, as they receive their orders and they must carry them out. But they will see: times will change. I have given instructions so that if they do not leave us alone ... although only one of us survives, we will make known who is responsible for the chaos in Guatemala.[134]

The attacks against Valiente Téllez, his family and his employees continued in 1981. In July his younger brother was killed, and National Police detectives attacked mourners after the funeral, gunning down eight members of "*The Vigilantes*". Unable to deny the detectives had killed them, Chief of Detectives García Arredondo claimed the victims had attacked them. In a press statement on 6 July Valiente Téllez again denounced not only the attacks against his family and employees, but accused both Arredondo and his third in command, Virgilio Gudiel Ortega, of other "kidnappings and murders".[135] He also described the techniques used to disguise police vehicles for "death-squad" operations:

(Valiente Téllez) said he had never had problems with the National Police, except the detective corps, Commando Six, and the Narcotics Division. He also said that in the past months 27 agents of "Los Vigilantes", including members of his family have been killed by the action of members of the detective corps. In this section they change license plates and the colour of vehicles in order to carry out assaults, he said.[136]

In early December 1981 Téllez was wounded by a sniper as he stood on his rooftop terrace, and on 29 December his house was attacked in an assault lasting over 20 minutes by heavily armed men with granades and submachine-guns; his wife and 17 year old daughter were killed, his two sons wounded. On 3 January, Valiente Téllez, in hospital recovering from his wound, slipped out and, with his three surviving brothers and three children, caught a place for Miami.[137]

Once out of the country he confirmed that the regular security forces were responsible for murders attributed to "death-squads", and declared that "as a head of the detective corps he had himself been involved in similar murder and 'disappearance' operations ordered by higher authorities."[138]

At the time of the Valiente Téllez affair the Detective Corps was divided into criminal and political investigations divisions (*Sección de Investiga-ciones Criminales* and *Sección de Investigaciones Especiales*);[139] it was also the base for and staffed Guatemala's branch of INTERPOL (the Guatemalan branch of the International Association of Criminal Police).[140] In the mid-1970s some tasks previously assigned to the Detective Corps were transferred to other special units within the National Police force in the capital. Amnesty International, in a 1981 report, noted that "Commando Six" and the *Pelotón Modelo* (Model Platoon) were "especially active during polical demonstrations and have been identified as having detained demonstrators who subsequently 'disappeared'."[141]

"Commando Six" (also known as "SWAT")[142] had considerably more responsibilities than the control of demonstrations, and was a rapid response force called on to deal with such emergencies as guerrilla assaults, raids on suspected hideouts of political or criminal suspects and narcotics control operations. "Commando Six" was equipped with the most sophisticated weaponry available to the National Police and provided with transport and communications equipment enabling it to reach any trouble spot in the capital in a matter of minutes of being notified of a crisis.[143] Its most widely publicized operation during the Lucas García regime was the assault on the Spanish Embassy occupied by Quiché Indians on 31 January 1980.[144] "Commando Six's" key role in the capital is illustrated by the reputation of its top officers. Police Colonel Juan Antonio Lima López, assassinated in January 1980, was well known to opposition groups as a top detective interrogator. Known as "El Chino Lima" in the mid-1960s, he was first denounced as a specialist in the torture of political prisoners in a clandestine publication in January 1966.[145]

Although the detective corps and special units such as "Commando Six" had, with the army's own (intelligence) units, primary responsibility in dealing with political suspects, every National Police zone headquarters both in the capital and the provinces also had special groups for investigations — and covert, extra-legal action.

The elimination of petty criminals and suspects from among the urban poor was frequently the task of these groups in conjunction with the Detective Corps. Although in the capital the Detective Corps and units from the 4th Division headquarters of the National Police were particularly notorious for "death-squad" killings of urban "undesirables", each police division likewise maintained "dirty squads" charged with picking up and killing suspected criminals and assisting the army's political murder operations. These "dirty squads" were based on a traditional system whereby patrolmen demoted for criminal or disciplinary offences must atone by taking on particularly hazardous or dirty work. Known as the "*rebajados*" (demoted) they provide a pool of men not officially part of the police force, but available to carry out any task assigned to them.

As far back as 1966, in the few weeks of press freedom that followed the inauguration of President Méndez Montenegro, a public denunciation was made by a lawyer who protested that his client, a prisoner held on criminal charges, had been held incommunicado in the charge of the "chief of the *rebajados* of the Second Police Division". He said he had been tortured with a rope around his neck, systematic beatings with a rubber hose, and "with the famous black hood".[146] A more recent account of the *rebajado* system was given by former Vice-President of Guatemala Francisco Villagrán Kramer after his resignation in 1980:

> The police in Guatemala have a system of agents, or let's say policemen, who have violated laws and regulations and thereby are separated and no longer active in the police force. They are relieved of their duties and placed in a different category, which is called '*rebajado*'. And this means they have been demoted, so these people ... are used for the purposes of assassination, and to pay them confidential funds are used. The word 'confidential funds' refers to ... a fund that all police in the world have to pay for information and things of that nature. So from these funds these elements are paid, a lesser salary than the policemen, but with the expectation of returning to the police force ...[147]

Although the detectives and regular forces of the National Police occasionally carried out political police activities in rural areas, the Treasury Police was the principal civilian security agency outside the cities. In October 1979, the peasant organization CUC described the Treasury Police as having evolved into:

> one of the most repressive of the police bodies in the country, above all in

the *Tierra Fria* ["Cold Lands", i.e. highlands] and in the border areas, like San Marcos . . . Before, they were simple employees who, with the excuse of preventing the making of *cuxa* [alcohol prepared from fermented fruit] and controlling contraband, abused the peasants by demanding bribes. . . Since 1974 they came to depend from the Ministry of Interior, in the times of General Arana. And so they changed to become a force of control and repression . . . With the pretext of seeking *cuxa* or contraband the Treasury Police enter houses to search papers and everything they can find . . . As well as entering to control the struggles of the people and their leaders, they enter to steal everything they can find, eggs, water, firewood, money . . .[148]

The CUC's assessment does not differ essentially from that of the US Army Area Handbook for Guatemala (1970):

[The Treasury Police] have been charged with being alert to any indication of subversive activity. They are expected to detect the entry, exit, internal movement or other activity of domestic or alien subversive elements. They are directed to enforce all laws relating to peace and public order, as well as to act as auxiliary to the military in case of national emergency. Under the conditions of instability existing during 1968, the latter responsibilities demanded more of their time and effort than did their primary functions. The training and experience gained in raiding illegal stills proved most valuable in ferreting out guerrilla arms caches.[149]

Backbone of the Security System: the Army

The army remained the backbone of the security system. By March 1982, when Lucas García was ousted from office, the regular army numbered some 18,000 and the Military Police had grown to an estimated 3,000.[150]

In 1980 the Guatemalan army of some 15,000 men was led by a corps of almost 1,400 officers, the vast majority of whom, recruited in adolescence, had attended one of the five military secondary schools known as "Adolfo V. Hall" institutes.[151] From the "Adolfo V. Hall" institutes suitable students go to the *Escuela Politécnica*, the military academy, in San Juan Sacatepéquez, just outside Guatemala City, and, after an eight month course graduate with a rank of second lieutenant.[152]

Immediately after graduation young officers may go on to university studies in Guatemala or abroad, or be immediately assigned to one of the military zones. Assignments are rotated and promotions follow fairly regularly at four month intervals. A leading authority on Guatemala's military sub-culture identifies the counter-insurgency specialists as an army elite.

The officers in the lower ranks have the opportunity to acquire experience in combat in the areas of guerrilla confrontation, and to take ranger and jungle fighting courses in the specialized centre for these studies ... in the department of Petén. Whether officers or soldiers, the Kaibiles are the elite troops of the Guatemalan army. Previously, there were frequent tours to military centres in the United States and the Canal Zone, but now these visits are rare and officers are sent instead to Taiwan or Israel.[153]

The top of the training ladder — the Guatemalan staff college, the Centre for Military Studies — provides "rather complete" technical training for top officers; promotion to senior ranks is contingent on candidates passing "intensive staff courses".[154]

Institutional perks that much improved even the junior officers' standard of living contributed to the cohesion of the officer corps throughout the 1960s and 1970s. Guatemalan sociologist, Gabriel Aguilera, in 1982, described this factor:

The officers' system of socialization tends to isolate them from the national social environment, favouring relationships among the military, even at the family level. Although salaries are low, there is a kind of social salary represented by privileges such as permits to import cars duty-free, the use of the commissary (a warehouse of imported duty-free merchandise), the use of the military club and other recreational facilities, family shopping holidays to Miami at low cast, educational facilities for their children in the pre-military "Adolfo Hall" institute, opportunities for young officers to enter universities, training and pleasure trips to Taiwan. In addition, each army officer receives a lot with a house of his own in the immense military colony which is being built in Zone 5 of the 'Santa Rosita' area of the capital. There, a new military hospital is also under construction for the use of the men in uniform. (The lots and subsequently the houses were granted to officers during the intra-military tension occasioned by the 1974 and 1978 electoral frauds.)[155]

Status and training of the officers and other ranks differs dramatically: the majority of the rank and file is recruited through press-gangs, methods not radically different from those used in the 19th Century. Conscription traditionally applies only to the rural poor, in particular the peasantry of indigenous origin who have the least power to resist. A Guatemalan army officer noted in a 1976 article that "recruitment focusses especially on people from the countryside: as they are the ones who least resist the fulfillment of this obligation".[156] As in the past, the military commissioners are responsible for fulfilling the periodic recruitment quotas. The increase in manpower needs and growing resistance to conscription, has, however, meant that military commissioners increasingly need the assistance of armed bodies of troops to fulfil their quotas.

Exemptions from military service were, in the past, formally provided for the 18-30 age group (who, by law, constituted the inactive "reserve") for various reasons, including being the sole support of a family, married with children, or studying. Exemption could, and to some extent still can, be bought with a small bribe; consequently, in practice, all but the rural poor are exempt from conscription.

General Ydígoras Fuentes, in his March 1963 Presidential message to the Guatemalan congress praised the army and gave his own rationale for its peasant composition:

> Fortunately our peasants, who constitute the cream of our Army, understand the land, love the life of the countryside, are extremely frugal, and can walk many leagues heavily burdened without tiring. These are the qualities we are using.[157]

He might have added that they were also easier to catch and less able to resist conscription.

A November 1966 classified US government report criticized conscription and training procedures:

> The system of obtaining and inducting Army conscripts is antiquated. Twice each year, one quarter of the Army's enlisted strength is replaced with new conscripts; a steady flow throughout the year would be preferable. There is no centralized training and assignment system. Other than minimum health standards, there are few if any criteria for selection of individual conscripts. If the conscript pays between $25 and $100 in Quetzales, he can avoid service.[158]

Recruits in the 1980s are still generally press-ganged at random, on market days, when dances are raided or rural buses stopped; Indian peasants remain the primary targets of conscription. Training, however, has developed since 1966. All recruits now receive three months' basic training at a "boot camp" at the Jutiapa army base "Aguilar Santa María", with 6-800 recruits in each "class"; the average period of active service in the late 1970s was 18 months.[159]

In July 1980 the Ministry of Defense issued new regulations for mandatory military service, reducing the range of exemptions and extending the period of active service to 30 months. Exemptions are still formally possible for the oldest sons of families who have exclusive responsibility for supporting younger siblings, and for young men with a brother already serving in the armed forces. The Defense Ministry held the revised "Recruitment Plan" represented a significant reform in conditions of (obligatory) service.

> The Military Service represents for the Guatemalan citizen, in accordance with the substantial modifications of the recruitment system, the

guarantee of a basic salary of $50.00 monthly with progressive increases and a proportional yearly payment every year. They will have a life insurance policy under the protection of the Instituto de Previsión Militar and will have the right to an additional $25.00 monthly, as assistance to their parents while they serve.[160]

The new regulations were in response to a need for a much higher level of manpower than in the past, to overcome the problem of rapid turnover in its largely conscript army (a problem also facing El Salvador as its civil war stepped up) and, through financial and social welfare inducements, to improve morale within the army's ranks. While the Guatemalan army had traditionally offered literacy training, the 1980 plan was promoted as offering recruits training opportunities in a number of trades — from nursing, mechanics, driving, building, baking, to repairing refrigerators. The recruits would also receive "the recommendation and certificates necessary for their success as a respected citizen, after having complied with their duty of service to the country".[161]

Whether or not the offers were made good, implementation of recruitment after 1980 was not less, but more arbitrary and violent than before. It continued to follow the traditional patterns, with exemptions determined in practice by the family's ability to pay bribes to the recruiting officers. Recruitment procedure is described in the OXFAM-America survey of on-the-spot workers cited previously:

Basically this is the way the army conscripts: they will enter a town, close off all roads, and start searching for teenagers between the ages of 15 and 21 ... They will grab anyone, especially if they do not have I.D.'s. The army takes all the new "recruits" to the nearest installation.
. . .
The army trucks enter town on market day, surround the market place and kidnap young men between 18 and 20 years old. No notice is given to their families. They simply do not return home, and their families must get the news from other adults in the marketplace. The captured youths are tied together and loaded into trucks.
. . .
I twice witnessed recruiting, once in the bus terminal and once in the center of the departmental capital. With machine guns pointed at the recruit and working in teams of three, soldiers rounded up youths one at a time and brought them to a holding area. The soldiers would even enter waiting buses and tear young boys away from their parents. The people all knew better than to resist or protest. Later, I found out that more wealthy families had about a day to arrive with sufficient money to buy the freedom of their sons. Often, the families never learned what had happened or where their sons were, since they were always taken to serve in remote areas of the country and never served as agents of repression in their own towns and villages.[162]

Conscript training is a process of indoctrination in anti-Communism and systematic brutalization; in interviews, former conscripts have described sessions in which recruits are obliged to submit to regular beatings and treatment that could accurately be described as torture. Maltreatment is ordered as part of a toughening and desensitizing process, with members of the same training units alternating in giving and receiving physical punishment. Discipline is enforced and instilled by physical punishment. One source gave the following account:

> It appears to me that the brutality of the Guatemalan soldier originates in his training. One very dear friend of mine willingly joined the army, against my own protests. He told me afterwards that he was tortured in training. He showed me one torture called *puente roto* [broken bridge] that they used against him, and I tried it. It leaves no marks, but is profoundly painful.[163]

Indoctrination of recruits reduces anti-Communism to an "us or them" scenario, with a special emphasis on the "protection of the army as an institution". In the interview with a former conscript published in Amnesty International's 1981 report on Guatemala he attributed his work in a military intelligence assassination squad to the "brain wash" ("*lavado de coco*") received in training:

> . . . they had already brainwashed me; they had already filled my head with their own ideology . . . They told us: 'You are going to get orders. You are going out now.' They sent us out on the street in an army car. That's how we used to go out, as civilians, but to keep an eye on things especially to control the students, because there [in G-2] we went to different classes where they told us that the students could be guerrillas and that they were the people who cause the disorder in the streets, and that according to the law in the army's constitution, you've got to kill all of these people . . . So I realized that the army is a school for murderers, it's as simple as that. They said to me, if you discover your father is in subversive movements — I didn't understand the word, 'subversive', they said, is whatever is against the government and is what causes disorder in Guatemala — if your father is involved in groups like that, kill him, because if you don't he'll try and kill us . . .[164]

Asked whether he would have killed his father, his mother, or his sister, he said he would kill "anyone who turned up, if we were ordered to".[165]

In the same interview the informant gave an account of arrests, torture and killings in Guatemala City and in rural areas. In one raid on a rural town, the unit was ordered to kill anyone found to have certain "papers" in their homes linking them to suspect organizations:

> We'd go off in a truck; we'd get to the place we had to search, yes, search and so forth; I mean if there were any people there who were, well, suspicious character. Yes, we have got the right to kill him, and even more organizations where a lot of people get together — and there are guerrillas there too... In... where they killed... where we went, about 20 of us went through all the houses to see if we couldn't find any papers, the ones they'd told us about. When we found a paper in a house, we took the family out, and if there was just one person we killed him. And that's what happened.[166]

Training transmits to the Guatemalan soldier the message that he is authorized to kill subversives without any particular formalities and that subversives are classified in very broad categories; "anyone who is a suspicious character"; it also instils the conviction that those who resist orders or instructions to kill will themselves be killed:

> The soldiers can kill people when they have orders to, but can they kill people without orders, just because someone is a suspicious character? Yes, certainly, any of us can be ordered to kill any man like that, who is a suspicious character. Yes, we have got the right to kill him, and even more so if we have been given strict orders to. Yes, we have the right to commit these offences.
> What did the officers say?
> Well, they say that if we don't carry out all the orders that they give us, if we disobey, instead of them they will kill us, so you have to be very careful about all this.[167]

Similar accounts have been given by acquaintances of other conscript soldiers:

> They undergo an intense 'brainwashing' and are frightened with the threat of communism. It is said that communism will take way their land and rape their mothers, wives and sisters. For this reason, they must shoot anyone the officer says is a communist. They are then sent to areas of the country where they do not know the people or their language. Some go out on kill missions, murdering people like their own families under orders of an official.[168]

Following completion of military service, former conscripts are closely watched through the military reserve system; the cream of the departing troops are offered an opportunity to serve in the security services and in particular in the Mobile Military Police:

> An effort is made to imbue them with the basic elements of military ideology and to maintain some kind of link with them when their period of service has ended. Those who demonstrate special abilities and loyalty

have the opportunity of enrolling in the mobile military police. This is a paramilitary corps which operates all over the country (i.e. not restricted to zones), and carries out repressive functions in the rural areas and police functions in the urban zones; members of the corps may also be 'rented' out to wealthy persons as bodyguards. Others go on to become military commissioners.[169]

The ideological indoctrination of army recruits is often accompanied by separating the recruit from his roots. Training is deliberately designed to break down identification with the many indigenous ethnic groups from which most of the recruits are drawn, through Spanish language instruction and a policy that recruits are never detailed to their home areas. This has become particularly important since the late 1970s when guerrilla groups emerged comprised largely of Indian peasants speaking their own languages.

Given the growing participation of some ethnic groups in political military organizations, the dispersion is necessary in order to avoid a possible identification by the soldier with the guerrilla of his ethnic group.[170]

Military service, moreover, leads to what Aguilera calls "*ladinización*": "the abandonment of the habits and forms of perception characteristic of the ethnic groups."[171]

In 1974, the permanent force of the Mobile Military Police (PMA) was officially given as 1,140, although reserve forces could be called up when private contractors required, and paid, for PMA services. Of the permanent force, 400 men were based at the Escuintla headquarters as a rapid deployment force, and 740 were detailed to roving detachments in the provinces.[172]Considerably more PMA personnel may have been assigned to serve private employers than comprised the permanent force itself; by 1974 most large farms and plantations had some PMA men on contract, as did many large businesses, banks and private individuals. The third major component of military forces, the military commissioners and their auxiliaries, probably numbered no less in 1974, and possibly considerably more than the estimated 9,000 reported serving in the late 1960s (no official figure has been released).

The leaflets and bulletins distributed by the CUC in the early 1980s included pointed descriptions of the different elements of the security system affecting the largely Indian peasantry. An October 1979 CUC leaflet outlined the principal military elements of the rural system, defining them as the military commissioners and the Mobile Military Police. At the local level the military commissioners provide a permanent presence,

people from the same communities, who after serving as soldiers remain tied to the army to repress our towns and villages ... That is how the army can be present even in the last corner of Guatemala.[173]

The commissioner system is described as the primary means for keeping an eye on rural organization:

The task of the military commissioners is to inform the Army of everything that happens in our communities and villages. They are watching wherever there is any seed of struggle, any meeting, any leaflet of protest, any leader, to go to denounce to their chiefs ... The other task of the Military Commissioners is to grab the kids to force them to go into the army. The commissioners have a chief of commissioners who communicates directly with an army officer to pass him lists of people who have meetings and try to organize themselves, of those who talk ... The chiefs of the commissioners pass the orders they receive from the army to the other commissioners and these pass them down to their "ears" [spies].[174]

The strongest criticism is reserved for the PMA, forces raised exclusively of former servicemen,

created to protect the plantations, the banks, the businesses of the powerful, the persons, homes and families of the exploiters. They are army and police at the same time ... They are the dogs who are most rabid, most cruel. In this corps they enlist those who have stood out in the army or in the police ... The planters and the capitalists go to the PMA and as if going to a market selling repression purchase the military police they want and take them to carry out the orders the powerful give them ... the letters PMA, above all on the south coast and in other areas where there are plantations are a signal of repression. They are hated and rejected by the honourable working population.[175]

In 1979, private contractors were required to pay about $120 per month for PMA services.[176]

The army's active and reserve forces, the PMA, and the military commissioners, were also augmented by an indeterminate, fluctuating number of plain-clothes civilian contract personnel serving as agents of military intelligence, and attached to each army garrison or headquarters. Military intelligence (G-2) had an officer in every garrison in direct communication with Section G-2 at the Army General Staff headquarters. The G-2 office controlled the intelligence service of each garrison, reporting directly to the top (by-passing the garrison commandant) on internal military affairs, but in consultation with the commandant on external security matters. The garrison G-2 officers administered the contracting of the *"confidenciales"* (confidential agents) and could issue arms permits and credentials to these agents. The *confidenciales* attached to each military establishment could be deployed locally, for intelligence gathering or operations, or shifted regionally to provide a manpower pool for covert operations, at the disposal of the Army General Staff or the presidential intelligence agency. The garrison or base commanders could also call upon the military commissioner network, the principal mechanism for intelligence collection, for covert operations.[177]

Many of the *confidenciales* attached to army garrisons, and the military commissioners, are civilians who also hold some allegiance to political parties of the far right, principally the MLN. One former Guatemalan official estimated that some 3,000 MLN members collaborated as paid *confidenciales* or as military commissioners or their auxiliaries, and explained the incorporation of armed MLN members into the army's apparatus as a means both to boost manpower and to *control* the MLN:

> The only way the Army can fully control the armed supporters of the MLN, who could threaten it in the future, is to know precisely who they are. The best way to keep an eye on them is by absorbing them. Some in the General Staff oppose this methodology on professional grounds. They use them only to control them; they don't like commanding civilians.[178]

The MLN has frequently claimed to have its own paramilitary forces; the majority of this manpower is, however, integrated into, and controlled by the army's intelligence and military commissioner system. MLN spokesmen perennially declare the readiness of the party's armed supporters to 'take up arms'. In 1975 the issue was Belize, when the MLN announced that "four thousand easterners were ready to take up arms without conditions or personal interests, awaiting the orders of President Laugerud to recover the territory of Belize."[179] In 1979 the MLN declared it would "push ahead with the creation of an 'anti-subversive' front to act as an "auxiliary force to the army in fighting the guerrillas".[180] In 1980, MLN leader Mario Sandoval Alarcón claimed the party kept a "paramilitary force of armed peasants and former police estimated by Sandoval to number 3,000".[181] By that time, however, the principal loyalties of most of the MLN's armed supporters probably went to the army, and not to the party or to its chief, Mario Sandoval Alarcón.

Intelligence Agencies: Assassination and "Disappearances"

At the top of the security system the presidential and military intelligence agencies worked in tandem, with Section G-2 of the Army General Staff providing most of the information, manpower and operational direction for intelligence collection and covert actions — including assassinations and "disappearances" — but with the presidential intelligence agency co-ordinating policy and action planning, and major operations. The presidential agency, under the Presidential General Staff, identified as the Regional Center for Telecommunications or called simply the Regional Center (*Centro Regional*), was based in the National Palace complex and provided the presidency with a communications and command nexus linking all parts of the security system, and a central intelligence agency with capabilities for special operations against intelligence targets.

The Regional Center was also the venue for high-level security meetings along the lines of those of the presidential security council established after the Castillo Armas coup in 1954; the group could include ministers responsible for defence and security, the heads of the police forces, and the President himself. According to one former official, Laugerud did not use the communications and logistic capabilities of the Regional Center only for security, but at times for beneficent purposes. After the great earthquake in February 1976, centralization of damage reports and co-ordination of relief and reconstruction operations were, according to this source, initially based in the Regional Center.[182] As under Arana, however, the Regional Center served Laugerud — and later Lucas — primarily as a security command centre, with co-ordination of a covert programme of selective assassination as part of the task. The Regional Center's direct involvement was convincingly alleged in several high-profile killings and attempted killings of leading political figures, among them Axel Mijangos Farfán, Vice-President of the Christian Democratic Party branch in Guatemala City, who was seized at his home in December 1975, tortured and killed, his mutilated body found dumped on a country road.[183] It was after a failed assassination attempt in 1976, however, that the Guatemalan public heard the first denunciation in the news media of a special operations unit operating from the Regional Center and described as the "Regional Police".[184] Manuel Colom Argueta, the capital's mayor from 1970 to 1974, leader of the FUR opposition party and a long-standing critic of military counter-insurgency tactics, was attacked by several men with submachine-guns, on 29 March 1976. Colom Argueta was wounded, but he and his own heavily armed bodyguards drove off the attackers; he subsequently took the unprecedented step of denouncing the "Regional Police" as behind the attack and naming the officers responsible:

> Colom immediately responded by addressing an open letter to President Laugerud, asserting that since his return to Guatemala one month previously his movements had been closely watched by plain clothes members of the Regional Police (Policía Regional), which he alleged to be a secret police force closely linked with disappearances and political assassinations. To facilitate investigations, Colom gave the names of three members of the Regional Police who had allegedly been watching him for

for the past month. When both the President's office and Interior Minister Vassaux denied the very existence of a Regional Police, Colom gave a press conference naming the leaders of this organization during the last three governments as Major Rolando Archila under Méndez Montenegro, Colonel Elías Ramírez under Arana, and Colonel Ramón Quinteros and Major Byron Lima under Laugerud.[185]

A further, detailed denunciation of the "Regional Police" was published in mid-1977 in a report issued by the National Committee for Trade Union Unity. Entitled *Fascism in Guatemala* (*El fascismo en Guatemala*) this report placed the repression of the trade union movement in a context of US security assistance and collaboration. The CNUS described the "Regional Police" as an aspect of US involvement in repression in Guatemala, stating that it operates under the name of Regional Communications Center (*Centro Regional de Comunicaciones*) and that it maintains daily radio contact with the other countries that are members of CONDECA (the Central American Defense Council) and with the Southern Command of the US army in the Panama Canal Zone.[186] CNUS also said "*La Regional*" receives orders directly from the head of state, and had a large staff which under Laugerud grew from 46 in 1974 to 71 in mid-1977.[187]

It was under the Lucas regime, however, that the presidential intelligence agency received widespread international publicity as the co-ordinating agency for Guatemala's "death-squad" killings. Amnesty International's 1981 report, *Guatemala: a Government Program of Political Murder*, concluded bluntly that the presidential agency co-ordinated "routine assassinations, secret detentions and summary executions" as part of a "clearly defined program of government". The report cited a wide range of sources in establishing the background of the agency, and its relation to the army's intelligence division:

> The National Palace complex makes it possible for the security services to centralize their communications and also to have access to the central files of the army intelligence division, which are reported to be housed in the Presidential Residence itself.[188]

The agency's head was identified as an army officer also serving as head of the Presidential General Staff.

At the time of the Amnesty International report, the presidential agency was officially known as either *Servicios de Apoyo a la Presidencia* (Presidential Support Services) or as *Servicios Especiales de Comuni-caciones de la Presidencia* (Special Communications Services of the Presidency); unofficially it was still known as the *Centro Regional*, or just *La Regional*. Opposition sources identified the head of the agency as the chief of the Presidential General Staff, Colonel Héctor Ismael Montalván, who chaired meetings of a special high level intelligence

171

group which could include the President, the Ministers of Defense and the Interior, the Army Chief of General Staff, the Chief of Military Intelligence, and the head of the National Police.[189] Apart from the President himself, only the Minister of Defense and the Chief of the Army General Staff had unrestricted access to information from the presidential agency. Under Lucas, the Minister of the Interior, although hierarchically in command of the civil police services, was a civilian and, according to one former official, needed written clearance from the Army Chief of Staff for access to specific information from the agency.

The presidential agency's operational side was primarily one of assessing threats, and delegating tasks. Opposition and other sources attributed responsibility for designation of targets for secret detention and murder, and approval of death lists prepared by other agencies, to the presidential agency.[190] Defector Elías Barahona distinguished between the preparation of death lists of supposed petty criminals (those whose killings would be attributed to the "*Escuadrón de la Muerte*") and those targetted on suspicion of political or trade union activity. The former could be chosen, with considerable discretionary powers, by the head of the Detective Corps in consultation with the head of the National Police; the presidential agency served only to establish policy guidelines for such killings. Lists of targets for clearly *political* killings, however, were prepared in the National Palace itself, and approved at the highest level:

> According to Elías Barahona lists of people to be eliminated were prepared from the records of Military Intelligence and the National Police. They included the names of 'trade union leaders and *campesinos* (peasants) provided by the Department of Trade Unions of the Ministry of Labour and by a sector of private enterprise'. Citing as his authority an officer of Military Intelligence, he said that the 'definitive lists' were prepared 'in a dependency of the army called "military transmissions" (transmisiones militares), on the fourth floor of the National Palace, and were approved at meetings held there attended by the Ministers of Defence and the Interior, and the Chief of the General Staff of the Army ... Decisions were carried out by 'the principal army and police headquarters of the republic'.[191]

The Democratic Front Against Repression (FDCR) made a similar assessment, distinguishing between "common" executions — determined by an "Operational Group" (*Grupo Operativo*) headed by National Police Director Colonel Chupina, and including other police chiefs — and more important political murders, which, as more sensitive operations, were the presidential agency's prerogative.[192]

The discretionary powers of the different levels of the security hierarchy to target suspects for murder, from the local military commissioner to the presidential intelligence agency, appears to depend largely on the prospective victim's social status. The 1981 Amnesty International report on Guatemala outlined a pattern of relatively indiscriminate government violence against victims of low social status — the peasants and the urban poor — in which killings could be carried out at the discretion of relatively low ranking personnel. A somewhat different practice was observed vis-a-vis those of higher status; prospective targets of great political significance, such as Fuentes Mohr, Colom Argueta, and the Roman Catholic priests "disappeared" or killed under the Lucas government, would have been determined at the presidential level:

> A more elaborate pattern is followed for dealing with Guatemalans of higher social or economic status, such as business people and professionals — doctors, lawyers, educators — or with leaders of legal political parties. Where people in these groups are suspected of 'subversive' activity, past or present, the discretionary powers of security service agents do not appear to be unrestricted. Such cases are thought to require consideration by high-ranking government officials before individuals can be seized or murdered; the system appears to function hierarchically, with the official level at which a decision may be taken corresponding to the status of the suspect.[193]

In cases of prospective victims of the highest status, the same report notes that:

> Policy decisions and the selection of who is to "disappear" and be killed are said to be made after consultations between the top officials of the Ministries of Defense and the Interior, and the Army General Staff, who command the forces responsible for the abuses.[194]

The Regional Center may have maintained its own group of special operatives for "death squad" activities, but the methods of operation described suggest a basic policy of deploying gunmen on temporary duty not traceable to the Regional Center or the Presidential Palace.[195] This was usually achieved by instructing army garrison commanders outside the capital to provide the temporary services of hand picked "*confidenciales*". A commander might be instructed to have four plainclothes agents travel to the capital and place themselves under the orders of the Regional Center; the commander would neither know nor wish to know the tasks to which these agents would be applied. The out of town agents would then be given an assignment; and, if ordered to carry out an assassination, provided with information on the prospective target's movements and, perhaps, photographs. The order would be to carry out the action and return immediately to their provincial garrison without contacting the centre. This operational routine was, however, only resorted to in cases of particular political sensitivity, i.e. the proposed murder of top political opposition leaders or other high profile targets whose deaths would be the subject of wide publicity and, perhaps, international inquiries.

According to a former government official, an example of a "death-squad" operation ordered and directed by the presidential agency, was the attempted murder of Víctor Manuel Valverth, a student member of the University of San Carlos executive committee.[196] Valverth was seized at gunpoint by two plainclothesmen in the university; as scores of university students and teachers seized in the same manner in previous months had "disappeared" or been found mutilated and murdered,[197] Valverth made a break for it, and was shot several times. He survived the attack, and his two assailants were tackled and overpowered by his classmates; one of the gunmen was subsequently killed when troops went on the campus to free them from the students. Although the two had identified themselves as members of the death-squad called the "Secret Anticommunist Army" (ESA), they were found to be carrying credentials as *confidenciales* as well as photographs of Víctor Valverth and other student leaders. The dead gun-man's credentials identified him as an agent of Military Intelligence (*Inteligencia Militar*) assigned to the "General Aguilar Santa María" army base at Jutiapa. The second carried a card issued by the Special Service (*Servicio Especial*) of the Treasury Police.

According to the same source, the procedure in the Valverth case, as in hundreds of others, involved a call from the presidential intelligence agency to provincial army garrisons (in this case Jutiapa) requesting *confidenciales* to be sent to the capital for unspecified purposes (such personnel could not in any event leave their base without the express leave of the base commander). National Police and Treasury Police *confidenciales* could also be contracted either through provincial army commanders or by direct contact with provincial commanders of the police services. Unless ordered to assassinate him on the spot, the plainclothesmen who set out to capture Valverth would have turned him over to one of the secret interrogation centres in or near the capital, where, eventually, he would have been shot or garrotted.

As a central command centre the presidential intelligence agency could also halt covert operations already in progress. In October 1980 in Costa Rica, a testimony made by a medical student who had been seized with his girl-friend by an army "death squad" in a highland Indian town — where he was working in the local clinic — described their arrest, in the presence of their landlady, and subsequent interrogation in an isolated rural area about his "political" activities.[198] Their captors said they were from the Secret Anticommunist Army (ESA) death-squad and had been ordered to "eliminate" the two prisoners. Before the interrogation began, however, a car radio call came through to the head of the unit, which the captives subsequently believed to have come from his superiors, and to have saved their lives. After about two hours of interrogation they were told that they were not to be killed, and would be returned to their homes because "someone in our organization wants you to be saved". About five hours from the time of their capture they were back at their homes. His girl-friend's family had appealed for their safety in the following way:

> ... when we came to X's home her mother told what they had done. Our landlady had contacted our families on the telephone. X's mother is Y, and a cousin of her's happened to visit the family that evening. He was a lieutenant when he left the army ten years ago, and his old mates from the military school are now majors and colonels. He himself is in agrobusiness and a terribly conservative man, but he saw this as a family matter. He also knows my parents. So they went to the *Estado Mayor Presidencial* (Presidential General Staff) ... and to its Security Department. The colonel in charge there was an old friend of X's uncle. He was very kind to them. He went to the president himself and came back with an oral order to 'all sections and all bases' to release her and me. X's uncle tried to get a written copy, but the colonel said it would not be necessary. We now found out that we had been released shortly afterwards. Our kidnappers must have received the order on the radio we heard. But X's mother and uncle did not know that we were about to be released. So they went on to the commander of the military operations in A and B. He was another friend of the old lieutenant. He was not in his office, but his ADC (adjutant) contacted him on the radio and received instructions to help them. He then went to a desk and took out a list with about 40 names on it, according to X's mother. 'They were a couple?' he asked. 'Then we had better hurry up so we do not execute a couple we have on this list.' He hurried out into another room. After a few minutes he came back. 'It was not the same couple, but everything is under control. There is no need for worry any more.' This happened at about 5 am.[199]

The direct involvement of the top-level presidential intelligence agency, "*La Regional*", was not, of course, necessary in most cases, which could be entrusted to the discretion of secondary commands. By far the greatest number of killings were carried out by the regular army, ordered through the regional command structures and guided by military intelligence officers. In an interview published by Amnesty International, a former army conscript seconded to a special operations unit of military intelligence in the capital described his selection for special duties and the methods used to kill "suspects" or bring them in for interrogation:

> ... they sent the three of us to the office of the S-2 [G-2], where we met officers. They stopped cropping our hair, instead they let us look really

good. They told us: 'Now you have been selected; you were chosen; you aren't just simple soldiers any more, like those in the unit.' What I thought then was that I was superior to everyone because I had managed to reach this position. They gave us separate training and each of us was given a .45 and left full of enthusiasm. [The .45 is] a weapon only officers use, with eight shots. They gave us one and we went out in civilian clothes ... And they gave us special identity cards so that if there were any police around ... we could show them these, so they wouldn't seize us and we could get away.[200]

The former soldier described surveillance techniques and arrest procedures, and the abduction of a student who was taken to the *Brigada Mariscal Zavala* (an army garrison in the capital) where he was interrogated under torture before being killed and his body dumped at night.[201] Agents were given the names of people to be watched or picked up, with details of their movements, yet they themselves were under observation by their superiors:

> there were always officers travelling around in private cars too, with radios. There might be one in the central park in zone 1, another could be in zone 6, or in zone 7, who were in contact . . .[202]

Standing orders for army intelligence special operations units demanded strict secrecy for extra-legal assassination details. "Need to know" procedures, under which only those giving the orders and the executors themselves are aware of an operation, appear similar to those in force for operations carried out on the instructions of the presidential intelligence agency. Intelligence officials are described as making assignments for surveillance to one unit, and then following up with an assassination squad chosen from a pool of potential operators. The soldier interviewed described the procedure used in a rural surveillance operation:

> ... you just ... note things down. You get to know them really well, and in order not to commit these crimes at that moment, you jot down the name of the house and such like, so that they can secretly order another commission to 'bring them to justice' [*ajusticiarlos*]. That's what you do, that's what we all do — I mean, get the name of the young man, the father and so on; find out what work he does, where he works, etc. The reports these commissions make are sent into the offices, such and such an office, circulated in such and such a way. The people there are in charge of finding a commission and secretly giving it its orders. Only they know where it's gone and what it's going to do. This is all done by Army G-2 — that's the way they work.[203]

From its inception, the data-base for the presidential agency drew upon the Army General Staff's military intelligence apparatus, also located in the Presidential Palace complex, on the third floor of the Casa Presidencial. According to former government officials, the General Staff is equipped with its own electronic data processing centre in the Palace complex, and can tap into the data-base of other government ministries and autonomous agencies, and the National Police computer centre.[204] The Ministry of Finance, according to the same sources, maintains computerized payroll and personnel records on every government employee, from rural school teachers to palace maintenance men, and all tax records, and provides a principal data-base for the intelligence and counter-intelligence work of the General Staff and the presidential agency.

The Ministry of Labour, although more limited in its functions, also has the attributes of a modern bureaucracy, including an efficient records system. The four years of the Laugerud regime were notable for the growth of the trade union movement, with many new unions registered, a development discussed in chapter 5. Legal requirements for recognition of labour unions, however, included registration of the names and addresses of each member of the union executive, with two photographs of each: one for a credential issued by the ministry, the other for a central file. According to informed sources, access to these records is routinely provided to the General Staff and the presidential intelligence agency, and their detailed information is an effective aid "when the time comes to pick them up".[205] There is some evidence that even the state-run telephone company links into the presidential intelligence agency; an account of a top level meeting of Guatemalan intelligence chiefs in January 1976 named those present as including Minister of the Interior General Vassaux Martínez, Lieutenant Colonel Mariano Rayo Ovalle, director of GUATEL (which, like the telephone company ANTEL in El Salvador, controls all telecommunication services in the country), the Chief of Army Intelligence, Colonel Guillermo Echeverría Vielman, and the Minister of Finance.[206]

From the mid-1970s virtually all government agencies, however innocuous, could be tapped for information useful to the top intelligence agencies. Records electronically available to the office of the Army Chief of Staff included the Ministry of Finance's tax and public employment records; the Ministry of the Interior's immigration and passport records; criminal and intelligence records of the National Police; and the records of military intelligence itself, built upon the data-base, compiled in the aftermath of Arbenz' overthrow, from the membership lists of the organizations outlawed by Castillo Armas. Immigration office records were computerized during the Laugerud administration, and served to clear passport applicants within 24 hours.[207] Rapid checking of more than one data-base was also possible; one source has described a vetting procedure in force for all staff employed in the presidential palace complex and other sensitive areas requiring the submission of applications to the Army General Staff. Within 24 hours the names would be checked against National Police, Ministry of Finance (tax and public employment), Ministry of Labour (records of labour leaders and activists), and military intelligence records and clearance granted or denied.[208] The same source described the improvement in the intelligence data base as a spin-off of the development of a modern system of public administration since the late 1960s, a development in which the US AID played a significant role:

> No single agency of government holds all the information, but all can be concentrated under the Army Chief of Staff. The information system is very refined — not that of an underdeveloped country; AID tried to catch us up. It may or may not have known it would go the way it did.[209]

The Balance of Terror: "Death-Squad" Killings

Few modifications were made to the security system — its structure or application — during the presidencies of Kjell Laugerud and Romeo Lucas García, apart from a gradual increase in personnel levels and, after 1977, a major increase in the number of Guatemalans killed by the security services. Although the scale of killings under Laugerud was somewhat less than that under his predecessor, Amnesty International, in submissions to the Inter-American Commission on Human Rights and in its publications in the first year of the new government, documented hundreds of cases of government killings, and by April 1976 had records on 379 cases "in which extra judicial execution is believed to have occurred",[210] the figure being acknowledged to represent only a small minority of the governmental killings and "disappearances" in the period, since only a fraction of the cases from rural areas were ever reported.

In a December 1976 *Briefing* on Guatemala, Amnesty International concluded that at least 20,000 Guatemalans had been killed or disappeared in custody since 1966:

> The vast majority of the "disappeared", when located, are found to have been the victims of violent death. Many are found with signs of torture or mutilation along roadsides or in ravines, floating in plastic bags in lakes and rivers, or buried in mass graves in the countryside. Other victims are shot in their homes or in the street ... Since 1966 the victims of covertly sanctioned murders or disappearances in Guatemala are believed by Amnesty International to number over 20,000, according to all available information.[211]

The selective assassination or "disappearance" of key political and trade union leaders under Laugerud has already been outlined. A relatively new phenomenon during Laugerud's government was the extension of the "death-squad" killings to an ever larger number of residents of the city slums tagged either as political organizers or as common delinquents. Killing petty criminals, with no clear political motive, along the lines of Brazil's *Escuãdrao da Morte*, was an innovation in Guatemala, where counter-terror killings had been introduced with an explicitly political objective. The "death-squads" that emerged in Brazil in the 1950s originally had no formal place within the security system and no political control function; and from all accounts were created to take vengeance on criminals who had killed policemen. In the 1960s, however, the "death-squads" were turned against Brazil's short-lived urban guerrilla movement, with "death-squad" leader, police inspector Sergio Fleury, credited with the ambush and killing of urban guerrilla theorist Carlos Marighela in 1969.[212]

By the end of the Laugerud Presidency, killings with no clear "political" motivation were on the upswing. The discovery of secret mass graves near the capital included bodies with the "skin-head" haircuts given convicts in the country's prisons, and the press frequently reported that prisoners, intercepted by "unidentified armed men" during transfers from one prison to another, were later found dead. Recidivist criminals released from Guatemala City's prison farm of "El Pavón" were by 1978 frequently picked up and killed by police "death-squads" almost as soon as they left the prison gates. In 1979, "El Pavón" prisoners, terrified of the prospect of release and murder, went on strike in protest.

Urban squatters and shanty town residents of the capital suffered most from the widening of the assassination squads' brief beyond limits defined by the victims' political activities. Some of the victims were, in fact, recidivist criminals. Press reports on the discovery of groups of bodies lined up at the side of streets in the poor parts of town often cited detailed police "fact sheets" on the victims' sometimes long criminal records, which the police had distributed to press sources almost before the bodies were cold. While consistently denying their involvement in these murders, the police went to great lengths to justify them as a service to law and order. Occasionally, however, the police records were false: victims characterized as vicious criminals had, instead, been active in trade unions or political opposition parties; or were victims of mistaken identity. The families, colleagues and friends of victims alleged to have criminal records sometimes vigorously denied this in paid advertisements in the press.

Extra-legal violence as a means of dealing with a specific problem of insurgency or opposition, was, under the Laugerud government, extended to apply to all aspects of law enforcement; the new methods saved time in dealing with conventional criminals, never more than a distraction from the government's overriding security objective, the extermination of insurgents and opposition leaders in general. The

179

expansion of the murder programme was also consistent with the overall objective of crushing opposition groups and intimidating potential supporters. Possibly, the regular appearance of bodies of executed "criminals" on the streets of the poorer sections of the capital was seen as a salutary lesson on the implacable and irresistible power of the state; those who stepped out of line did so at their peril. Behind the liquidation of common criminals the government could also conceal its specifically political killings. Portrayal of the "death-squad" murders as "vigilante" acts cleansing the society of vicious criminal elements distracted domestic and international public opinion from the government's policy of systematic political murder. Under the Lucas García regime the killing of alleged "criminals" became more widespread and more widely publicized, coinciding with a dramatic rise in the number of political dissidents and suspected dissidents murdered by the state.

It was under the Lucas García regime that a government publicity campaign made most use of the killings of alleged "criminals" by issuing regular statistics on deaths attributed to one of two "death-squads": crediting what they called the *Escuadrón de la Muerte* (Death-Squad) for the murder of "criminals", and the *Ejército Secreto Anticomunista* (Secret Anticommunist Army, ESA) with the murder of "subversives". Amnesty International, in its 1981 report on Guatemala, debunked the government's campaign as a mechanism to evade accountability for its own actions:

> The government does not deny that people it considers to be 'subversives' or 'criminals' are seized and murdered daily in Guatemala — but it lays the whole blame on independent, anti-communist 'death squads' . . . National Police spokesmen told the local press in 1979 that the Escuadrón de la Muerte had killed 1,224 'criminals' ('1,143 men and 82 women') from January to June 1979 and that the ESA had killed 3,252 'subversives' in the first 10 months of 1979 . . . Amnesty International believes that abuses attributed by the Government of Guatemala to independent 'death squads' are perpetrated by the regular forces of the civil and military security services.[213]

One source connecting the "Death-Squad"/ESA dichotomy to a careful government publicity strategy was the former press spokesman of the Minister of the Interior, Elías Barahona, who after serving both the Laugerud and Lucas governments resigned in September 1980 to join the Guerrilla Army of the Poor:

> Elías Barahona y Barahona, who had been the ministry's press representative since 1976, described his job there as that of carrying out a press policy to explain governmental violence in terms of fighting between 'clandestine groups of the extreme right and left'. He said that

blank letter-head stationery of the alleged 'death squads', Ejército Secreto Anticomunista and Escuadrón de la Muerte, was stored in the office of the Minister of the Interior, who is responsible for internal security.[214]

Another Guatemalan commentator on the government's murder policy, Manuel Colom Argueta, interviewed shortly before his own assassination, described "the government's strategy of selective repression" and the willingness of the extreme right "to accept the blame for a lot of the crimes the army commits". Colom Argueta also placed the enormous escalation of the government's political killings in the context of the September 1978 bus fare conflict and the advance of the Nicaraguan revolution:

> The current strategy of power is selective. It intends to destroy all organized popular resistance, which has grown steadily since 1963. If you look back, you'll see that every single murder is of a key person. They are not all of the same ideological orientation, they are simply the people in each sector or movement who have the capacity to organise the population round a cause . . . There is another reason for the repression: the civil war in Nicaragua. The September bus fares conflict gave the government the excuse it needed to act . . . More people are dying here than in Nicaragua, but no-one knows there's a war going on against the population. We estimate that in the last three months there have been over 2,000 murders.[215]

The scale of political killings by the Laugerud and Lucas García governments could not be concealed from international public opinion. First CNUS, and then the Democratic Front Against Repression made systematic efforts to get word out of the country on events there: sending delegations of trade union and political leaders to visit European capitals, and regularly publishing news summaries, often just digests, on killings and "disappearances" published in Guatemala's daily newspapers. Another factor was the murder, in 1979, of Manuel Colom Argueta and Alberto Fuentes Mohr, both internationally known and linked to the Socialist International.

Killings and "disappearances" of leaders of the Christian Democratic Party — also part of a powerful international political organization — and of the trade unions linked to international labour federations, stirred up worldwide attention. Other factors related to external forces: the increasing activity of international human rights organizations towards the end of the 1970s; the opening of some US congressional committees as fora for presenting information on human rights in Central America; a growing activism by international religious organizations in defence of human rights; and increased interest in Central America on the part of public opinion and the news media due to the Nicaraguan revolution.

7. Human Rights and Security Assistance

Outflanking the United States Congress

When Kjell Laugerud García took office as President, in July 1974 the United States' commitment of dollars and personnel to assist Guatemala's security system had declined considerably from its peak in 1971 under Colonel Arana Osorio. In 1976 the strength of the US Military Group had been reduced from 34 (1969-71) to 15.[216] A progressive reduction in annual MAP budgets after 1971 meant smaller grants of arms and equipment; training allocations, however, remained at about their 1970 levels, or increased, up to and including 1975.[217] Overseas officers' training under the International Defense Education Program (IDEP) continued at about the 1969 level, while in-country training, as in the 1960s, was provided both by the Military Group and Mobile Training Teams.

The decrease in Military Group personnel in Guatemala in the early 1970s (as also in El Salvador) accorded with an overall reduction in postings of military personnel to Latin America, in response to congressional criticism of the political cost of their presence, and a changing view of the state of insurgency there. In 1969 congressional hearings a Defense Department spokesman declared that "insurgency and terrorism" no longer threatened to overthrow "any particular Latin American government", and attributed this to two factors: (1) insurgencies had failed to attract support, and notably failed to attract peasant support; and (2) the 1960s assistance programme had been successful:

> ... the Latin American internal security forces have improved markedly over the last 10 years. They are now organized and trained and equipped to handle an insurgency-type threat.[218]

> As the internal security capability of Latin American military forces has improved, it has been possible to reduce the level of military assistance provided by the United States. The level has receded from a high of $82.8 million in fiscal year 1966 to $22.8 million in the current

fiscal year and a proposed $21.4 million for fiscal year 1970 . . .[219]

Reduction in size of the Military Groups in Latin America was described in the hearings as proportional to the decline in scale of the overall assistance programme; from about 700 personnel in Military Groups in 17 Latin American countries in 1969 (with the largest — 126 — in Brazil) to about 500 in 1971.[220] Any limitation on the smaller Military Groups' capability to provide training within each country would be compensated "through Mobile Training Teams which can be dispatched wherever specific assistance is required."[221]

This reduced US assistance in arms and equipment was compensated by a massively expanded provision of credit under the Foreign Military Sales Program. The phasing-out of large-scale Military Assistance Program (MAP) grants of material (and scaling down of Military Groups) responded directly to congressional considerations of economy and human rights. Considerably before the Carter administration, congressional hearings of the late 1960s had repeatedly castigated the military (and Public Safety Program) over human rights abuse by their Latin American clients and counterparts. The 1968 and 1969 hearings to assess the Alliance for Progress and consider the 1970s US policy towards Latin America dealt in detail with allegations of serious human rights abuses by US-aided military and police bodies and sought to assess the potentially deleterious ethical and public image effects associated with US security assistance.

US Army Latin Americanist John Childs described the extensive review of US policy on Latin America initiated by Senator Frank Church in 1969 in the Senate Foreign Relations Committee as having been a major factor in the programme's curtailment. As early as 1969, according to Childs,

> Senator Church was threatening to end the MAP/SAP [Security Assistance Program] in Latin America completely if the Executive did not voluntarily curtail them.[222]

In 1972, congress took the first steps to radically change the 1960s system of Military Groups world wide, by requiring congressional authorization for each group; legislation provided for a reduction of the total number of authorized Military Groups after 1976 to 34.[223] By 1979 the total personnel assigned to Military Groups in Latin America had been reduced from 700-800 to about 100, with a number having been phased out altogether: Guatemala and El Salvador, however, retained active Military Groups throughout that period.[224]

Since 1961, foreign assistance legislation in the US had included a human rights component; Section 502B of the Foreign Assistance Act of 1961 declared that "... a principal goal of the foreign policy of the United

States shall be to promote the increased observance of internationally recognized human rights by all countries."[225]

Not until the early 1970s, however, did human rights provisions in the Foreign Assistance Act go beyond vague expressions of good intentions, or provide a serious legislative stricture on executive actions. It was Section 502B of the Foreign Assistance Act of 1974 that was designed to make human rights a measurable factor in foreign assistance, and to provide US congress with both a monitoring role and control of the purse strings to enforce human rights provisions in the law. Section 502B states that:

> ... no security assistance may be provided to any country the government of which engages in a consistent pattern of gross violations of internationally recognized human rights ... [Gross violations are defined to include:] ... torture or cruel, inhuman, or degrading treatment, causing the disappearance of persons by the abduction and clandestine detention of those persons, and other flagrant denial of the right to life, liberty or the security of persons.[226]

The Foreign Assistance Act of 1974 established the same human rights criteria for all programmes of security assistance funded under the act, including the Military Assistance, the IMET, the Foreign Military Sales Program, and the Economic Support Fund. Also defined as security assistance under the act were all *commercial* exports of goods classified as "defense items and services" or "crime control and detection instruments and equipment".[227]

The International Security Assistance and Arms Export Control Act repeated the language of the 1974 Foreign Assistance Act, and required the Secretary of State to present to congress an annual report on human rights conditions in each of the countries receiving security assistance.[228]

Although US law after 1974 required the administration to apply a human rights yardstick to the security assistance programme, only with the Carter administration did the foreign assistance bureaucracy pay more than lip service to its obligations under the law. Security assistance policy for Central America was the object of intensive congressional scrutiny for the first time in hearings in the House of Representatives Committee on International Relations (Subcommittee on International Organizations) in 1976. This hearing, on human rights in Nicaragua, Guatemala and El Salvador, and their implications for US policy, heard extensive testimony from a broad range of witnesses who described in detail the practices of torture and extra-judicial execution, prolonged secret detention and "disappearance" as well as other gross violations of human rights in each of the three countries. In contrast, Assistant Secretary of State Hewson Ryan's testimony was a rather pathetic presentation suggesting allegations could not be followed up because

Embassies were short staffed, and the US could not "conduct investigations in a foreign country ... a sovereign country".[229] This lack of information notwithstanding, Secretary Ryan told the hearing that in the three countries

> a review of all the hard evidence we could assemble did not yield the judgement that there had emerged a consistent pattern of gross violation of human rights.[230]

When challenged by Subcommittee Chairman Donald Fraser on specific allegations, Ryan's response was:

> We try to obtain as much information as possible about these allegations ... Every allegation, of course, has its counter-allegation, and very often we are left with pages and pages of allegations, and pages and pages of counterallegations...[231]

This cut little ice with a committee which had been provided with abundant hard human rights information from individual experts and non-governmental organizations.

Congressional frustration with the Executive's apparent flouting of the law since 1974 — by decision or institutional inertia — found expression when Chairman Fraser summed up his assessment of Secretary Ryan's testimony:

> Mr. Ambassador, you make a poor case before this committee. For instance, you have been unable to ascertain the statutory foundation for the continuation of aid to these three countries. You speak of charges and countercharges cancelling out each other. You state that you are understaffed, and that you have no authority to investigate. You ought to just quit ... I find nothing concrete in what you say ... What good does it do for the Congress to pass legislative provisions that will limit military aid to the countries which engage in systematic violations of human rights, when you say: 'Well, a lot of charges and countercharges cancel each other out.'
> Mr. Ryan. We have been precisely unable to document ...
> Mr. Fraser. It is quite clear, from the way that you are approaching this, that you have not tried to document them.[232]

Assistant Secretary of State Ryan's evasive response to specific questions suggested simple ignorance of the human rights situation in Latin America, but the record of the hearings notes that he was then a 25 year veteran of Foreign Service duty in Latin America, and in other posts related to US policy towards Latin America.

When Jimmy Carter became President in January 1977, the law already required satisfactory respect for human rights as a precondition for US security assistance: all it lacked for implementation was political will. Carter brought a long absent idealism to the Presidency and sought to execute the law of the land, including the Foreign Assistance Act's human rights provisions previously circumvented. Carter and the few outsiders appointed to push human rights in the State Department made a considerable effort to do so. In the final analysis, the efforts of Carter and a few outsiders to push the human rights issue in the State Department were insufficient, in the Central American case, to overcome the institutional resistance within the foreign assistance and defence establishment to wholeheartedly implement human rights legislation.

The State Department's first annual report on human rights conditions in aid receiving countries was released in April 1977. By that time security assistance to Chile and Uruguay had been cut off on human rights grounds, although without formally attributing the gross and consistent violations of human rights to the two governments' responsibility. The government of Guatemala got off relatively lightly in the report (which failed to hold it in any way responsible for the "death-squad" murders) but President Laugerud, along with President Arturo Armando Molina of El Salvador, chose to join the heads of state of Brazil and Argentina in "renouncing" most US security assistance. Their ostensible motive was that the US Department of State's publication of this compendium of human rights information was an affront to their national sovereignty.[233] In retrospect, neither Guatemala, El Salvador, nor Brazil, faced serious security assistance cuts, but their official rejection of aid eliminated the embarrassing possibility that it might be cut off; it was also consistent with the nationalist strain in the military doctrines of Brazil and Argentina — best formulated in Brazil's Doctrine of National Security.[234] Military aid to Brazil and Argentina had, moreover, been dramatically wound down since the late 1960s and was relatively insubstantial by 1977. Guatemala's and El Salvador's renunciation of aid is less easily explained in terms of wounded nationalism. Both countries had been severely censured in congressional hearings in July 1976 (although not by the Department of State) but had shrugged that off: the government of El Salvador sent a curt diplomatic note declaring its concern that such hearings represented a form of "intervention in El Salvador's internal affairs"; the government of Guatemala did not deign to comment.[235]

In the 1977 (Section 502B, human rights) report neither Guatemala nor El Salvador had been harshly criticized.[236] The Guatemala section emphasized the supposedly independent nature of the "death-squads" and suggested that these killings were balanced by left-wing opposition violence:

> Kidnappings and assassination of government officials by leftist terrorists continue ... as do politically motivated murders by rightists and leftist groups.[237]

The implication was that most victims were government officials, the balance divided between two antagonistic forces, the government uninvolved. The section on El Salvador could be characterized as a full whitewash:

> The Salvadoran Government does not condone nor is there evidence of a pattern of torture, inhumane or degrading treatment or punishment. There have reportedly been some isolated instances, however, of actions perpetrated by government agents which could be considered repressive.[238]

When Guatemala and El Salvador jointly renounced military assistance both had largely concluded a period of extensive refitting for counter-insurgency and had contracts with Israel for the provision of counter-insurgency aircraft, light submachine-guns (Uzi and Galil) and other equipment. The acquisition of further armaments on the open market presented neither country with financial problems. The net effect of the gesture of renunciation for El Salvador turned out to be virtually nil. For Guatemala it would prove significant only by 1979, with unprecedentedly strong internal guerrilla resistance, and as the escalation of government forces' killings put Guatemala in the international spotlight as a world leader in the perpetration of atrocities. For the US to renew security assistance at such a time was a decision requiring a convincing rationale for a human rights conscious congress: either a real improvement in human rights performance or a "reformist" coup was needed.

The major impact of four longstanding US clients renouncing assistance was to take four military regimes out of the dock and provoke criticism of the Carter administration's human rights policy for having alienated valued allies. With the addition of Chile and Uruguay, six allied states were effectively exchanging sanctions or potential sanctions for principled stands, thereby placing the onus of the spoiled relations on Carter and his political appointees in the Department of State. Overnight, military regimes under fire for gross violations of human rights presented themselves as injured parties. As one US army authority wrote "Latin reaction was characterized by indignation"; the southern cone nationals in particular saw the US action as a "betrayal".[239] The result of what they saw as "arrogant interventionism" — the linking of security assistance to human rights performance — when combined with the "dramatic decline in the Latin American Military Assistance Programme in terms of dollars, arms and personnel" was a dramatic loss of US "influence" in the region.[240]

The Guatemalans' renunciation however, occasioned neither hardship nor sacrifice to the Guatemalan military, and did little to interrupt good relations with their counterparts in the US military establishment. The Carter administration's estrangement from the Guatemalans did not actually mean all military aid was cut off. Dealings between the military of each country continued — although congress was unaware of this at the time; and, simultaneously, close US allies (particularly Israel and Argentina) were increasingly involved in taking up the slack in military assistance — with the apparent encouragement of the US military and intelligence establishment.

In the 1981 congressional hearings on "Human Rights in Guatemala" information was requested of the Department of State on the record of assistance to Guatemala. One chart provided gave figures for "Military Assistance" ranging from $2.1 million in 1976 to zero in 1977, 1978 and 1979; however, more detailed breakdowns by budget heading, in almost illegible, reduced-size format, indicated that major arms and equipment transfers had gone ahead almost as if relations had remained undisturbed. While, ostensibly, these transfers, under the Foreign Military Sales, and the Military Assistance Programs, were in fulfillment of agreements or contracts pre-dating the Carter administration's clash with Laugerud, to the Guatemalans the uninterrupted flow of deliveries and continued presence of the Military Group to assist in putting new equipment to use, signalled a less than total implementation of the "human rights" policy, and the US military establishment's continued support for their counter-insurgency effort. The 1981 hearings' record confirms that funding for the Military Assistance Program proper dropped dramatically from $134 million in 1976 to $6 million in 1977.[241] MAP funding had, however, been steadily dropping since 1974, as military assistance policy prescribed a progressive change from the provision of grant material to equipment and transfers through the Foreign Military Sales programme (FMS) (which gives credits, rather than grants towards acquisitions) and the Commercial Sales programme. The 1977 rupture in relations between the United States' human rights advocates and the Guatemalans interrupted neither the FMS nor the Commercial Sales deliveries, nor even the delivery of grants previously approved under MAP. Table 7.1 gives the dollar value for actual *deliveries* under FMS, MAP and Commercial Sales.

Table 7.1

Military Assistance Agreements and Deliveries, 1974–1980 (Dollars in thousands) *

	1974	1975	1976	1977	1978	1979	1980
FMS Deliveries	1,464	3,370	3,041	2,169	2,410	3,327	2,254
Commercial Export Deliveries	209	471	345	1,020	550	665	417
MAP Program	430	162	134	6	1	6	—
MAP Deliveries	1,539	260	280	104	46	1	71

* All figures from Hearings, "Human Rights in Guatemala", 1981, pp. 38–39, "Additional Material Submitted by the Department of State; figures for FMS *agreements* in the hearing record are illegible.

The July 1981 hearings on Guatemala paid particular attention to *commercial* exports of military or police equipment to Guatemala that potentially were in breach of Section 502B of the Foreign Assistance Act.[242] Regulation of export controls depended on a license system (administered by the Department of Commerce) for commercial sales of items on the Department of State's "Crime Control and Detection List" (the "munitions list"). On 5 April 1981, the Reagan administration had bypassed legislative restrictions on sales of military and crime control equipment to Guatemala by simply changing the rules regulating such sales. The export of 50 two-and-a-half ton trucks and 100 army jeeps was made possible by removing both items from the "Crime Control and Detection List" and reclassifying them as goods for "Regional Stability Controls"; the sale went ahead in June 1981.[243]

Relatively complete information on licensed commercial sales is available from the 1981 hearings. Only after 1979 are more than a few isolated disapproved licences on the record. Over one million cartridges were exported each year up to 1981, plus varying quantities of firearms (for 1978-80 these included a total of 2,279 pistols and revolvers; 1,380 rifles and carbines; and 10 submachine-guns).[244] Other items listed as military equipment and licensed for export included tank spare parts, armoured vests, military vehicles and explosives. Among the more unusual items requested by the Guatemalans and licensed for export in 1979 were 22 Tasers (model "Taser TF-76"), a relatively exotic item that might logically be expected to be misused in a torture state. Classified as a "non-lethal" weapon, the Taser is advertised by its California makers as having the stopping power of a small handgun. This weapon simultaneously fires two darts trailing fine wires and on impact ("effective even through heavy clothing") conducts the electric charge into the target's body.[245] A 1975 report by the California-based Center for Research on Criminal Justice says the Taser:

> Fires small, barbed electrical contactors . . . Electric charge administered through barbs. Victim is paralyzed until electrified contacts are removed or current shut off.[246]

Non-military crime-control equipment licensed for export from 1978 to 1981 included shotguns, protective vests and Kevlar "bulletproof" fabric, trucks and truck parts, two aircraft, and one "Psychological Stress Analyzer".[247]

Other major transfers of military equipment occurred in 1980 and 1981, still under the Carter administration, when the Department of Commerce licensed the sale of helicopters for conversion to military purposes. In these years the Guatemalan military acquired three Bell 212 and six Bell 412 helicopters at a cost of some $10.5 million; these aircraft are civilian models of the UH1H "Huey" and were promptly converted for military use, according to *Washington Post* reporter Christopher Dickey who confirmed the transfer:

> Those helicopters were bought with Commerce Department approval . . .
> . . . At least two of the new helicopters are now equipped with .30 calibre machine guns. At garrisons such as this one in northwestern Guatemala, amid rough mountainous terrain where leftist and Communist guerrillas have their strongest forces, this new equipment appears to be essential to Guatemala's counterinsurgency campaign. The army moves its troops overland in US-made trucks and jeeps. A Bell 212 helicopter with door guns is used to strafe nearby guerrilla positions while a just-arrived 412, still with its 'executive' interior, carries troops to the scene of a battle and evacuates the casualties.[248]

While throughout the Carter period the flow of military equipment and aid to Guatemala was sufficient to conclude that the military assistance bureaucracy was "playing the end against the middle" in failing to enforce the human rights policy, economic assistance from the US and from strongly US-influenced international lending agencies after 1979 continued at about the same level as before. This included allocations under US Public Law 480 (PL–480, "Food for Peace") and through the AID, credits through the Inter-American Bank of Rural Development (IBRD) and the Inter-American Development Bank (IDB); see Tables 7.2 and 7.3.

Table 7.2
AID and "Food for Peace" (PL–480) allocations 1974–81*

	1974	1975	1976	1977	1978	1979	1980	1981
AID	2.5	9.4	29.0	14.3	4.5	17.4	7.8	9.1
PL–480	1.2	3.4	12.5	4.5	4.6	5.3	3.3	7.5

* In millions of dollars. Figures from Hearings, "Human Rights in Guatemala", 1981, p. 37 and US Department of State, "Report on Human Rights Practices in Countries Receiving US Aid", 1981. p. 449.

Table 7.3
Assistance from International Agencies, 1977–1981*

	1977	1978	1979	1980	1981
IDB	25	35.7	0.3	66	25.5
IBRD	55	72.0	0.0	17	26.5

*In millions of dollars. Figures from US Department of State, "Report on Human Rights Practices in Countries Receiving US Aid, 1980", p. 333 and 1981, p. 449.

AID and PL-480 funding continued at about its 1981 level until 1983. Major IDB loans were approved in November 1981, including $20 million toward a project to control and combat livestock diseases; $22.5 million for water and sewerage projects, and two loans totalling $70 million to help complete a major hydroelectric project.[249] A further IDB loan request at the end of 1981 was apparently the first such loan in which human rights considerations played a part:

> An application for an $18 million IDB loan for rural telecommunications was temporarily withdrawn by the Guatemalan government in December 1981, following hearings in the US Congress. House Banking Sub-committee Chairman Jerry Patterson (D-California) told State Department witnesses that the telephone project loan had tremendous potential for military applications, that it did not meet basic human needs, and that he considered it to be 'flat-out illegal'.[250]

In addition to the Inter-American lending agencies a high level of IMF and World Bank lending continued without any consideration of Guatemala's human rights record. According to a report by the Washington-based Institute for Policy Studies the IMF provided the government of Guatemala with a $110.1 million facility in November 1981, reported to "impose few conditions" on the borrower, while the World Bank was considering funding loan requests for projects in "telecommunications, electricity, and education".[251]

That Guatemalan regimes suffered no economic hardship as a result of the restriction on US security assistance can be illustrated by the budgets for defence spending published in Guatemala's official *Boletin Estadistico*. The clash with the Carter administration occurred after several years of rapid increases in the defence budget, increases in real numbers of *quetzales* (until recently equivalent to dollars), and in the proportion of the overall budget. Despite the aid cut the defence allocation continued to grow in 1978. The $27.4 million 1974 budget rose by 64% to $42.9 million in 1975; the $49.8 million 1976 budget increased by 64% to $77.1 million in 1977, jumping to $91 million in 1978.[252] Analyst Gabriel Aguilera has compared the quadrupling of the defence budget between 1974 and 1978 with the figures for education, which did not even double.[253] Similarly, while in 1974 the defence budget was about the same as for public health, by 1978 it was nearly twice that for public health. Aguilera notes that the leap in the defence budget after 1976 "coincided with the time when equipment was being replaced and recruiting was being stepped up in the army as well as the police forces."[254] The rise related in part to increased tensions over Belize, but also, perhaps more significantly, "to medium-range preparatory measures for internal war" in response to the resurgence of guerrilla operations in 1975.[255]

Although the US continued to provide funds and equipment

throughout the Carter years, major military purchases to regear Guatemala's security system for major counter-insurgency offensives in the late 1970s were also made from non-traditional suppliers, including Italy, Belgium, Yugoslavia and Israel. It was Israel, however, that became the main supplier of arms and expertise for counter-insurgency after 1975, even before US human rights policy took shape. Israel's arms transfers and advisers compensated for the reduction of the US military presence in Guatemala after 1977.

Israel: US's Partner in Security Assistance

Israel's contribution to the Guatemalan security system after 1975 included sales and grants of large numbers of counter-insurgency aircraft, and provision of light automatic weapons. Between 1975 and 1982, a minimum of 15,000 Galil submachine-guns (technically 'light assault rifles'), 11 Arava Short-take-off and Landing Aircraft (STOL), 10 armoured cars and other equipment were provided by Israel.[256]

By 1980 the Galil was the Guatemalan army's and security service's standard weapon. An interview with a conscript soldier, transcribed and published by Amnesty International, refers to the arrival of the Galils and the belief within the ranks that the arms were provided because Israel was in Guatemala's debt (Guatemala has consistently voted with Israel in the United Nations). The Galil is referred to in the context of an account of the soldier's training and indoctrination, and his selection to serve in a special operations assassination squad:

> *Weren't you afraid that one day an officer might have ordered you to kill someone?*
> I wasn't afraid. At that time I was full of the ideas they filled me with. I wasn't afraid they might tell me to kill someone. I used to do it because my mentality by then had changed completely — that's what happened to me.
> *You could kill people without any problems?*
> Yes, without problems. Once they saw that I was really keen and understood the things they had taught me, they took me out of my unit with two others. Afterwards, we didn't stay in the same unit but were instructed separately. They didn't discipline us much then; we had already suffered enough, so they didn't discipline us so much, although the men in the unit did get disciplined.
>   Then they gave us a little black 'galil' that had only just arrived.
> *Is that a weapon?*
> Yes, 'galil'.
> *It's very sophisticated isn't it?*
> Yes, it's very new. They said Israel sent them to Guatemala, because it owed Guatemala something and other arms arrived. This one can fire a maximum of 350 shots a minute.

So they gave us this weapon and we were happier because we were better equipped. When these weapons arrived they gave us one each, then stopped giving us the M-1 rifles. They collected those and stored them. When they gave us this weapon, the took me out of the unit but the others stayed on.

They then sent the three of us to the office of the S-2 [Intelligence] where we met officers. They stopped cropping our hair, instead they let us look really good. They told us: 'Now you have been selected; you were chosen; you aren't just simple soldiers any more'.[257]

In the late 1970s opposition sources reported that Israel was providing special help to the Guatemalan military in the field of communications and organization of co-operatives for counter-insurgency purposes. NACLA has also reported on the evidence that Israeli advisers were training the Guatemalan security forces in "urban counterinsurgency":

A US journalist recently returned from Guatemala reported discussions with Guatemalan military police who had participated in a two week urban counterinsurgency course taught by Israeli advisers. It is unknown whether the advisers represented the Israeli military or were working as private citizens.[258]

Defector Elías Barahona in his September 1980 statements upon leaving his post at the Ministry of the Interior claimed Israeli advisers were "permanently" based in Guatemala, "as technicians and experts to train youth leaders, in dissemination of information and propaganda, and in the formation of terrorist commandos."[259] Barahona added that the only publicly acknowledged Israeli assistance was "in the field of cooperatives", and that this had been the pretext for Interior Minister Donaldo Alvarez Ruiz to visit Israel in September 1979, to buy arms and anti-riot equipment.[260] Spokesmen for the Democratic Front Against Repression also claimed Israeli advisers and technicians were working in Guatemala and with US advisers in the telecommunications and intelligence facilities in the National Palace complex.[261] In 1980 Israel's military assistance became an issue in its own internal politics when Israel's Histadrut Labour federation wrote Prime Minister Menachem Begin to demand arms transfers to Guatemala be stopped, and described human rights violations in Guatemala as "an affront to all humanity and civilization".[262]

Israel's government and military establishment has consistently refrained from acknowledging either arming or training the Guatemalan security establishment, but Guatemalan authorities have been less reticent. Israeli assistance to Guatemala's security communications and intelligence was confirmed on 4 November 1981 when a new training and intelligence centre was opened by President Romeo Lucas García and his brother, Chief of Staff Benedicto Lucas García:

In November 1981, Generals Romeo and Benedicto Lucas García inaugurated in Guatemala City the Army Electrónics and Transmissions School(Escuela de Transmisiones y Electronica del Ejército) built with Israeli assistance and technology. During the ceremonies, attended by the Israeli ambassador to Guatemala, President Lucas García stated that 'thanks to the assistance and transfer of electronic technology provided by the State of Israel to Guatemala', the Guatemalan Army has enhanced its ability to stay on top of the latest technological developments.[263]

The Israeli daily *Ma'ariv* reprinted a remark by General Benedicto Lucas García praising the "gigantic job" done by Israel on behalf of Guatemala's armed forces.[264] He was not just being polite: by 1982 the dollar value of Israeli military assistance was estimated at \$90 million.[265]

The first important contact between the Guatemalan and Israeli military establishments possibly took place in August 1975, when a delegation of top Guatemalan army officers travelled to Israel, ostensibly seeking Israeli expertise in organizing agricultural co-operatives. Press reports at the time said the delegation was headed by a special adviser to President Laugerud, and included five army colonels and lieutenant colonels.[266] According to most sources the first sales of Israeli equipment to Guatemala (and El Salvador) were in 1975, and military transfers of equipment ranging from Galil submachine-guns to armoured cars and aircraft continued throughout the balance of the decade.[267]

It was Israel's provision of shiploads of arms and counter-insurgency aircraft to the Somoza regime in the years just before its overthrow that attracted the sympathy of some Arab countries to the Nicaraguan Revolution, and prompted Arab assistance to the new Nicaraguan government after Somoza's was ousted.Expressions of gratitude for this assistance have been wrongly interpreted by some observers and propagandists as proof of the present Nicaraguan government's anti-Semitism; conversely, evidence of authentic anti-Semitism on the part of top Guatemalan army officers and their Salvadorean counterparts has been overlooked or concealed. Ironically, only shortly after Israel first agreed to provide arms, and, perhaps, advisory assistance to Guatemala, *Revista Militar de Guatemala* (Guatemalan army's Staff College review) published a prominent feature article by a Guatemalan officer in praise of Adolf Hitler. National Socialism, and the "Final Solution".[268] Entitled "*El Nacional Socialismo*", it quotes extensively from *Mein Kampf*, concluding that Hitler's anti-Semitism originated in his "discovery" that Communism was part of a "Jewish conspiracy". The author, Captain Angel M. Cantoral Dávila, explains that Germany had to fight against the Jews "in self defense", as part of its battle against a Russia "dominated by the strength of a Marxist-Jewish nucleus and converted into an instrument for the domination of other peoples."[269]

He asserts, moreover, that the Nazis had a bad press precisely because they had slaughtered *Communists*:

> Greater Germany at war went through an essentially anticommunist phase, and this has garnered it persistent enemies that are even now producing films against the crimes of nazism ... while there isn't a single one about the present and greater crimes of Communism.[270]

Captain Cantoral Dávila cautions the reader that Nazism is not "a political panacea", to be applied across the board, but urges each country to develop its own variation of National Socialism "like the Spanish Falange, which is eminently nationalist and Catholic".[271]

Sympathies and, indeed, identification with the Nazis as champions of anti-Communism in the Guatemalan military are also reflected in the ideology of the most powerful of the right-wing political parties that since 1954 has worked hand in hand with the military. The National Liberation Movement (MLN), which originally described itself as "the party of organized violence", is ideologically close to groupings modelled on German or Italian fascism in Argentina, Uruguay and Paraguay, as well as other groups linked in the Taiwan-based World Anti-Communist League (WACL), itself described in the US press as composed of "anti-semitic, neo-fascist groups".[272]

In 1980, MLN in turn, reportedly provided financial and organizational assistance to El Salvador's right-wing semi-official party ARENA, headed by Major Roberto D'Aubuisson. MLN founder Mario Sandoval Alarcón's nephew, Carlos Midence, has been quoted as taking credit for helping set up ARENA, and as expressing admiration for Hitler and Nazism:

> 'ARENA, that's my baby', exclaimed Midence, a roly-poly former MLN organizer who sports a swastika medallion he says was given to him by the private secretary of Hitler's former propaganda minister in Argentina.[273]

D'Aubuisson, too, reportedly told three reporters: "You Germans are very intelligent. You realized that the Jews were responsible for the spread of Communism, and you began to kill them."[274]

That Israel's part in Central America was preconceived, has been suggested by the timing of its initiative in Guatemala and its regional application. Israel's aid to Nicaragua's Somoza government in its last battle to retain power, and the Carter administration's blind eye turned at the time, is, perhaps, the best documented instance when Israel stepped in to compensate for the US cutting off direct military assistance to accord with its human rights policy. In 1978, credit sales and deliveries of aircraft, ammunition, radios and rifles to Nicaragua were apparently unique in Israel's cash-only arms trade experience (unless costs were secretly guaranteed by the United States). Most sources indicate that the US at least passively approved of Israel making the arms sales banned to the US itself:

> Despite its own cutoff of military aid, the US government raised no objections to Israel's efforts to help the dictator [Somoza]. As a State Department official explained: 'If Somoza goes we would prefer to see him go peacefully. We would not like to see him toppled in an armed revolt.'[275]

That the US could instantly stop the flow of Israeli weapons to Somoza's Nicaragua (or elsewhere in Central America) is indicated by an incident in Somoza's final weeks, when, on recommendations from Washington, a ship with the last of a series of Israeli arms packages was turned back.[276]

In July 1983 the *New York Times* published a report claiming the Israeli arms and advisory assistance programme in Central America was not solely an Israeli initiative, motivated by profit or by strictly Israeli political interests. The *Times*, quoting senior Reagan administration officials, said that Israel had agreed to a US request to send arms — including artillery, mortar rounds, mines and hand grenades — to Honduras for use by anti-Nicaraguan forces. Shipments of the arms, said to have been captured from PLO forces, had already begun, as

> part of an enlarged Israeli role in Central America encouraged by the United States as a way of supplementing American military aid to friendly governments and supporting insurgent operations against the leftist Nicaraguan government.[277]

The same source cited American officials who

> told the newspaper that the Israeli co-operation in Central America was a factor in the recent improvement in Israeli-US relations.[278]

It is only natural to speculate that the massive influx of Israeli arms and advice to Central America after 1976 followed an invitation or request to do so by either the Department of State, or by US defence or intelligence agencies acting semi-independently.[279]

When Military Assistance is not Military Assistance

Although human rights legislation served to block most traditional training programmes after 1977, some US advisers continued to train the military inside Guatemala, and, despite the ostensible embargo, some Guatemalan officers were trained at American bases. The scale of these concealed programmes remains unknown, but inadvertently revealed evidence is sufficient to conclude that the Pentagon made every effort to continue traditional training activities, and succeeded in signalling their counterparts that a special relationship between the two armies remained whatever the exigencies of Carter's foreign relations policies. Under the Reagan administration concealment of ongoing relations between the two military establishments gradually broke down.

In October 1982, reporter Allan Nairn revealed that at least one US adviser was stationed in Guatemala despite the much publicized ban. In a televised interview US Army Captain Jesse García acknowledged that he was employed to teach Guatemalan army cadets ambushing techniques, surveillance, combat arms, artillery, armour, patrolling, demolition, the full range of Special Forces skills. Congressman Michael Barnes characterized García's work as in direct violation of the congressional stricture that "no military assistance including training [can] be provided for Guatemala without the approval of Congress."[280] The Defense Department subsequently explained García's presence as part of a previously unknown programme, apparently not funded under the Foreign Assistance Act:

> According to Pentagon spokesman Henry E. Catto, Jr., on October 21, the Personnel Exchange Program '. . . is not designed to provide liaison, security assistance, a US intelligence source, or help for MAAG's or MilGroups.' Captain García is 'a professor of English to cadets at the Escuela Politecnica. He is also responsible for teaching military-related subjects as prescribed by the curriculum of the Escuela Politecnica. This includes staff supervision over all military instruction and the weekly field training exercizes conducted by the cadets.'[281]

Further training and advisory assistance was provided during the embargo period by members of the US Military Group, and by civilians from other agencies, although the importance of the civilian component of the United States mission in Guatemala is difficult to gauge. There is some evidence, both from opposition groups and other sources that after 1977 US intelligence personnel continued without pause to play an important training, consultancy, or advisory role in security matters. When a car bomb exploded in front of Guatemala's National Palace on 6 September 1980, killing eight and injuring some 150 bystanders, the Guatemalans called in experts from the US Embassy to inspect the scene: press reports said "two AID bomb specialists" were there within ten minutes.[282] More significantly, opposition sources maintain, convincingly, that US intelligence officers worked closely with the Presidential intelligence agency, throughout the embargo period. The level of US intelligence and covert military assistance presumably leapt after the election of Ronald Reagan.

Although training of Guatemalan forces at US military bases was largely stopped after 1977, in early 1983 students at the School of the

Americas in the Canal Zone included two Guatemalan officers. According to the school commander, Colonel Nicolas Andreachio, "The two were admitted at the special request of the State Department."[282] Other Guatemalans have been trained in the US, (presumably with the go-ahead of the Departments of Defense and State) by private corporations. Principal trainees have been the army's helicopter pilots, sent to Texas under the Reagan administration to be trained by the makers of their new helicopters. Civilian contractors have also reportedly undertaken to provide repairs and replacement parts for counter-insurgency aircraft inside the US, with a wink and a nod — if not covert funding — from the Reagan administration. The extent of the Reagan administration's effort to circumvent congress was partially revealed in late 1982, when it was discovered that between 1981 and 1982 helicopter exports had been licensed to permit the expansion of the Guatemalan army's fleet from eight to 27 ("The Guatemalans have been buying the commercial version of a range of Bell helicopters and then converting them to military use at the rate of one a month").[284] Documents purportedly recovered from the wreck of an air force helicopter shot down by ORPA guerrillas also tended to confirm that a major effort was being made in the US to pull the teeth of congressional sanctions. ("A letter to the dead pilot, Colonel Mario Enrique Vasquez, from the Comex company of Florida details the repair work carried out in the United States on Guatemalan air force A-37 counterinsurgency aircraft. The document also alludes to the supply of 200 lbs of material from the logistics section of the US air force to the Guatemalans".)[285]

Other backdoor security assistance from the Reagan administration may be forthcoming in the near future, ostensibly intended to help Guatemala prepare for democratic presidential elections. While the Reagan administration would find it difficult to win congressional approval for a programme to assist Guatemala's army to establish totalitarian control over the population, aid for elections is, on the surface, innocuous. Current proposals for "election" aid include assistance to develop a central, computerized population registry, with universal identity cards with photographs. The registration programme has already begun, and has attracted some criticism:

> ... the various municipalities and townships throughout Guatemala have begun the army-sponsored re-registration of all citizens. Signing up with the new government population office is compulsory, and applicants are charged $2.50 for the service, which includes a passport-type photograph. The price is equal to a day's wage in many parts of the country, and there have been protests. There is evidence that the new registration will serve purposes other than elections. An army officer explains: 'This is one way to know who everyone is and where he is supposed to be'.[286]

Although the Reagan administration has provided not insubstantial security assistance, and fundamental political support, to Guatemala's army since 1981, the US congress has to date proved of sufficient backbone to resist being railroaded into formally lifting the sanctions the Guatemalans unwisely called down upon themselves in 1977. The Reagan administration, however, has never stopped trying to restore a major, overt security assistance programme to Guatemala, and to signal Guatemala's army that the problem is not a question of human rights but an intransigent congress. On 7 January 1983 the Department of State announced a $6.3 million sales agreement to provide spare parts for Guatemala's UH-1H counter-insurgency helicopters and other equipment previously under embargo in response to "significant steps" taken by the Guatemalan regime to improve its human rights record.[287] The aid release was justified by what was described as a "dramatic decline" in human rights abuse, and a stated intention to strengthen the army's "moderate" officers; a rationale much like that used initially to support military assistance to El Salvador after the October 1979 coup. The package included a US commitment to provide for helicopter inspection and repairs, apparently by US military personnel, $1.12 million in spare parts for A-37B aircraft, and $170,000 earmarked for training.[288]

Congressional opposition stopped most of the package. House of Representatives Appropriations Committee Chairman Clarence Long went on record in May 1983 that he would not budge on the matter:

> After describing a litany of abuses against Guatemalan Indians by government forces, Long asked Under Secretary William Schneider Jr. at a hearing: 'What on earth are we doing giving military aid to a country responsible for these monstrosities? I know of no redeeming features in Guatemala to justify our putting money in, to continue the murder and torture, the burning of villages, of poor, pathetic Indians.'[289]

Notes to Part 3

Chapter 5

1. For biographical information on Kjell Laugerud see *Revista Militar de Guatemala*, October-December 1970.
2. For biographical information on Vassaux Martínez, see *Revista Militar*, July-September 1970. Vassaux Martínez was trained at Fort Gulick in 1953 and at Fort Benning in 1962.
3. NACLA, *Guatemala* (1974), "Teachers Everywhere", p. 189. The same source (p. 190) illustrates the importance of cross-sector unity in the teachers' conflict.
4. Roger Plant, *Guatemala: Unnatural Disaster*, London: Latin America Bureau (1978).
5. *Panorama*, January 1974, p. 6.
6. Ibid.
7. *El Gráfico*, 26 February 1974.

8.   *La Tarde*, 11 March 1974.
9.   *La Noche*, 22 March 1974.
10. NACLA, *Guatemala* (1974), p. 191, citing *New York Times*, 8 March 1974.
11. Plant, op. cit., p. 47 citing *La Nación*, 26 February 1974.
12. Plant, op. cit., p. 47.
13. Ibid., p. 46, citing Dirección General de Estadística, *Censo de Población y Habitación, 1973*. Official estimates for 1980 suggest the move into manufacturing stalled in the early 1970s; the manufacturing sector remained at about 14% of the economically active population of 2.137 million; agricultural workers at about 58% (respectively 289,641 and 1,237,748). *Europa Yearbook, 1983*, London, 1983, p. 421.
14. Plant, op. cit., p. 46; government statistics registered only 27,486 union members.
15. Ibid. The CTF was an affiliate of the World Confederation of Free Trade Unions and a member of its Western Hemisphere body, ORIT.
16. See Brian Murphy in Richard Adams, *Crucifixion by Power*, chapter 9, "The Stunted Growth of Campesino Organizations", for a detailed discussion of union organization up until the mid-1960s.
17. Plant, op. cit., p. 46.
18. Ibid. Surprisingly, FASGUA grew from an organization founded by the Castillo Armas government in 1955 as a "tame" labour federation (the *Federación Autónoma Sindical*) which moved rapidly to the left and, in 1957, changed to its present name. Eventually FASGUA completed its ideological shift by affiliating with the Prague-based World Confederation of Trade Unions.
19. Statement, *Central Nacional de Trabajadoves*, 1979.
20. See Brian Murphy, in Adams op. cit., "The Stunted Growth . . ." pp. 445-7, for an excellent analysis of peasant organization in the context of changing legislation before and after the revolutionary period. Murphy explains the distinction between peasant *sindicatos*, created for, and limited to, explicitly economic purposes, and *uniones*, which were associations of private landowners.
21. Ibid., pp. 158-60.
22. Ibid., pp. 163-4.
23. Ibid., p. 357, Table 7-1.
24. Ibid., p. 365, Table 7-2.
25. Plant, op. cit., p. 76.
26. Adams, op. cit., pp. 181-2.
27. These included forced recruitment by military commissioners who doubled as labour recruiters; peasants were offered the choice of joining the army or working on the plantation.
28. Plant, op. cit., p. 82.
29. Adams, op. cit., p. 369 citing Lester Schmid, "The Role of Migratory Labor in the Economic Development of Guatemala", Ph.D. dissertation, University of Wisconsin, 1967.
30. Plant, op. cit., p. 82.
31. Adams, op. cit., "The Costs of Growth: Cotton"; Plant, op. cit., pp. 80-89; NACLA, op. cit. *Guatemala* in particular.
32. Adams, op. cit., pp. 371-8.
33. Ibid., p. 378.
34. *Europa Yearbook, 1983*, p. 425. Exports to the People's Republic of China, zero in 1977 were $28 million in 1978, $66 million in 1979, and $62.5 million in 1980 and consisted primarily of cotton. A 1981 Guatemalan trade mission to China led by Minister of the Economy Valentín Solórzano was reportedly told by the Chinese that they "sympathized with the Guatemalan struggle against Soviet and Cuban Aggression" (*Central America Report*, 14 November 1981, "Guatemala: Red cotton candy").
35. *Latin America Regional Reports*, 9 July 1982, "Business Unhappy with Rios Montt".

36. *Latin America Regional Reports*, 8 January 1982, "Rural Crisis Helps the Guerrillas".
37. Plant, op. cit., p. 88.
38. OXFAM-America, *Witness to Political Violence in Guatemala* (1982), p. 14.
39. Ibid.
40. Adams, op. cit., p. 201 for reference to the co-operatives in El Quiché; Plant, op. cit., p. 87.
41. Plant, op. cit., p. 87; 227 were agricultural co-operatives, 26 artisan, 192 savings and loan and 86 consumer.
42. Ibid.
43. Speech by Gen. Kjell Laugerud García, from his collected speeches, *Discursos . . .* (Editorial del Ejército, Guatemala, 1976).
44. Luis Reina's death at the hands of the EGP apparently precipitated the army assault on co-operatives set up in the area. See *El Imparcial* (Guatemala), 22 December 1966 for an account of the founding, in April 1966, of the co-operative "Ixcán Grande" in the border area between the departments of El Quiché and Huhuetenango. The account describes the arrival of several hundred families of Mam Indians from nine *municipios* of southern Huhuetenango department. Catholic charities provided funds for a clinic and a co-operative store, and provided each co-operative member with 300 cuerdas (30 acres) of land. Ixcán Grande was one of the co-operatives wiped out by the army in the late 1970s. See also *Uno más Uno*, 17 February 1980, "Con la muerte del Tigre de Ixcán, en junio de 1975 comenzó la militarización en Guatemala", by Marco Aurelio Carballo.
45. *Uno más Uno*, 17 February 1980, and Plant, op. cit., p. 91.
46. OXFAM-America, 1982, op. cit., p. 17; statements by former development workers.
47. From a photograph of the message signed by the *Movimiento Armado Nacionalista Organizado* (Organized National Armed Movement) in *La Tarde*, July 1975, "La Organización Clandestina 'La Mano' Amenaza de Muerte . . .".
48. Plant, op. cit., pp. 74-5; Adams, op. cit., pp. 166, 341.
49. The scheme was widely described as a "resettlement" or "colonization" project; the area involved was officially reported to cover 914,000 hectares (*Latin America and the Caribbean 1980*: (World of Information, UK) p. 163.
50. Plant, op. cit., p. 90, citing *Inforpress Centroamericana*, 5 August 1978.
51. Ibid., p. 89.
52. Amnesty International, *Guatemala*, 1976.
53. Plant, p. 90, citing *El Gráfico*.
54. Ibid.
55. Interviews, 1979. Laugerud, in particular, whose brother Hans directed the Agrarian Reform Institute (*Instituto Nacional de Transformación Agraria*, INTA), reportedly owned a vast estate near Cobán in Alta Verapaz. Lucas García owned vast tracts at Raxruja, near the Rubelsanto oil field in northern Alta Verapaz.
56. Plant, op. cit., p. 5.
57. See, for example Susan Jonas, "Class-Quake in Guatemala", *Guatemala and Central America Report*, cited in Hearings, "Human Rights in Nicaragua, Guatemala and El Salvador: Implications for US Policy", 1976.
58. Plant, op. cit., p. 5.
59. Ibid.
60. Ibid., p. 1.
61. Amnesty International, *Guatemala*, 1976, pp. 5-6.
62. OXFAM-America, op. cit., 1982, p. 15.
63. Plant, op. cit., p. 6.
64. Ibid.
65. Ibid., p. 47; see also OXFAM-America, op. cit., p. 17 and the *Frente Democrático Contra la Represión*'s (FDCR) *Informador Mensual*, November 1979, p. 7, for accounts of the creation of CNUS and its significance.

66. Plant, op. cit., p. 58.
67. Ibid., p. 48.
68. Ibid.
69. Speech to the graduating class of the *Escuela Politécnica*, published in *Ejército*, January 1966.
70. Plant, op. cit., p. 7.
71. Ibid., p. 29.
72. Ibid., p. 59; the Ingenio Pantaleón refined the sugar from its own surrounding plantations and for some 100 other plantations on the coast.
73. Ibid., p. 85; $1.12 was the minimum daily wage for cotton, sugar and cattle ranch workers; for coffee workers it was $1.04.
74. Ibid.
75. Plant, op. cit., pp. 51-3 for Lopéz Larrave's background.
76. Ibid., p. 53.
77. Ibid.
78. Amnesty International, *Report*, 1978, p. 124 and FDCR, *Informador Mensual*, November 1979, p. 7.
79. FDCR, op. cit., p. 7.
80. Amnesty International, "Repression of Politicians in Guatemala", 28 June 1979, mimeograph, AI Index AMR 34/13/79.
81. On this occasion the MLN split from the army's "official" coalition, running former president Col. Enrique Peralta Azurdia as its candidate. The Christian Democrats, the Authentic Revolutionary Party, and the Popular Participation Front all joined to field a single candidate, who would represent their National Unity Front: this was General Ricardo Peralta Méndez, Peralta Azurdia's nephew, and the former head of the agency created in 1976 to co-ordinate reconstruction after the earthquake. See *Keesing's Contemporary Archive*, 9 June 1978, for statistics on the presidential and congressional elections.
82. NACLA, *Report on the Americas*, November-December 1978, "Guatemala Bus Fare Rebellion", p. 43.
83. *Latin America Political Report*, 13 October 1978, "Guatemala: Bus Fare Crisis", and FDCR, *Informador Mensual*, November 1979, p. 7.
84. NACLA, op. cit. For detailed reporting on the progress of the bus fares conflict see the short-lived Guatemalan newspaper *Nuevo Diario* from October 1978.
85. *Latin America Political Report*, 13 October 1978, op. cit.
86. *Nuevo Diario* (Guatemala), 10 October 1978.
87. Amnesty International, *Report*, 1979, p. 65.
88. Ibid.
89. Ibid.
90. Ibid., and Amnesty International, *Report*, 1981, p. 150.
91. Amnesty International, *Guatemala: A Government Program of Political Murder*, 1981, p. 12.
92. Ibid., p. 7.
93. *Latin America Political Report*, 13 April 1979, "Guatemala: rot in the state of Denmark".
94. *Latin America Political Report*, 30 March 1979, "Guatemala: At the price of his head".
95. Ibid. and *Latin America Political Report*, 6 April 1979, "Colom Argueta's last interview", in which he is quoted as saying "The government is attempting to give itself a democratic veneer, which is why they are recognizing my party (FUR). But in exchange, they want my head."
96. Amnesty International, Mimeograph, "Repression of Politicians in Guatemala", 28 June 1979.
97. Amnesty International, 1981, *Guatemala: A Government Program of Political Murder*, pp. 6-7. Father Conrado de la Cruz and his assistant Herlindo Cifuentes were detained with at least 44 others in a May Day demonstration in the capital in 1980

and "disappeared". Those killed included Spanish priests José María Gran (a Philippine national) and Faustino Villanueva, as well as Belgian priest Walter Voordeckers.

98. OXFAM-America, op. cit., 1982, p. 15.
99. Ibid.
100. Ibid., p. 16.
101. Ibid., p. 17.
102. Amnesty International Report, 1980, pp. 141-2.
103. Ibid.
104. *Comité de Unidad Campesina (CUC)*, 1 May 1978, leaflet: "*El Comité de Unidad Campesina al Pueblo de Guatemala*".
105. Ibid. This urban-rural solidarity was a major CUC objective; see statement of CUC representative Domingo Hernández Iztoy, December 1982: '. . . it was very frightening to the government that on the first of May, we appeared in demonstrations — Indians and *Ladino* workers — side by side. Because for a long time, one method of continuing the system of exploitation was to use divisions between Indian and *Ladino* peoples."
106. See *Frente* (Guatemala), January 1980 for summaries of press reports. The pattern of limited direct action then reported, particularly community action to free leaders from local jails, is essentially the same as in the 19th Century. This pattern changed in the 1980s, as the Indian population turned to open warfare.
107. For summaries of press reports on the "El Izotal" protests and the October 1979 demonstrations see FDCR, bulletin, November 1979, Vol. 1, pp. 13-14, and *Panorama*, October 1979, pp. 6-7. On 14 October two students distributing CNT leaflets, protesting the murder of Miguel Najarro of "El Izotal", were detained on the steps of the Supreme Court building and "disappeared" for a period before an army officer relative of one intervened; both were, however, badly tortured. 16-year old Yolanda Aguilar Urizar was found to be blind as a result of torture; she did eventually recover her eyesight. Her mother, Yolanda de Urizar, is a labour lawyer who was herself detained in 1983 and remains "disappeared".
108. *Panorama*, October 1979, p. 8.
109. The first reference to the Salvadorean minimum wage decree appeared in an illustrated mimeographed leaflet: "*El CUC exige 5 quetzales por tonelada de Caña y por quintal de algodón*", undated, probably December 1979; this was also mentioned in another mimeographed leaflet dated December 1980; "*El Comité de Unidad Campesina -CUC- Al Comité Nacional de Unidad Sindical -CNUS- a todas sus organizaciones sindicales y a los demás sectores populares y democráticos*".
110. CUC, undated leaflet, probably December 1979.
111. CUC, January 1980 leaflet.
112. See *Inforpress* from November and December 1979.
113. EGP, *Campañero*, July 1982, no. 6.
114. Ibid.
115. The 17,000 figure is cited in Washington Office on Latin America (WOLA), *Update*, February 1983.
116. Transcript from taped interview by Alaíde Foppa for Radio UNAM, Mexico City.
117. Ibid.
118. See, for example, OXFAM-America, op. cit., p. 21, quoting development workers who reported an increase in emigration to the urban slums, and a tendency for migrant workers on coffee plantations in the south of Mexico to remain there.
119. From *Uno más uno* (Mexico City), reproduced in *American Poetry Review*, "Journey to the Depths", (trans. Patricia Goedicke) January/February 1983, pp. 23-5. This gives the speaker's name as Rigoberto Menchú. For an account of the "disappearance" of Rigoberto's mother, Juana Tum de Menchú, after arrest by an army patrol on 19 April 1980, see Amnesty International, *A Government Program of Political Murder*, 1981, p. 14.

120. Its membership as of 1982 included the *Núcleos Obreros Revolucionarios "Felipe Antonio García"*, NOR; the *Comité de Unidad Campesina* (CUC); the *Coordinadora de Pobladores "Trinidad Gómez Hernández"*, CDP: The *Cristianos Revolucionarios "Vicente Menchú"* CRVM; an indigenous peasant organization from El Quiché; and university and secondary school branches of the *Frente Estudiantil Revolucionario "Robin Garcia"*, FERG (as listed in an FP-31 leaflet, dated 14 May 1982, issued after the occupation of the Brazilian Embassy in mid-1982.
121. FDCR, bulletin, January 1980.
122. Piero Gleijeses, "Guatemala: Crisis and Response", (manuscript) Johns Hopkins University (SAIS) 1982, pp. 9-10. Prof. Gleijeses refers the reader to an account of the EGP's organizational work by a participant, Mario Payeras, *Los Días de la Selva* (Mexico, Ediciones Bloque de Apoyo a la Revolución Centroamericana, 1980).
123. See *Compañero*, the EGP English/Spanish monthly for July 1982, and *El Gráfico*, 30 November 1975.
124. *El Día* (Mexico), 13 January 1981, "Guatemala: represión brutal", by Teresa Gurza.
125. Ibid.
126. OXFAM-America, 1982, p. 29.
127. Ibid., p. 32.
128. Gabriel Aguilera Peralta, "The Process of Militarization in the Guatemalan State", LARU Studies, September 1982, p. 46.
129. Frente Popular 31 January -FP-31-,"*El FP-31 desenmascara la política genocida de la junta militar golpista*", leaflet, 14 May 1982.

Chapter 6
130. Office of Public Safety, Termination Phase-Out Study, 1974.
131. Gabriel Aguilera, op. cit., notes press reports in July 1975 announcing the creation of 640 additional police posts; further rises in the authorized force level occurred irregularly in subsequent years.
132. Plant, op. cit., pp. 31-2.
133. Ibid.
134. *Prensa Libre* (Guatemala) 17 November 1980; see also 23 August 1980.
135. *El Día* (Mexico City) 9 July 1981, "La policía Guatemalteca Culpable de Asesinatos: un Ex-Jefe de Detectives."
136. *El Gráfico*, 8 July 1981, " 'Yo Acuso' de Manuel Valiente Téllez."
137. *Noticias de Guatemala*, 16 January 1982; see also the Guatemalan daily press of the period. The international news media disregarded Valiente's own attribution of the attacks to the security services, which was common knowledge in Guatemala City, and implied the attacks had been carried out by the guerrillas; see in particular *New York Times*, 30 December 1981 (AP) and *Reuter*, 29 December 1981.
138. Amnesty International *Report*, 1982, p. 140.
139. The death of security chiefs is often the only occasion on which the news media may refer to political police agencies; in November 1980 the Guatemalan press reported the assassination of Justo Rufino Hernández, Deputy Head (*Segundo Jefe*) of the Special Investigations Section of the Detective corps. (See *El Gráfico*, 5 November 1980.)
140. Interpol was placed within the detective corps in accordance with a congressional decree of March 1967. The head of Guatemalan Interpol under Lucas García was arrested by the army after the 23 March 1982 coup, and mysteriously died in custody soon afterwards.
141. Amnesty International *Report*, 1981, p. 11.
142. Commando Six was called a "SWAT" team because it was modelled on the "Special Weapons and Tactics (SWAT)" teams developed in the US in the mid-1960s in response to urban unrest and fears of urban guerrilla warfare. In the US context they were distinguished from conventional police bodies in their use of automatic weapons, military tactics, elite police status and high motivation. Unlike

the plainclothes detectives, Commando Six personnel wore a distinctive uniform modelled on those worn in an American television series about a SWAT team: dark blue flight suits and baseball caps. See *Miami Herald* 16 January 1980 for reference to Commando Six's mimicking of American television.

143. In a 1979 interview a former Guatemalan official maintained Commando Six could be on the scene of a bank raid or similar incident in the capital within about five minutes of the alarm being given. Press reports in the 1970s frequently showed heavily armed members of the SWAT unit at the scene of bank robberies, wearing bullet-proof vests (see for example *La Tarde*, 18 October 1979).

144. The Spanish Embassy fire has never been convincingly accounted for. Some observers claim the cause was a bomb thrown into the building by police as they charged in, firing automatic weapons; many of the dead were confirmed to have bullet wounds. Other sources said that four students accompanying the Indian delegation had molotov cocktails which exploded at the time of the police assault. A third explanation might be found in comparing the Embassy assault with perhaps the most widely publicized action by SWAT teams in the US: in May 1974, a house used by members of the "Simbionese Liberation Army" in Los Angeles, California was attacked with firearms and tear gas, exploding into flame in an eerily similar way to the Spanish Embassy fire. One source concludes that the types of tear gas projectiles used "can ignite a firestorm when used indoors"; see Center for Research on Criminal Justice, *The Iron Fist and the Velvet Glove* (Berkeley, California, 1977, 2nd edition). This study also includes a resumé and bibliography on the origin of the SWAT concept (pp. 93-7). Whether tear gas projectiles were fired into the Embassy prior to the assault is not known; objects identified by onlookers as "bombs" may, however, have been projectiles of flammable tear gas.

145. *Correo de Guatemala*, 16 January 1966.

146. *El Imparcial*, 22 July 1966.

147. Transcript, "File on 4", produced by Gerry Northam for British Broadcasting Corporation, Radio 4, February 1981.

148. CUC, October 1979, untitled mimeograph.

149. John Dombrowski, et. al., *Area Handbook for Guatemala*, 1970, p. 323; this source uses the term "Border Patrol".

150. Estimates of force levels for the army in 1974 range from 12,500 to 15,000. A 1969 breakdown reported the standing force as 900 officers and 11,000 enlisted men; 2,500 of the enlisted men were classified as "specialists" (*especialistas*) contracted because of their particular technical skills; they served with higher pay and the right to resign. The military commissioners were not accounted for in the published force level; they received a supplementary payment of $47 a month in addition to their stipend as members of the army's "active reserve". (See C. Sereseres, "Military Development and the US Military Assistance Program for Latin America: The Case of Guatemala, 1961-69", PhD dissertation, University of California at Riverside, 1971, p. 106.) *This Week*, 30 November 1981, gave the army force level at 18,000 at that time; this may have reached 22,000 by the first quarter of 1982; official figures are not available.

151. Gabriel Aguilera, op. cit., p. 48; the Adolfo V. Hall schools are located in Guatemala City, Zacapa, Mazatenango, Cobán and Quetzaltenango.

152. Ibid., p. 49.

153. Ibid.

154. Ibid .

155. Ibid.

156. Captain José Luis Quilo, "Trascendencia del Servicio", in *Revista Militar de Guatemala*, October-December 1975, January-March 1976.

157. Presidente Ydígoras Fuentes, *Mensaje*, March 1963.

158. US Department of State, *Internal Security Programs in Latin America, Guatemala*, p. 20.

159. See *El Gráfico*, 31 July 1980, and Gabriel Aguilera, op. cit., p. 50.

160. *La Nación*, 29 July 1980, "Nuevas normas para el servicio militar dicta Ministro de Defensa".

161. Ibid.

162. OXFAM-America, 1982, pp. 29-30. For a summary of conscription procedures, see also Marlise Simons, "Indians resist Military Service: Guatemalan Army's Contempt for their Culture Breeds Spirit of Revolt", *Washington Post*, 28 March 1980.

163. OXFAM-America, 1982, p. 31.

164. Amnesty International, *Guatemala . . .*, 1981, p. 21.

165. Ibid.

166. Ibid. , pp. 23-4.

167. Ibid., p. 24.

168. OXFAM-America, 1982, p. 30.

169. Aguilera, op. cit. (September 1982), p. 50.

170. Ibid.

171. Ibid .

172. Sereseres, Dissertation, op. cit., p. 113.

173. CUC, October 1979, untitled mimeograph.

174. Ibid. The leaflet also notes that the principal income of the military commissioners consists of bribes provided by the parents of potential conscripts.

175. Ibid.

176. Aguilera, op. cit. (September 1982), p. 50.

177. Interview, December 1979, with former Guatemalan official on G-2. Plainclothes men carrying credentials establishing their identity as "confidential" agents of military intelligence are most frequently revealed in the Guatemalan news media when they are killed in vendettas or by guerrilla groups. For example, *Prensa Libre*, 23 March 1981, reported the submachine-gun slaying of "Adonis García Navas, 35, and Marco Antonio Pérez Cortez, 30, who carried credentials as '*confidenciales*' of the army" ("The victims attempted to return the fire").

178. Interview, December 1979: the identities of Guatemalans interviewed in the course of the study cannot be made public for reasons of security.

179. *Prensa Libre*, 8 November 1975.

180. *Latin America Political Report* (London) 14 December 1979.

181. *Washington Post*, 6 April 1980, "Feared Guatemalan Rightist Battles Rising Left Tide", by Marlise Simons.

182. Interview, December 1979.

183. Ibid.

184. The 1967 *La Violencia en Guatemala* (Mexico City) apparently made the *first* published reference (outside Guatemala) to the "*Policia Regional*", then identified as just one of several "death-squads".

185. Plant, op. cit., p. 28. Col. José Elías Ramírez Cervantes, head of the Military Academy under Laugerud, was himself assassinated in April 1976.

186. CNUS, *El Fascismo en Guatemala: Un Vasto Plan Represivo Contra el Pueblo y el Movimiento Sindical*, cited in Plant, op. cit., pp. 51, 113; and Latin America Working Group, *Letter* (Canada), No. 1, December 1977, p. 9.

187. Cited in Latin America Working Group, op. cit., p. 9.

188. Amnesty International, *Guatemala . . .*

189. See, for example, the statement of defector Elías Barahona y Barahona, September 1980, or the FDCR's newspaper, *Frente*, January 1981. The latter, in an article entitled "La Caja Negra", describes the top security group as including seven members, and known as the "Caja Negra" (Black Box). In addition to the officials noted above *Frente* maintains that the "Black Box" included a North American advisor of Puerto Rican origin and a representative of Guatemalan private enterprise.

190. Amnesty International, for example, *Guatemala . . .* attributes policy decisions and

the selection of targets for "disappearance" and killing to the special intelligence group at the centre of the agency.

191. Ibid., p. 8.
192. *Frente*, January 1981.
193. Amnesty International, *Guatemala* . . . p. 6.
194. Ibid.
195. This account of operational methods is based on an extensive interview with a former top Guatemalan official who asked not to be identified; it is consistent with accounts given in other interviews by opposition leaders, and with the evidence available from analysis of cases of "death-squad" killings.
196. Amnesty International *Report*, 1981, p. 153, outlines the details of the Valverth case.
197. In January 1981 the Democratic Front Against Repression (FDCR) published statistics on government killings in 1980, giving a total of 3,719 Guatemalans killed; 389 were university or secondary school students, 86 were university teachers, and 326 were primary school teachers. Others killed included 300 peasant leaders, 110 trade unionists, 30 social-democratic party leaders, 16 journalists and four Roman Catholic priests.
198. Typescript, dated 28 October 1980; names and places have been deleted at the request of the recorder of the testimony.
199. Ibid.
200. Amnesty International, *Guatemala* . . . p. 22.
201. Ibid. Reference is also made to two secret cells at Mariscal Zavala, one called "The powder magazine" ("El Polvorín"), the other "the olive" ("la aceituna") (possibly because it was painted green).
202. Ibid.
203. Ibid.
204. Interviews, December 1979.
205. Interview, December 1979.
206. "A view of Recent Activities in Central America: 1972-1977", unsigned typescript, Miami, 1978. The Christian Democratic Party alleged that GUATEL played a principal role in the electoral fraud that placed Kjell Laugerud in the Presidency in 1974. A paid advertisement by the party claimed that telexed election returns received in the sixth floor offices of GUATEL were systematically falsified when favourable to the National Opposition Front (which supported Ríos Montt); (see *Diario de la Tarde*, 7 March 1974, paid advertisement, cited in Carlos Caceres, *Aproximación a Guatemala*, Universidad Autónoma de Sinaloa, Culiacán, Sinaloa, México, 1980, p. 200.)
207. Interview.
208. Interview.
209. Interview.
210. Amnesty International Briefing: *Guatemala*, December 1976, p.16.
211. Ibid., p. 1.
212. There are several excellent studies of the Brazilian death-squads, notably Helio Pereira Bicudo, *El Escuadron de la Muerte*, Madrid; Ultramar, 1978, and Helio Bicudo was Sao Paulo's District Attorney. Aderito López, *L'Escuadron de la Mort: Sao Paulo*, translated by Antonio Tavares-Telez, Casterman, Belgium, 1973.
213. Amnesty International, *Guatemala* . . ., pp. 5-6.
214. Ibid., p. 8.
215. *Latin America Political Report*, 6 April 1979, "Colom Argueta's Last Interview".

Chapter 7

216. US Congress, Hearings, "Human Rights in Nicaragua, Guatemala, and El Salvador: Implications for US Policy", 1976, p. 111.
217. Ibid., pp. 185-6.
218. US Congress, Hearings, "New Directions for the 1970's: Toward a Strategy of Inter-

American Development", 1969, p. 527, testimony of William E. Lang, Deputy Assistant Secretary of Defense for Africa and Western Hemisphere.

219. Ibid., pp. 498-9.
220. Ibid., p. 500. The same source notes that: "... the functions of the attaché and the missions are quite different. The attachés are members of the ambassador's staff and their functions are to deal in the sphere of what I would call overt intelligence. The military missions are in an entirely different field. Their function is to provide technical advice and assistance to the Latin American security forces."
221. Ibid., p. 499.
222. John Childs, op. cit., p. 498.
223. Ibid., p. 499.
224. Ibid.; Childs adds that in 1980 all "MilGroups" were to become "Offices of Defense Cooperation" while retaining their prior functions; this provision has not been implemented.
225. Americas Watch/American Civil Liberties Union (ACLU), *Report on the Situation of Human Rights in El Salvador*, New York, January 1982, p. 210, note 6; chapter 13 outlines in detail US legislation on foreign assistance as regards human rights, and information on the human rights implications for second countries of legislation such as the US War Powers Resolution of 1973.
226. Ibid., pp. 211-15.
227. Ibid., p. 212.
228. John Childs, *Unequal Alliance: The Inter-American Military System, 1938-1978*, Westview Press, Boulder, Colorado, 1980, p. 212.
229. US Congress, Hearings, "Human Rights in Nicaragua, Guatemala, and El Salvador: Implications . . . ", p. 112.
230. Ibid.
231. Ibid.
232. Ibid., pp. 113-7.
233. John Childs, *Unequal Alliance . . .*, p. 212.
234. The Brazilian doctrine built upon the concepts of internal defence (security) and development, which were at the heart of US counter-insurgency doctrine, while retaining a strong nationalistic position and building upon the conventional role of the armed forces in defending the nation's sovereignty. Based on already well developed policy formulation at Brazil's *Escuela Superior de Guerra* (War College), the "*Doutrina de Seguranca Nacional*" was to be cited in support of the 1964 coup. John Childs, *Unequal Alliance . . .*, p. 193 summarizing the Brazilian doctrine wrote: "... the concepts of 'development' and 'security' are inseparable and constitute the essential doctrine of the 1964 Revolution: national security and development are not merely military concepts, but stem from the integration of economic, social, political and military development. In a sense the doctrine is merely a contemporary expression of the 19th century Positivist current of thinking in Brazil which caused the words 'Ordem e Progreso' to be placed in Brazil's national flag. In the context of the latter half of the 20th century, 'security' has replaced 'order' and 'development' has replaced 'progress' ".
235. US Congress, Hearings, "Human Rights Conditions . . .", 1976, p. 235.
236. US Department of State, "Human Rights Practices in Countries Receiving US Security Assistance"; report submitted to the Committee on International Relations, House of Representatives, 25 April 1977 (Washington D.C., US Government Printing Office, 1977). This is known as the "502B Report".
237. Ibid., pp. 119-20. The 1977 502B Report, however, included a summary of pertinent information on "death-squad" killings published by Amnesty International, in its *Report on Torture*, (1973) and in its 1975-76 *Annual Report*.
238. Ibid., pp. 117-8. The 1977 country reports were so bad the Subcommittee on International Organizations of the Committee on International Relations commissioned its own country reports (on 19 countries), prepared by the Congressional Research Service, to "help to identify and highlight some of the

issues relating to executive reporting on human rights conditions". The reports responded to questions "concerning the adequacy of and usefulness of the submissions provided by the Department of State" and resulted in an analytical study of criteria pertinent to human rights reporting, as well as individual country by country chapters. (See US Congress, House Subcommittee on International Organizations, Committee on International Relations "Human Rights Conditions in Selected Countries and the U.S. Response", (Washington D.C., US Government Printing Office, July 1978).

239. Childs, *Unequal Alliance . . .*, p. 212. Lt. Col. Childs ascribed these feelings to the Latin American military solely as a result of the publication of the 1977 country reports; he was, however, overstating their sensitivity to mere words, and understating the possibly very real confusion over the cut-off of aid to Uruguay and Chile, both favoured client states in the formative years of their military governments.

240. Ibid., p. 207. Ironically, the ruffled US Latin American relations resulting from the renunciation of security assistance became the American right's stalking horse in demanding a policy of unlimited military aid for the 1980s. See, for example, a policy paper prepared for the right-wing Council for Inter-American Security, Inc., "A New Inter-American Policy for the Eighties", by "new right" policy makers L. Francis Bouchey, Roger W. Fontaine, David C. Jordan, Gordon Sumner, and Lewis Tambs (1980): "Human rights, . . . a culturally and politically relative concept that the present Administration has used for intervention for political change in countries of this hemisphere, adversely affecting the peace, stability and security of the region, must be abandoned and replaced by a non-interventionist policy of political and ethical realism . . . It has cost the United States friends and allies and lost us influence in important Latin American countries. It has even contributed to the destabilization and loss or prospective loss of countries like Nicaragua, El Salvador, Guatemala, and Costa Rica."

241. US Congress, Hearings, "Human Rights in Guatemala" (Washington D.C.: US Government Printing Office, 1981), pp. 38-9, "Additional Material Submitted by the Department of State".

242. US Congress, Hearings, "Human Rights in Guatemala", 1981, p. 10.

243. Ibid., p. 11.

244. The full listing of license requests for "munitions list" exports is reproduced in ibid., pp. 41-51; figures cited here are from a summary of exports in IPS, *Resource*, Update No. 1, Flora Montealegre and Synthia Arnson, "Background Information on Guatemala, Human Rights and US Military Assistance", July 1982, pp. 14-5.

245. Advertisement.

246. Center for Research on Criminal Justice, *The Iron Fist and the Velvet Glove*, p. 226, citing Security Planning Corporation, Non-Lethal Weapons for Law Enforcement, Washington, 1972.

247. US Congress, Hearings, "Human Rights in Guatemala", p. 52.

248. *International Herald Tribune*, Washington Post News Service, "Guatemala Gets Arms from US Despite Ban", by Christopher Dickey, 25 January 1982.

249. Institute for Policy Studies, *Resource*, Update No. 1, July 1982, p. 11.

250. Ibid.

251. Ibid .

252. Cited in Aguilera, op. cit., (September 1982), p. 47.

253. Ibid., p. 56, Table 4; citing Bank of Guatemala, *Boletin Estadistico*, January, February, March 1980, p. 31; the 1978 figure is a projection.

254. Ibid.

255. Ibid., p. 48.

256. NACLA Report, January-February 1982, "Israel Arms Trade", by Ronald Slaughter.

257. Amnesty International, *Guatemala: A Government Program . . .*, pp. 20, 21.

258. NACLA Report, January-February 1982, "Israel . . .", p. 52.

259. Elias Barahona statement, op. cit. (September 1983). See also *Latin America Regional Reports*, 6 May 1983, "Transforming the Indian Highlands", for reference to Israeli assistance in establishing co-operatives in the context of the government's "beans and rifles" counter-insurgency offensive under President Rios Montt.
260. Barahona, op. cit.
261. *Frente*, January 1981.
262. Institute for Policy Studies, *Resource*, Update No. 1, p. 13.
263. Ibid., p. 14.
264. Cited in *The Guardian*, (London), 27 August 1982, "Caribbean Boomerang Returns to Sender", by Ignacio Klich. The *Washington Post* news service reported that "The Israelis... recently opened a military communications school in Guatemala... and there have been reports of Israeli advisers here as well" (Christopher Dickey, "Guatemala Gets Arms . . .").
265. *Keesing's Contemporary Archive*, 23 July 1982, pp. 31, 607.
266. *Panorama*, citing *Prensa Libre*, 12 August 1975.
267. See, for example, Institute for Policy Studies, *Resource*, Update No. 1, p. 13, and NACLA, "Israel . . .", pp. 51-2.
268. *Revista Militar de Guatemala*, April-December 1976, "*El Nacional Socialismo*" by Captain Angel M. Cantoral Dávila.
269. Ibid.
270. Ibid.
271. Ibid.
272. Craig Pyes, "D'Aubuisson's Fledgling Party finds a Mentor in Guatemala", *Albuquerque Journal*, 18 December 1983.
273. Ibid.
274. Mary McGrory, "US is Learning to Love the Mean Little Major", in the *Washington Post*, 27 April 1982; the article cites Mexican paper *El Dia* as the original source.
275. NACLA, "Israel . . .", p. 52.
276. Piero Gleijeses, "The United States and Turmoil in Central America", draft paper prepared for the panel "The 1980's: The Decade of Confrontation?", published in US Department of Defense, Department of the Air Force, *Current News: Special Edition*, 15 April 1982. Professor Gleijeses concludes Carter could have stopped the Sandinistas only by military intervention: "It is true that in the last weeks of the regime, Washington stopped supplying weapons (both as a way to persuade Somoza to resign and in response to the international outcry). It is also true that at the very end Washington diverted an Israel ship bringing military supplies to the dictator. But Somoza didn't fall for lack of weapons".
277. Reuter, 21 July 1983.
278. Ibid. *Central America Report*, 17 December 1982, commented on the 6 December 1982 three day official visit to Tegucigalpa, Honduras, of Israel's Defence Minister Ariel Sharon only shortly after Reagan's visit there. His time was mostly spent meeting top army officers, including Gen. Gustavo Alvarez Martínez, then the Honduran army commander. See also *This Week*, 1 August 1983, "Taking Heat off US Role".
279. The principal evidence is that no formal US demarche to Israel, critical of its role, came to light — even under the Carter administration — suggesting that major arms transfers to states facing US human rights sanctions were not considered against the US's interests.
280. Allan Nairn, *Washington Post*, 21 October 1982, cited in Institute for Policy Studies, *Resource*, "Background Information on US Military Personnel and US Assistance to Central America", November 1982, pp. 1-2.
281. Institute for Policy Studies, *Resource*, "Background Information . . . ", note 3, citing telephone interview, 22 October 1982 with Pentagon spokesman Henry E. Catto Jr.
282. Guatemalan daily press, 7 September 1980.

283. Paul Ellman "The School that Trains Democrats and Dictators", in *The Guardian*, 1983.
284. *Latin America Regional Reports*, 14 January 1983, "Reagan to Resume Arms Sales".
285. Ibid.
286. *This Week*, 29 August 1983. Previous municipal registration cards did not require photographs.
287. Institute for Policy Studies, *Resource*, Update No. 8, p. 14.
288. Ibid.
289. *Newsweek*, 2 May 1983, p. 14.

Part 4: Into the 1980s: Mass Counter-Terror and Resistance

8. A Last Chain of Coups

The great wave of terror launched by General Romeo Lucas García's government against the trade unions, moderate opposition parties, co-operatives and peasant organizations, and independent labour and opposition groups occurred at the height of the United States' efforts to temper human rights abuses in Guatemala by restricting military aid. United States foreign policy after the fall of Somoza was intended to help regional governments contain the revolutionary left while encouraging the rise of moderate opposition parties and political leaders who could give an acceptable face to Central American governments. Only by encouraging partnership between the military establishments and such moderate political figures and parties as Alberto Fuentes Mohr and his social democrats, Manuel Colom Argueta and his FUR, or the Christian Democrats, did US policy makers see a means to complement the military aspects of the counter-insurgency programme with economic and politial reforms and give the US an opportunity to lend military and economic assistance on a large scale.

The Guatemalans, however, received mixed signals from the start. A 1980 report from the Washington-based Center for International Policy described how not only the US military but also the State Department establishment undermined the human rights policy:

> Ideological preferences and 'clientism' made many State Department professionals uncomfortable with a policy which put them at odds with former Latin allies. Most career officials were unenthusiastic and some actively sought to subvert the policy.[1]

An example of the former was Terence Todman, Carter's first Assistant Secretary of State for Inter-American Affairs:

> [Todman] accused those advocating a more public and aggressive human rights policy of being 'zealots' with an inherent bias against established authority. He locked the Latin American Bureau (ARA) into a persistent, stubborn battle against those outnumbered political appointees and loyal

215

professionals seeking to implement their interpretation of Carter and [Secretary of State] Vance's views on human rights. When travelling abroad, Todman used code words that contradicted the rhetoric of his superiors. In Central America, he repeatedly referred to 'the right of governments to protect themselves against terrorism'.[2]

In a similar mould was Carter's first ambassador to Guatemala, career officer Frank Ortiz, who was eventually removed, partly because of his less than enthusiastic support for the administration's human rights policy.

High profile visits by top *former* US army and intelligence officers also undermined the human rights policy. In December 1979 General Daniel O. Graham, ex-director of the US Defense Intelligence Agency; General John K. Singlaub, formerly an American general staff officer, and Colonel Jan McKeney (all retired), visited Guatemala as members of the "American Security Council". Their meeting with General Romeo Lucas García and — at which they reportedly discussed the Communist threat to Guatemala — was widely reported in the Guatemalan press as a top level army to army visit. The US Embassy was obliged to inform the press that the "Security Council" was a private entity and had no official status.[3]

The most convincing signal to the Guatemalans that they should not take the United States' foreign policy seriously came from the US military itself. The steady flow of material assistance through MAP and FMS suggests that the US military establishment took every opportunity to continue relations as they were before Carter, whatever the official US foreign policy. Direct relations between the US military (and intelligence agencies) and their Guatemalan counterparts were apparently neither interrupted nor soured during Carter's short-lived effort to apply US law in its foreign relations. Available evidence suggests that Guatemalans were encouraged to see Carter and his political appointees at the State Department as a short-term problem they must bear with but which they could outlast. Guatemalan officers continued to attend the Inter-American Defense Board and College at Fort McNair in Washington, regional events such as the annual conferences of representatives of the American Armies, and to meet top level US military officials in Guatemala and the US. Defense Department representatives made highly publicized visits to Guatemala when the two governments were ostensibly estranged over human rights matters; private talks on these occasions were described by the Guatemalan press as votes of confidence for the regime's refusal to kowtow to Carter's human rights concerns. Press reports in January 1980 described a series of recent visits by top American military officials to Guatemala, and reported the "particular satisfaction" the Guatemalan regime derived from the visits:

Conspicuously isolated in Central America after the overthrow of Somoza and the reformist coup in El Salvador, Guatemala was in much need of a vote of confidence from the Pentagon.[4]

The Guatemalan government's response to the conflicting signals was to reject the Department of State's calls for improvement in human rights conditions and toleration of moderate opposition groups Washington might collaborate with in the future. Lucas García chose to exterminate the moderate opposition groups, along with the new mass organizations that had emerged under Laugerud's Presidency and grown increasingly powerful under his own regime. Lucas García and the Guatemalan civilian and military elites perceived President Carter's human rights policy as a minority policy, backed only by a small clique of "Communists" in the Department of State and by Carter himself:

> The Guatemalan ruling class — never known for its political sophistication — became increasingly convinced that the State Department was dominated by Marxists (including men like William Bowdler and James Cheek, who they believed had cunningly persecuted and finally removed from his post the staunchly anti-Communist Ambassador Frank Ortiz). Continuing pressure and public chastening from Washington led only to a break in communication between the two governments, while within Guatemala repression wrought havoc among those centrist groups that enjoyed Washington's support.[5]

A policy debate within the US foreign policy establishment (the Department of State, the National Security Council, the Department of Defense) in the last year of the administration pitted advocates of a restoration of military aid to Guatemala (who claimed the human rights policy had failed) against advocates of Carter's human rights policy.[6] The major factor favouring the continuation of Carter's policy towards Guatemala was that Lucas García's government — unlike that of El Salvador — faced no serious threat by revolutionary forces. Even the "liberals", however, were committed to preventing a Nicaragua-style revolution in Guatemala by fair means or foul:

> ... it is important to understand the rationale of those State Department 'liberals'... They would have advocated military assistance for the regime, had they believed that it was necessary for its survival. But in their eyes Lucas was not yet seriously threatened — hence the United States could afford to wait (while military assistance was provided by Argentina, Israel and other countries). In this fashion, the Carter administration would avoid dirtying its hands and would preserve the facade of its human rights policy as long as possible.[7]

The Guatemalans were, apparently, aware that the US commitment to prevent more Nicaraguas was deeper than the commitment to the human rights policy. And, too, they could afford to wait for renewed direct US assistance, while taking care of subversion with the proven techniques of US counter-insurgency doctrine.

The Reagan Presidency began as Lucas García approached his last year in office, and as Guatemala's guerrilla organizations launched the first of a series of co-ordinated offensives. Guerrilla forces attacked army and police posts throughout the country, destroyed convoys, blocked highways — particularly in the Indian highlands of the North-west — and carried out major assaults in the capital. In turn, the Reagan administration scrambled to rehabilitate Lucas García's image in the US, and repudiated Carter's policies by clearing the sale of $3.2 million in military trucks and jeeps, circumventing the congress and the Foreign Assistance Act. Despite efforts to publicize the growing threat of the guerrilla opposition and to obscure Lucas García's policy of state terror, 1981 congressional hearings and growing international attention to human rights violations in Guatemala made restoration of a large military assistance programme to the Lucas García government virtually impossible. Johns Hopkins University Guatemala authority Piero Gleijeses described the 1981 situation:

> US efforts to improve the image of the Guatemalan regime proved an abject failure. Assuredly, the administration was unlucky: its campaign had just begun to unfold when Amnesty International released the most incriminating report it had ever published on Guatemala. By documenting conclusively, for the first time, that 'tortures and murders are part of a deliberate and longstanding program of the Guatemalan government', Amnesty struck an untimely blow to Washington's emerging argument that rightwing terror was independent of government responsibility.[8]

According to Gleijeses, a major plank of the Reagan government's programme for restoration of military aid to Guatemala was that the military agree to place a civilian in the Presidency in 1982:

> ... such a civilian would have better served the image-building efforts of the State Department, which was stressing the importance of the March 1982 elections in the 'democratization' under way in Guatemala.[9]

But Lucas García refused to consider such an alternative, and named his Defense Minister, General Aníbal Guevara, as the official candidate. Guevara was presidential candidate of the Revolutionary Party (PR), the Democratic Institutional Party (PID) and the small Front of National Unity (FUN). As in 1978 the MLN opposed the army's choice and fielded its own candidate, Mario Sandoval Alarcón. The Christian Democrats, as part of the National Opposition Union (UNO) and General Carlos Arana Osorio's own far right party, renamed

National Authentic Central (*Central Auténtica Nacional* (CAN) formerly the *Central Aranista Organizada*, (CAO)) each fielded their own candidates.[10] Lucas García's choice for the Presidency put him out of step both with his own Guatemalan far right (who had also begun to sense slippage in the war against the guerrillas) and his allies in the Reagan administration.

In mid-July 1981 Lucas García launched a successful co-ordinated offensive against guerrilla organizations in the capital. The principal target was a network of ORPA safe houses of which authorities claimed to have destroyed 20. The successes were confirmed some time later in the guerrilla's own publications; the Guerrilla Army of the Poor's international review *Compañero* described the offensive as having been carefully prepared by military intelligence over two years:

> Based on military intelligence, in a spectacular series of raids hundreds of troops backed up by tanks and helicopters surround and destroy safehouses of the revolutionary movement. Right in the city center gunbattles lasting hours rage. The 'security' forces cordon off whole neighborhoods and evacuate the entire population living in the affected zones. . . Guerrilla losses during the first two months of the campaign rise to almost 100. In August, when the offensive has reached its climax, General Aníbal Guevara, former Minister of Defense, is declared the candidate for the Presidency.[11]

Foreign observers attributed the success of this offensive in the capital to vastly improved military intelligence capability, attributed variously to US, Israeli and Argentine intelligence assistance. London-based *Latin America Weekly Report* gave principal credit to the Argentines:

> One tangible reason for the army's better performance against the guerrillas is its improved intelligence work, attributed by some observers to its Argentine counter-insurgency advisers. . . Argentine expertise is also seen behind the army's successes against the ORPA group's infrastructure in Guatemala City earlier this year. Some observers believe that the Argentines have introduced the technique of network analysis, which involves, among other things, the elaborate computerised review of telephone calls, and electricity and other bills for suspect houses. One of the 20 ORPA safe-houses was identified, for example, because of its abnormally high electricity bill. . .[12]

Lucas García's own acknowledgement that Israel had worked with the army in the fields of "communications and electronics", key components of the intelligence system, came in January 1982, with the opening of the army's new communications and electronics training centre (see Chapter 7); as yet no similar horse's mouth acknowledgement of the Argentine role in Guatemalan intelligence has emerged.

A rural offensive launched in August 1981 under the direction of the new Army Chief of Staff, President Lucas García's brother, General Benedicto Lucas García, was less immediately successful than Lucas García's 1981 urban counter-insurgency initiative. Forces of up to 4,000 troops, backed by the army's formidable counter-insurgency aircraft, moved against suspected guerrilla supporters in the Pacific coast region, with new tactics involving large scale massacres by regular army troops in communities believed sympathetic to the guerrilla opposition. Major troop movements into the central highlands of Huehuetenango, El Quiché and Chalatenango followed in September. By November 1981, the level of killings among the Indian peasants of the highlands perhaps surpassed even the bloodshed of the Zacapa campaign of 1967–69. Most observers, however, found the offensive relatively ineffective, but indicative of a new strategy that, in the long term, might erode the guerrillas; popular support by physically eliminating suspect social sectors:

> The main victims were peasants, who supported the guerrillas but were rarely armed. This was partly a result of deliberate government strategy to destroy the guerrillas' social base. But it was also simply because the army rarely managed to hit the guerrillas themselves. Despite improved intelligence on their movements . . . and despite the relatively more dynamic leadership of General Benedicto Lucas García, who took over as army chief of staff in August, the army made little headway in tracking down elusive and highly mobile guerrilla columns. The guerrillas invariably managed to break through army efforts to surround them.[13]

An expressed objective of the campaign to "clear" the guerrillas and suspect population from the highlands of Chimaltenango and El Quiché departments was to eliminate threats to the Pan-American highway, the main route through the highlands which guerrillas had repeatedly cut off. In a late November 1981 appearance before the foreign press Lucas García announced the initial success of the operation, which he characterized as a strategy in which "the army is acting on a large scale to annihilate subversion in Guatemala in a short time".[14]

In spite of the offensives in the highlands, guerrilla actions increased in the last months of 1981, and in February 1982 the EGP, ORPA, FAR and PGT groups joined forces in a guerrilla umbrella organization, the Guatemalan National Revolutionary Unity (*Unidad Revolucionaria Nacional Guatemalteca*, (URNG)) and published a five-point platform deliberately designed to attract the broadest possible support, with a special appeal to army officers to turn against the government.[15] The platform called for an end to repression against the people, to cultural oppression and discrimination, and repressive economic and politial domination by the local and foreign "wealthy class", and pledged to form a representative government and adopt a non-aligned foreign policy.[16] Shortly after the creation of URNG, and perhaps equally threatening to the status quo, was the creation of an umbrella *political* organization — the Guatemalan Committee of Patriotic Unity (*Comité Guatemalteco de Unidad Patriótica* (CGUP)). This grouped distinguished Guatemalan exiles, led by writer Luis Cardoza y Aragón, and united the organizations of the Democratic Front Against Repression and the FP-31 and others opposed to the government.[17] Both the URNG and the CGUP denounced the March 1982 elections as a farce.

Although General Benedicto Lucas García's counter-insurgency campaigns of late 1981 and early 1982 failed to crush the guerrillas in the promised short order (and this failure would weigh against his brother) innovations introduced by the chief of staff largely set the pattern for the coming years. Benedicto Lucas García introduced what the guerrillas quite correctly described as a "campaign of extermination against the Indian peoples unprecedented in Guatemalan history", through a systematic "scorched earth" policy in Indian areas thought to have gone over to the guerrillas.[18] The policy was to annihilate the guerrillas' social base across the board in the most seriously "infected" areas and to establish mechanisms for population control throughout the rural areas in order to strangle the guerrilla movement. A February 1982 report described the procedures and evidence that they were beginning to take effect:

> The effects of his policies are beginning to be felt. There are constant troop movements along the Pan-American highway to the west, where heavily armed soldiers are posted at regular intervals. All vehicles and their occupants are subjected to stringent checks at military road blocks. Virtually all the buildings close to the road have been abandoned, including schools and hotels; most of the small villages visible from the road, which is littered with the remains of burnt-out vehicles, have been razed.[19]

As Army Chief of Staff the President's brother also initiated the expansion of the regular army, of its reserve forces, and of the forces of civilian irregulars; a process which was further developed after the change of government. At the end of the year press reports stated that, in the course of 1981, the strength of the regular army had risen to 21,000.[20] In November 1981 the army announced the creation of an auxiliary force within the army's permanent (active) reserve system. The new forces, partly raised by calling up former servicemen, were described as local territorial forces which would serve in their home areas under the local army commandant's or military commissioner's orders. The numbers involved were not initially publicized; in two areas of the highlands alone, however, 1,800 men — mostly *ladinos* in the largely Indian areas — were reported to have been raised:

Gen. Benedicto Lucas García... announced that some 1,800 campesinos in the highlands are being trained, armed and incorporated into the regular reserves who now number about 3,000. The reserves are ex-soldiers who undergo periodic training and are available for active duty when called upon. Gen. Lucas disclosed that about 1,000 men were being trained in Rabinal, a rebel-infested area in Baja Verapaz Department, while another 800 were being organized in Joyabaj in the trouble-ridden Quiché. The organization of a home guard in situ will release regular soldiers for duty elsewhere, military experts say.. the new units organized as part of the reserves will be assigned militia type tasks — guard duty, local logistics and communication, etc.[21]

The speech announcing the new force was made at a 1960s style anti-Communist rally staged in Joyabaj, El Quiché, in mid-November, when some 4,000 peasants were brought together "to express their support and complete collaboration in the struggle against subversion".[22] Benedicto Lucas García said the peasants incorporated into the new force would become part of "the permanent reserves of the army, as the Constitution prohibits the formation of militias apart from the reserves".[23] By January 1982 military authorities reported having raised 11,000 men for the active reserve units, or "home guard", in the departments of Alta and Baja Verapaz alone; most were described as "veterans" and most were *ladinos*.[24] By early 1982 an estimated 30,000 men had been recruited to swell existing army auxiliary forces, and serve as adjuncts to the local military commissioner network or attached to rural army garrisons.[25]

Most accounts of the army's expanded irregular force described it as a "civilian militia" raised to implement the army's policy of eliminating the guerrillas' base of support by killing or driving the highland Indian population from their communities; a policy also benefiting the non-Indian elite recruits by driving the Indians from the land they desire:

... the army has commissioned 30,000 civilian militamen to serve as guides and fight alongside troops. The army's reliance on the militiamen — many local landholders itching to oust Indians from choice lands — is the principal cause of violence in the area, Guatemalan opposition party members claim... The leaders said the language barrier between Indians and the mostly Ladino army troops makes other Ladinos in the communities — often relatively wealthy local elites — the army's natural ally. 'What the ladinos do is take advantage of the army's force to settle what are essentially local political problems,' a peasant leader said. 'They tell the local garrison commander, 'So and so is a Communist.' The troops and the militiamen kill these people."[26]

The thousands of auxiliaries raised under General Benedicto Lucas García were, in origin and organization, much the same as those developed by the army in the 1960s to boost its manpower in the eastern parts of the country, turning the local elites and *ladino* population as a whole against the Indian peasantry. A final organizational innovation — known as the Civil Defense Patrol system — that placed the men of the Indian communities themselves under army orders, was introduced in the course of 1982. But only the army's *ladino* auxiliaries, or militias, and the traditional auxiliaries administered through the military commissioner system, were armed and given discretionary power to pursue counter-insurgency warfare. Conversely, the compulsory Civil Defense Patrols were armed with sticks, and directed at gunpoint by members of the army itself.

Presidential Elections, Corruption, Pre-emptive Coup

As the 7 March 1982 Presidential elections approached, the failure of the army's counter-guerrilla offensive to halt a steady onslaught of guerrilla activity in town and countryside was a factor in the progressive estrangement of Guatemala's civilian elites from the Lucas García government, and Lucas García's chosen successor, General Aníbal Guevara. Guevara, in particular, was accused of incompetence in dealing with the guerrillas as Minister of Defense, and so seen to offer little as President.[27] Both Guevara and Lucas García were also identified with the spread of corruption within the military, corruption that had been growing in scale since the 1960s and distressed civilian elites and young army officers largely excluded from a share in the spoils.

When Aníbal Guevara was declared the victor in the elections, despite evidence of massive fraud, hardly anyone was pleased. The political parties of the far and moderate right that had ranged candidates against him were united in protest against the fraud and demanded the poll be annulled and a new election held within 60 days. On 9 March the three defeated candidates led a demonstration to the National Palace to present a petition to this effect; the demonstration, made up of supporters of the extreme right MLN and CAN parties, Christian Democrats and others, was attacked by the police, with many protesters injured while the three candidates were briefly detained and questioned at police headquarters. The President refused to consider their petition.[28]

On 23 March, President Romeo Lucas García was placed under house arrest by the representatives of a majority sector of the army's officer corps. The nearly bloodless coup (some resistance was reported in Huehuetenango and El Quiché) was announced as a measure to repudiate the electoral fraud and the corruption of the Lucas García government. Although backed by the army's young officers, it was promoted particularly by officers close to the MLN party; and the coup makers never promised the sort of social and economic reforms that had been offered in the 1979 coup in El Salvador. In any case no representatives of the young officers were incorporated into the subsequent junta. The first statement by the officers involved in the coup was in a radio broadcast by MLN leader Leonel Sisniega Otero.[29]

Called from the beginning to head the junta was General Efraín Ríos Montt, former army chief of staff under the Arana presidency, and a candidate for the Presidency himself in 1974; like El Salvador's Napoleón Duarte in 1972, Ríos Montt was often considered to have won the vote but lost the count. During 23 March three statements on the composition of the new junta went out from the National Palace; the initial formula placed Ríos Montt in a junta with junior officers, the second in a junta including civilians. The third and final formula placed Ríos Montt at the head of a junta composed of himself, Brigadier General Horacio Egberto Maldonado Schaad (previously commander of the Honour Guard Brigade in the capital) and Colonel Francisco Luis Gordillo Martínez (formerly head of the army general headquarters in the capital).[30] The three were all graduates of specialist training by the US Army Special forces at Fort Gulick in the Canal Zone; Ríos Montt had also studied at Fort Bragg, North Carolina, where he completed Course 33- G-F6, 1-61 "Counterguerrilla operations" as well as an 18 month course at the Italian Army's School of War.[31] His command experience was considerable, with posts in the late 1960s including commander of the Honour Guard brigade, the Mariscal Zavala brigade, Deputy Chief of the Army General Staff, and Director of the Polytechnic (Military) School. Under Arana Osorio he became Chief of the Army General Staff. Ríos Montt was exceptional in the army hierarchy as he had joined the army (in 1943) and risen through the ranks, eventually graduating from the Polytechnic School in 1950.[32]

The background to the 23 March coup involved internal military dissension, the estrangement of the traditional civilian supporters of military government from Lucas García and his generation of army officers, and international factors. The proliferation of corruption and personal enrichment at the top of the army hierarchy was of particular concern both to the civilian elites, with whom the army hierarchy had come to compete, and the junior officers, who considered the extraordinary levels of corruption reached in the 1970s to interfere with their own safety and with the conduct of the counter-insurgency war. Personal enrichment had been a feature of the military governments in power since 1963: Peralta Azurdia had become a top industrialist; Arana Osorio, Laugerud, Lucas García and others acquired interests in industry and vast landholdings.

The process whereby the military hierarchy began actively to compete in the economic sphere with the traditional elites took off under Colonel

Enrique Peralta Azurdia's government (1963–66). In this period the institutional means for the military to provide for its own welfare — the army bank, military health care facilities, insurance, and so on — were developed. By the mid-1970s Peralta Azurdia was himself a member of the economic elite and the principal spokesman for the private sector's major commercial and industrial groups. The entry of top army officers into the private elites continued under the military governments of the 1970s; Colonel Arana Osorio was widely quoted as having defended the process as a trade-off: "If the military are to combat subversion, they don't have to be the employees of the rich, but their partners."[33]

Moderate economic security, if not wealth, was also provided to the officer corps as a whole. While this was acceptable to the younger officers as long as their military duties entailed little risk or sacrifice, the increased size and strength of the guerrilla movements in the mid to late 1970s meant their risks grew proportionately. One factor in the young officers' support for the coup against Lucas García and his hand-picked successor was dismay at the increasing casualties they themselves were suffering while the Generals waxed fat; and a conviction that, under Lucas García, with Aníbal Guevara in the Defense Ministry, corruption had reached a scale that seriously hampered the conduct of the counter-insurgency war, and placed the junior officers' lives in jeopardy.

Young officers had borne the brunt of casualties in clashes with the guerrillas, with, according to officers interviewed unofficially in July 1981, 23 officers and 250 soldiers killed in the first four months of 1981 alone, and, by the end of June, a total of some 1,000 army personnel dead.[34] The unhappy course of the war was believed to be partly due to the army high command's excessive skimming of arms procurement funds for their personal profit, and the consequent acquisition of inadequate arms and equipment:

> According to their information, eight leading generals are running a successful arms-buying racket. Over the past six years, the group is said to have spent US$175 m. on Italian, Belgian, Yugoslav and Israeli weapons, but to have claimed their value at US $425 m. The difference has gone into private bank accounts in the Cayman Islands.[35]

While dissatisfaction in the officer corps was essential for a viable coup against Lucas García, the coup was also supported by the civilian economic elites which had traditionally ruled in tandem with the military. *Latin America Weekly Report* wrote in March 1982 that relations between the Lucas García government and the civilian elites had been "less than cordial", with disputes over "taxation and other aspects of economic policy" and noted that "Private businessmen almost all dislike Guevara, who has little if any understanding of economics". This was laid to the vested interests of the military elites:

> The army high command has formed a bureaucratic elite, which has very different interests to those of the private sector. . . The army has set up its own bank, and military men are in charge at 46 semi-autonomous state institutions. Also officers enjoy access to special shops where consumer goods such as whisky can be bought at much reduced prices.[36]

Allied to the military elite were bureaucratic and technocratic elites, which shared the military's economic interests (and spoils) while offering political support through the two "official" parties identified with the military government:

> The army has formed alliances with the leaders of such parties as the Partido Revolucionario and the Partido Institucional Democrático. . . State employees must be members of the parties, the main social base of this new bureaucratic elite.
>
> The official alliance's policies reflect the elite's interests. Formally to the left of any opposition group, it advocates maintaining present levels of state intervention and a more aggressive nationalist economic policy. . .[37]

The same source notes that, with the MLN, the CAN party had been the most strident in opposition to the Lucas García-Guevara economic policies and the electoral fraud of 1982, despite General Carlos Arana Osorio (founder of the CAN, comprised of his supporters) having been the first of the three army officers to enrich themselves in the Presidency since 1970.

The role of the Reagan government in the 23 March coup remains obscure, but may have been decisive. The Lucas García regime's indifference to public relations problems as it went ahead with its programme to exterminate not only the guerrillas, but the Indians believed to help them, and even the Christian Democrats, had stymied even the best efforts of Reagan's government to rationalize the restoration of large amounts of military aid. In May 1981, Reagan had sent General Vernon Walters, former deputy director of the CIA, as a special envoy for talks with Lucas García about restoring aid; a month later these talks were followed by the agreement to export US military vehicles as a contribution to "regional security". By bending over backward, however, the Reagan government could not convincingly represent the Lucas García regime as having changed for the better in 1981; church sources put the toll of the government's counter-insurgency operations at up to 11,000 deaths in 1981 alone. The US Embassy estimated more than 3,600 deaths (attributed to ambiguously defined "death-squads") and in January 1982 the Christian Democrats complained that 238 party officials had been slaughtered in the previous 18 months.[38] By mid-1981, prospects for restoring military aid to Guatemala were dismal: the Lucas García regime's policies provoked

... deep abhorrence among an overwhelming majority in Congress ... as a dispirited lobbyist lamented, 'nobody wants to put himself on the line on the Hill by asking for weapons for Guatemala — even conservative Congressmen don't want to get involved'.[39]

Initially, Reagan administration proponents of renewing military aid chose to wait; by the end of 1981, however, the administration came to see Guatemala as under serious threat from the guerrillas which only a large assistance programme could pre-empt. As one commentator wrote:

> ... by the end of 1981 a sense of urgency began to emerge within the Reagan administration, following a year of growing guerrilla military strength and popular support while the economy sharply deteriorated. Some US officials even began to wonder whether Guatemala would replace El Salvador as the next 'domino' in Central America.[40]

The change in perceptions took effect with the inclusion of a request in the Security Assistance Act for Financial Year 1983 for $251,000 allocation for IMET training of Guatemalans, and discussion of a request for some $2 million in helicopter spares with the Lucas García government.[41]

The barrier to total restoration of military assistance was Lucas García's pig-headed failure to compromise with the US either on his policies or on the choice of his successor. In February 1982, impending coups intended to pre-empt the election and installation in power of General Aníbal Guevara, identified with the army's corrupt old guard, were widely rumoured. Ironically, one of the prime contenders as potential rival was the President's brother, General Benedicto Lucas García, described as having raised morale in the army, and who claimed to have transformed it into ". . . an aggressive, flexible and highly mobile army that will hit the guerrillas in their strongholds rather than their hitting us in ours."[42] Characterized as a modern professional, trained by the French in counter-insurgency, one source reported that his "rapid rise to power as the national strong man has prompted rumours that he might be tempted to launch a coup against the official presidential candidate. . ."[43] But after the coup he was removed from his post as chief of staff; yet, a year later, was reportedly in charge of counter-insurgency operations in the Petén. The policies he introduced in the campaign in the Indian highlands, moreover, remained in force under his brother's successor in the Presidency.

Replacing Lucas García's hand-picked successor with General Benedicto Lucas García would hardly have achieved a principal objective of the Reagan administration: a new face for the regime. Some semblance of change was needed in order to rush through what, by then, was seen as urgently needed US military assistance. A more suitable formula was to combine the forces of the young officers authentically disturbed by the corruption of the old regime with a retired army officer who, previously, might have won a Presidential election. The United States' role in encouraging the coup, or in influencing the composition of the junta, directly or indirectly remains unknown, but the response of the US was enthusiastic. Having waited discreetly for the dust to settle before recognizing the new regime, on 30 March, in the traditional note to the Foreign Minister the United States expressed a desire to continue relations and co-operation between the two governments. Three weeks after the coup US Ambassador Frederic Chapin was sufficiently impressed by the new faces to declare that Guatemala had "come out of the darkness into the light" and that he would support restoration of military assistance.[44] About the same time Assistant Secretary of State Enders credited Ríos Montt with changing Guatemala's policies and practices virtually overnight, claims facilitated by the new junta's temporary restriction of "death-squad" killings in the capital; Enders claimed that:

> . . . since last month's coup led by junior officers, violence not directly connected to the insurgency has been brought virtually to an end. . . Concrete measures have been taken against corruption. . . All political forces have been called to join in national reconciliation.[45]

On 26 April, White House spokesman Dean Fisher told the press that restoration of military assistance was being "very seriously considered", while other US officials made more specific references to administration plans:

> . . . [they said] that the Administration planned to approve the sale of $4,000,000 worth of spare parts for US-made helicopters, to restore $50,000 in military training funds for the current fiscal year, and to resume support for loans to Guatemala in the Inter-American Development Bank and other international financial institutions, and that it had already requested $250,000 in training funds for the 1983 fiscal year. . .[46]

If evidence of the scorched earth counter-insurgency operations in the Indian highlands, which were uninterrupted by the coup and escalated in its immediate aftermath, had been concealed from the international news media and US and international human rights monitors, the Reagan administration would have been able to convince a tractable US congress to give the Ríos Montt junta the benefit of the doubt. The State Department's claims that the Guatemalan government had changed its nature and should be given a fresh start with renewed military assistance (along the lines of the rush to aid El Salvador after the October 1979 coup) fell flat by the end of May. News trickling out with the tens of thousands of refugees crossing Guatemala's northern border into Mexico, and from observers on the spot, testified to an unprecedented slaughter of the Indian peoples of the highlands that in some cases — particularly that of the Ixil people of El Quiché — appeared to approximate genocide.

The Ascension of General Efraín Ríos Montt

In public relations terms the 1982 coup was similar to the July 1966 innauguration of Julio César Méndez Montenegro, a civilian stepping in after a long period of military rule, and, to the young officers' reformist coup in neighbouring El Salvador in 1979, two years before. The young officers who initially took credit for the Guatemalan coup had put forward a three-point plan calling for new elections within 60 days, for army officers to be ineligible for election, and for an end to government corruption.[47] Before the day was out, however, the junta of top officers led by Ríos Montt had overruled their young colleagues and issued a revised platform retaining only the commitment to end corruption. The junta's final 14-point platform appeared tailor-made to satisfy Washington's need for high profile gestures to mollify congressional human rights advocates and clear the way for military assistance. Stated objectives were, among others:

> . . . to made the people feel that the authorities are at the service of the people;
> to achieve the reconciliation of the Guatemalan family for the benefit of national peace and harmony;
> to achieve individual security and happiness on the basis of absolute respect for human rights;
> to eliminate administrative corruption;
> to achieve the recovery of the economy under a free enterprise system;
> to reorganize the electoral system so that political participation could be respected in true democracy. . .[48]

The junta's rhetoric was strong on human rights, vague on democracy, and non-committal on elections.

In the first few weeks of the new regime some 20 government officials, all civilians, were arrested, to be prosecuted for "abusing their authority, embezzlement, extortion, and continuous fraud". They included the former prison director, officials of the Ministry of Finance, and the former Attorney-General.[49] Detective Corps chief, Lieutenant Colonel Pedro García Arredondo, was dismissed (but not prosecuted) and replaced by International Police Academy graduate Oswaldo Xolon Xat; the Detective Corps itself was given a new image by changing its name to Department of Technical Investigations (*Departamento de Investigaciones Técnicas*, (DIT)).[50] Perhaps the most dramatic event of the post-coup period was the sacking, on 24 March, of the home of former Minister of the Interior Donaldo Alverez Ruiz, a civilian (who was out of the country) after troops arrested his guards. Press reports the day after described Alvarez Ruiz, who had formal authority over the police, as having directed the "death-squads" under Lucas García.

In practice, the Ríos Montt regime called a halt to "death-squad" killings in the capital for a time: fewer bodies with signs of torture and gunshot wounds were reported found in the weeks immediately after the coup. Indeed, in his first television address to the nation Ríos Montt promised that under the new order the "death-squad" killings of the past would be ended; instead there would be proper executions: "There will be no more dead bodies on the roadsides. We will execute by firing squad whoever goes against the law. But no more murders."[51]

Ríos Montt, since 1978 a convert to the charismatic Christian movement, and an active member of the fundamentalist California-based Christian Church of the Word, from his first statement as chief of the junta attributed his rise to power to God's own decision. Dubbed the "Ayatullah Ríos Montt", his pledges to rid Guatemala of corruption and crush subversion in an orderly manner were widely taken at face value. He was not seen as a man who would lie, although there was an unhealthy element of the eccentric and even the frankly bizarre in his public statements after 23 March.[52]

Ríos Montt's promise to replace the anonymous terror of urban "death-squads" with the formal procedure of an army firing squad led, on 1 July 1982, to a decree establishing the death penalty for a wide range of offences; the setting up of a system of special, secret courts empowered to impose the death penalty; and secret trials without defence or appeal. Ríos Montt warned that subversion would be dealt with drastically:

> Whoever is against the instituted government, whoever doesn't surrender, I'm going to shoot. It is preferable that it be known that 20 people were shot, and not just that 20 bodies have appeared beside the road.[53]

Or, as he said in an August statement, with the state of siege the government would "kill people legally".[54]

The composition and location of the special courts, the dates of hearings and executions, and the place of burial of those executed would remain secret. Defence before the new courts was to be no more possible than it had been in the face of the strictly administrative procedures applied for targetting the victims of the extra-judicial executions attributed to "death-squads". Ríos Montt told an interviewer that the courts were part of "a merciless struggle" to combat subversion, that all captured rebels would be put before the courts, and that "I stress that those whom the courts find guilty of the crimes that I have listed will be sentenced to death."[55] Ríos Montt himself was to be responsible for appointing three army officers to sit in each of the special courts, or remove them if appropriate.[56]

Despite Ríos Montt's rhetoric, and the new legislation legalizing secret summary trial and execution, past procedures for extra-judicial execution continued to be applied after a brief moratorium in Ríos Montt's first month in office. There was no lull in rural counter-insurgency operations and their attendant massacres; and in June, "death-squad" killings were already beginning to pick up in number.

On 22 May the junta decreed an amnesty law which was widely reported abroad and touted by the US Embassy as proof of Ríos Montt's "conciliatory" intentions. The decree declared its purpose to be the restoration of "social peace" and to give "subversives" the chance to reenter society free from criminal responsibility.[57] The law's provision freeing from criminal responsibility "the members of the Security Forces of the State who in fulfilling their duty participated in counter-subversion activities"[58] was not widely publicized. Subversives were given 30 days to turn themselves and their arms over to the army; there was no time limit set for security personnel to benefit from the amnesty.

The amnesty for "subversives", like previous Guatemalan amnesties, was designed primarily for foreign consumption, and offered little but the risk of torture and death to any subversive foolish enough to appear at the local barracks to take it up.[59] Ríos Montt's own comments on the amnesty for *security personnel* illustrate his line of thinking on human rights; on 1 June he attacked critics of amnesty for those who had violated human rights. These actions were undertaken to confront Communism, he said, and to prevent the Soviets "from raising their hammer and sickle" over Guatemala.[60] At the end of the amnesty period Ríos Montt declared a state of siege and the suspension of civil rights, and announced that the death penalty would be applied to anyone found with large quantities of weapons, or caught while carrying out "terrorist acts".[61]

The state of siege law, which remained in force throughout Ríos Montt's government, added little to *de facto* army and police powers; it merely formalized powers for arrest without warrant, secret detention, and unlimited powers of search and seizure. It did add a veneer of legality to established practice, although contravening — as did past practice — the international human rights instruments to which Guatemala is party.[62] Other provisions of the law introduced controls on the news media and organizations of all kinds, in a manner reminiscent of Peralta Azurdia's 1963 Law for the Defense of Democratic Institutions: Article 4 suspended all trade union activities and Article 14 imposed censorship on the news media and prohibited the publication of "any information of trouble-making groups"; Articles 5 and 6 authorized the President to place under army administration public services and any other services or institutions, including schools, and to take over or dissolve groups, organizations, entities or associations of any kind that performed "acts that are subversive or contrary to public order or to the measures taken by the military."[63]

The lull in urban "death-squad" killings after the overthrow of Lucas García coincided with a rapid escalation of scorched earth counter-insurgency operations in the Indian highlands. In a July 1982 report, Amnesty International presented evidence that the Guatemalan army was "sweeping" the Indian highlands through indiscriminate massacres of the suspect population, describing incidents in which over 2,600 people had been put to death by the army.[64] Cases reported from the first weeks after the coup included burning of the villages of Sacatalji, Crumax, San Isidro and Samuc de Cobán, and an unknown number of killings in the course of army operations in the department of Alta Verapaz on 24 March; on 26 March the murder of the members of nine peasant families, a total of 54 people, and the "disappearance" of three other prisoners at the hands of troops in the village of Pacoj in Chimaltenango. On 31 March the village of Estancia de la Virgen, in San Martín Jilotepeque, in Chimaltenango, was largely burned to the ground and troops killed 15 peasants and burned four others alive. Between 30 March and 3 April 55 people were killed by troops in the El Quiché village of Chinique and about 29 peasants were burned alive, bound to the roof-poles of their houses in the El Quiché villages of Chocorales and Semejá I.[65]

In mid-May the Guatemalan Conference of Bishops issued a pastoral letter condemning the army's brutal sweeps through the highland departments, protesting that "Not even the lives of old people, pregnant women or innocent children were respected... Never in our history has it come to such grave extremes."[66] Guatemalan newspaper owner Jorge Carpio Nicolle reacted to the bloodbath by risking his own life in a signed editorial; an unprecedented gesture, even though its careful wording stopped short of identifying the army as the instrument of what he described as genocide:

> To anyone who has any sympathy with his fellow men, the type of genocidal annihilation that is taking place in the Indian zones of the country is truly horrifying... There has been much talk of improving our image abroad, but this image will continue to blacken itself more and more with this new resurgence of blind and absurd violence. This new resurgence of mass murders sends the message that Guatemala is very far from peace, or even a decrease in violence. In the outside world they will once more close their doors to us, because in fact we do not deserve any aid as long as this keeps occuring.[67]

And *Latin America Regional Reports* in a 7 May 1982 edition described the strategy backed by the Ríos Montt regime as one of naked terror:

The army strategy is to clear the population out of the guerrilla support areas. Troops and militias move into the villages, shoot, burn or behead the inhabitants they catch; the survivors are machine-gunned from helicopters as they flee.[68]

On 12 May 1982 the FP-31 occupied the Brazilian Embassy. The occupiers, primarily members of the CUC, demanded the publication of a manifesto outlining in detail the nature of the counter-insurgency offensive launched in the Indian highlands by General Ríos Montt. At the risk of a repetition of the massacre in the Spanish Embassy, the Brazilian Embassy occupation proved a success: the Brazilian government made it clear that it would not accept a police attack on the building and facilitated the safe departure of the occupiers into exile after the publication of an account of their grievances. Mexico granted asylum to the group, largely comprising Indian members of the CUC from El Quiché; their stories, once in Mexico, were widely publicized.

The document the CUC/FP-31 wished to make known, breaking through the domestic censorship by force, as well as the *de facto* censorship at an international level imposed by their isolation, was entitled "The Army Continues to Massacre our Communities". It declared the intention of the "Indian and poor ladino peasants of the Committee of Peasant Unity — CUC — to denouce the brutal repression our Indian communities in Guatemala are suffering at the hands of the Army of the Military Junta." The document explicitly countered the new President's image-building efforts which, they said, wrongly claimed the human rights situation in Guatemala had improved:[69]

> We want it to be known that this Junta of generals and colonels, since 23 March not only has followed the policy of massacres and destruction of the previous military government, but in some regions has intensified the massacres to levels we have never previously known. At the same time, it has invented new and more cruel ways to attack us, seeking to break our spirit to resist. It has disguised its criminal acts with a demagoguery of God and human rights, to try to fool some people in Guatemala and international public opinion. Because of this, so no one is fooled, we want to make known the terrible reality we live today in the Guatemalan countryside.
>
> Since the 23rd of March we have seen how, far from ending the massacres, the army of the Junta has continued and increased them. The army has occupied our communities and has massacred in Chimaltenango, El Quiché, Sololá, Huehuetenango, Alta and Baja Verapaz and in other places. More than 3,000 people — men, women, children and old people — have been massacred in the most barbaric ways, in this month and a half alone. They have been tortured, their throats cut, or burned

alive in their houses. . . We have seen how the army comes into our communities, burning all of the houses, all of the corn which sustains us, destroying or stealing our property, clothes and anything of value, and killing and stealing all of our chickens and pigs.

It was several months before independent organizations and the international news media discovered the full extent of what was happening in the Indian highlands of Guatemala in the first months under General Ríos Montt's terror offensive. When they did, the accuracy of the CUC document was confirmed.

The rise and radicalization of the CUC, and the incorporation of the Indian peasantry as a group into the political process through the CUC and similar organizations, provided the background to the insurgency in the highlands and the transformation of the guerrilla organizations ORPA and EGP into largely Indian organizations. The *levee en masse* of the Indian peoples feared by the Guatemalan elite since the colonial period appeared to have begun with the 1980s, in an unexpected partnership of the urban poor, the trade unions and sectors of the middle classes. The response was an adaptation of the 1960s counter-insurgency doctrine to isolate and destroy the Indian population.

Ríos Montt's Fall from Grace

The junta established in March 1982 was dissolved on 9 June by order of its chief, General Efraín Ríos Montt, who declared himself President and sole repository of both executive and legislative powers. General Maldonado Schaad and Colonel Gordillo were dropped from the junta and stripped of their ministerial posts. Concentration of the powers of the government in Presidential hands (Ríos Montt's) was extended even to the municipal level. The country's 324 elected municipal mayors (municipalities are the equivalent of townships) were replaced by Ríos Montt's appointees, a measure reminiscent of General Ubico's 1930s system of appointed municipal *intendentes*.

To the irritation of the MLN and other parties of the civilian elite, Ríos Montt's dissolution of the national congress immediately after the coup appeared, by late 1982, more of a permanency than they might originally have expected. On 15 September 1982 a "Council of State" of representatives from diverse social sectors — hand-picked by Ríos Montt — came into being. As a body limited to *advising* the executive, the Council was seen as a step in the institutionalization of Ríos Montt's autocratic rule; although invited to send representatives the principal political parties boycotted the assembly.

Ríos Montt also dismayed the civilian far right by changing past practices of handing out ministerial and other top posts to top civilian party leaders. In a way unprecedented since Peralta Azurdia's three-year military government, Ríos Montt put military men into key state administrative jobs which had traditionally been the province of civilians, with army officers taking over such agencies as the Social Security Institute (*Instituto Guatemalteco de Seguridad Social*, (IGSS)), which operated the country's major hospitals.[70]

The coup that placed Ríos Montt in power was backed by the civilian far right, on the understanding that they were backing officers who favoured the army's withdrawal from interference in the economy, and that under the new regime far right parties would be given a major role in co-governing the country with the army. Ríos Montt's first months in power dashed hopes for an immediate restoration of the MLN-CAN partnership with the army. Both Maldonado Schaad and Gordillo had been close collaborators of the MLN; their removal from the junta suggested Ríos Montt wanted to rule without interference either from them or from the MLN.[71] Although Ríos Montt had nothing to do with reformist young officers (and a good case can be made that there is, in fact, *no* reformist faction in the officer corps)[72] he did provoke the ire of some senior officers by creating an advisory council of junior officers, based in the Presidential palace itself, and making them his principal advisers. Soon known as the "Seven Dwarfs", these young officers (considered military "technocrats") backed the ousting of Maldonado Schaad and Gordillo in June 1982 (and became highly unpopular with many top officers).

Ríos Montt's conflicts with senior officers and civilian elites centred on his autocratic refusal to share power, his reliance on junior officers as advisers, his advocacy of control of state agencies and enterprises by army technocrats, and his meddling with Guatemala's *laissez-faire* economy. His economic concepts were not unrelated to the fire and brimstone speeches in which he excoriated corruption in government and among the wealthy classes, including the business sector:

> 'We have a strong and intelligent private sector', he said 'which has impoverished itself and the nation by its tax-dodging and its illegal export of dollars, which has made us all poor, not only in money but in men'.[73]

If being accused of moral lapses by Ríos Montt was galling, he infuriated the wealthier classes by introducing a 10% value added tax on sales and talking of tax reform. This interference in the private pursuit of wealth was without precedent in Guatemalan history; as one source notes

> Taxation in any form is virtually non-existent in Guatemala, whose fiscal revenue still comes mainly from what a US diplomat recently described as one of the few remaining 'mercantilist' customs systems.[74]

Ríos Montt's professed Christian beliefs served to garner support for his regime from Guatemalan and US fundamentalist churches, and initially aided apologists (mainly the Reagan administration) for the regime's excesses in making a case for supporting his government. For a time Ríos Montt's religious and anti-corruption rhetoric served to distract international attention from human rights abuses.[75] When maintaining that this man could not be presiding over any army programme of murder, apologists could point to Ríos Montt's regular sermonizing, and his tendency to drop to his knees requesting divine guidance during press conferences.

Although initially the officer corps welcomed the international public relations benefits of Ríos Montt's religiosity and the assistance provided by fundamentalist church groups to the rural counter-insurgency campaign,[76] his proselytizing from the Palace, including weekly Sunday television appearances, and having brought two church elders to the Palace as Presidential advisers, did not go down well in all quarters. The Roman Catholic church hierarchy was particularly concerned by Ríos Montt's elevation of a Protestant cult to the status of a semi-official religion in an overwhelmingly Catholic country. Church-state tension was aggravated on the occasion of Pope John Paul II's visit to Guatemala, in March 1982, by seemingly deliberate insults proferred by Ríos Montt, beginning with a highly publicized refusal to provide public funding for the visit and topped off by going ahead with a series of executions of secretly tried and sentenced political prisoners on the eve of the Pope's visit — after the Pope had publicly pleaded for clemency on their behalf.[77]

Although by the end of 1982 important sectors of the officer corps and the civilian elites of Guatemala had many reasons to wish to be rid of Ríos Montt, these did not include major disagreement on the conduct of the counter-insurgency war. To a large extent Ríos Montt was simply following through with the campaign strategy inaugurated in the last months of the previous government; after Ríos Montt's 16 months in the Presidency counter-insurgency strategy would remain unchanged.[78]

In June 1983, retired army intelligence chief General José Guillermo Echeverría Vielman published an open letter to General Ríos Montt demanding the removal of the young army officers serving as special Presidential advisers; the expulsion of religious advisers from the Palace, and a pledge to agree on a programme for return to constitutional" rule.

Immediately after publication of this letter signs that a coup was in the making appeared; the first reported act of insubordination was the refusal of the Quetzaltenango garrison commander "to carry out the presidential order to bombard a village that had fallen under guerrilla control".[79] This was not, as it might seem, a daring and altruistic refusal to execute a brutal order but an indicator that machinations for a coup were already in motion. "The fury of Ríos Montt grew when he learned that the Guatemalan air force and the Huehuetenango, San Marcos and

Santa Cruz del Quiché garrisons had also decided to rebel."[80] On 29 June, former junta member Colonel Francisco Gordillo seconded calls for a coup in a television news conference, explaining that "Ríos Montt thinks it was God who made him President, but in reality it was we who appointed him".[81] MLN leader Leonel Sisniega appeared on the same programme openly calling for a coup and characterizing Ríos Montt as a "traitor" and "religious fanatic".[82]

Ríos Montt won a little more time in office by acceding to the demands to oust the "Seven Dwarfs" from the Palace and return them to other duties and by dissolving the group of "evangelical advisors who had created a network of preachers up and down the country".[83]

The United States' position on Ríos Montt was by this time influenced by several unfavourable factors, not least of which was Ríos Montt's refusal to go along with the United States' call for Central America's governments to gang up militarily on Nicaragua through a revived CONDECA. Concerned with Guatemala's own insurgency problem, Ríos Montt irked the US government by refusing to go along with this proposal and declaring Guatemala's neutrality in the region's conflicts. At that point Ríos Montt's place in US plans for the region blurred. He was no longer an asset on the human rights score, too much had been broadcast and published on his extermination policies in the Indian highlands, and his loquacious eccentricity had lost much of its charm. He no longer served to unite a divided officer corps, and he had antagonized the civilian political leaders with whom he should have been governing. In the absence of any possibility that the Guatemalan army would repeat the "reformist coup" formula (there were simply no suitable reformist officers and no army faction willing to support a civilian alternative) the US may, logically, have supported Ríos Montt's ousting.

Army commanders meeting on 6 and 8 August at the barracks of the Honour Guard Brigade in Guatemala City decided that Ríos Montt must go. The army hierarchy was united in the decision, and the Presidential succession went to the second in the army's hierarchy after the President, Ríos Montt's hand-picked Minister of Defense, 52 year old Brigadier General Oscar Humberto Mejía Víctores. Army Chief of Staff Colonel Héctor Mario López Fuentes backed the coup and retained his position at the top of the army command.[84]

Ríos Montt did attempt some resistance. Called to the Honour Guard Brigade barracks on 8 August and asked to resign, he was allowed to return to the Palace to close up shop; Ríos Montt made one last effort to reach regional commanders, ordered the Presidential Guard to repel attackers, and held out for two hours as guards and rebels exchanged desultory gunfire, and helicopters and A-37 Dragonfly counter-insurgency jets buzzed the palace. The official death toll was two civilians and one soldier, though considerably more were wounded before Ríos Montt surrendered.[85]

The new President, sworn in shortly after Ríos Montt abandoned the Palace (in civilian clothes), had a background similar to other recent presidents of Guatemala, and was a member of the "Zacapa group". At the time of the Zacapa campaign (1966–68) General Mejía, then a lieutenant colonel, served as head of S-3 in the Zacapa army headquarters at the *Brigada Militar "Capitán General Rafael Carrera"*. In later years he had served as base commander in Escuintla, Quetzaltenango and the capital, and as Inspector General of the army.[86] Both General Mejía and Colonel López Fuentes, chief of the army general staff, were described in one account following the coup as "the leading figures of the core of higher-echelon survivors from the Lucas García days".[87] More to the point, they had presided over the army's scorched earth, mass counter-terror campaign during the previous 16 months.

Mejía was, indeed, a throwback to the Lucas García days in his inability to disguise his contempt for human rights and human rights advocates. As Minister of Defense he had clashed with Chairman of the US House of Representatives Appropriations Committee, Dr Clarence Long, a man not easily pushed around by generals or presidents. After a meeting in February 1983 Mejía responded to Long's human rights concerns by accusing him of "sounding like a member of the *Ejército Guerrillero de los Pobres* (EGP)".[88] After the coup which but Mejía in power, Long was quoted as assuring that "we can see to it that we don't give any military or economic aid to this crowd".[89]

General Mejía may be at odds with the US congress, but is apparently on good terms with the US military, and strongly backed by the Reagan administration. On the day before the coup, Mejía flew to a snap meeting with the deputy chief of the US military's Southern Command and the army chiefs of Honduras and El Salvador on the aircraft carrier *Ranger*.[90] Subsequently General Mejía told others he had advised the US of the coup in advance, and there was "no objection".[91] Although US officials claimed they heard only "rumours" of a coup, the evidence that the US military mission was fully aware of its planning and execution is considerable. No doubt to his considerable embarrassment, US Army Major William McArdoe was caught by Guatemalan television cameras lurking in a National Palace portico while talking into a walkie-talkie as troops scrambled around in the final stage of the coup.[92] Questioned about the involvement of their man in the events at the Palace, a US government spokesman responded indignantly that Major McArdoe was carrying out a "routine" investigation, and that "The United States did not favour a coup: we had no prior knowledge of the coup, and we reject these allegations".[93]

The coup did benefit United States hardliners in two ways, and the public relations problems attached to Mejía's assumption of power — mainly arising from his known stance on human rights — were by then no worse than those produced by Ríos Montt's human rights record and eccentric behaviour. Getting Ríos Montt out of the Palace removed an unpredictable rightist upon whom the US could no longer depend as an unconditional ally in the region. General Mejía had none of Ríos Montt's personality quirks, was a dependable counter-insurgent, and shared the Reagan's administration's viewpoint on the regional threat represented by the Nicaraguan and Salvadorean revolutions. Although Mejía himself insisted that "there has not been a change of government, but merely a replacement of Ríos Montt"[94] there was a very real shift in external policies. *Latin America Regional Reports* wrote that:

> The clearest feature of the regime which ousted Efraín Ríos Montt. . . is its overt alignment of Guatemala with the Washington-Tegucigalpa-San Salvador axis in the struggle against the Sandinistas in Managua and the Salvadorean rebels.[95]

The shift was obvious in some of his first measures, among them the dismissal of Foreign Minister Eduardo Castillo Arriola, who had formulated Ríos Montt's policy of neutrality vis-à-vis Nicaragua, and non-involvement in the Salvadorean conflict. It was equally evident in his statements:

> Mejía included in the new regime's manifesto 'our commitment to Guatemala to struggle by every means to eradicate the marxist-leninist subversion threatening our liberty and sovereignty'. He also stated publicly that in his view the Contadora Group 'has nothing to do in Central America'; instead, what was needed was support for the struggle against the Sandinistas in Nicaragua.[96]

In General Mejía the Reagan administration had evidently found a kindred spirit. That the US will assist General Mejía's government, either overtly or covertly, appears a foregone conclusion. Just 24 hours after the coup, the US welcomed the change, and efforts to rehabilitate General Mejía began immediately. State Department spokesman John Hughes said Mejía had promised the US Ambassador that he would lift the state of seige, abolish the secret courts and "continue the process of returning the government to democratic leadership".[97]

It seems probable that General Mejía will accede to the domestic and international pressures for some form of elections in the foreseeable future, and a return to a political accommodation with the far right political parties. The army, however, with or without a civilian in the Presidency, cannot be expected to surrender its political prerogatives easily, and will do so only when it has no alternative.

9. Counter-Insurgency: A Final Solution

The counter-insurgency campaign involving new tactics and a radical expansion of regular and paramilitary forces launched in the last months of the Lucas García regime, continued without interruption after the change of government on 23 March 1982. The tactics were new in part because of the scale of the operations; although the precise death toll will never be known, the dead probably numbered tens of thousands in 1982 and 1983 alone.[98] Application of the strategy for the highlands involved organizational innovations whereby the army would endeavour to control all aspects of the lives of those highland Indians not exterminated outright. Population control measures were designed to place the rural population under permanent surveillance and at the disposal of the army. A principal means was to require all males in the Indian communities between the ages of about 15 and 60 to serve in a new structure of the army reserve force, formalized in 1982 as the system of *Patrullas de Autodefensa Civil*, (PAC) (Civil Self-Defense Patrols).

A "National Plan for Security and Development", signed by Ríos Montt and his junta colleagues on 1 April 1982, outlined the public face of the army's "internal defense and development" strategy. Restating the points of the junta's "platform" of national objectives, the document proposed:

> The improvement of the structure and function of the Army and the internal security corps for confrontation and efficient combat with the subversive groups and movements.[99]

and gives particular emphasis to the need to co-ordinate all parts of the counter-insurgency effort at the highest levels, and centralize intelligence collection:

> Create at the highest political level, an agency to direct the antisubversive effort, that in accordance with the corresponding national policies, will issue instructions and general directives, integrate the measures agreed in every field and efficiently coordinate their realization ... Optimize the organization of the Central Intelligence Agency, adding to its means,

240

modernizing its systems and extending its action to every corner of the country and internationally in order to detect in all fields and areas the conditions that can give rise to subversive movements or can contribute to their growth. Locate and identify the subversive groups, including their essential character and their activities.[100]

Some major steps to centralize co-ordination of the counter-insurgency war did follow in the course of the next year. Perhaps the most far-reaching measure was the transfer of responsibilities for the police services from the Ministry of the Interior to the Ministry of Defense, taking effect on 15 January 1983.[101] Although the police had traditionally been commanded by serving army officers (with the exception of the Detective Corps, which traditionally went to a civilian chief) police personnel were not under military discipline and had none of the benefits accruing to army personnel (under the new system police would benefit, receiving health services through the Military Social Security Institute). More significantly, the measure continued the trend of the previous decade towards increased centralization of the security system, police and military, and ended the past practice of giving civilian political leaders — such as PID chief Donaldo Alvarez Ruiz — even partial control of the system. The simplified chain of command was similar to that of El Salvador's Ministry of Defense and Public Security.

At the municipal level the army created a structure designed to co-ordinate political and military aspects of counter-insurgency, a proposal considered in the 1960s but never implemented. This co-ordinating structure, in combination with the army's civilian irregulars, was seen as reflecting the guerrillas' own organization:

> Colonel [Gustavo Adolfo] Méndez put it succinctly in Huehuetenango: 'We have destroyed them with their own weapons', he declared. The guerrillas had set up a network of some 25,000 'local irregular forces' in Huehuetenango and the Government replaced them with its civil patrol groups. The EGP also set up 'local clandestine committees' which collected arms, intelligence and supplies, and recruited sympathizers. The Government's equivalent are 'Municipal Coordinating Bodies', which also help organize food and work for the peasants.[102]

Tight control of counter-insurgency operations, even in isolated rural areas, would be the order of the day. Procedures for supervision and control of operations and tactics were described in an interview with Army Lieutenant Romeo Sierra, commander of a 20-man patrol base in the highlands, and responsible for co-ordinating patrols throughout a 20 square kilometre area:

> According to Lieutenant Romeo Sierra ... the sweeps were directed from

241

the top. Field commanders like Sierra receive their orders through a chain of command which places only three steps — the minister of defense, the army chief of staff, and a colonel in the provincial capital — between themselves and Ríos Montt. The commanders receive daily orders from the colonel, and maintain hourly radio contact with his headquarters. 'I advise him that I'm going to Tutzuhil with 20 men. He knows everything. Everything is controlled.' All field tactics must be reported in the commanders' daily 'diary of operations' which is reviewed and criticized in monthly face-to-face evaluations. 'We're on a very short leash,' Sierra said.[103]

In July 1982 Ríos Montt launched what he dubbed the "Rifles and Beans" (*Fusiles y Frijoles*) programme, rifles standing for security and beans for development. Ríos Montt and his public relations officers declared enthusiastically that beans would be provided for those with the government, and the government's defenders would be issued rifles. The "beans" end of the strategy related primarily to residents of Indian communities forced into army "model villages" often primitive refugee camps at the army's main bases, and required to provide forced labour on army road building or related projects. Ironically, international aid agencies, including the United Nations World Food Program, have provided most of the commodities distributed by the army to those in its camps and to its active supporters.

Americas Watch, in a January 1984 report, notes that the World Food Program has a policy to provide only food aid to national governments, and that in Guatemala this, almost by definition, means it will be distributed by the army, although officially this is denied:

> Indeed, Americas Watch researchers saw the military distributing World Food Program food in rural areas. Thus international food aid becomes another instrument of military control. That is, hungry peasants must pledge allegiance to the government, work on government projects, and obey military commands in order to obtain food.[104]

While aspects of Ríos Montt's "beans" policy are reprehensible, particularly the way peasants have been driven to concentrate in the army's camps by hunger induced through the destruction of crops and livestock, the "rifles" end of the policy was the more dramatic. Far from giving the peasants rifles to defend themselves, the slogan "Beans and Rifles" was generally, correctly, interpreted to mean those with the government would have their beans and live, those against it would be on the receiving end of the rifles and die. Americas Watch's 1982 report describes the policy as "Beans *or* Rifles", and quotes an army officer in Cunen, El Quiché, who succinctly defined the policy as "If you are with us, we'll feed you, if not, we'll kill you."[105] The same report describes the strategy as one of total war against the Guatemalan people:

... we believe the government of President Ríos Montt is committed to total war. It asserts that it offers the people of Guatemala 'fusiles o frijoles' — guns or beans. In other words those who are with the government are fed; those who are not with the government are shot. No one is permitted to remain neutral.[106]

A secret Army General Staff document dated 16 July 1982 gives the code name for the counter-insurgency offensive as "Victory 82" (not "Beans and Rifles"), and outlines general orders for the campaign. The document is a classic expression of 1960s counter-insurgency doctrine; the objective is stated as simultaneously aiding the population, and annihilating those among the population supporting the guerrillas, or linked to suspect organizations:

> *Military Attitude in Countersubversive Operations*
> 1) Countersubversive Operations are always in support of the population and never against it;
> 2) The mission is to annihilate the guerrilla and parallel organizations; The Operations and our conduct should be intended to deny the guerrillas access to the civilian population, from which it supports itself and within which it hides.[107]

The permanent orders use terminology distinguishing community members supporting the guerrilla; Local Irregular Forces (*Fuerzas Irregulares Locales*), (FIL); members of mobile guerrilla units called Permanent Military Units (*Unidados Militares Permanentes*, (UMP)), and members of the guerrilla "infrastructure", called Local Clandestine Committees, (*Comités Clandestinos Locales*, (COL)). The strategy provides for members of the local FIL, low level guerrilla supporters to be "rescued" under certain circumstances: "Rescue the individuals of the Irregular Local Forces (FIL) neutralizing or eliminating those who do not wish to integrate themselves into normal life."[108] Members of the guerrilla proper or its "infrastructure", the CCL and the UMP, are simply to be killed: "Annihilate the Local Clandestine Committees (CCL) and the Permanent Military Units of the enemy UMP."[109]

Tactics recommended to achieve counter-insurgency objectives are outlined in easily memorized form: Fool them, Find them, Attack them, Annihilate them:

> 1. Fool them: Subversion must be fought with its own methods and techniques. Always have in operation a Plan of Disinformation.
> 2. Find them: The major problem is always to find the military units of the guerrillas who in accordance with their own systems of fighting remain in hiding. Use local intelligence and saturate the area with patrols.
> 3. Attack them: When you have found the guerrilla force, maintain

contact at all cost and immediately inform the Superior Unit so that it can support the operation and achieve the annihilation of the enemy that has been found.

4. Annihilate them: The destruction of the guerrilla forces is the mission. The control of territory is a means to complete this mission but not its end or final objective.[110]

In practice the army's tactics after March 1982 varied in accordance with intelligence assessments of the degree of support the guerrillas found in different parts of the country.

In areas bordering Mexico the army concluded the population was disloyal, and set about creating a no-mans-land, destroying virtually all the Indian communities in the area and killing as many inhabitants as could be caught. Similar tactics of fire and extermination were used in other highland areas where the population was believed to have gone over to the guerrillas, or to organizations like the CUC, considered parallel to the guerrillas' own movements. Vast areas of El Quiché department, of Huehuetenango, Chimaltenango and Alta Verapaz were the target of army operations designed to wipe out communities considered suspect and to drive other inhabitants of the region into army controlled camps. Several remarkable reports have been produced by international human rights organizations based on interviews with refugees from the terror who fled across the border into Mexico's southern state of Chiapas; in a 1983 report Survival International published summaries of many interviews with survivors of army attacks on Huehuetenango communities. Testimonies consistently report the arrival of troops in trucks or helicopters who assembled the villagers, told them they were "all guerrillas", and then began systematically to kill them. One account described the arrival of truckloads of soldiers at a village on 15 June 1982:

> They said that all the people in the village were guerrillas, even the women and children. He ran and hid, then watched as the soldiers killed fifteen people, including women, with machetes. They set fire to the houses, and sometimes opened the doors of the huts and threw hand grenades inside. In all, fifty people in the village were killed . . . Two of those killed were his uncles. From a kilometre away, he saw some women from his village who were hung by their feet without clothes . . .[111]

Americas Watch, in its May 1983 report on Guatemala, gave accounts of similar testimonies from numerous refugees. A member of a group of 207 refugees from the village of Kaibil Balam, municipality of Chajul in El Quiché, described the destruction of his community by the army at the end of 1982:

> . . . Guatemalan army soldiers entered their village and began shooting

men, women, children and livestock. Soldiers murdered children by cleaving their heads with machetes, strangling them with rope, and throwing them in the air and then bayonetting them. Women who did not escape were raped. Those who survived fled to the hills and tried to live off the crops and food supplies the army had not destroyed. In January and February 1983, the army again returned to the village and burned crops that the survivors had recently cultivated in nearby *parcelas*. No longer able to subsist in the mountains, 221 survivors from Kaibil Balam fled to Mexico. They were pursued intermittently by army patrols . . .[112]

Americas Watch found that refugees from many different parts of the highlands had similar accounts of army procedures used in the destruction of their communities:

Time and again, we listened to detailed eyewitness accounts of the use of planes and helicopters to bomb villages, settlements, and cooperatives, followed by ground assaults by soldiers who opened fire on men, women, and children. Other refugees told us that when the soldiers entered their village, rather than shooting randomly, they separated the men from the women and children; the men were taken into the local Catholic church and shot; the women and children were placed in separate buildings where they were burned alive or shot after first being raped by soldiers.[113]

Testimonies also consistently described the murder of women and children as a mechanical task of particular brutality:

Most of the testimony reveals that the army does not waste its bullets on women and children. We were repeatedly told of children being picked up by the feet and having their heads smashed against the walls, choked to death by hand or with ropes or killed with machetes or bayonets.[114]

The practice of killing entire families has been a special feature of the post-1982 period, and according to press reports has been openly justified by some Guatemalan army commanders. Several top army officers have explained the logic of the killings: that the foundation of the guerrillas' organization was what they called "family nuclei", and so the extermination of the guerrillas required the destruction of the "family nuclei".[115] The killings are described by officials in many press interviews as a "military necessity", the offensive against the Indian communities as an unpleasant, but unavoidable aspect of the "dirty war" against the guerrillas.[116] Guatemala's counter-insurgency programme is aimed at extirpating insurgency at its roots, thus eliminating current and future threats. Guatemala's army chose to kill the children with their parents to foreclose the option of their own future incorporation into the guerrillas, whether impelled by a desire for personal vengeance or from political conviction. That some aspects of the highland offensive — the near extermination of some Indian peoples — approximate genocide — defined under international law as killings "committed with intent to destroy, in whole or in part a national, ethnical, racial or religious group" — [117] is discussed further below.

Some areas not targetted for total depopulation were the object of army operations designed to drive the people from their communities into army camps where they would be under direct supervision. In many cases the army carried out successive raids on communities, with several residents "disappeared" or killed on each occasion; eventually, residents responded to raids by wholesale flight. This, in turn, was interpreted by army officers as evidence that they were guilty of collaborating with the guerrillas. Once villagers flee into the hills from the army another phase of the operation is introduced: the community's huts are burned down, livestock, crops and tools are destroyed. The scorched earth policy is carried out to cut off the suspect population (and, of course, the actual guerrillas) from food and shelter.

This process is illustrated by an account of the experience of residents of one village in the municipality of Patzún, Chimaltenango. The village of "Ama"[118] was raided by the army on five occasions in 1982. Each time troops burned the houses of suspects (who were not present at the time) and captured and killed or took away several villagers; on one occasion the victims were the mayor and his 10 year old daughter, as a reprisal for villagers having not reported the presence of guerrillas in the area. On 25 April villagers had advance warning of an army raid and fled en masse into the mountains: a response interpreted by the army as evidence that they had all gone over to the guerrillas. The level of violence then increased dramatically. On 26 April the neighbouring hamlet of Chipiacul was raided: its people did not attempt to flee, but 22 men were detained and killed. On 2 May a second hamlet was raided, the women taken to the evangelical church where some were raped; ten men were killed. At "Ama" the troops burned houses, destroyed or confiscated tools and food stores, and destroyed crops in the fields. The 300 people of the community spent three months living in the mountains on roots, river crayfish, and wild fruits, with some help from neighbouring villages; throughout their wandering they were pursued by army patrols. Finally, after an army attack on their encampment the community disintegrated: some fled toward the cities of the coast, some toward the capital, some were killed.

The destruction of villages, crops and even forests on which the Indian people of the highlands depend for survival has been widely reported. The practice has driven the people from their land to Mexico or to the cities, into army refugee centres where they must surrender to, and rely upon the army for their basic needs. Americas Watch described the twin goals of the counter-insurgency strategy as to rapidly destroy the guerrillas, and to "reassert the government's control over — i.e. 'pacify' — the Indian population":

The principal tactics of this strategy are bombing, shelling, selective killings, and massacres in suspected 'subversive' villages, combined with a scorched earth policy of crop-burning, confiscation of harvests and slaughter of livestock, calculated not only to deny the guerrillas food but also to force peasants to near starvation. Unless they reach the relative safety of Mexico, civilian survivors of these army operations face a choice between surrendering and seeking the protection of the army or of living in hiding, on the edge of starvation. The army provides food to those who surrender in 'strategic hamlets'.[119]

In a number of widely reported cases, refugees from communities destroyed by the army have hidden in the mountains for months, but finally surrendered themselves at regional army bases, driven by hunger. Although army public relations teams promise refugees fleeing from "the guerrillas" food and shelter at army refugee centres, once there refugees suspected as "subversives" are culled, interrogated and killed. As a consequence it has generally been the old, and women with small children who have come down from the mountains to take up the army's offer of beans and security. In October 1982 some 3,000 to 5,000 survivors of attacks on Indian and *ladino* communities in Chimaltenango and El Quiché surrendered to the army after hiding out in the mountains for months.[120] After being placed under guard in an army camp in San Martín Jilotepeque some 200 men were reportedly taken away and killed: according to a Cakchiquel Indian who fled the camp, the several thousand refugees,

> hungry and miserable and thinking that they would not be harmed . . . went to the Army's village. They were mostly the older men, the women and children and those who were sick. In the next few days, the soldiers killed about 200 people.[121]

An international outcry followed the surrender of several thousand more refugees at San Martín Jilotepeque in late October when word of an impending cull of the new group reached the outside world.[122]

Latin America Regional Reports reported in September 1983 that massacres of suspected supporters of the guerrilla movement continued to increase in number and were characterized by "clinical savagery". Tactics were varied "according to specific counter-insurgency goals":

> The killing is sometimes selective, with community leaders, such as teachers or Church activists, and their families being singled out. In other instances whole villages have been wiped out. Everything depends on the army's perception of the level of local support for the guerrillas. In areas where military intelligence points to a guerrilla 'push' 'preventive terror' is used. In several cases army and civil defense units have visited villages masquerading as guerrillas, killed indiscriminately and then returned

later in uniform to 'rescue the survivors' and organize them into civil defense units.[123]

Where the entire population was not classed as supporting the guerrillas the people were subjected to "screening" operations. Although in some areas screening procedures after March 1983 involved the obligatory civil patrol system set up in 1982, most reports of operations of this kind are identical to those of previous years. They begin with the cordoning off of the village or town, often on a market day, and a systematic identity check of all residents. All are assembled, and hooded informants are escorted down lines of villagers; those pointed out by them to accompanying soldiers are taken away and killed. A New Orleans *Times Picayune* report in September 1982 quoted an interview with a regional army commander in the Indian highlands who gave his own account:

> 'Our intelligence unit supplies the names of local insurgent forces in each place that has been contaminated by subversion. We go in and make a roll call, asking those individuals why they collaborated. If they admit they were coerced, we rescue them, through psychological action. Otherwise', he said, 'they are neutralized or eliminated.'[124]

The same article cited civilian witnesses of screening procedures directed by the colonel. They described the army's use of masked informants during the "roll calls" in Indian communities to point out people accused of aiding the guerrillas, and the practice of immediate execution of those singled out — often with their entire families — by shooting, hanging, machete, clubbing or burning to death.

Accounts of the "screening" or "cleansing" operations describe methods similar to standard procedures used in Vietnam, called "County Fair operations", in which South Vietnamese or US forces cordoned off a village so that police could interrogate and, hopefully, arrest the local "infrastructure".[125]

Heavy reliance on the army's own informants in Guatemalan screening operations was frequently combined with compulsory involvement of community civil defence patrols in the execution of suspects. In this way community members were forced to share responsibility for the army's actions. An account from Joyabaj, El Quiché, in early 1983 describes "screening" operations in which "a man with a green hood over his head" accompanied an army patrol and identified suspects, and members of the community's own "civil defense patrol" were ordered to carry out the executions:

> The operations work like this: the army enters a village, bearing lists of suspected guerrilla sympathizers. 'One man from the village is hooded', my informant, politically a centrist, tells me. 'He is made to walk among

the people pointing out the suspects.' After one such walkabout, the village civilian defense patrol was ordered to execute four people in public. 'The men were struggling and shouting as they were held down, their heads yanked back by their hair. Then their heads were hacked from their bodies with machetes. The severed heads were presented to the local military commander by the villagers, as proof that the execution had been carried out.[126]

The Civil Defense Patrols

The civil defence system was developed in two stages, and combined a rationalization of the army's 1960s system of trustworthy, politically motivated civilian auxiliaries, with a programme to place the highlands Indians under military command and control. The first stage was begun in the latter half of 1982, as the Lucas García regime expanded the army's auxiliary forces in much the same way used since the mid-1960s: army veterans, and civilians considered politically sound, generally members of right-wing parties, like the MLN, were brought into the army's "reserve" network, under the orders of military commissioners and regional army commanders. These irregular forces, largely comprising *ladinos*, were to form the active, armed contingents of the civil patrol system. In organizational terms they appear to have differed little from the large forces raised by the army in the eastern parts of the country in the late 1960s, prior to the launching of the Zacapa campaign. The numbers estimated in the force of armed civilian irregulars by March 1982 range up to 30,000. By mid-1983 Ríos Montt claimed over 300,000 had been incorporated into civil patrols. Most of these recruits, however, were involuntary conscripts and armed only with sticks and machetes, not trusted with firearms. The armed civilian auxiliaries fully trusted by the army probably did not exceed 30,000.

The civil defence system may have had some quasi-legal basis in the 1968 army law, the *Ley Constitutiva del Ejército*, which provides for all adult males to perform military service, and remain nominally part of the army's reserve force until the age of 50.[127] Call up of males between 18 and 50 (and often in practice, those from 15 up to about 65) in the civil patrol system appears, however, to be done selectively, concentrating in the areas of heavy Indian population and without consideration of the legal niceties of conscription laws and regulations.

The civil patrol system was most thoroughly developed in the western highlands, in areas designated "areas in conflict". There the patrol system was applied primarily as a system of population control whereby members of the tight-knit Indian communities could be collectively held hostage against subversion.

To some extent the civil patrol system is a reversion to the community policing systems of the 19th Century and the colonial period. Then as now, however, failure of the indigenous community to fulfil its obligations to the state could provoke the state's violence against the community as a whole or its leaders. Americas Watch has compared the civil patrol system to colonial systems of forced labour:

> ... [the system requires] the conscription of all males, from older boys to old men, into an endless rotating system of compulsory policing and vigilante service, unpaid and unavoidable. Failure to supply the necessary manpower for intense local policing and population control entails severe penalties inflicted by the military authorities.[128]

Although theoretically in force throughout the rural areas of the country, the civil patrol system has been established on a comprehensive basis only in the Indian communities of the western highlands, where virtually every adult Indian male has been conscripted into the system. Already in May 1982 the *Comité de Unidad Campesina* (CUC) had denounced the system as a strategy "to turn the poor against the poor":

> Now they have added a new treachery to present their massacres as confrontations between the guerrilla and so-called civil patrols, where peasants supposedly of both sides are killed ... The army in many areas has forced all of the peasants to participate in these bands, saying that if we do not do so they will kill us for being subversives.[129]

Those doing the killing, however, are described as "no more than paramilitary groups led by soldiers and by military commissioners and spies in each locality."[130]

On creation of a civil patrol the men of a community must provide personal information and register with local army commanders, and henceforth perform a series of tasks. Interviews with refugees who fled to Mexico describe the registration procedure:

> The army has ordered us to participate in civil militias ... These civil militias are something new. It's a way of controlling the people ... They said [we should] present ourselves to them, and enlist ourselves in their programs by giving them our personal data such as our addresses, a photograph, and they're going to give us a card in order that we can be identified as Guatemalans and legal in our homes.[131]

The introduction of the civil patrol system in its two aspects, as an obligatory system of population control in the Indian areas, and a rationalized system of voluntary civilian auxiliaries in the army's armed counter-insurgent forces, was reflected in several of the policy documents of the Guatemalan military in the first months of the Ríos Montt regime. The 1 April 1982 "National Plan for Security and

Development" concludes that in the military sphere the army's existing system of organization was inadequate to deal with "the different fronts presented by armed subversion": "The successes of the Army against the Guerrilla *focos* have not reflected a significant weakening that would permit us to predict their eradication in the short term."[132]

The document proposes that steps be taken immediately to "increase efforts on intelligence and for the establishment of a model for control of the population." The civil patrol system was central to this new model and specified as such in a 16 July 1982 document, "Standing Orders for the Development of Countersubversive Operations" for campaign plan "Victory 82". The documents outline the military strategy for the campaign as based fundamentally on cutting off the guerrillas from their supporters. As a principal means to do so, listed under "Psychological Operation", the army was "To organize in the Areas of greatest conflict the patrols of Civil Self-Defense, to be fully supervised and controlled by each Command." Civil patrols were also to be made part of a programme of population control outlined in the "Victory 82" document:

> Prevent sabotage on the cotton, sugar cane and other plantations and other areas of production, during the harvest months; Institute controls over the personnel in seasonal labour who travel from the *altiplano* of the Republic to the South Coast; Institute control of the roads and control of the population through: a) Patrols; b) Check-points; c) Censuses; d) Control of documents, etc.[133]

The civil patrols were most useful to the army in this area of population control, through surveillance and regimentation of the Indian communities. Americas Watch, in their January 1984 report, summarized the tasks of patrolling and reporting required from the civil patrols:

> The civil patrols officially require that all men from ages 18 to 60 participate in 24-hour tours of duty patrolling their community against 'subversives' on a rotating basis. The frequency of rotation depends somewhat on the supply of males available in particular localities, with 24-hour shifts recurring once a week in some areas. More typically, however, it appears that men serve one such shift per fortnight... On each patrol, there is a leader and from 10 to 20 patrolmen serving with him.[134]

A main objective of the patrolling is to monitor movement through the area and report to local army officers on a regular basis:

> They are required to patrol the streets, roads, and hillsides day and night, registering all comings and goings of the population. In heavily patrolled areas and strategic places such as main roads, the patrols must record the

251

names of all arrivals, where they are going, the reasons for their movements, and where they have come from. In addition to this intensive surveillance over the boundaries of their communities, they are required to report on any suspicious people walking about at night, the language they speak, and what they are saying. These reports are delivered to the local military authorities, two officials whose titular responsibilities are '*comandante*' and '*ideas ideológicas*'.

Civil patrol members' failure to report strangers moving through the area, or inform on local people may be punished by their own execution.

Civil patrols are also regularly required to accompany troops; although unarmed, they serve to draw the fire of ambushers and act as a human screen for the regular troops. Many civil patrollers are required to carve wooden guns, not to frighten off guerrillas, but to enhance their role as decoys.

> [The patrols] would not be effective against either armed guerrillas nor against the military authorities themselves, who evidently have no great confidence that their new recruits will not turn on them if truly armed. This charade is taken so far that the patrols are required to arm themselves with wooden toy guns (some even painted black) which might at a distance be mistaken for real arms and cause these civilians to be placed in vulnerable positions... Moreover, on patrol in insecure areas, it is alleged that the military requires the civilian patrols to enter first to see if they, with their antique or wooden guns, draw fire from the enemy.

Local army commanders maintain files on patrol members, and supervise the performance of tasks assigned to each patrol. Petitions requesting permission to be absent from a patrol shift, or to hire a substitute for specific duty shifts, must be made to the local army commander. Americas Watch, in its January 1984 report, concludes that the civil patrol system transforms the traditional society of the indigenous communities into a totalitarian police state:

> ... the creation of the civil patrol system reporting to the local military commanders, effectively displaces traditional forms of self-government and maintenance of order . . . It represents a complete disregard for community elders and elected leaders, and for judicial settlement of disputes. The countryside is transformed into a police state. It is difficult to overemphasize the extent to which the civil patrol system contributes to a totalitarian control of the indigenous population.[137]

In many ways the regimentation introduced into Indian life by the civil patrol system resembles the days of the vagrancy laws of the early 20th Century, when Indian men were required to carry pass-cards signed by large private landowners to prove they were fulfilling their legal obligation to work. Under the current system exemptions from civil patrol duties are permitted for seasonal work on private plantations, conditional upon provision of a substitute, and that, on return the civil patrol members present a "receipt" signed by the plantation owners or their representatives. Failure to have such a "receipt" can mean summary execution. As Americas Watch notes:

> ... [the system] can create pressure on a peasant to accept any wage rather than return home after weeks of searching for work without any such receipt, and gives leverage to plantations to use their precious signatures as an additional control over the migrant work force.[139]

In the long term, new forms of economic subjugation of the Indian peasantry may be introduced. In 1983, army spokesmen described plans reminiscent of the 1880s programmes to oust the Indians from potential coffee growing lands while keeping them on hand as a captive labour force. Interviews with Guatemalan Colonel Eduardo Wohlers, head of the "Program of Help to Areas in Conflict" (*Programa de Ayuda de Areas en Conflicto*, (PAAC)), part of Ríos Montt's "guns and beans" policy, outlined the means by which the army sought to retain control of highland areas from which guerrillas had been cleared by putting the Indians to work in agro-business. "Rural development" in Guatemala is to involve assistance to existing landowners for the expansion of export agriculture: "Without tampering with the existing pattern of land ownership, the army intends to turn the Indian highlands into a vast factory farm."[140]

Indians brought into the area, closely controlled, would provide the labour force. Politically trusty civilians (the equivalent of ORDEN in El Salvador) would provide the manpower for a security infrastructure based on the "civil patrols" concept:

> Last summer, as the army occupied many former guerrilla strongholds, numerous highland villages were placed under permanent military control. 'Under previous governments', Wohlers explained, 'the problem was that we pulled out, leaving the subversives to take advantage of our absence to win back villages. Now the army intends to remain in permanent occupation, aided by the pro-government militia (defensa civil) service which is mandatory for all males aged between 18 and 50.'[141]

The first stage of the PAAC plan, after clearance operations, is to boost local food production "to meet local demand", and deploy displaced peasants "... in the so-called food-for-work units, which build roads and irrigation facilities in exchange for daily subsistence food rations."[142]

The tens of thousands of internal refugees fleeing the counter-insurgency sweeps in the north-west can thus be controlled, in camps or "model villages", while being put to work at minimal cost.

Once government control was reestablished and reinforced through the civil defence "militia", the second stage was to be the building of an economic infrastructure based on increased production by existing medium and large farms. Models for this agricultural plan, according to Colonel Wohlers, included Taiwan and Israel, with Israeli advisers providing "technical assistance and training". Funding for the scheme is being sought from the United States:

> Colonel Wohlers confirmed that USAID had given the green light to the new export crop plan and had assured him in private that funding would be available. AID officials in Guatemala City agree that a favourable decision is likely later this year.[143]

Just how realistic the second stage of the plan is remains to be seen. The concentration of the Indian population in controlled villages will, however, probably remain a feature of the highlands until the government falls.

Early in the civil patrol system's development reluctance by the men of a community to form a patrol was one of the many indicators taken by the army to mean that the community sympathized with the guerrillas. During 1982, most Indian communities not destroyed by violence or abandoned by the flight of their people were obliged to form civil patrols or be destroyed. There were cases in which whole villages refused and suffered the consequences.[144] But even if they accepted, a community was not exempted from the murder of its people by troops directing the patrols. Civil patrol members could be forced at gunpoint to kill their own community leaders with machetes, or could themselves be put to death on army orders for suspicious activities or unsatisfactory performance of patrol duties.[145] Fulfillment of the obligation to form civil patrols brought the Indian communities neither reward nor protection. Periodic selective killings of the communities' men, who by 1983 were almost all members of the patrols, continued even in areas from which the guerrillas had by and large been "cleared". Troops would appear with a list, and men identified as collaborators with subversive organizations, or considered guilty of lapses in their civil patrol tasks, would be dragged from their homes and shot. The terror sustained through these casual murders tended to ensure that patrol members were not "won over" to the government. The principal benefit conferred by patrol membership was an uncertain permission to survive, which could be withdrawn whenever their names appeared on the commander's death list.

The army has also used the patrol system among the almost exclusively Indian highlands' communities to divide them against themselves and their neighbours. Civil patrols are forced at gunpoint to execute members of their own families or communities; civil patrols of one community are forced to accompany troops in raids on neighbouring communities, and bloody their own hands by killing the army's prisoners with their machetes or with firearms handed them by the troops.[146]

The application of the civil patrol system has differed radically between the largely autonomous, closely knit Indian highlands' communities and the cities or towns and other areas with a significant *ladino* population.[147] In practice, *ladinos* have generally been exempted from serving in civil patrols,[148] yet many have become armed auxiliaries in the army's "active reserve", as has traditionally been their privilege. In some largely *ladino* populated areas however, they have been recruited, armed, and placed in command of civil patrols composed mainly of Indians. In these areas the army used traditional recruitment methods, drawing on army veterans and members of right-wing parties to set up forces they called civil patrols whose activities and organization differed little from the armed auxiliary groups set up under the military commissioner system; except that these *ladino* "civil patrols" were apparently even more systematically organized and centrally controlled than in the past.

Outside the exclusively Indian areas of the western highlands most observers have stressed the dual nature of the civil patrol system: forced levies of patrollers from the Indian villages, trusted only with their machetes, subordinated to heavily armed army commanders or commissioners and their subordinates; the armed *ladino* civilians appointed as patrol commanders.

In some areas the patrol system has been reported as a mechanism to use the Indians as forced labour on roads and private farms. In a November 1983 interview Christian Democrat leader Vinicio Cerezo described the civil patrols as used to reinforce rural power structures by totally subordinating the Indian peasants to the army and the local elites:

> Apart from killings allegedly carried out by the patrols, the Christian Democrat Party claims it has evidence that Indians have been forced by the patrols to work for no wages. Cerezo alleged that the patrols were also being used by the Army to reinforce the domination over the Indians of the *Ladino* (mixed race) group who have traditionally run Guatemala. 'The Army has based its repressive structure on the *Ladinos* who command the patrols', Cerezo said.[149]

In the Indian highlands the community structures to some extent prevented the civil patrol from becoming the grass-roots vigilante system prescribed by counter-insurgency doctrine. The army's terror tactics and the lack of reward (not even that of guaranteed survival) for co-operation with the army contributed to this failure. But the civil patrols provided the army with a major tool for control of the civil patrollers themselves.

In areas where the population was not overwhelmingly Indian, communities were more easily divided against themselves: *ladinos* placed in command of civil patrols could be trusted not to resist army instructions and were delegated some real authority over their fellows. In some areas the army could even trust *ladino* civil patrolmen to carry out the kind of "death-squad" operations traditionally entrusted to the military commissioner network — sometimes the killers serving as civil patrol leaders had previously worked in "death-squads" wearing a different hat. Civil patrols were reported to be particularly active as executors of army death lists on the South Coast. In November 1983 the Christian Democrat Party protested that "civil defense patrols" had carried out systematic assassinations of the party's local leaders and previously elected municipal officials on the South Coast, particularly in Escuintla.[150]

Ladino-led civil patrols also proved to be obedient executors of army orders to detain and execute local people in other areas. Press reports described a September 1982 visit by Guatemalan-based foreign diplomats to an area near Chichicastenango where the civil defence patrol had reportedly killed 25 people. During the visit, a diplomat asked the commander of the local patrol, in the presence of an army officer, what had happened.

> 'The head of the local civil defense patrol asked an army officer if he could tell the truth,' the diplomat said. 'When told to go ahead, he admitted that they had killed 11 civilians in June, 11 in July and three others at a later date. He said that the first 11 had been macheted but this was too messy so the rest were garrotted to death.' Asked why the killings had taken place, the civil defense patrol commander reportedly replied: 'Because they were on the list'.[151]

The Question of Genocide

Since 1982 the Guatemalan army has carried out a campaign of systematic extermination in many parts of the western highlands; the mass of the population there was considered, probably correctly, to have sympathized with the guerrilla movement, or collaborated in such mass organizations as the Committee of Peasant Unity (CUC), considered by the army to be collaborators of the guerrillas. Most inhabitants of the area were Indian peasants, and the victims of the extermination campaign, from suspect areas or villages, were members of the many distinct Indian peoples of the country. Where not killed outright, many survivors of these groups who failed to flee the country are reduced to captivity in internal "refugee centres" or "model villages".

Of Guatemala's seven million people an estimated four million do not speak Spanish as a mother tongue and identify themselves as members of one of 23 Indian peoples distinguished by their language and customs. The largest groups are the Kekchi, Mam, Cakchiquel, and the Quiché, numbering altogether some three million people. Smaller groups include the Kanjobales, Chujes, Jacaltecos, Aguacatecos, Uspantecos, Ixiles, Achíes, Pocomchíes, Pocomames and Tzutuhuiles; together some 600,000 to 700,000 people.[152] Among the Indian peoples hardest hit by the army's counter-insurgency policies are the Ixil (an estimated 45,000 in 1969), concentrated in the triangle (the "Ixil triangle") between the El Quiché towns of Chajul, Nebaj and Cotzal.[153] The Ixil have a long history of clashes with the *ladino* landowners of the area, including a short-lived insurrection in Chajul in 1925; and in 1936 the army commandant and his garrison of seven *ladino* soldiers were disarmed and beaten after an insulting response to Indian grievances over the compulsory labour system and changes in the status of debts; when troops arrived seven Ixil men were captured and shot.[154]

The "Ixil triangle" was one of the first targets of Ríos Montt's counter-insurgency drive, and the first area announced by the army to have been "pacified" through the organization of the "civil defense" system.[155] In November 1982 Americas Watch reported that "One of the twenty-three linguistic groups, the Ixil in El Quiché, has been all but wiped out as a cultural entity."[156]

The American Friends Service Committee, in an October 1982 paper, reported signs that "the Indian cultures themselves are beginning to disintegrate" as a consequence of the army's policies, and that, as in El Salvador in 1932, ". . . people stop wearing traditional dress because it indicates where they are from and may make them suspect."[157]

In a statement from the occupied Brazilian Embassy, in May 1982, the CUC warned that Indians from the highlands, distinguished by their regional dress, native language and customs, were hunted down and killed even outside their home areas, and movement to the coast or the cities to find work could no longer be undertaken

> . . . for fear of being murdered on the roads or the plantations, for the simple fact of being poor Indians who live in certain municipios, and cantons, especially in El Quiché, Chimaltenango and Huehuetenango, since the army and the gunmen of the landowners accuse us of being subversives and murder us. The same thing happens to those of us who go to sell or do business in other towns or in the capital city. We have had to stop this because the "guides" of the army have gone to the city to point out the people of certain cantons and hamlets, who are then murdered.[158]

With the frightened people of the Indian highlands hiding from execution squads, discarding the traditional dress by which each

Indian community can be distinguished, and seeking to pass as acculturated *ladinos*, the parallel with the extermination of most of El Salvador's Indian cultures in 1932 is striking.

Is the Guatemalan government guilty of genocide? International law defines the crime largely in terms of the identity of the targets of the killing: the mass murder of a group defined only by its political beliefs, as in the Indonesian massacre of Communist Party members in 1965, does not necessarily qualify. In the Guatemalan case, however, the top secret directives of campaign plan "Victory 82" appear to have selected many of the Indian peoples for extermination because their ethnic group as a whole was judged to have been infected by subversion. The Ixil were hunted down and killed because they were Ixil, and, therefore, subversives — much as Cambodia's Khmer Rouge targetted the Muslim Cham people for extinction. Under the 1948 United Nations Convention on the Prevention and Punishment of the Crime of Genocide this deliberate annihilation of Indian peoples — in the name of the fight against Communism or motivated by racial hatred — qualifies as genocide. This Convention defines acts of genocide as all those, including killings "committed with the intent to destroy, in whole or in part, a national, ethnical, racial or religious group".

Ríos Montt and his press spokesmen have been quoted as justifying the mass killings in the Indian communities:

> When asked about army killings of unarmed civilians Gen. Efraín Ríos Montt . . . replied: 'Look, the problem of the war is not just a question of who is shooting. For each one who is shooting there are 10 working behind him.' His press secretary, Francisco Bianchi, explained 'The guerrillas won over many Indian collaborators', he said. 'Therefore, the Indians were subversives, right? And how do you fight subversion? Clearly you had to kill the Indians because they were collaborating with subversion. And then they would say, "You're massacring innocent people". But they weren't innocent. They had sold out to subversion.'[159]

When meeting the press in December 1982 Ríos Montt clarified his position further: " 'We have no scorched-earth policy', he said. 'We have a policy of scorched Communists.' "[160]

Support for Ríos Montt's policies from Guatemala's far right resembled that given Salvadorean President Maximiliano Hernández Martínez for the 30,000 deaths in the 1932 pogrom which virtually exterminated the Indian population of eastern El Salvador: the targets seen as both Communists and Indians — extermination justified on either count. In an interview with a US based reporter one wealthy Guatemalan saw the counter-insurgency offensive as an opportunity to *complete* the extermination of the Indians:

> 'The massacre of Indians is simply the continuation of the work of the

conquest', said one wealthy Ladino — one of the mixed Indian and European people, who make up less than half Guatemala's population but control most of its wealth. 'You finished off the Indians in your country nearly 100 years ago.'[161]

A spokesman for a Guatemalan landowners association was less outspoken, but supported a similar position: "If the guerrilla areas have to be cleared of these people, the Indian population, then it must be done."[162]

Whatever the rationale, observers in Guatemala from the first month of the Ríos Montt regime all described the counter-insurgency offensive as aimed specifically at the Indian population. A priest in Huehuetenango told a reporter that: "The army is trying to kill every Indian alive."[163]

Claims that the regime had reformed were wrong a diplomat told the *New York Times*: "Indians are systematically being destroyed as a group . . . There is no break with the past."[164]

Of all the crimes of contemporary counter-insurgency, the mass murder of the Indian peoples of Guatemala's highlands will be remembered the longest, and with the greatest shame by those who permitted, or assisted, its unfolding.

Notes to Part 4

Chapter 8

1. Center for International Policy, *International Policy Report*, October 1980, Vol. VI, No. 1, "US Human Rights Policy: Latin America", by Richard E. Feinberg, p. 3.
2. Ibid., Todman was transferred to Spain after a February 1978 speech in New York attacking the administration's human rights policy.
3. *El Imparcial*, 12 December 1979.
4. *Latin America Regional Reports*, 11 January 1980.
5. Piero Gleijeses, "Guatemala: Crisis and Response", (manuscript) Johns Hopkins University (SAIS) 1982, p. 14.
6. Ibid., p. 15.
7. Ibid.
8. Ibid., p. 18.
9. Ibid., p. 19.
10. For information on Guatemalan elections, including official results, see *Keesings Contemporary Archives*.
11. *Compañero*, July 1982, English Language Edition, p. 7.
12. *Latin America Weekly Report*, 6 November 1981, "Testing time for military solutions in Guatemala and El Salvador".
13. *Latin America Regional Reports*, 4 June 1982, "Counter-insurgency at the crossroads".
14. *Inforpress*, 26 November 1981.
15. Institute for Policy Studies, *Resource*, July 1982, p. 4.
16. Ibid.
17. Ibid. For accounts of guerrilla actions in January and February 1982 see *Latin*

America Regional Reports, 12 February 1982, "Army steps up actions against guerrillas", and *Campañero*, July 1982.

18. *Campañero*, July 1982, p. 7.
19. *Latin America Regional Reports*, 12 February 1982, "Guatemala: Army steps up actions . . .".
20. See, for example, *Central America Report*, 9 January 1982, p. 2.
21. *This Week*, 30 November 1981, "Homeguard is Organized".
22. *Inforpress*, 26 November 1981.
23. Ibid.
24. See, for example, *This Week*, 11 January 1982, p. 11.
25. See *Latin America Regional Report*, 30 April 1982, "New government orders clean-up of the police"; "The government claims to have organized and armed up to 30,000 peasants, some . . . with sophisticated weaponry such as M-16 rifles . . ."; and Institute for Policy Studies, *Resource*, July 1982, p. 7.
26. Arthur Allen, "Guatemala's Indians still die as government, guerrillas fight on", *The Sun* (Baltimore), 1 June 1982.
27. Gen. Guevara became army chief of staff in mid-1979.
28. See *Keesings Contemporary Archive*, 23 July 1982, p. 31, 605, for a summary of post-election events.
29. Ibid.
30. Ibid.
31. *El Gráfico*, 26 March 1982, "Perfil de los tres nuevos gobernantes"; *Diario de Centro América* (Guatemala), 23 March 1982 and 26 March 1982.
32. *Diario de Centro América*, 26 March 1982.
33. Quoted in *Hoy*, 9-15 April 1980.
34. *Latin America Weekly Report*, 31 July 1981, "Graft among Guatemala's generals threatens the war effort", citing an interview with a group of officers published in *Uno más uno* (México City).
35. Ibid.
36. *Latin America Weekly Report*, 19 March 1982, "Private Sector Finds its Voice".
37. Ibid.
38. Loren Jenkins, "Leader Insists Vote to be Fair in Guatemala", Washington Post Service, *International Herald Tribune*, 6-7 March 1982.
39. Piero Gleijeses, op. cit., pp. 20-21.
40. Ibid.
41. Ibid., p. 21, note 24, citing *New York Times*, 7 March 1982, "Sanitizing Guatemala" and *Washington Post*, 22 December 1981, "Regime Blamed for Violence in Guatemala", Jack Anderson. Anderson reported that State Department officials had secretly sounded out key congressmen about the proposed release of the parts, and received 'almost universal negative responses . . .'
42. *Latin American Regional Reports*, 12 February 1982; these were Gen. Benedicto Lucas' words to describe his objectives in an interview.
43. Ibid.
44. The remark was widely reported; see *Keesings Contemporary Archive*, 23 July 1982.
45. Robert Kaiser, "Reagan May lift ban on Military sales in Guatemala", *Washington Post*, 22 April 1982, quoted in Gleijeses, op. cit., p. 25.
46. *Keesings Contemporary Archive*, 23 July 1982.
47. Institute for Policy Studies, *Resource*, July 1982, p. 3.
48. The junta's programme is reproduced in *Keesings Contemporary Archive*, 23 July 1982.
49. Institute for Policy Studies, *Resource*, July 1982, p. 5.
50. *El Gráfico*, 27 March 1982, "García Arredondo sustituido ayer"; *El Día* (Mexico City) 21 April 1982; the DIT in turn would be "purged" in April 1983 with the arrest of some 20 officers and men on corruption charges; Roberto Cruz Gudiel, identified as the former head of Guatemala's Interpol (a part of the DIT) was found

dead in his cell shortly afterward; see *Uno más Uno*, 14 April 1983, *El Gráfico*, 16 April 1983, and *Times of the Americas*, 11 April 1983.

51. "The Coup That Got Away", *Time*, 5 April 1982.
52. Gleijeses, op. cit., p. 27, notes that concern rapidly grew over Ríos Montt's "mental equilibrium"; "Ríos Montt's psychological condition is a source of concern to several sympathetic but increasingly apprehensive US officials. A reading of his own public statements since March 23 makes US uneasiness understandable."
53. Statement by Ríos Montt, reported in the *Miami Herald*, 6 June 1982 and the *Eureka Times Standard*, 9 September 1982.
54. Survival International, *Witness to Genocide*, 1982, p. 8.
55. Americas Watch, *Human Rights in Guatemala: No Neutrals Allowed*, 23 November 1982, p. 92. The report includes an extensive review of Decree law No. 46-82 of 1 July creating the Special Courts, how the system violates international human rights standards and the first executions under the new system. See also *Amnesty International Report 1983*, p. 141, and Amnesty International, "Proceedings under Decree Law 46-82", AI Index 34/18/83.
56. Americas Watch, *Human Rights in Guatemala . . .*, p. 92.
57. Ibid., p. 79.
58. Ibid.; the amnesty law was Decree-law No. 33-82, taking effect on 1 June 1982.
59. The government announced on 30 June that "430 guerrillas" had turned themselves in; this claim has not been substantiated and appears unlikely. See Institute for Policy Studies, *Resource*, July 1982, p. 5, citing UPI, 1 June 1982.
60. Ibid.
61. Ibid.
62. See Americas Watch, *Human Rights in Guatemala . . .*, part II, "The Laws" for a discussion of Guatemalan law and international standards.
63. Ibid., pp. 84-5.
64. Amnesty International, "Massive Extrajudicial Executions in Rural Areas under the Government of General Efraín Ríos Montt: Special Briefing", July 1982, AI Index: AMR: 34/34/82.
65. Ibid.
66. Episcopal Conference of Guatemala, 27 May 1982.
67. Americas Watch, *Human Rights in Guatemala . . .*, p. 22, citing Jorge Carpio Nicolle, from *El Gráfico*, 20 May 1982.
68. *Latin America Regional Reports*, 7 May 1982.
69. Comité de Unidad Campesina, (CUC), "El Ejército de la Junta Militar Sigue Masacrando a Nuestras Comunidados", Guatemala, May 1982 (mimeo, 5 pages).
70. *Latin America Regional Reports*, 25 March 1983.
71. Ibid.
72. Gleijeses, op. cit., p. 27, concludes that "there is no significant modernizing group among the young Guatemalan officers. Neither Ríos Montt, nor the young officers — nor even the technocrats brought into the government — have proposed or intend to introduce the social reforms that any formula of the Modernizing Right desperately requires."
73. *Latin America Regional Reports*, 24 September 1982.
74. *Latin America Regional Reports*, 19 August 1983.
75. *This Week*, 15 August 1983, citing Acting Archbishop Ramiro Pellecer, and American Friends Service Committee, "Questions and answers about the current situation in Guatemala", October 1982. Until Cardinal Casariego's death, efforts by bishops and clergy to speak out on human rights issues were systematically blocked by the church hierarchy.
76. American Friends Service Committee, op. cit., pp. 3-4.
77. See, for example, Iain Guest, "Deaths at dawn shock UN", *The Guardian*, 5 March 1983.

78. Some — apparently insignificant — criticisms were made; some complained that placing army officers in administrative positions reduced the available commanders for operations in the field.
79. *Latin America Regional Report*, 15 July 1983.
80. Ibid.
81. Ibid.
82. *Newsweek*, 11 July 1983, "A Colonel Plots a Coup".
83. Ibid.
84. See *Latin America Regional Report*, 19 August 1983, "Guatemala: a Risky Step to the Right" for reference to the positions on the coup of the various factions within the officer corps.
85. *Time*, 22 August 1983, puts the toll at three dead, 16 wounded ("From Preacher to Paratrooper", p. 10).
86. *Diario de Centro América*, 31 March 1982 includes an extensive c.v. of the then newly appointed Deputy Minister of Defense.
87. *Latin America Regional Report*, 19 August 1983.
88. Ibid.
89. Ibid.
90. Ibid.
91. *Time*, 22 August 1983.
92. Ibid.
93. Ibid.
94. *Latin America Regional Report*, 19 August 1983.
95. Ibid., the same source notes that Mejía also represented a severe shift to the right on domestic issues.
96. Ibid.
97. Ibid.

Chapter 9

98. Amnesty International's count of individual deaths attributable to extra-judicial execution reached 2,600 between 23 March and the end of September 1982, although Amnesty's press release announcing the continued massacres in the countryside (11 October 1982) stressed that full figures were almost certainly far higher. Both the Guatemalan Committee for Justice and Peace and the Guatemalan Commission for Human Rights estimated at least 8,000 deaths for the same period (cited in Americas Watch, *Human Rights in Guatemala . . .*, p. 13).
99. Although an internal army document, and never published, the *Plan Nacional de Seguridad y Desarrollo* was widely circulated in the capital as a 5-page photocopied typescript. Although signed by the three junta members, it was prepared by a Working Group (*Comisión de Trabajo*) of the Guatemalan Army General Staff and the Center for Military Studies.
100. Ibid.
101. *Prensa Libre* (Guatemala), 15 January 1983, "Security Forces to be Part of Defense Ministry". A further innovation was the creation of a special force (*Comando de Operaciones Especiales*, (COE) (Special Operations Command)) within the National Police to serve as a counter-guerrilla brigade. According to its commander, army Major Juan Francisco Cano, this force included picked men aged 18 to 22 trained in the use of special weapons. The COE was explicitly raised for rural operations, a role traditionally played by the Mobile Military Police. (See *El Día* (Mexico City) 21 April 1982, "Crearon un Nuevo Cuerpo de Contrainsurgencia en Guatemala").
102. John Rettie, "A Regime Goes for the Heart", *The Guardian* (London), 29 October 1982.
103. Allan Nairn, "Dead Reckoning", *The Guardian* (London), 13 April 1983.
104. Americas Watch, *Guatemala: A Nation of Prisoners, January 1984*, (pre-publication manuscript, p. 8). Pagination differs in the published text.

105. Americas Watch, *Human Rights in Guatemala* ..., p. 10, citing Raymond Bonner in *The New York Times*, 18 July 1982.
106. Ibid., p. 2.
107. ANEXO "H" *(Ordenes permanentes para el desarrollo de operaciones contrasubversivas) al Plan de Campaña "Victoria 82"* (ANNEX "H" to Campaign Plan "Victory 82", Standing Orders for Countersubversive Operations); a heading in the top right hand corner, reads: Estado Mayor General del Ejército, Palacio Nacional, (Army General Staff National Palace) 16 July 1982, LEMG-1800; from photocopy of numbered typescript copy.
108. Ibid.
109. Ibid.
110. Ibid.
111. Craig W. Nelson and Kenneth I. Taylor, *Witness to Genocide: The Present Situation of Indians in Guatemala*, Survival International, (London, 1983) p. 19.
112. Americas Watch Report, *Creating a Desolation and Calling it Peace*, May 1983 Supplement to the Report on Human Rights in Guatemala, p. 16.
113. Ibid., p. 17.
114. Ibid., pp. 13-14.
114. Ibid.
115. *Washington Post*, 4 January 1983.
116. Since November 1981, the term "dirty war" or "*guerra sucia*" has been reported in general usage by both Guatemalan army officers and US Embassy staff who have briefed reporters. The term is most frequently associated with Argentina's counter-insurgency campaign of the late 1970s when up to 15,000 people were detained and "disappeared"; its usage could stem from Argentine advisers' use of the term, or a natural association of the current bloodbath with the Argentine experience. The term "dirty war" above all was used by the Argentines as an expression to rationalize the use of state terrorism against the "dirty" tactics of the enemy.
117. The definition of genocide cited above, established in the 1948 Convention on the Prevention and Punishment of the Crime of Genocide of the United Nations, explicitly omits, in a manner controversial in 1948 and still controversial to date, inclusion of "political groups" as potential victims of genocide. See Amnesty International, *Political Killings by Governments*, (London 1983) p. 94, quoting the Convention on the Prevention and Punishment of the Crime of Genocide. Article II defines as "genocide" acts including killings "committed with the intent to destroy, in whole or in part" the abovementioned groups.
118. Ricardo Falla, S.J., "El Hambre y Otras Privaciones Inducidas por el Ejército de Guatemala sobre la Población Civil", *Estudios Centroamericanos*, October 1983, p. 852. "Ama" is not its real name.
119. Americas Watch, *Creating a Desolation* ..., pp. 9-10.
120. Nelson and Taylor, op. cit., p. 31.
121. Ibid.
122. Ibid.
123. *Latin America Regional Reports*, 24 September, "Ríos Montt Faces Problems on the Right ... but has Some Success Against the Left".
124. New Orleans *Times Picayune*, September 1982.
125. Richard A. Hunt, "Strategies at War: Pacification and Attrition in Vietnam" in Hunt and Shultz, p. 29.
126. Gill Brown, "The Hooded Agents of Death", *The Sunday Times* (London), 20 March 1983.
127. The *Ley Constitutiva del Ejército*, signed into law on 5 September 1968 by President Méndez Montenegro, categorizes the army's manpower into active, reserve, and retired. Active forces included the Permanent Force (*Fuerza Permanente*), comprising active service officers and men, and the Available Force (*Fuerza Disponible*), sometimes called the Active Reserve (*Reserva Activa*), including the Military Commissioners and their auxiliaries who, when performing military

duties, were considered to have the rights and obligations of members of the Permanent Force under military law. Reserves included the Available Reserve: citizens aged 18 to 30 who have completed, or were undergoing, training in reserve units, or had served in the Permanent Force. (All veterans of regular army service, or Sunday marching to fulfil their service requirement if under 30, are subject to recall as part of the Available Reserve.) The Mobilizable Reserve (*Reservo Movilizable*) includes men aged 30 to 50 who have seen active service or had weekend training. All other men aged 18 to 50 are part of the Territorial Reserve (*Reserva Territorial*) and also subject to call up.

128.   Americas Watch, *Guatemala: A Nation of Prisoners*, p. 32.

129.   Comité de Unidad Campesina (CUC), 15 May 1982, *El Ejército... Sigue Masacrando a Nuestras Comunidades*, p. 3.

130.   Ibid.

131.   Cited in testimony presented by Angela Berryman, of the American Friends Service Committee, to a subcommittee of the US House of Representatives, on 5 August 1982.

132.   *Plan Nacional de Seguridad y Desarrollo*, 1 April 1982; source a 5-page photocopy of the document, signed by Brigadier General Efraín Ríos Montt and two other members of the military junta, with a heading attributing it to a Working Commission of the General Staff of the Guatemalan Army.

133.   ANEXO "H", *Campaign Plan "Victory 82"*.

134.   Americas Watch, *Guatemala: A Nation of Prisoners*, p. 33.

135.   Ibid., pp. 33-4.

136.   Ibid., pp. 35-6; in the Indian communities firearms described by Americas Watch as "antique" have been issued to select members of patrols only when accompanied by a superior force of armed troops: firearms are turned in after every expedition.

137.   Ibid., pp. 42-3.

138.   Ibid., pp. 43-4.

139.   Ibid.

140.   *Latin America Regional Reports*, 6 May 1983, "Guatemala: Transforming the Indian Highlands".

141.   Ibid.

142.   Ibid.

143.   Ibid.

144.   See, for instance, *Uno Más Uno*, 13 May 1983, "Denuncian Matanza de Cien Campesinos Guatemaltecos", reporting that villagers from the hamlet of Xoraxaj, Municipality of Joyabaj, in El Quiché, declared that on 15 April 1983 civil patrols killed some 100 peasants of their village because they refused to become part of the civil patrols. The villagers also expressed their fear that the neighbouring villages of Zacualpa, Xuturbala and Pocop, would be likewise victimized on refusing to participate in the civil patrols.

145.   Americas Watch, *Creating a Desolation . . .*, pp. 23-4.

146.   Gill Brown, "The Hooded Agents of Death", op. cit.

147.   It should be restated that the term *ladino* as used in Guatemala is applied both to people of mixed race, and those who, although of Indian background, speak Spanish and no longer consider themselves Indians.

148.   Americas Watch, *Guatemala: A Nation of Prisoners*, p. 47, observes that in El Quiché "as in colonial times and in other repressive eras in Guatemalan history, the more well-to-do Ladino population is de facto not subjected to civil patrol conscription"; this is attributed partly to economic ability to buy exemption.

149.   Paul Ellman, "Civil Defense Force 'is Slaughtering Indians'", *The Observer* (London), 4 December 1983.

150.   Ibid.

151.   Ibid.

152.   See, for example, *El Dia* (Mexico City), 23 April 1982, José Ventura, "Los Indígenas en la Revolución Guatemalteca".

153. Benjamin N. Colby, Pierre L. Van den Berghe, *Ixil Country: A Plural Society in Highland Guatemala*, University of California Press, Berkeley, 1969, p. 131.
154. Ibid., p. 155.
155. *El Dia*, (Mexico City), 25 April 1982, "La ORPA Guatemalteca Incendió un Puesto Policial".
156. Americas Watch, *Human Rights in Guatemala* . . ., p. 7.
157. American Friends' Service Committee, testimony by Angela Berryman.
158. Comité de Unidad Campesina, *El Ejército* . . .
159. Allan Nairn, *The New York Times*, 20 July 1982.
160. "Guatemala Vows to Aid Democracy", Reuters, *The New York Times*, 6 December 1982, cited in Americas Watch, *Creating a Desolation* . . ., p. 9.
161. Arthur Allen, "Guatemala's Indians Still Die as Government, Guerrillas Fight On", *The Sun* (Baltimore), 1 June 1982.
162. *Prensa Libre*, quoted in WOLA, *Update*, October 1982.
163. Survival International, *Witness to Genocide*, Nelson and Taylor, op. cit., p. 12, citing *The New York Times*, 3 June 1982.
164. Ibid., citing John Dinges, "Why We Are in Guatemala", *Inquiry*, November 1982.

Part 5: The Age of Counter-Insurgency

10. The Age of Counter-Insurgency: An Assessment

Liberals and conservatives in the United States both saw the 1960s as a decade for introducing new initiatives in Latin America, to halt the spread of Communist subversion, and simultaneously, to promote development and democracy. The Alliance for Progress, combined with the innovative doctrine of counter-insurgency, was to offer a humane, alternative way to lasting security, economic reform, and accelerated evolutionary political development away from traditional brutal tyranny. The doctrinal and material means to crush latent or active insurgency was, generally, under the supervision of the military, to combine with development programmes and sweep away the legacy of social and economic oppression. In the long term, in their improved circumstances, the people of the region were no longer to be prey to foreign advocates of subversion and insurgency.

By the end of the 1960s, early advocates of the new counter-insurgency and "nation-building" programmes were already expressing their disillusionment with the results of the new initiatives. The tactics of counter-insurgency — torture, "disappearances" and "death-squad" killings — which gradually became known outside the target countries, provoked protests in and out of government. At a different level, the combined US assistance programmes of the 1960s were seen to have promoted a trend toward institutionalized military rule never seen before in the Americas. Authorities on the Latin American military, such as Edwin Lieuwen, took issue with the 1960s focus on strong military institutions as the instrument of combined development and security, and criticized the proponents of "a kind of myth of military salvation for the Latin American area".[1]

Although Latin American armies had never been aloof from politics, and national strongmen often rose through the military to claim personal power, 1960s regearing for counter-insurgency coincided with a new phenomenon of institutional military government. No longer content to support traditional, personalist rulers indefinitely, armies established systems for the institutional control of government, rotating army officers through fixed term presidencies, and expanding military control throughout most areas of government bureaucracy. In Guatemala, after Colonel Enrique Peralta Azurdia's 1963–66 "government of the armed forces" army officers alternated in the Presidency; the army itself curtailing the terms of those officers who aspired to personal power outside their institutional mandate, or rejected the advice of their peers. In El Salvador a regular rotation of military men in the Presidency continued uninterrupted after 1961 until the 1979 coup. To the south, Brazil and Peru exemplified the new kind of long-term military regime.

Institutional military rule was defended in the late 1960s by theorists developing the concept of the authoritarian regime as a key to effective counter-insurgency *and* economic development. Both proponents and critics of the shift explained the trend toward authoritarian military rule in terms of changing perceptions of their role and behaviour within the military institutions themselves. The new orientation redirected military concerns from external to internal defence, considered that the military itself should lead the development of the nation, and promoted the expansion of the military role from the specialized tasks of defence to all aspects of government. Some social scientists described this changing orientation as a "new professionalism" oriented to the internal warfare, fomented directly by US military assistance programmes "devoted to exporting doctrines concerned with the military's role in counterinsurgency, civic action and nation building."[2]

That the US government itself held that military regimes were organizationally the best equipped, and more significantly, legitimate institutions for "nation building" was, by the 1970s, cause for some concern. Combined with the excesses committed by the new military governments against their own populations, this US role in the militarization of the Americas prompted blistering criticism by such as Senator William Fulbright, who concluded that US security assistance had "brought change and progress toward democratic processes to a standstill." (Professor Lieuwen, following the Senator, added "Well, I don't know that we have done this deliberately".)[3]

The 1960s saw radical change not only in the role of armies in government, but in many aspects of their basic military doctrines. Like most of the military forces in Latin America, the military institutions of El Salvador and Guatemala developed, however unevenly and imperfectly, in rough accord with classic military models provided by the armies of Europe and the United States. Developed under the tutelage of Spanish, French, or Prussian-trained Chilean military missions, the two armies' foundation on the European military ideal was subsequently reinforced by the doctrine and practice promoted by successive US military missions. The departure from this classic military model, in both practice and theory, awaited the new military doctrine originated by the United States for export to developing countries in the 1960s.

The importance of doctrine to military institutions, and to government where armies hold political power, is at the core of recent Central American history. Writers on civil-military relations and on the military as an institution have stressed the central role of *doctrine* in guiding military structure and behaviour, and defined classic military doctrine variously as "*l'idée militaire*", or as a "professional *weltanshauung*",[4] concepts suggesting a somehow timeless quality. US theorist Samuel Huntington wrote of a "professional ethic", and posited a military "ideal type" with a standard set of "values, attitudes, and perspectives which inhere in the performance of the professional military function".[5] Morris Janowitz put forward a less romantic view, suggesting that doctrine — which is central to military behaviour — must incorporate both an element of tradition, and a capacity to change:

> Generals and Admirals stress the central importance of "doctrine'". Military doctrine is the "logic" of their professional behavior. As such, it is a synthesis of scientific knowledge and expertise on the one hand, and of traditions and political assumptions on the other. The military profession of each nation develops a military doctrine which reflects its social environment [. . .] There is something to be gained by describing the doctrine of the military elite as an "operational code". The term implies that professional thought has significant elements of historical continuity, but at the same time, undergoes change as a result of experience and self-criticism. The importance of an operational code, or a doctrine, is that it supplies leaders with guidelines for estimating whether a particular set of policies is appropriate for achieving a desired goal.[6]

The doctrine of counter-insurgency introduced a new operational code for military institutions linked only remotely to the codes or guiding doctrines developed from classic models. Among the larger armies of the Americas the elements of the doctrine were incorporated unevenly. Argentina's armed forces fully embraced the concept of "counter-terror", killing some 30,000 Argentines in cold blood, but turned their own expanded intelligence services to the task. No vast paramilitary forces such as "ORDEN" or today's "Civil Defense" groups were created to assist the regular armed forces and police services in the bloodbath of Argentina's "disappearances" and death camps. The perversion of traditional military values during the "counter-terror" years has been described as a major factor in the decay of the Argentine military, and its humiliation in the Malvinas/Falklands war. Some core of institutional strength and classic values appears to have survived the holocaust years, however, its presence reflected in the current experiment of democratic restoration.

In contrast to the Argentine experience, military conduct during Peru's 12 years of military government after 1968 showed no evidence of the influence of counter-insurgency doctrine's prescriptions of terror and paramilitary organization.

As case studies of the influence of counter-insurgency doctrine on events since 1961, Guatemala and El Salvador are perhaps not typical, as, arguably, the military institutions and governments of these countries were more intensively shaped and directed to this end than elsewhere. In both countries, to a greater extent than in other states now facing insurgency, operational codes were more thoroughly revised to make the liquidation of domestic oppositionists through "counter-terror" the primary military objective and to seek this end through a proliferation of paramilitary forces. In the process, the traditional military values of the regular armies of both countries have been destroyed and an armature of internal logic, arguably not military but paramilitary, has been substituted. The armed forces are dedicated exclusively to irregular, internal warfare against the domestic population; covert, extra-legal action has become the military norm. Army organization and strategy are semi-military or paramilitary, not military.

It is important to stress that the military doctrines put forward by the US security establishment in the 1960s and embraced by Guatemala's and El Salvador's armies were never imparted by the US military to its own conventional forces. Counter-insurgency's logic of "anything goes", and inherent disregard for law and the rules of war, were not permitted to infect these forces. In practice, counter-insurgency doctrine was the exclusive province of special irregular warfare units, somewhat isolated from other units, notably the US Army Special Forces. These were known as the *paramilitary* specialists: specialists in paramilitary skills and paramilitary organization. They, and the US intelligence agencies they sometimes served on detached duty, were the instruments whereby the new doctrine was imparted to foreign counterparts. And Special Forces — and presumably CIA — paramilitary specialists are the trainers working with the Salvadorean, Guatemalan and Honduran armies today. The new professionalism of counter-insurgency warfare is, then, in paramilitary skills and organization, in the tactics of irregular warfare outside the limits of the rules of war and oblivious to conventional military ethics or ideals.

In countries facing an active, or seemingly imminent insurgency, the 1960s saw both a reinforcement of pre-existent paramilitary police organizations — such as El Salvador's National Guard or Guatemala's National Police and Mobile Military Police — and the development of networks of civilian irregulars. In Guatemala these forces were organized under the direction of rural military commissioners and the regular army. In El Salvador, irregulars fell within the para-political, paramilitary organization ORDEN, also subordinated to the regular army. Both organizations rapidly outstripped regular army force levels, rising to between 30,000 and 80,000 men in arms in the 1960s. In the 1980s both networks were transformed into "Civil Defense" organizations.

Other paramilitary networks emerged in the 1960s almost everywhere major US security assistance programmes were to be found. South Vietnam's many 1960s paramilitary "Civil Defense" forces have already been described. The Philippines' principal paramilitary organization on the US model — the "Civil Home Defense Forces" — is still today a main aspect of its counter-insurgency programme. A 1972 study commissioned by the US Department of Defense examined the response to insurgency in Thailand, Bolivia, India and Guatemala and identified a common denominator in their "effective" counter-insurgency programmes: "all four countries did establish paramilitary organizations to supplement their police and armed forces".[7]

Although little research has been published concerning paramilitary, as opposed to military institutions, there is some evidence that the role of paramilitary forces has changed significantly, and their numbers swelled around the world since the 1960s. Civil-military relations authority Morris Janowitz, in a 1977 essay, published findings of a preliminary, quantitative analysis of paramilitary organization on a global basis in the "developing nations". Although statistics cited in this pilot study are incomplete (for example, no militia-like organizations are registered for Central America), Janowitz found:

> The available data indicate that in the developing nations there has been a dramatic increase in the size of the agencies of internal coercion, especially the paramilitary units. This trend has been conspicuous from 1965 to 1975.[8]

The same author also notes that paramilitary expansion was directed not to meet the everyday demands of law enforcement in modernizing societies, but primarily at exerting "political control", and he offers a very tentative finding that the quantitative growth was matched by a rise in regime violence:

> After 1965 the level of violence by ruling groups against unorganized, quasi-organized, or organized opposition elements seems to have increased to some degree. This is at best an impression, and careful scholarship will be required to document and explicate it.[9]

An argument of the present study is that counter-insurgency doctrine both provided the blueprint for paramilitary expansion and launched a trend to naked regime violence in states facing active or potential insurgency. These organizational and strategic concepts in the main sufficed to restrain the pressures of insurgency, in the short term. While temporarily compensating for the political failings of minority regimes to adapt economic and political structures to changing situations, the increasing reliance on paramilitary proliferation and regime violence ultimately provoked mass resistance and political breakdown. Morris

Janowitz' essay suggests the growth of paramilitary organizations and reliance on police powers are in compensation for political failings, but a somehow natural reaction:

> It must be emphasized that in general we are dealing with a reactive trend; that is, the increased emphasis and reliance on coercive agencies are not, initially or primarily, the result of a grand design or explicit intention. Instead, the absence of or the failure to develop more effective patterns of political and social control leads military regimes or military-based regimes to rely more heavily on internal police control.[10]

But the opposite, too, might be said; having introduced mechanisms for more extensive political control through a paramilitary apparatus and untrammelled regime violence, regimes put off the necessity of dealing with the population through other means. Counter-insurgency doctrine, moreover, reinforced and systematized the reactive trends to paramilitary expansion, and prescribed they be raised to take advantage of existing cleavages in societies facing insurgency. From Vietnam to El Salvador the very composition of the new paramilitaries — raised from highly motivated local elites, defined by economic privilege, religious or ethnic background, or proven ideological commitment — contributed directly to the subsequent levels of regime violence. The paramilitary militia concept at the core of counter-insurgency doctrine, in practice, provided for the creation of an armed elite set apart from the bulk of the society, with in some cases life and death discretionary powers. Often the conflict between the new paramilitary elite, and the potential insurgent overlay, and exacerbated, ancestral conflicts between antagonistic population sectors. A classic example was the experience of the British militias called out in the 19th and early 20th Century to deal with public order problems and threats of insurgency. Militias, motivated by differences in social class and religion, were most apparent in Ireland, where militiamen were raised primarily among the middle classes in Protestant, loyalist Ulster, for repression of the Catholic peasantry of the South:

> The troops used in public order roles were usually Yeomanry, or sometimes Militia Infantry, embodied for short periods for this purpose. The fact that these were usually Ulster units, and that the Yeomen were socially of a level above the peasantry, hardly helped to restore peace. It did however solve the usual problem of motivating troops for security duties.[11]

And in Britain itself, militia raised from the middle classes were pitted against organizing industrial workers:

> It was the local Yeomanry who carried out the Peterloo massacre, and the

regular cavalry who had to interfere and beat them off when they became altogether too violent for politically responsible officers to tolerate. Regular troops could only be used in situations . . . where the dissidents themselves came from the middle class which provided the Yeomanry.[12]

In Guatemala since the 1960s the Indian peasantry became fair game for death at the hands of the *ladino* partisans of the far right political parties, incorporated as a group into the new paramilitaries. In El Salvador, too, the peasant-elite dichotomy, and the potent motivator — ideological fanaticism — underlay the new paramilitaries. Combined with a state policy of terror and extermination for the suspect population, the very nature of the new paramilitary organizations provided an impulse to a kind and level of political violence beyond all previous experience.

Rehabilitating Counter-Insurgency Doctrine

It was only during the 1975–79 period that the United States military and intelligence establishment reduced its commitment to the active promotion of counter-insurgency doctrine and its active involvement in covert and overt assistance to Third World counter-insurgents. The change was a reaction both to the failure of counter-insurgency warfare in Vietnam, and the trend to rein in the United States' intelligence agencies in the mid-1970s. It was measureable to the extent that both the regular armed forces and the intelligence agencies reduced their forces of "paramilitary" specialists trained specifically to organize paramilitary irregulars in second countries, and to carry out covert paramilitary operations. While counter-insurgency doctrine was to some extent reduced to a simmer in the US military's policy and training establishments the doctrine was neither abandoned nor significantly modified in the wake of the Vietnam War. The doctrine of the early 1960s, with the concepts of counter-organization and counter-terror at its heart, remained intact for implementation to meet the crisis of insurgency in the 1980s.

The rehabilitation of counter-insurgency doctrine, and a campaign to regear the US military and intelligence establishment for its active promotion and execution began in the last two years of the Carter administration. Counter-insurgency advocates turned to the public through books and articles by former CIA and military officers calling for a return to the strategies of the 1960s; in some cases they creatively rewrote the history of US experience in counter-insurgency over the previous 20 years to suggest it had been a resounding success. Long-time CIA South-east Asia hand, Theodore Shackley, to a large extent led the field in the public rehabilitation of counter-insurgency doctrine with his 1981 book *The Third Option: An American View of Counterinsurgency*

Operations. Shackley deplored the limitations placed by Congress on CIA and other paramilitary activities since 1975 as a decision to reduce foreign policy options to either nuclear war or "doing nothing". He proposed a reopening of "the third option", defined as "the use of guerrilla warfare, counterinsurgency techniques, and covert action to achieve policy goals."[13] This, the author maintains, was thoroughly successful in the past in dealing with "wars of national liberation", its organizational systems and techniques "field-tested in the unforgiving school of two decades of practical experience."[14] Examples given of successful counter-insurgency initiatives that should be repeated included the creation and deployment of the paramilitary Provincial Reconnaissance Units — once known as Counter-Terror Teams' — which served Vietnam's Phoenix programme as "death-squads", and the raising of Laos' Meo tribesmen as mercenary "counter-guerrilla" irregulars. Neither the Vietnamese nor the surviving Meo, however, are cited to support Shackley's view that any but the most ephemeral advantage was won through the actions of the PRU and the tribal "counter-guerrilla" experiments (and, indeed, where are the Meo tribesmen today?)

In assessing institutional readiness for an aggressive programme of counter-insurgency in the 1980s, Shackley notes that CIA Director Admiral Stansfield Turner's 1976 budget cuts "forced drastic personnel reductions and maintained equipment inventories at levels below what I believe are necessary to sustain the third option".[15] Over 2,800 intelligence officers are said to have been forced out of the CIA in the late 1970s, most of them specialists in irregular, counter-insurgency warfare;[16] the rationale for the house-cleaning, however, was not trimming the budget. To restore the CIA to its former self, "To train a new cadre of guerrilla warfare and counterinsurgency experts" would, in Shackley's view, take at least three years.[17] In 1984, evidence of vast overt and covert assistance programmes in Central America's counter-insurgency states, and semi-covert military action against the Nicaraguan government, suggests the CIA's paramilitary capability was rapidly restored under the Reagan government, and perhaps outstripped even its previous peak force levels.

Like the CIA, the US Army's Special Forces, which in the past worked closely with the CIA in the creation of paramilitary, indigenous or mercenary forces, were to some extent run down in the aftermath of the Vietnam War. But they, too regained lost strength in the first years of the 1980s. A 1982 article by two eminent US defence analysts deplores the failure in the late 1970s to maintain and improve the United States' "low intensity warfare" capability, one element of which is the Army Special Forces:

> Reductions ... affected the Special Forces, one of the units most effectively prepared for the various forms of unconventional low intensity

conflict. From a high of over 9,000, the size of the Special Forces declined after their 1971 withdrawal from Vietnam to approximately 2,000 by the latter half of the 1970s. Recently, the size of the Special Forces has increased to three 1,400-soldier groups stationed in the United States.[18]

In a series of policy recommendations, the same authors state that 'we concur with Theodore Shackley that the United States must develop what he terms the 'third option'; military and security assistance must be boosted, to include training and supply of military equipment.

> Unlike the long-term objectives of development assistance, security assistance is specifically designed to address short-term problems in countries experiencing rapidly intensifying unconventional challenges. A case in point is the current situation in El Salvador.

Security assistance, including "the introduction of US technical training personnel to assist friendly armed forces or insurgents", in turn requires a "reemphasis and expansion of US security assistance personnel and appropriations."[19]

Two recommendations in particular relate to the US capability to train and direct paramilitary forces in second countries, either as auxiliaries to the regular forces of "friendly governments" or as "insurgents" to be unleashed against enemy states. This is to include "a serious ugrading of Special Forces units", with their focus of action to be, as in the 1960s, "organizing and advising either friendly government or resistance forces in unconventional techniques." Secondly, they recommend:

> Restoration of a powerful paramilitary capability within the CIA . . . CIA paramilitary experts made significant contributions to prior US counter-insurgency and guerrilla efforts (especially in recruiting, training, logistics, and planning), and they will be equally important in the future given the proper authority.[20]

After the Iranian revolution of February 1979, and the collapse of Nicaragua's Somoza regime only months later, the foreign policy reforms of the Carter administration were subjected to aggressive reappraisal, and the checks introduced on the paramilitary operations and wherewithal of the intelligence and defence establishment reconsidered. Ironically, the fall of Somoza and the Shah was blamed by the covert action and counter-insurgency advocates both on the human rights policy, and on their own hands having been tied in those final days of *levee en masse* in the two countries; and not on the programmes of the US military and intelligence agencies that over decades had constructed the fragile authoritarian edifices which collapsed in 1979. That it was precisely the open-ended support of the

US that created the aura of dynastic invulnerability in Nicaragua and Iran, halted political development, and led inexorably to a tidal wave of overwhelming resistance was not considered in the post mortem. The Carter administration responded to criticism by gradually restoring the lost prerogatives of the intelligence agencies, and building up the force levels of the "paramilitary" and covert action specialists of these agencies and of the military.

In the 1980s there was compelling evidence that the rehabilitation of counter-insurgency doctrine, and of the apparatus for its execution was complete. The introduction of El Salvador's "Operation Wellbeing", openly promoted as a look-alike to Vietnam's Civil Operations and Rural Development CORDS programme, which administered Operation Phoenix, and since 1981, the open support for vast paramilitary "Civil Defense" systems in El Salvador, Honduras, and Guatemala, all reflected a new commitment by the US military and intelligence establishment to aggressively apply 1960s counter-insurgency doctrine, and their mandate to do so. Policy failures of previous decades, the fruit of identical programmes, were swept under the carpet.

Central America and United States Foreign Policy: A Juncture

That by 1984 the 1960s counter-insurgency doctrine had become accepted as a doctrine for the 1980s even outside the rarified circles of the military and the intelligence agencies was confirmed by the January 1984 report of the National Bipartisan Commission on Central America. Set up by the Reagan White House, and chaired by Henry A. Kissinger, the Commission had been requested to advise on the formulation of a long-term US policy toward the region, taking into account both social and economic factors, and the immediate "internal and external threats to its security and stability."[21] In almost every way the report was indistinguishable from quasi-academic policy papers prepared in the 1960s' hey-day of counter-insurgency and the Alliance for Progress. The diagnosis of the *problem* was broken down into elements domestic in origin — notably, the heritage of social and economic inequality — and those of foreign paternity. Reference to the latter restated 1960s views of Cuba as the arch-enemy Soviet proxy, but added to the pantheon of menace Nicaragua's still non-aligned regime. Domestic problems, while acknowledged, are found amenable only to long-term solutions; the foreign (insurgent) threat, to immediate military action.[22]

As in the period of the Alliance for Progress, military assistance in the 1980s is proposed as an essential precondition to eventual reform, to win time for long-term objectives of social, economic and political development. A major US policy goal defined by the Kissinger

Committee for El Salvador was "to give democratic forces there the time and the opportunity to carry out ... structural reforms"; the key to providing this breathing space was defined as an effective counter-insurgency programme.[23]

What, then constituted an effective programme in the view of the Kissinger Committee? Ironically, it is the Guatemalan model that is described as effectively incorporating all the features of a classic counter-insurgency programme.

> The Guatemalan Army continues to apply counter-insurgency tactics developed through 20 years of experience in the field. At the heart of these tactics is aggressive and persistent small-unit patrolling in areas of guerrilla activity. A key organization of about 400,000 *campesinos* and Indians into Civil Defense Forces. There forces are poorly armed — only about one in ten men in some units is armed with a gun, usually an M-1 rifle — but they provide security for villagers, go on patrol regularly and have taken heavy casualties in contacts with insurgents.
>
> The positive aspect of the counter-insurgency program is civic action, in which the Guatemalan Army has a long tradition. Under Rios Montt, the armed forces provided food and housing materials to villages participating in the Civil Defense program. The Guatemala government's financial crisis, however, has led to a slowdown of the civic action efforts. [24]

That state terror is at the core of the Guatemalan strategy is not entirely overlooked; the Commission's report acknowledges the "brutal behavior" of the security services, but as an anomaly in the model programme. State terror is seen as endemic, but not policy.

> In the cities they have murdered those even suspected of dissent. In the countryside, they have at times killed indiscriminately to repress any sign of support for the guerrillas Such actions are morally unacceptable.[25]

The report is emphatic, moreover, in that both the laudable tactical and organizational components of the Guatemalan counter-insurgency programme and the abhorrent, if effective counter-terror element were of strictly Guatemalan inspiration: 20 years of intensive US counter-insurgency assistance in Guatemala are tastefully left out of the equation. Guatemala is seen to have developed an effective system *on its own*. US assistance is proposed to help the Guatemalans hold the line, and, perhaps, to permit the Guatemalan armed forces to perform the counter-insurgency task without the wholesale extermination of the domestic population.

> The Guatemalan armed forces have been able so far to contain the insurgency without assistance from abroad ... But financial restrictions on the Guatemalan government and shortage of military supplies and

spare parts could soon begin to limit the effectiveness of the Guatemalan counter-insurgency effort.[26]

Similar assessments are made of the Salvadorean situation in the Kissinger Commission report although atrocities are not so directly laid to the armed forces themselves:

> There is, of course, a darker side as well in El Salvador. The United States obviously cannot accept, let alone support, the brutal methods practiced by certain reactionary forces in Central America. Some of these actions are related to counter-insurgency. Their common denominator is the systematic use of mass reprisals and selective killing and torture to dissuade the civil population from participating in the insurgency or from providing any help for the insurgents.[27]

The references to El Salvador's "dark side" are consistent with the routine explication of "death squad" terror there by US military and diplomatic spokesmen: the terror is strictly local; there have always been such killings. Colonel Eldon Cummings, head of the US military mission in 1979, for example, told the press that stopping the "death squad" killings "is not simple . . . You can't change 50 years of the normal way of doing things overnight."[28] Perhaps the prize statement attributing state terror to political culture appeared in a November 1983 Reuters report. Citing US Embassy and Salvadorean military sources, it states that the Central Intelligence Agency had "penetrated" police and military intelligence years before and had full information on the officers and agencies running the "death squad" programmes. According to an Embassy spokesman, however, the US's hands were tied in so far as stopping the killings; El Salvador might not survive the disruption of these traditional practices:

> "If you pursue the squads it is going to cut so far back into the fabric of Salvadorean society you may face the destabilisation of the society", one US Embassy official said.[29]

The vision of selective assassination and mass executions as a hoary, time-honoured tropical custom essential to Central American society runs through most of the official statements of US government spokesmen on Central America since 1979, as well as the Kissinger Commission's report. And the latter notes that, however repugnant, El Salvador's use of naked terror has been both traditional, and an effective response to insurgency:

> Historically, such reprisals . . . have often proved capable of preserving colonial rule and unpopular governments for a very long time, even centuries. Other violence has in fact nothing to do with insurgency at all. It

is designed to terrorize opponents, fight democracy, protect entrenched interests, and restore reactionary regimes.[30]

The Kissinger Commission consequently proposes massive rises in military assistance, and the injection of US counter-insurgency wherewithal and advice on the premise that this would represent an alternative to the savage, but effective programmes now in progress; US assistance is justified as a kind of trade-off. The baser instincts of reactionary locals, and their effective use of mass murder, can be tempered only by upgrading military assistance programmes, not by harping on human rights. US counter-insurgency methods are described as a humane alternative to the savage tactics of the untutored Central American armies.

The blind spot centres on US counter-insurgency doctrine's substance, and its past. Neither the Carter nor Reagan administrations, nor the Kissinger Commission recognized that the doctrine of counter-insurgency put forward by the US security establishment for Central America in the 1980s is, in form and substance, precisely the same formula exported throughout the Americas two decades before, and faithfully adopted in Guatemala and El Salvador as the basis of military organization and strategy. Discussions of the "dark side" of counter-insurgency methods in Central America are posited on a local tradition of savagery exculpating the US of even modest co-responsibility in the atrocities of its allies. In contrast, it is suggested that there is no place for brutality, let along "counter-terror" in the US concept of counter-insurgency. It is as if the United States had neither interests nor involvement in Central American counter-insurgency programmes before the 1980s, and entered the fray only then, a late-coming missionary seeking to stop the savages from bashing out each other's brains.

> Whatever their aims, [terroristic] methods are totally repugnant to the values of the United States. Much more enlightened counter-insurgency models were pursued [by United States allies in the Americas] in the 1960s when military action was combined with positive economic and political measures. The methods of counter-insurgency developed over the last generation by the armed forces of the United States are consistent with such methods. They depend upon gaining the confidence and support of the people and specifically exclude the use of violence against innocent civilians. Yet these methods are expensive.[31]

The Guatemalans and Salvadoreans, then, can be persuaded to moderate their reliance on naked terror if the United States provides more assistance, and imposes its own enlightened counter-insurgency model. A qualitative change toward more humane methods of counter-insurgency is presented as primarily a matter of cost, and US commitment. The crux of the argument is that the Guatemalan and Salvadorean counter-insurgents are *expected* to adopt humane tactics if only, and only if, it provided an open-ended US commitment to provide arms and funding; why they should change their methods in such a case is not entered into. Human rights linkage to aid is ruled out as leverage.

> The present level of US military assistance to El Salvador is far too low to enable the armed forces of El Salvador to use these modern methods of counter-insurgecy effectively. At the same time, the tendency in some quarters of the Salvadoran military towards brutality magnifies Congressional and Executive pressures for further cuts in aid. A vicious cycle results in which violence and denial of human rights spawn reductions in aid, and reductions in aid make more difficult the pursuit of an enlightened counter-insurgency effort ... In the Commission's view it is imperative to settle on a level of aid related to the operational requirements of a humane anti-guerrilla strategy and to stick with it for the requisite period of time.[32]

Although a tenet of the Kissinger Commission's report is that current US counter-insurgency doctrine provides the modern, humane model by which counter-insurgency should be pursued, the substance of that doctrine is barely discussed either in that report or in other contemporary, declassified US government reports. The general outline of US counter-insurgency methods provided by the Kissinger Commission, however, confirms that little has changed since 1961. Counter-terror, as in the 1960s, is not openly acknowledged as a legitimate strategic concept. But counter-organization remains a basic, undisguised principle, as in the 1960s, justified as a means of "self-defense" for the vulnerable population against guerrilla coercion. The past and present roles of such irregular forces in taking counter-terror to the countryside is ignored.

> In addition to continued action on the economic and social fronts, [US methods] require two forms of military action, to be carried out by two distinct types of forces. First, local popular militias must be formed throughout the country (with whatever minimal training is feasible and with only the simplest weapons) to prevent the insurgents from using terror to extract obedience . . . Since this localized protective militia cannot be expected to resist any sustained guerrilla attack, US counter-insurgency methods also require the availability of well-trained and well-equipped regular forces in adequate numbers. These methods assume that the regular units will be provided with efficient communications and suitable transport, notably helicopters, to enable them to provide prompt help for village militias under attack, and to allow them to pursue guerrilla bands on the move.[33]

These, then, are modern counter-insurgency methods in a nutshell, seen as innovations by the Kissinger Commission. But it was precisely the raising of civilian irregulars, whether termed paramilitary groups, Civil Defense groups, or "localized protective militias" that dominated the elaboration of today's counter-insurgency systems in Guatemala and El Salvador in the 1960s and 1970s. And it was these civilian irregulars who served the regular armed forces in conflict situations as a key mechanism for the execution of counter-terror, and in doing so rapidly advanced the polarization of entire populations in the counter-insurgency states.

Although the Kissinger Commission does not directly refer to a legitimate concept of counter-terror in today's counter-insurgency doctrine (or acknowledge its past existence), evidence that counter-terror remains a core element of US doctrine is considerable. Some of this evidence has already been summarized in the two parts of this study, and month by month, new evidence emerges from the Central American arena of counter-insurgency warfare. The most recent substantive reports of US involvement in programmes of counter-terror, one indicator of the continued viability of counter-terror theory, have come from El Salvador. The US government's public estrangement from Guatemala, and the consequent highly covert work of the US military mission still based there, and the associated US intelligence teams has contributed to a natural hermeticism over this most explosive of counter-insurgency's arsenal of tactics. Reports from El Salvador, however, have progressively revealed both evidence of direct US involvement in organizing and assisting the Salvadorean intelligence agencies, which launched counter-terror in the 1960s and 1970s, and direct involvement in the continuing programme of counter-terror in El Salvador to the present.

The background to US involvement in organizing and collaborating with the work of ANSESAL, *Agencia Nacional de Seguridad*, El Salvador's top intelligence agency, and ANSESAL's primary responsibility in creating the first "death squads" is detailed in Volume I of this study. So, too, is evidence that after the October 1979 coup, which marked a watershed of a massive increase in US assistance in the 1980s, ANSESAL was renamed, but continued its co-ordinating function in the military's programme of selective assassination and counter-terror; and that US intelligence personnel continued to monitor the execution of this programme. In May 1984, the respected *Christian Science Monitor* added new evidence of direct involvement both of CIA and US military advisers in the covert counter-terror programmes of ANSESAL's successor, ANI, *Agencia Nacional de Intelligencia*. The *Monitor* cites two high-level principle sources, one a civilian, one a top army officer, in describing the US role in ANI and the intelligence command centres in the Army General Staff headquarters after ANSESAL was nominally dissolved in October 1979.

[ANI] is an operations-oriented counter-intelligence group originally set up under CIA direction about four years ago, and still financed and advised by the CIA. As part of its function, the two sources say, ANI keeps watch over, detains, interrogates, generally tortures, almost always beats, and sometimes kills suspects that it believes have links with leftist organizations. ANI is under the command of Col Renaldo Goelcher and Col Gabriel Contreras who, according to the military sources, are in close and regular contact with the CIA station chief at the American Embassy. [. . .] The conservative civilian source adds that ANI has also participated in the more traditional death squad activity of "disappearing" people — that is, kidnapping victims, often from their homes, killing them, and then dumping their bodies into the sea or remote areas.[34]

The US army, in turn, is directly involved in advising the Army General Staff's liaison offices with ANI, Departments 2 (Intelligence) and 5 (Civil Affairs):

. . . closely connected to ANI are the two intelligence departments of the Salvadorean armed forces general staff, Department 2 and Department 5. While ANI is operations-oriented, they add, these general staff departments are directed toward intelligence-gathering and have US military advisers who are mainly Cuban-Americans. According to the civilian source, the two departments pick victims up and torture them, sometimes to death. The tortures, he says — usually beatings, burnings, and electric shocks — are often conducted in the building housing the headquarters of the armed forces general staff in San Salvador. He stresses that the existence of the torture activities is common knowledge at Salvadorean general staff headquarters and rules out the possibility that the US advisers are unaware of them[35]

The same source outlines the covert intelligence apparatus' role in ongoing "death squad" activity, and its long and intimate relations with both the CIA and the United States military:

According to the civilian source, US army Col David Rodriguez, a Cuban-American, helped to organize general staff Departments 2 and 5 several years ago. Both ANI and general staff Departments 2 and 5 grew out of the original Salvadorean National Security Agency (ANSESAL). According to leading military sources in El Salvador ANSESAL was created in 1962 with heavy CIA and US military participation [. . . .] Over the years, ANSESAL received consistent CIA advice and training. [. . . .] After ANSESAL was dissolved, there was a restructuring of the military junta (more conservative members were added) and ANI and general staff Departments 2 and 5 were organized to replace ANSESAL in the early '80s. Thus the connection between ANI and the general staff departments on the one hand and the CIA on the other has a longstanding institutional base.[36]

Also confirmed were earlier reports in the *New York Times* that at least one of El Salvador's top officers in the years since October 1979, when mass counter-terror reached its greatest heights was, at the time, on the payroll of the US government. This was Colonel Nicolas Carranza, successively Vice-Minister of Defense, head of the telecommunications agency ANTEL, a key intelligence post, and head of the Treasury Police. According to the *Monitor*, the *Times'* claim that Carranza had received $90,000 a year through the CIA "was confirmed by sources in the CIA, the Senate's Select Committee on Intelligence, and the State Department."[37]

The evidence grows that personnel of the CIA and the US regular army work closely with, and perhaps control top members of the Salvadorean military responsible for formulating counter-terror policy, and directly with the intelligence agencies responsible for executing policy through torture and political murder. The methods used are, in any case, consistent with past United States' doctrinal prescriptions for the use of selective counter-terror as a tool of counter-insurgency; their continued practice is one indicator that counter-terror remains a viable concept both in Salvadorean and United States counter-insurgency doctrine. Despite the protests of the Kissinger Commission, US counter-insurgency doctrine and practice in the 1980s is neither enlightened, nor humane, nor ultimately effective. But there is an extreme reluctance among even the more enlightened members of the US foreign policy establishment to pursue the facts when discussing military doctrine and strategy; and an overwhelming tendency to permit ideology to dominate analysis and judgement of foreign policy issues.

The Central American dilemma resides both in the United States' assessment of the nature of insurgency, and the proffered solution of its policy makers, the same counter-insurgency doctrine "field tested in . . . two decades of practical experience". Reagan administration ideologues have been reluctant to consider domestic conflicts as other than manifestations of a global, ideological battle between East and West. New right ideologues close to the administration present a vision of Central America within a world view of unshaded absolutes, elevating the influence of International Communism to almost supernatural levels, and claiming inside knowledge of the Soviet master plan of conquest. Historian Lewis A. Tambs, for example, presented a lengthy outline of what he called the Communists' own game plan to a 1981 congressional hearing on human rights in Guatemala. Tambs described the "four phases" of the Soviet plan of action to win power, and enumerated "the six Communist principles of retaining power in Latin America". And he warned that this will inevitably succeed *unless* drastic counter-action is taken.

> The Soviets have developed for Latin America a historically and currently successful plan of action for starting, waging and winning a war of

National Liberation. This will eventually lead to hegemony of all of Latin America.[38]

In Tambs' view, Central American insurgencies were clockwork operations directed by the Soviets down to the last detail, with interchangeable parts:

> Information I picked up yesterday indicated there are some 400 Salvadoreans who were originally being trained in Nicaragua to go to the El Salvador front, but after the sweep operation [there] they [the Soviets, presumably] decided to divert these people to Guatemala . . .[39]

Although new right advocates with pretensions to expertise in geopolitics have had a rough ride in congressional hearings, they have swept the field in the executive branch, and made policy. Jeane Kirkpatrick has advanced arguments similar to, but considerably more fluent than those of Lewis A. Tambs, and won the ear of President Reagan. Kirkpatrick has also gone to the public with slick articles on "The threat America cannot ignore":

> It's almost unbearably unfashionable to say so, but there is a plan to create a communist Central America which, if successful, will have momentous consequences for our security and that of our European allies, for Israel's international position, and for the unfortunate people of Central America.[40]

Here again insurgency is seen solely as part of a vast plan; an ideological vision of geopolitics dictates policy: change in Central America today will mean the fall of Europe, and even Israel, tomorrow. Linkage of foreign policy to ideological preconceptions is absolute, and the outcome is an aggressive policy of counter-insurgency.

Although the Kirkpatricks represent the extreme end of the foreign policy establishment, even US liberals drawn into the Central America debate have failed to effectively challenge certain basic ideological tenets on which current policy rests. The report of the Kissinger Commission, attacked by the hard right for its sometimes liberal recommendations, lays down two fundamental reasons revolutionary forces must under no circumstances be permitted to overthrow existing governments in Central America. These are dependent on perceptions of: 1) the nature of contemporary insurgencies, and the role therein of International Communism; and 2) a doomsday prophecy as to what these revolutionary forces would do upon gaining power:

> Cuba and Nicaragua did not invent the grievances that made insurrection possible in El Salvador and elsewhere [. . .] But it is important to bear in mind three facts about the kind of insurgencies we confront:

* They depend on external support [. . .]
* They develop their own momentum, independent of the conditions on which they feed;
* The insurgents, if they win, will create a totalitarian regime in the image of their sponsors' ideology and their own.[41]

The arguments to counter each of these premises go unheard. That insurgencies in the region did not originate with, or *depend* on external support; that the insurgencies depend primarily on local conditions; and that today's insurgents cannot be conveniently labelled ideologically, or presumed to aspire to Gulag society. Data that contradicts the articles of faith of the Cold Warriors' assessment of the Central American conflicts falls by the wayside.

The Reagan administration requires Central American insurgencies to be recognized as manifestations of Soviet power and ideology. If the facts do not support this determination, the facts must be covered up, and resources dedicated to propaganda designed to support the administration's ideological mindset. A prime illustration of ideological assertion packaged as fact was Jeane Kirkpatrick's half-page newspaper feature in April 1983, reproduced *in extenso* around the world. A key assertion was that the Salvadorean insurgency was utterly dependent on the material support of International Communism, and indigenous neither in origin nor direction. And by repetition even the crudest misrepresentations gain credibility:

> The pretence that the [Salvadorean] FMLN is an indigenous guerrilla movement without significant foreign support has also been largely abandoned. Too many truckloads, planeloads, boatloads of arms from Cuba, Nicaragua, and the Eastern bloc have been found . . .[42]

The Salvadorean guerrilla movement, then, is an alien import initiated, supplied, and, by implication, manned by foreigners; but Kirkpatrick's affirmation on truckloads, etc. of arms from outside is unsubstantiated. A former Marine and CIA officer responsible for CIA's assessment of evidence of arms transfers to the Salvadorean guerrillas, David Macmichael, cites his own experience in tracking arms supplies there after April 1981, and has stated that in his two year stint no single transfer of arms from Nicaragua to El Salvador was intercepted or report of such transfer confirmed.[43] He contrasted this dearth of evidence of outside interference with the abundance of evidence collected on US arms supplies to its proxies waging war on Nicaragua:

> "I do not believe there is Nicaraguan Government involvement or use of Nicaraguan territory in any significant way for the supply of arms or other war material," he said. "If you have good solid information, you are going to intercept something. If you have air drops, planes crash. The planes we

allegedly send into Nicaragua crash all the time. Stuff gets dropped in the wrong place, parachutes hang up in trees."[44]

And the Salvadorean guerrilla groups were active long before the Sandinista revolution took shape, or power in Nicaragua.

Policy, then, from the Kissinger Commission to the hard-liners of the Reagan administration pivots around a perception of the enemy's omnipresence in all Central American conflict, and presupposes insurgent subordination to enemy ideology and intentions. These perceptions determine the priorities in defining the United States' national interests regarding Central America, and provide the impetus behind counter-insurgency doctrine's rapid resurrection and rehabilitation in the 1980s after nearly a decade under a cloud.

A major strategic flaw in arguments for a renewed export of counter-insurgency doctrine resides both in the faulty analysis of the nature of today's insurgencies, and their international context, and in the past record of counter-insurgency itself. The small insurgencies present in Guatemala and El Salvador in the 1960s and 1970s, when counter-insurgency doctrine was first introduced there, have undergone a transformation. *Foco* guerrilla movements have been superseded by true mass uprising, like Michael Waltzer's *levee en masse*, when an anti-guerrilla war cannot be fought, "because it is no longer an anti-guerrilla but an anti-social war, a war against an entire people . . . " And the broader international context of Central American insurgency has changed; it could be a miscalculation to presume the field of battle will remain within these small conflict states should state terror, and United States intervention in Central America, become a war of attrition.

It is in the prospects for perpetual war in Central America that parallels with Vietnam must inevitably be drawn. Like Vietnam, a commitment of US ground forces and air power to the Central American conflicts might indefinitely postpone the final disintegration of these countries' armies and the collapse of their governments. Although considerably larger than the united North and South Vietnam — 372,000 square kilometres compared to 300,000 — the conflict states of Nicaragua, Guatemala, El Salvador and Honduras have a considerably smaller population. But unlike Vietnam, the actors, and the victims of Central America's civil wars are members of a much larger community with a shared language, religion and culture. In the short-run this facilitates US counter-insurgency assistance. Military advisers today are largely Spanish-speakers, of Mexican or Puerto Rican or Cuban descent. In the long-run, as the atrocities which have been part and parcel of the counter-insurgency war continue, and whole societies face destruction, Latin Americans may develop more than a passive sympathy with the underdogs, and a new brand of antipathy toward the United States and its interests.

Already US intervention in El Salvador — and Nicaragua — is a prime concern in much of Latin America. Unlike the 1960s, the new anti-Americanism goes considerably beyond the universities and the fringes of radical politics. The formation of the Contadora Group is one indicator that the centre-right or moderate democratic governments of the region are no longer to be a full party to US interventionism; perhaps a forerunner of a further, future estrangement. And should Central America become the theatre of a larger United States war against a Latin American people, it would seem probable that far from intimidating potential insurgents in those countries still unconditionally supporting US policies, it would legitimize and foment insurgencies within their borders.

And so, while the ideologues now formulting US policy warn that *permitting* or *abetting* changes in the government and economic systems of Central America must inevitably lead to a domino destruction of US influence and interests in the Caribbean and Mexico, it should be argued precisely to the contrary, that such a domino effect could *only* occur if the United States continues to block reasonable political and economic reform in the region, and perpetuates and expands its military intervention in El Salvador and Guatemala.

Counter-insurgency organization and tactics now being promoted as a Central American final solution to insurgency are no longer an innovation, but have been the norm in Guatemala and El Salvador for over 20 years. All the United States offers today in the military sphere is more wherewithal to pursue a bankrupt strategy for internal warfare. Today's *levee en masse* is in part the fruit of the counter-insurgency doctrine wholeheartedly implemented in Central America since the 1960s, an unexpected harvest of dragons' teeth. A new age of counter-insurgency will mean a second sowing of dragons' teeth, and a further harvest of legions of dead and ever widening fields of conflict.

Notes to Part 5

Chapter 10
1. *Hearings*, "Survey of the Alliance for Progress", op. cit., p. 304; testimony of Dr Edwin Lieuwen on "The Latin American Military".
2. Alfred Stepan, "The New Professionalism of Internal Warfare and Military Role Expansion', in Alfred Stepan (ed.) *Authoritarian Brazil: Origins, Policies, Future* (New Haven: Yale University Press, 1973), p. 50.
3. *Hearings*, "Survey of the Alliance for Progress", p. 304.
4. Samuel P. Huntington, *The Soldier and the State: The Theory and Politics of Civil-Military Relations* (New York: Vintage Books, 1964), p. 61.
5. Ibid.
6. Morris Janowitz, *The Professional Soldier: A Social and Political Portrait* (New York: The Free Press of Glencoe, 1960), p. 257.
7. Norman A. Lacharite, Jean Rodman Wolfgang, "The Police Role of Internal Security Forces in Internal Defense", American Institute for Research, Kensington, Maryland, May 1972.
8. Morris Janowitz, *Military Institutions and Coercion in the Developing Nations*

(Chicago: University of Chicago Press, 1977) p. 70. Janowitz breaks down the meaning of paramilitary into three categories: "National Police Force — Full-time militarized police units, domiciled in part in barracks, equipped with light military weapons and military vehicles, and organized under the central government. Includes frontier guard units. Often called gendarmerie.

Local Defense Units — armed local personnel, domiciled at home, typically without or with only partial uniforms, and deployed in their own area. Essentially part-time military defense units in connection with internal armed insurrections. In some developing countries, called militia.

Workers' Militia — Part-time personnel recruited on the basis of criteria of political reliability. Industrialized societies' equivalent of local defense units designed mainly for domestic security; mobilized in ceremonial and politically critical situations. Domiciled at home. Partially uniformed and only partially armed, but can include units with military reserve functions." (See p. 28.)

9. Ibid., p. 18.
10. Ibid., p. 7.
11. John James, Royal Air Force, "The Military and the Police", draft manuscript, 21 September 1973, p. 4.
12. John James, "Violence and the Functions of an Armed Force", IUS, Manchester, April 1976 (manuscript). The same study notes that the State militias of the United States fell into disfavour after the Civil War: until industrial conflict began in the North ("After the labour troubles of 1877, they were revived in most states specifically for riot control during strikes, often with financial support from the big industrial corporations...") Then, and in their present incarnation as the National Guard, their largely middle class composition figures directly in their suitability, and inbuilt motivation, for deployment in industrial conflict.
13. Theodore Shackley, *The Third Option: An American View of Counterinsurgency Operations* (Reader's Digest Press: New York, 1981) pp. 17–18.
14. Ibid., pp. 155–6. Shackley also maintains that the counter-insurgency methods outlined as a prescription for the future in the book "have also been appraised by a panel of experts I brought together informally after my retirement", a group of 12 who are said to have "dissected and endorsed all aspects of the concepts outlined in the book". This claim is somewhat borne out by the reference to *The Third Option* in an analysis by Richard Shultz, Jr. and Alan Ned Sabrosky in *Lessons from an Unconventional War*.
15. Ibid., pp. 19–20.
16. Ibid., p. 18.
17. Ibid., p. 20.
18. Richard Shultz, Jr., and Alan Ned Sabrosky, "Policy and Strategy for the 1980s: Preparing for Low Intensity Conflicts", in Hunt and Shultz, *Lessons from an Unconventional War*, pp. 210–11.
19. Ibid., p. 208.
20. Ibid., p. 212.
21. White House, *Report of the National Bipartisan Commission on Central America*, January 1984 (Washington, D.C.; US Government Printing Office), introductory statement.
22. Ibid., pp. 37–8 outline "US interests in the Crisis", and illustrate the overwhelming preoccupation with the Soviet Union.
23. Ibid., p. 86.
24. Ibid., p. 99.
25. Ibid., p. 100.
26. Ibid.
27. Ibid., p. 95.
28. Al Kamen, "Brutal Murders Routine — Who Kills Salvadorean Civilians", *Washington Post*, 9 April 1981.
29. Robert Block, "US Knows Death Squad Chiefs But Cannot Stop Killings", *Reuter*, 3

November. A US Embassy official is also cited as stating that the threat of withdrawing aid "was not the key to stopping the squads". "There have to be significant changes in the top officers. If not, they will always revert to their violent ways and there will always be death squads", the official said.

30. White House. *Report* of the National Bipartisan Commission . . . , p. 95.
31. Ibid.
32. Ibid.
33. Ibid., pp. 95–6.
34. Dennis Volman, "Salvador death squads, A CIA Connection?", *Christian Science Monitor*, 8 May 1984.
35. Ibid.
36. Ibid.
37. Ibid.
38. *Hearings*, "Human Rights in Guatemala", 1981. "Prepared statement of Lewis A. Tambs, Department of History, Arizona State University", p. 167.
39. Ibid. For more thinking along similar lines, see the Council for Inter-American Security's "A New Inter-American Policy for the Eighties" (Washington, D.C., 1980), co-authored by Lewis Tambs, a member, with Roger W. Fontaine, David C. Jordan, Gordon Sumner, and L. Francis Buchey of the Council's Committee of Santa Fe.
40. Jeane Kirkpatrick, "The threat America cannot ignore", *International Herald Tribune*, April 1983.
41. White House. *Report* of the National Bipartisan Commission . . . , pp. 86–7.
42. Jeane Kirkpatrick, op. cit.
43. Editorial, "Nicaragua, Pro and Contra", *New York Times*, 18 June 1984.
44. Harold Jackson, "Former CIA man says Nicaraguan arms for Salvador ceased three years ago", *The Guardian* (London), June 1984.

Bibliographic Note

Primary sources, largely United States, Guatemalan and Salvadorean government documents, were used for each of the three major areas covered in the present study: the United States doctrine of counter-insurgency in theory and general application, and the Salvadorean and Guatemalan experience of counter-insurgency. Principal primary sources and a selection of secondary sources are noted below; full bibliographic references for a much larger selection of sources is provided in the end notes to the text.

Sources on El Salvador and Guatemala, from independence to 1910, include legislation governing the organization of the state and its institutions: the laws of municipal and departmental organization; the organic laws and regulations of evolving military and police institutions; and the legislation developed to regulate and control labour. Some 19th and early 20th Century codes and regulations were consulted in their original form; other legislation and related executive decrees, orders and proclamations were mostly consulted in contemporary and subsequent compilations: Isidro Méndez' *Recopilación de las Leyes del Salvador en Centroamérica* (Guatemala: Imprenta La Luna, 1855, republished in facsimile in San Salvador: Imprenta Nacional, 1956), and Rosendo P. Méndez' *Recopilación de las Leyes de Guatemala*, a regularly updated multi-volume series. Useful indexed compilations of Guatemalan law include Alfonso Bauer Paiz' *Catalogación de Leyes y Disposiciones de Guatemala del Período 1870 a 1930* (Guatemala: Universidad de San Carlos, 1965) and Jorge Skinner Klee, *Legislación Indigenista de Guatemala* (Mexico City: Instituto Indigenista Interamericano, 1954). Some use was also made of the official gazettes of the two countries for the texts of laws, decrees and edicts, and for commentaries on new legislation and political events; these sources were most heavily consulted for the 1910-60 period. El Salvador's national gazette, now called *Diario Oficial*, has undergone several name changes: *Gaceta Oficial de El Salvador*; *El Constitucional*; *El Faro Salvadoreño*; *Gaceta Oficial*; *Boletín Oficial*; *Diario Oficial*. Guatemala's gazette has also had many names: *El Guatemalteco*; *Diario de Centroamérica*; *El Centroamericano*; *Diario Oficial*; and *La Gaceta*.

The legislation and official gazettes of the two countries were also consulted for the period of the two governments adaptation to counter-insurgency doctrine, between 1960 and 1984. Cited extensively for the 1910-60 and 1960-84 periods were the annual reports (*Memorias*) of the Ministries of War and of Government, and of the Presidency. Reports of the Ministries of Government (variously termed *Gobernación*, or *Interior*) provided useful data on internal security matters, including police statistics for the 1931-44 regimes of General Martínez (El Salvador) and General Ubico (Guatemala).

Serial publications of the armies and police services of the two countries were also of considerable value. These included El Salvador's *Revista de la Guardia Nacional* (from 1912) and *Boletin Oficial de la Policía Nacional* (from 1932), and Guatemala's *Revista de la Policía Nacional*, all three published up to 1944, and, from 1944 to 1954, the *Revista de la Guardia Civil* (Guatemala). Of great importance as sources of doctrinal material were the military reviews published after 1940: the *Revista Militar de Guatemala* (more or less monthly from 1942, with interruptions), *Ejército* (Guatemala, from 1963), and the review of El Salvador's Staff College, *Revista de la Escuela de Comando "Manuel Enrique Araujo"* (from January 1963). These publications frequently carried articles by army officers on aspects of counter-insurgency, texts of speeches by army chiefs, and reprints of articles on counter-insurgency from US military publications.

The US National Archive was a major source of documents on political affairs and on the development of military and police systems in El Salvador and Guatemala for the 1910-48 period. Three areas of records were consulted in the Modern Military and Diplomatic divisions of the Archive: Record Groups 165, 84 and 59. Files consulted included country files on El Salvador and Guatemala, and, for comparative purposes, Nicaragua. By far the richest untapped source of information in published material was found in Record Group 165, containing records of the War Department and Special Staff. This section holds the field dispatches from US military attachés in Central America, called G-2 or Military Intelligence reports. G-2 reports cited included translations and copies of press cuttings, texts of recent legislation, letters from informants, and other important documents as well as the Military Attachés' assessments. With only a single Military Attaché assigned to cover the five Central American states from San José, Costa Rica, the detail and apparent accuracy of reporting is of high standard. Numbered chronologically, G-2 Reports are classified by country and subject category, for example General Conditions, Population and Social Conditions, Military Establishment, Public Order and Safety, etc.

Next in importance was Record Group 84, containing diplomatic records of US legations and, later, embassies in Guatemala and El Salvador. The Legation Files contain both documents forwarded to and received from Washington, and materials not found in the State Department's central files.

Record Group 59, which holds the State Department's central files, was also consulted, both at the National Archive and in microforms. Record Group 59 files are known as the Decimal Files and classified by country and category in accord with a decimal coding system. Files consulted were those in Class 8, relating to the Internal Affairs of States, from several sub-categories of files 814. (Guatemala) and 816. (El Salvador). Numbers to the right of the decimal point in the system indicate the sub-categories dealt with: 814.00 concerns political affairs in Guatemala; 814.10, public order and safety; 814.20, military affairs and the army. Specific aspects of each major category are indicated by a number building on that of the larger generic category, i.e., military organization is under 814.22, military laws under 814.203. Work with Record Group 59 materials centred on the political affairs, public order and safety, and military affairs' categories of the 814. and 816. series. The annual volumes of *Foreign Relations of the United States*, which reproduce selected documents of the diplomatic records of the Department of State, were also consulted.

Declassified materials from Canadian and British archives concerning 1932 events in El Salvador were made available to the author by Prof. Dermot Keogh of the University of Cork, Ireland. They included materials from Record Groups 24 and 25 of the Canadian Public Archives, Ottawa, Canada, and from FO 371, files 5293 and 5313, in the British Public Records Office, Kew, London. Most valuable were the accounts prepared by Canadian naval officers on the ship *Skeena*, present during the 1932 revolt and massacre in El Salvador, particularly a nine page report by Commander V.G. Brodeur, "General Resume of Proceedings of HMC Ships whilst at Acajutla, Republic of San Salvador. January 23rd-31st, 1932".

Sources on 1960s counter-insurgency doctrine and programmes for its implementation include a broad range of unclassified and declassified US government documents. The latter include declassified documents from the Agency for International Development's Office of Public Safety; the Department of the Army; the Joint Chiefs of Staff; the CIA; the Department of State; and the White House. White House documents of particular importance include the series of National Security Action Memoranda of the Kennedy administration establishing the "Special Group (Counter-Insurgency)" and laying the basis for 1960s police and military assistance programmes. State Department documents of particular interest are those concerning "Threat Assessment" and "Internal Defense Plans" for Guatemala, El Salvador and other countries considered to face active or incipient insurgency. Inter-agency policy papers on security assistance produced by the Department of State in the 1960s outline the scope of the counter-insurgency programmes initiated, and indicate the substance of the doctrine and policy on which they were based.

Some CIA material on counter-insurgency in Latin America has been declassified; most important for this study, however, were CIA declassified *Situation Reports* and *National Intelligence Estimates* on rural pacification in Vietnam, particularly on the application of the concepts of counter-organization and counter-terror.

Declassified documents from the Department of the Army evaluating combined US Army Special Forces and CIA programmes in Vietnam provided further insight into the practical application of counter-insurgency doctrine, and complemented declassified US Army Special Forces reports from Latin America to the Joint Chiefs of Staff.

Published material from the US military consulted on aspects of counter-insurgency doctrine and practice included army handbooks and field manuals, and articles and monographs from serial publications from within the US military establishment. Journals and periodical publications reviewed included *Army*, *Military Review*, *Air University Review*, *Naval War College Review*, and *Proceedings of Annual Conferences*, *US Army Human Factors Research and Development*.

Some declassified, unclassified, or leaked documents, such as *Pentagon Papers*, have been commercially published, or are on the shelves of public libraries. A great body of declassified documents from the 1950s and 1960s, were consulted through the Carrollton Press Declassified Documents Reference System, a microfiche collection of documents systematically published as they become declassified. Abstracted, cross-referenced, and indexed by subject and originating agency in quarterly indexes, the system provides ready access to key documents of the Departments of State and Defense, Joint Chiefs of Staff, White House, National Security Council and other government agencies found in the Truman, Eisenhower, Kennedy and Johnson Presidential Libraries. Carrollton Press microfiche references in this study include the date of the index volume in which the document is abstracted, or *R* for those items catalogued in the retrospective index through 1976, the relevant page number, and a letter identifying the specific item; for example, (242D) (1981) would refer to item D, page 242 of the 1981 index, identifying the appropriate fiche.

In addition to these, many documents used for the present study were declassified following Freedom of Information Act requests by the author between 1979 and 1984. Documents of particular importance included reports on US Public Safety Program projects in Guatemala and El Salvador, and inter-agency policy papers on security assistance programs in Latin America.

A series of US diplomatic cables, correspondence, and heavily censored ("sanitized") transcripts of interviews with informants were released to the author through the Freedom of Information Act in May and November 1982, concerning the detention, "disappearance", and presumed torture and execution of US citizen Ronald Richardson in El Salvador in 1976. The material includes a letter from Secretary of State Cyrus R. Vance to Salvadorean President Colonel Arturo Armando Molina, and a series of memoranda on the case from the US Embassy in El Salvador, and Department of State officials responsible for Latin American affairs. The material is of particular interest as a case study of the Carter administration's human rights policy when put to the acid test.

Unclassified Department of State publications consulted include occasional "White Papers" and bulletins, and the reports prepared annually since 1978 in accordance with Sections 116 (d) and 502 (b) of the Foreign Assistance Act, known as "Country Reports on Human Rights Practices", or simply "502B Reports". Published at the demand of Congress, the reports include sections assessing human rights observance in each country covered.

Public documents of the US Congress, particularly the records of hearings on foreign assistance, regional policy toward Latin America, and, since the early 1970s, hearings on human rights observance in countries receiving US assistance, are cited throughout the study. As full references are provided in the end notes, only the responsible chamber (House of Representatives or Senate), the title of the report, and date of publication are indicated in the bibliography; all hearings cited were published by the US Government Printing Office, Washington, DC.

Several original documents of importance for this study have been attributed to US government personnel, although their authors remain anonymous. One key document is a typescript paper known as "The Miami Document". Circulated widely in photocopies in Washington, DC and in Central America in 1977, the unsigned document purports to outline the involvement of top army and intelligence officers of El Salvador and Guatemala in combined action with Miami-based Cuban exiles in criminal fire-arms and narcotics traffic as well as political terror activities. The document appeared after the arrest of Salvadorean army chief of staff Col. Manuel Alfonso Rodríguez in New York on a charge linked to US organized crime and involving the sale of 10,000 sub-machineguns (he was subsequently convicted). Central American sources have speculated that the document was written and disseminated by Miami-based officers in a US law enforcement agency, possibly the FBI or the Treasury Alcohol, Tobacco and Firearms Strike Force, after tracing criminal activities affecting the United States to Central American military personnel who for political reasons were untouchable.

A second key document on Central America is the "Dissent Paper" distributed in Washington DC in November 1979. In the introduction its authors claim that it was prepared in the foreign policy establishment's "dissent channel", and incorporates in-house criticism of policy trends in the wake of the Nicaraguan revolution. The lengthy document, whatever its precise paternity, provides valuable insights on the practical substance of the human rights policy of the Carter government, and makes a case that the restoration of major military assistance to the region would lead directly to policy failure.

Other primary sources used for this study included photocopies of correspondence between members of the US Congress and the Department of State and other agencies, made available to the author by Washington based organizations. This material includes copies of correspondence between Senator James Abourezk and the Agency for International Development regarding the International Police Academy's secret "Bomb School" in Texas, and between Senator William Fulbright and CIA Director William Colby regarding the restrictions on police assistance programmes, legislated in 1974.

Many Central American and other newspapers, journals, newsletters and news digests were consulted. Of particular importance from El Salvador were the journals *Universidad*, produced irregularly by the National University, and *Estudios Centroamericanos*, produced by the Universidad Centroamericana "Simeón Cañas" in San Salvador; the latter is by far the most important social science journal of Central America and has provided reporting and analysis of contemporary issues and events since its foundation. Salvadorean newspaper sources were used for the present study only for the 1960-84 period, and included the two major dailies, *El Diario de Hoy* and *La Prensa Gráfica*, the short-lived *La Crónica* of the 1970s, and the newspaper of the Archbishopric of San Salvador, *Orientación*, for the late 1970s.

Material from the Guatemalan newspapers *El Imparcial*, *El Gráfico*, *La Prensa Libre*, and other dailies was used in researching the 1960-84 period. *El Imparcial*, described as the closest thing to a newspaper of record for Guatemala, was reviewed on microfilm for the key years 1965-71. Press cuttings from most Guatemalan dailies after 1966 were also reviewed. News summaries of reporting in the Guatemalan and Salvadorean press were available in the monthly publication *Panorama* (Guatemala), and, after 1972, in the weekly news digest *Inforpress Centroamericana*; both sources give full references identifying newspaper sources. Other newspaper sources on Guatemala included the weekly news digest *Noticias de Guatemala* and the short-lived *Nuevo Diario* of the late 1970s; the newspaper and digest of photocopied press cuttings produced by exiles in Mexico, *Correo de Guatemala* (1970-72), and the periodic news digests and photocopied press cuttings published by the Guatemalan *Frente Democrático Contra la Represión*.

Summaries of Central American newspaper and radio news reports in the 1970s and 1980s were consulted through the US Department of Commerce *Foreign Broadcast Information Service* reports.

Of major importance were some periodicals published outside Central America, such as the newsletter *Latin America Weekly Report* (from 1967) and its later incarnations, the *Latin America Political Report* and *Mexico and Central America Report*, published by Latin America Newsletters, London, England. The *Latin America and Empire Report*, and other publications of the North American Congress on Latin America, NACLA (New York), were also of considerable value. Reference is also made in this study to major US newspapers ranging from the *New York Times* to the *Albuquerque Journal*, to the weeklies *Time* and

Newsweek, and to such specialist publications as the *Journal of Inter-American Studies and World Affairs*. European newspapers cited include *The Guardian, The Sunday Times*, and *The Observer* (London), and *Le Monde* (Paris).

The papers and publications of several human rights organizations were essential sources on political developments and US intervention in Central America in the 1970s and 1980s. Amnesty International's annual reports since 1973, its special country reports, and its regular background and case reports provide basic information on the changing human rights situation in El Salvador and Guatemala. So, too, do country studies published by the Inter-American Commission on Human Rights. Periodic bulletins published by the Washington Office on Latin America (WOLA) were particularly useful for tracing the nature of US military assistance to the region after 1977. Of great value for research on both El Salvador and Guatemala since 1979 and the US role there were the reports of the Americas Watch Committee (New York).

Of particular importance in tracing US military and security assistance were the publications of several research organizations such as NACLA (New York), since 1967, and, since the mid-1970s, the Institute for Policy Studies (Washington, DC). The reports of the London-based Latin America Bureau (since the late 1970s) have also been particularly useful.

Human Rights organizations within El Salvador and Guatemala have provided much of the basic human rights information collected by US-based or international human rights organizations, and their bulletins and reports have contributed to this study. Notable among such organizations are *Socorro Jurídico, Socorro Jurídico Cristiano, Tutela Legal* and the *Comisión de Derechos Humanos de El Salvador* for El Salvador, and Guatemala's *Comité de Familiares de los Desaparecidos, Bufete Jurídico* (the Legal Aid Office of the University Students' Association), the *Comisión de Justicia y Paz*, and the *Iglesia Guatemateca en el Exilio*.

Guatemala: Selected Sources

Adams, Richard N., *Crucifixion by Power*. Austin Texas: University of Texas Press, 1970.
> *Political Changes in Guatemalan Indian Communities: A Symposium*, New Orleans: Tulane University Press, 1957.
Aguilera, Gabriel, "El Proceso del Terror en Guatemala". Mimeographed, Sept. 1970, with Dec. 1970 Appendix.
> *La Violencia en Guatemala como Fenómeno Político*. CIDOC, Cuaderno No. 61, 1971.
> "The Process of Militarization in the Guatemalan State", in *Central America: a Contemporary Crisis, LARU Studies*, Vol. V, No. 1, September 1982.
Americas Watch Committee, *No Neutrals Allowed*, New York: Americas Watch, November 1982.
> *Creating a Desolation and Calling it Peace*, New York: Americas Watch, May 1983.
> *Guatemala: a Nation of Prisoners*, New York: Americas Watch, January 1984.
Amnesty International, *Guatemala: Amnesty International Briefing*, London, 1976.

Guatemala: a Government Program of Political Murder, London: 1981.

Guatemala: Massive Extrajudicial Executions in Rural Areas under the Government of General Efraín Ríos Montt, Amnesty International Special Briefing, London, July 1982.

Baker, Ross Kenneth, *Military Intervention and Status Deprivation in Postwar Latin America*, Ph.D dissertation, University of Pennsylvania, 1966.

Buttrey, Jerrold, "The Guatemalan Military, 1944-1963: An Interpretative Essay", University of Texas, Austin, 1967 (manuscript).

Cáceres, Carlos, *Aproximación a Guatemala*. Culiacán, Sinaloa, México: Universidad Autónoma de Sinaloa, Colección Nuestro Continente, 1980.

Comité Guatemalteco de Defensa de los Derechos Humanos, *La Violencia en Guatemala*. México: Fondo de Cultura Popular, 1969.

Comité Nacional de Unidad Sindical (CNUS), *El Fascismo en Guatemala: Un Vasto Plan Represivo Contra el Pueblo y el Movimiento Sindical*. Guatemala, 1978.

Comité de Unidad Campesina (CUC), "El Ejército Sigue Masacrando a Nuestras Comunidades", leaflet, 15 May 1982.

Corro, Alejandro de, *Guatemala: La Violencia*. CIDOC Dossiers No. 19, 20, 21, Cuernavaca, Morelos, México: CIDOC, 1968.

Cruz, José Luis, *El Ejército como una Fuerza Política*, Guatemala: Instituto de Ciencias Políticas, mimeographed, 1971.

Dombrowski, John, et. al., *Area Handbook for Guatemala*. Washington, DC: US Government Printing Office, 1970.

Durston, John W., *La Estructura de Poder en una Región Ladina de Guatemala*. Guatemala: Seminario de Integración Social Guatemalteca, 1972.

Einaudi, Luigi, Brian Jenkins and César Sereseres, "US Military Aid and Guatemalan Politics". Paper for the Problems of US Foreign Policy Working Group, California Arms Control and Foreign Policy Seminar, March 1974.

Einaudi, Luigi, and César Sereseres, "Arms Transfers to Latin America: Toward a Policy of Mutual Respect", manuscript, June 1973.

Galeano, Eduardo, *Guatemala: Occupied Country*, New York: Monthly Review Press, 1969.

Gleijeses, Piero, "Guatemala: Crisis and Response". Washington, DC: Johns Hopkins University, 1983 (manuscript).

"The United States and Turmoil in Central America", in Department of the Army, *The 1980's: Decade of Confrontation, Proceedings of the Eighth Annual National Security Affairs Conference, 13-15 July 1981*. Fort McNair: National Defense University Press, 1981.

Grieb, Kenneth, *Guatemalan Caudillo: The Regime of Jorge Ubico*. Athens, Ohio, USA: Ohio University Press, 1979.

Hernández Méndez, Colonel Jorge H., "Incidencias de la Política en Decisiones Militares", in *Revista Militar de Guatemala*, April-June, 1965.

Geopolítica. Guatemala: Ministerio de Defensa, 1969.

Institute of Policy Studies, "Background Information on Guatemala, the Armed Forces, and US Military Assistance". Washington, DC: Institute of Policy Studies, June 1981, and "Update No. 1", July 1982.

"Background Information on US Policy and US Military Assistance to Central America, Update No. 8", Washington, DC: Institute of Policy Studies, March 1983 (all three publications prepared by Cynthia Arnson).

Jenkins, Brian, and César D. Sereseres, "US Military Assistance and the Guatemalan Armed Forces", in *Armed Forces and Society*, Vol. 3, No. 4, 1977.

Johnson, Kenneth, *Guatemala: From Terrorism to Terror*, Conflict Studies, No. 23, May 1972.

North American Congress on Latin America (NACLA), *Guatemala*. New York: NACLA, 1974 (Jonas, Susanne and David Tobias, editors).

Latin American Studies Association (LASA), *Report of the Ad Hoc Committee on Guatemala*. Gainesville, Florida: LASA, 1973.

Le Bot, Yvon, *Les Paysans, La Terre, Le pouvoir: Etude d'une Société agraire à dominante Indienne dans les hautes terres du Guatemala*. Paris: Ecole des Hautes Etudes en Sciences Sociales, Ph.D dissertation, 1977.

López Alvaro, "La Crisis Política y la Violencia en Guatemala", in *Diez Años de Insurrección en América Latina*, Santiago: Ediciones Prensa Latinoamericana, 1971.

"Luchar contra el Comunismo en Todos los Frentes", in *Ejército*, Guatemala, 1967.

Melville, Thomas and Marjorie, *Guatemala: Another Vietnam?* London: Pelican, 1971.

Monteforte Toledo, Mario, *Centroamérica: Subdesarrollo y Dependencia*. México, DF: UNAM, 1972.

Moore, Granville A., *Social and Ritual Change in a Guatemalan Town*. Ph.D dissertation. New York, 1966.

Munson, Dana, *Zacapa*. Canoga Park, Cal. USA: Challenge Books, 1967.

Nelson, Craig W. and Kenneth I. Taylor, *Witness to Genocide*. London: Survival International, 1983.

OXFAM America, *Witness to Political Violence in Guatemala*. Boston, Mass. USA: OXFAM America, 1982.

Pereira Echeverría, Adalberto, *La Policía*. Guatemala: University of San Carlos, 1951 (dissertation).

Plant, Roger, *Guatemala: Unnatural Disaster*. London: Latin America Bureau, 1978.

Sereseres, Céar D., "The Guatemalan Armed Forces: Military Development and National Politics". Paper presented at the Sixth Annual Meeting of the Latin American Studies Association, March 1976.

   Military Development and the US Military Assistance Program for Latin America: The Case of Guatemala, 1961-1969. University of California at Riverside, 1971 (dissertation).

Silvert, Kalman H., *A Study in Government: Guatemala*. New Orleans, La. USA: Middle American Research Institute, Publication No. 21, Tulane University, 1954.

   "Guatemala 1955: Problems of Administration", American Universities Field Staff Report, 1955, Vol. II, No. 2.

Weaver, Jerry L., "The Political Style of the Guatemalan Military Elite", in *Studies in Comparative Political Development*, Vol. V., 1969-70.

   "The Military Elite and Political Control in Guatemala, 1963-66", in *Social Science Quarterly*, Vol. 50, No. 1, June 1969.

Select Bibliography

Selected US Government Sources

Agency for International Development, Office of Public Safety

Brown, Theodore D., Chief Public Safety Advisor, El Salvador, "End of Tour Report, August 31-December 11, 1962", 11 December 1962. Declassified 31 March 1980 through FOIA request.

Costello, Peter F., Chief Public Safety Advisor, Guatemala. "End of Tour Report, December 9, 1965-20 November 1969", 25 December 1969.

Crisostomo, D.L., Chief Public Safety Advisor, Guatemala. "Report on Public Safety Program", 6 December 1963.

    "Report on Police Progress and Development in Guatemala, January 1961-December 1965", 10 December 1965. Declassified 31 March through FOIA request.

    "Briefing Report for the OPS/Washington Evaluation Team on the Public Safety Program in Guatemala", 23 October 1964.

Laughlin, David, Chief Public Safety Advisor, Guatemala. "Completion of Tour Report", 27 April 1960.

Martinez, Richard R., *Termination Phase-Out Study, Public Safety Project El Salvador*, May 1974.

Naurocki, Alfred W., Public Safety Communications Advisor. "End of Tour Report", 27 June 1964.

Stewart, Ambassador C. Allan (ret)., *Report on Visit to Central America and Panama to Study AID Public Safety Programs*, May 18-June 14, 1967. Classified Secret; declassified 2 April 1980 through FOIA request.

Termination Phase-Out Study: Public Safety Project Guatemala, July 1974.

Central Intelligence Agency

Colby, William. "The Situation"/"Colby Draft", 11 May 1964. Typescript manuscript including draft "Vietnam Special Action Section", 5 May 1964 proposing new concept for counter-insurgency, "integrating the military, paramilitary and civilian efforts" in successive target areas, and creating a central coordinating agency.

Directorate of Intelligence, Office of Current Intelligence, "Intelligence Memorandum", "The role of public opinion in Latin American Political Stability", 13 May 1965. Declassified, sanitized, 5 May 1976, Johnson Presidential Library, National Security File, Latin America.

"Intelligence Report: The Situation in South Vietnam", 24 July-30 July 1967. Carrollton Press.

'Special National Intelligence Estimate", No. 14-69, "The Pacification Effort in Vietnam", 16 January 1969. Carrollton Press (355B) (1979).
"Survey of Latin America", 1 April 1964. Johnson Presidential Library, National Security File, Latin America.
Sayre, Robert M., Memorandum to McGeorge Bundy, 12 June 1965, "Task Force Report: Guatemala". Johnson Presidential Library, National Security File, Latin America.

Congress of the US House of Representatives

Alleged Assassination Plots Involving Foreign Leaders (Hearings, Senate, 1975).
Citizens Guide on How to Use the Freedom of Information Act and the Privacy Act in Requesting Government Documents, Thirteenth Report by the Committee on Government Operations. Union Calendar No. 412, House Report No. 95-793, 1977.
Guatemala and the Dominican Republic (Hearings, Senate, 1971).
Human Rights Conditions in Selected Countries and the US Response (Hearings, House, 1978).
Human Rights in Guatemala (Hearings, House, 1981).
Human Rights in Nicaragua, Guatemala, and El Salvador: Implications for US Policy (Hearings, House, 1976).
New Directions for the 1970s: Toward a Strategy of Inter-American Development (Hearings, House, 1969).
The Recent Presidential Elections in El Salvador (Hearings, House, 1977).
Religious Persecution in El Salvador (Hearings, House, 1977).
Review of State Department Country Reports on Human Rights Practices for 1981. (1981).
The Situation in El Salvador (Hearings, Senate, 1981).
Survey of the Alliance for Progress: Compilation of Studies and Hearings (Senate, 1969).
US Policies and Programs in Brazil (Hearings, Senate, 1971).

Department of the Army

Army Concept Team in Vietnam, "Employment of a Special Forces Group", 20 April, 1966. Carrollton Press (204B (R).
Civil Affairs Operations, Field Manual 100-1, September 1959.
Continental Army Command, *Counterinsurgency Operations*, Pamphlet No. 516-3, Fort Monroe, Virginia, October 20, 1964.
Counterinsurgency Operations, Field Manual 31-16, 1963.
Counterinsurgency Operations, Field Manual 31-16, 1967.
Doctrinal Guidance, Field Manual 100-1, September 1959.
5th Special Forces Group (Airborne), 1st Special Forces, "Subject: Operational Report Lessons Learned", 9 May 1967. Carrollton Press.
Guerrilla Warfare and Special Operations, Field Manual 31-21, 1963.
Headquarters, *Handbook of Counterinsurgency Guidelines for Area Commanders: An Analysis of Criteria*. Department of the Army Pamphlet No. 550-100.
Operational Report No. OT-RD-760787, "Civilian Irregular Defense Group Forces", February 15, 1967. Carrollton Press (204B) (R).
Operations against Irregular Forces, Field Manual 31-15, 1961.
Stability Operations; US Army Doctrine, Field Manual 31-23, 1967.

Department of Defense

Office of the Assistant Secretary of Defense for National Security Affairs, "US Policies toward Latin American Military Forces", 25 February, 1965. Johnson Presidential Library, National Security File, Latin America.

Department of State

"Airgram for information to all diplomatic posts, for action to: Caracas, Guatemala, Phnom Pen, Quito, Rangoon, Tehran, Yaounde, A joint STATE/DEFENSE/AID/USIA message", 6 July 1962, no. CA-236. Concerns the creation, composition, and function of the "Special Group (CI)"; ongoing surveys of "US and overseas indigenous internal defense resources"; and requesting the preparation of "Country Internal Defense Plans (IDP)". A two-page model plan in outline is included. Classified Secret; declassified 1979 following FOIA request.

American Embassy, Guatemala. Airgram no. A-125, 29 May 1962 to the Secretary of State. "Assessment of Local Police Forces". Declassified 1979 through FOIA request.

Airgram, 15 September 1962 to the Secretary of State. "Subject: Internal Defense Plan Guatemala. Declassified 1979 through FOIA request.

Telegram, 27 February 1964, Ambassador Bell to Assistant Secretary of State Mann, Concerns military and security assistance. Carrollton Press (60E) (R).

American Embassy, Peru. Telegram 449, 3 November 1965 to Secretary of State for Gen. Maxwell Taylor. Concerns updated Internal Defense Plan, and Peruvian resistance to US counter-insurgency proposals. Carrollton Press.

Bureau of Intelligence and Research. "Latin America: Impact of Foreign Military Assistance", 22 November 1971. Carrollton Press (1981).

Bureau of Inter-American Affairs (State) and Bureau of Latin America (AID), Internal Security Programs Evaluation Group. *US Internal Security Programs in Latin America*, 30 November 1966. Volumes I-IV, including Volume II, *Guatemala*, of six declassified 2 April 1980 through FOIA request.

Hardin, Herbert O. Chief Latin American Branch PSD/ICA and David Laughlin, Chief Public Safety Advisor Central America and Caribbean Area. "Subject: Internal Security in El Salvador", 24 August 1960.

Policy Planning Staff. *A New Concept for Hemispheric Defense and Development*, 15 January 1961. Declassified January 1977.

Interdepartmental Technical Subcommittee on Police Advisory Assistance Programs, *Report of the Interdepartmental Technical Subcommittee on Police Advisory Assistance programs*, 11 June 1962. Declassified 2 April 1981 through FOIA request.

Washington Internal Security Asssessment and Programming Team. Telegram to American Embassy in San Salvador, "Assessment of Threat". Report of assessment team after visit to El Salvador from 5 to 9 May 1961. Declassified 1979 through FOIA request.

International Cooperation Administration. Public Safety Division Report on the National Police of the Republic of El Salvador, November 1956. 53pp.

Report on the National Police in the Republic of Guatemala, 9 April 1956, 82pp.

Joint Chiefs of Staff

"Combined GVN-US Efforts to Intensify Pacification Efforts in Critical Provinces", 19 June 1964. Carrollton Press (90A) (1979).

Dictionary of US Military Terms for Joint Usage. JCS Publication No. 1, 1 February 1964.

Lemnitzer, General L.L., Chairman. "Memo for the Special Assistant to the President for National Security Affairs", 17 July 1962, "A Summary of US military Counter-Insurgency accomplishments since 1 January 1961", Carrollton Press (R).

Memorandum for the Special Group (CI), 30 January 1962. "Subject: Military Training related to Counter-Insurgency Matters (U)". Carrollton Press (241F) (R).

Memorandum for the Special Group (CI), 17 July 1962. "Subject: Counter-insurgency Organization (U)". Carrollton Press (242) (R).

Office of the Special Assistant for Counter-Insurgency and Special Activities, MJCS 331-66, 15 November 1966. *Counterinsurgency Blue-book Fiscal Year 1966*. Carrollton Press (242D) (R).

Yarborough, Gen. William. Report, "Subject: Visit to Colombia, South America by a Team from Special Warfare Center, Fort Bragg, North Carolina (Special Warfare Mobile Training Team)" and "Secret Supplement Colombia Survey Report", 26 February 1962. Carrollton Press (154D) (R).

White House

Bundy, McGeorge. Memorandum to President Johnson, 10 September 1964. Briefing for meeting with Latin American Ambassadors. Johnson Presidential Library, Confidential files, White House Central Files, CO-1-8, Latin America.

Bundy, McGeorge. Memorandum to the Secretary of Defense, National Security Action Memorandum no. 56, 28 June 1961. "Subject: Evaluation of Paramilitary Requirements". Carrollton Press (896F) (R).

Davies, Thomas W. Memorandum to the Attorney General at the request of Mr. Dungan, 16 January 1963. "Subject: A Future Role of the Special Group (CI)". Carrollton Press (902A) (R).

Memorandum to McGeorge Bundy, 12 January 1963. "Subject: Internal Defense Plans". Carrollton Press (901F) (R).

Eisenhower, Gen. Dwight D. Memorandum to Secretary of Defense, 24 October 1953. "Psychological Warfare". Carrollton Press (R).

Jackson, D.D. Memorandum to General Eisenhower, 17 December 1952. "Psychological and/or Political Warfare". Carrollton Press (219F) (R).

Komer, Robert W. Memorandum to McGeorge Bundy, 10 April 1962. Concerns the role of the Special Group (CI). Carrollton Press (901A) (R).

National Security Action Memorandum 124, "Establishment of the Special Group (Counter-Insurgency)", 2 January 1962. Carrollton Press (900C) (R).

National Security Action Memorandum 182, "Counter-Insurgency Doctrine", 24 August 1962. Carrollton Press (901E) (R).

Report of the National Bipartisan Commission on Central America. January 1984.

Other Selected Sources

Advanced Research Projects Agency (ARPA). "A Historical Survey of Patterns and Techniques of Insurgency Conflicts in Post-1900 Latin America", ARPA Project No. 4860, 15 January 1964.

Barber, Willard F. and Ronning, C. Neale. *Internal Security and Military Power: Counterinsurgency and Civic Action in Latin America*. Columbus, Ohio: Ohio State University Press, 1966.

Barnett, Frank R. "A Proposal for Political Warfare", *Military Review* (US), March 1961.

Barton, F.H. *Salient Operational Aspects of Paramilitary Warfare in the Asian Areas*. Baltimore: Operations Research Office, 1954.

Bjelajac, Slavko N., Office of the Deputy Chief of Staff for Operations, US Department of the Army. "Establishment of Principles of Counter-insurgency", *Proceedings of Annual Conferences, US Army Human Factors Research and Development*, October 1968.

Bellinger, Major John B. "Civilian Role in Anti-guerrilla Warfare", *Military Review* (US), September 1961.

Bicudo, Helio Pereira. *Mi Informe sobre El Escuadron de la Muerte*. Madrid: Ultramar Editores, SA, 1978.

Blaufarb, Douglas S. *The Counterinsurgency Era: US Doctrine and Performance, 1950 to the Present*. New York: The Free Press, 1977.

Bowden, Tom. *Beyond the Limits of the Law: A Comparative Study of the Police in Crisis Politics*. Harmondsworth: Penguin, 1978.

Breunig, Lt. Colonel Joseph T., US Army, Office of the Chief of Staff. "Counter-guerrilla operations - A preventive aspect", *Proceedings of Annual Conferences, US Army Human Factors Research and Development*, November 1969.

Calvert, Brigadier J. Michael. "El Patron de la Guerra de Guerrillas". *Revista Militar de Guatemala*, October-December 1966.

Cantoral Davila, Captain Angel M. (Army of Guatemala). "El Nacional Socialism". *Revista Militar de Guatemala* April-December 1976, pp. 61-6.

Center for Research on Criminal Justice. *The Iron Fist and the Velvet Glove: An Analysis of the US Police*. Berkeley, California, 1977.

Chacon Arevalo, Lt. Col. Mario Modesto. "Consideraciones sobre la Defensa Civil". *Revista de la Escuela de Comando y Estado Mayor "Manuel Enrique Araujo"* (El Salvador), no. 2 April-June 1967.

Childs, Lt. Col. John. "The Inter-American Military System". Ph.D dissertation, American University, 1978. Also published as *Unequal Alliance: The Inter-American Military System, 1938-1978*. Colorado: Westview Press, 1981.

Collazo Davila, Vincente. "The Guatemalan Insurrection", in Bard E. O'Neill, William R. Heaton, and Donald J. Alberts, eds., *Insurgency in the Modern World*. Colorado: Westview Press, 1980.

Council for Inter-American Security. "A New Inter-American Policy for the Eighties". Washington, DC: 1980.

DiGiovanni, Jr. C. "US Policy and the Marxist Threat to Central America". US Heritage Foundation, "Backgrounder". Washington, DC, 15 October 1980.

Donovan, James A. *The US Marine Corps*. New York: Praeger, 1967.

Eckstein, Harry (ed.), *Internal War: Problems and Approaches*. New York: Free Press, 1964.

Enloe, Cynthia H. *Ethnic Soldiers: State Security in a Divided Society*. Harmondsworth: Penguin Books, 1980.

"Police and Military in the Resolution of Ethnic Conflict", *Annals of the American Academy of Political and Social Science*, September 1977.

"Military Police Relations in the Third World: The Militarization of Domestic Order", Manuscript, September 1978.

Epstein, David. "The Police Role in Counter-insurgency Efforts", *Journal of Criminal Law, Criminology and Political Science*, Vol. 54, 1968.

Fitzgerald, Frances. *Fire in the Lake: The Vietnamese and the Americans in Vietnam*. New York: Vintage, 1973.

Gott, Richard. *Guerrilla Movements in Latin America*. London: Nelson, 1970.

Guatemala, Estado Mayor General del Ejercito (General Staff). *Plan Nacional de Seguridad y Desarrollo*. Palacio Nacional, 1 April 1982. Photocopied typescript, 5 pages; includes 23 March 1982 text "Objetivos Nacionales Actuales", signed by Junta president Gen. E. Rios Montt.

    Ordenes Permanentes para el Desarrollo de Operaciones Contrasubversivas, Anexo "H" al Plan de Campaña "Victoria 82". Palacio Nacional, 16 July 1982. Photocopied typescript, 5 pages, signed by

    Decalago PAAC, Plan de Asistencia para las Areas en Conflicto. Palacio Nacional, July 1982. Photocopied typescript, ten point outline of counter-insurgency principles in the "Victoria 82" campaign, including the "Fusiles y Frijoles", "Rifles and Beans" concept.

Guatemala, Army. "Guia para el planeamiento de la contrainsurgencia". Texto Especial 31/176, nd, translation from text of US Army School of Special Warfare. Photocopied typescript reproduced in A. Corro, *Guatemala: La Violencia*, CIDOC Dossier 19, 1968.

    "La Tercera Guerrilla o Guerrilla Criminal". *Revista Militar de Guatemala*, January-June 1970.

Guzman Aguilar, General Carlos (Army of El Salvador). "La subversion comunista y las acciones guerrilleras". *Revista de la Escuela de Comando y Estado Mayor "Manuel Enrique Araujo"*, no. 18, July-December 1970.

Heilbrunn, O. *Partisan Warfare*. New York: Praeger, 1962.

Hernandez, Major Gustavo Atilio (Army of El Salvador). "Guerra Irregular en el Ambiente Centroamericano". *Revista de la Escuela de Comando y Estado Mayor*, no. 4, January-March 1964.

Hernandez Mendez, Colonel Jorge H. (Army of Guatemala). "Defensa Integral de una Nacion". *Revista Militar de Guatemala*, January-June 1963.

    Geopolitica. Guatemala: Ministerio de Defensa, 1969.

Hunt, Richard A. and Shultz, Richard H., eds., *Lessons from an Unconventional War: Reassessing US Strategies for Future Conflicts*. New York: Pergamon Press, 1982.

James, John (Royal Air Force, UK). "The Military and the Police", Manuscript, September 1973.

    "Violence and the Functions of Armed Force". Manuscript, April 1976.

Janowitz, Morris. *Military Institutions and Coercion in Developing Nations*. Chicago: University of Chicago Press, 1977.

Johnson, Chalmers A. "Guerrilla Conflict", *World Politics*, July 1962.

Kitson, Frank. *Low Intensity Operations: Subversion, Insurgency, and Peacekeeping*. London: Faber and Faber, 1971.

    Gangs and Countergangs. London: Barrie and Rockliff, 1960.

Klare, Michael T. "Arms and Power: The Politics of US Arms Sales to Latin America", *NACLA Latin America and Empire Report*, Vol. IX, no. 2, March 1975.

"Operation Phoenix and the Failure of Pacification in Vietnam", *Liberation*, May 1973.

War Without End. New York: Vintage Books, 1972.

Lacharite, Norma A. and Wolfgang, Jean Rodman. "The Police Role of Internal Security Forces in Internal Defense". Kensington, Maryland, American Institute for Research, commissioned by US Department of Defense, May 1972.

Langguth, A.J., *Hidden Terrors*. New York: Pantheon, 1978.

Lefever, Ernest W. for the Brookings Institute, *US Public Safety Assistance: An Assessment*. Washington, DC: December 1973 (Commissioned by the Office of Public Safety).

Marchetti, Victor and Marks, John. *The CIA and the Cult of Intelligence*. New York: Dell, 1974.

McCuen, Lt. Col. John J. (US Army). *The Art of Counterinsurgency Warfare: The Strategy of Counterinsurgency*. Harrisburg, Pa.: Stackpole Books, 1967.

Medrano, General Jose Alberto (Army of El Salvador). "La Guerra de Vietnam". *Revista de la Escuela de Comando y Estado Mayor*, no. 18, July-December 1970. Speech delivered 23 November 1970.

Monge, Major Roberto (Army of El Salvador). "Guerrillas y Contra-guerrillas". *Revista de la Escuela de Comando y Estado Mayor*, no. 6, July-September 1964.

Paget, Julian. *Counter Insurgency Campaigning*. London: Faber and Faber, 1967.

Pan American Union, Department of International Law. *Strengthening of Internal Security*. Washington, DC, 1953.

Powers, Thomas. *The Man Who Kept Secrets: Richard Helms and the CIA*. New York: Pocket Books, 1979.

Pustay, Major John S. (US Air Force). *Counterinsurgency Warfare*. New York: Free Press, 1965.

Rodriguez, Lt. Col. Manuel Alfonso (Army of El Salvador). "La guerrilla y la contra-guerrilla en la guerra revolucionaria". *Revista de la Escuela de Comando y Estado Mayor*, no. 10, January-March 1966.

"Será efectiva la defensa movil ante le guerrilla?" *Revista de la Escuela de Comando y Estado Mayor*, no. 2, April-June 1967.

Saxe-Fernández, John. "The Central American Defense Council and Pax Americana", in *Latin American Radicalism*, edited by Irving Luis Horowitz, John Gerassi and Joshua de Castro. New York: Vintage, 1969.

Shackley, Theodore. *The Third Option: An American View of Counterinsurgency Operations*. New York: Readers Digest Press, 1981.

Sheehan, Neil; Butterfield, F.; Kenworthy, E.W.; and Smith, Hedrick. *The Pentagon Papers: The History of the Vietnam War . . . as Published by the New York Times*. New York: Bantam Books, 1971.

Stepan, Alfred, *The Military in Politics* Princeton: Princeton University Press, 1971.

"The new professionalism of Internal Warfare and Military Role Expansion", in Alfred Stepan, ed., *Authoritarian Brazil*. New Haven: Yale University Press, 1973.

Thompson, Robert. *Defeating Communist Insurgency*. London: Chatto and Windus, 1967.

No Exit from Vietnam. London: Chatto and Windus, 1969.

Walter, E.V., *Terror and Resistance, A Study of Political Violence*. Oxford: Oxford University Press, 1969.

Waltzer, Michael. *Just and Unjust Wars. A Moral Argument with Historical Illustrations*. New York: Harper, 1977.

Watson, Peter. *War on the Mind: The Military Uses and Abuses of Psychology*. Harmondsworth: Penguin, 1980.

Index

FUN   *Frente de Unidad Nacional* (Front of National Unity)
FUR   *Frente Unido de la Revolución* (United Front of the Revolution)
ICA   International Cooperation Administration
IMET   International Military Education & Training Program
IMF   International Monetary Fund
LASA   Latin American Studies Association
MAP   Military Assistance Program
MILGROUP   US Military Group (Guatemala)
MLN   Movement of National Liberation
MTT(s)   Mobile Training Team(s) (US)
NACLA   North American Congress on Latin America
NOA   *Nueva Organizacion Anticomunista* (New Anticommunist Organization)
ORPA   Organization of the People in Arms
PAC   *Patrullas de Autodefensa Civil* (Civil Defense Patrol System)
PAAC   Program of Help to Areas in Conflict
PGT   Guatemalan Workers' Party
PID   *Partido Democrático Institucional* (Democratic Institutional Party)
PLO   Palestine Liberation Organization
PMA   *Policia Militar Ambulante* (Mobile Military Police)
PR   *Partido Revolucionario* (Revolutionary Party)
URNG   *Unidad Revolucionaria Nacional Guatemalteca* (Guatemalan National Revolutionary Union)
WACL   World Anti-Communist League

LATIN AMERICAN AND CARIBBEAN TITLES FROM ZED BOOKS

Fidel Castro
THE WORLD CRISIS
Its Economic and Social Impact on the
Underdeveloped Countries
Hb and Pb

Donald Hodges and Ross Gandy
MEXICO 1910-1982: REFORM OR
REVOLUTION?
Hb and Pb

George Beckford and Michael Witter
SMALL GARDEN, BITTER WEED
The Political Economy of Struggle
and Change in Jamaica
Hb and Pb

Liisa North
BITTER GROUNDS
Roots of Revolt in El Salvador
Pb

Ronaldo Munck
POLITICS AND DEPENDENCY IN
THE THIRD WORLD
The Case of Latin America
Hb and Pb

George Beckford
PERSISTENT POVERTY
Underdevelopment in Plantation
Economies of the Third World
Pb

Tom Barry, Beth Wood and Deb
Preusch
DOLLARS AND DICTATORS
A Guide to Central America
Hb and Pb

George Black
TRIUMPH OF THE PEOPLE
The Sandinista Revolution in
Nicaragua
Hb and Pb

George Black
GARRISON GUATEMALA
Hb and Pb

Cedric Robinson
BLACK MARXISM
The Making of the Black Radical
Tradition
Hb and Pb

Teofilo Cabastrero
MINISTERS OF GOD, MINISTERS
OF THE PEOPLE
Hb and Pb

Chris Searle
WORDS UNCHAINED
Language and Revolution in Grenada
Hb and Pb

George Brizan
GRENADA: ISLAND OF
CONFLICT
From Amerindians to People's
Revolution 1498-1979
Hb and Pb

Maurice Bishop
IN NOBODY'S BACKYARD
Maurice Bishop's Speeches, 1979-
1983: A Memorial Volume
Hb and Pb

Carmelo Furci
THE CHILEAN COMMUNIST
PARTY AND THE ROAD TO
SOCIALISM
Hb and Pb

Latin American and Caribbean
Women's Collective
SLAVES OF SLAVES
The Challenge of Latin American
Women
Hb and Pb

THIRD WORLD WOMEN TITLES FROM ZED

Bobby Siu
WOMEN OF CHINA:
Imperialism and Women's
Resistance, 1900-1949
Hb and Pb

Ingela Bendt and James Downing
WE SHALL RETURN:
Women of Palestine
Hb and Pb

Miranda Davies (editor)
THIRD WORLD — SECOND
SEX:
Women's Struggles and National
Liberation
Hb and Pb

Juliette Minces
THE HOUSE OF OBEDIENCE:
Women in Arab Society
Hb and Pb

Margaret Randall
SANDINO'S DAUGHTERS:
Testimonies of Nicaraguan Women
in Struggle
Pb

Maria Mies
THE LACEMAKERS OF
NARSAPUR:
Indian Housewives Produce for the
World Market
Pb

Asma el Dareer
WOMAN, WHY DO YOU WEEP?
Circumcision and Its Consequences
Hb and Pb

Raqiya Haji Dualeh Abdalla
SISTERS IN AFFLICTION:
Circumcision and Infibulation of
Women in Africa
Hb and Pb

Maria Rose Cutrufelli
WOMEN OF AFRICA:
Roots of Oppression
Hb and Pb

Atar Tabari and Nahid Yeganeh
IN THE SHADOW OF ISLAM:
The Women's Movement in Iran
Hb and Pb

Bonnie Mass
POPULATION TARGET:
The Political Economy of
Population Control in Latin
America
Pb

Nawal el Saadawi
THE HIDDEN FACE OF EVE:
Women in the Arab World
Hb and Pb

Else Skjonsberg
A SPECIAL CASTE?
Tamil Women in Sri Lanka
Pb

Patricia Jeffrey
FROGS IN A WELL:
Indian Women in Purdah
Hb and Pb

June Nash and Helen Icken Safa
(editors)
SEX AND CLASS IN LATIN
AMERICA:
Women's Perspectives on Politics,
Economics and the Family in the
Third World
Pb

Latin American and Caribbean
Women's Collective
SLAVES OF SLAVES:
The Challenge of Latin American
Women
Hb and Pb

Christine Obbo
AFRICAN WOMEN:
Their Struggle for Economic
Independence
Pb

Gail Omvedt
WE WILL SMASH THIS
PRISON!
Indian Women in Struggle
Hb and Pb

Agnes Smedley
PORTRAITS OF CHINESE
WOMEN IN REVOLUTION
Pb

Raymonda Tawil
MY HOME, MY PRISON
Pb

Nawal el Saadawi
WOMAN AT ZERO POINT
Hb and Pb

Elisabeth Croll
CHINESE WOMEN
Hb and Pb

Arlene Eisen
WOMEN AND REVOLUTION IN
VIETNAM
Hb and Pb

Mi Mi Khaing
THE WORLD OF BURMESE
WOMEN
Hb and Pb

ANGOLAN WOMEN BUILDING
THE FUTURE
From National Liberation to
Women's Emancipation
Hb and Pb

Madhu Kishwar and Ruth Vanita
(editors)
IN SEARCH OF ANSWERS
Indian Women's Voices
Hb and Pb

Kumari Jayawardena
FEMINISM AND NATIONALISM
IN THE THIRD WORLD
Hb and Pb

Zed titles cover Africa, Asia, Latin America and the Middle East, as well as general issues affecting the Third World's relations with the rest of the world. Our series embrace: Imperialism, Women, Political Economy, History, Labour, Voices of Struggle, Human Rights and other areas pertinent to the Third World.

INTERNATIONAL RELATIONS/IMPERIALISM TITLES
FROM ZED BOOKS

Albert Szymanski
IS THE RED FLAG FLYING?
The Political Economy of the Soviet
Union Today
Hb and Pb

V.G. Kiernan
AMERICAN — THE NEW
IMPERIALISM:
From White Settlement to World
Hegemony
Hb

Satish Kumar
CIA AND THE THIRD WORLD:
A Study in Crypto-Diplomacy
Hb

Dan Nabudere
THE POLITICAL ECONOMY OF
IMPERIALISM
Hb and Pb

Yan Fitt et al
THE WORLD ECONOMIC CRISIS:
US Imperialism at Bay
Hb and Pb

Clyde Sanger
SAFE AND SOUND
Disarmament and Development in the
Eighties
Pb

Frederick Clairemonte and John
Cavanagh
THE WORLD IN THEIR WEB:
The Dynamics of Textile
Multinationals
(Preface by Samir Amin)
Hb and Pb

Henrick Secher Marcussen and Jens
Erik Torp
THE INTERNATIONALIZATION
OF CAPITAL:
Prospects for the Third World
Hb and Pb

Malcolm Caldwell
THE WEALTH OF SOME
NATIONS
Hb and Pb

Georgi Arbatov
COLD WAR OR DETENTE: THE
SOVIET VIEWPOINT
Hb and Pb

Rachel Heatley
POVERTY AND POWER:
The Case for a Political Approach to
Development
Pb

Ronald Graham
THE ALUMINIUM INDUSTRY
AND THE THIRD WORLD:
Multinational Corporations and
Underdevelopment
Pb

Petter Nore and Terisa Turner
OIL AND CLASS STRUGGLE
Hb and Pb

Rehman Sobhan
THE CRISIS OF EXTERNAL
DEPENDENCE:
The Political Economy of Foreign Aid
to Bangladesh
Hb and Pb

Zed Books' titles cover Africa, Asia, Latin America and the Middle East, as well as general issues affecting the Third World's relations with the rest of the world. Our Series embrace: Imperialism, Women, Political Economy, History, Labour, Voices of Struggle, Human Rights and other areas pertinent to the Third World.

You can order Zed titles direct from Zed Books Ltd., 57 Caledonian Road, London N1 9BU, UK.